Jon E. Lewis was born in 1961. His many previous books include *The Mammoth Book of the Secrets of the SAS & Elite Forces, D-Day as They Saw it, The Mammoth Book of How It Happened World War II, The Mammoth Book of Soldiers at War, The Mammoth Book of Life Before the Mast* and *The Mammoth Book of True War Stories*.

Also available

The Mammoth Book of 20th Century Ghost Stories
The Mammoth Book of Arthurian Legends
The Mammoth Book of Astounding Word Games
The Mammoth Book of Battles
The Mammoth Book of Best New Horror #11
The Mammoth Book of Bridge
The Mammoth Book of British Kings & Queens
The Mammoth Book of Cats
The Mammoth Book of Chess New Edition and Internet Games
The Mammoth Book of Comic Fantasy II
The Mammoth Book of Dogs
The Mammoth Book of Dracula
The Mammoth Book of Egyptian Whodunnits
The Mammoth Book of Endurance and Adventure
The Mammoth Book of Eyewitness Battles
The Mammoth Book of Eyewitness History 2000
The Mammoth Book of Eyewitness WWII
The Mammoth Book of Fantastic Science Fiction (1970s)
The Mammoth Book of Fighter Pilots
The Mammoth Book of Future Cops
The Mammoth Book of Haunted House Stories
The Mammoth Book of Heroes
The Mammoth Book of Heroic and Outrageous Women
The Mammoth Book of Historical Detectives
The Mammoth Book of Historical Whodunnits
The Mammoth Book of the History of Murder
The Mammoth Book of Humor
The Mammoth Book of Jack the Ripper
The Mammoth Book of Killer Women
The Mammoth Book of Life Before the Mast
The Mammoth Book of Literary Anecdotes
The Mammoth Book of Locked-Room Mysteries and Impossible Crimes
The Mammoth Book of Love & Sensuality
The Mammoth Book of Men O'War
The Mammoth Book of Movie Detectives and Screen Crimes
The Mammoth Book of Murder and Science
The Mammoth Book of New Sherlock Holmes Adventures
The Mammoth Book of Nostradamus and Other Prophets
The Mammoth Book of Oddballs and Eccentrics
The Mammoth Book of Private Lives
The Mammoth Book of Pulp Fiction
The Mammoth Book of Road Stories
The Mammoth Book of Sex, Drugs & Rock 'n' Roll
The Mammoth Book of Soldiers at War
The Mammoth Book of Sword & Honor
The Mammoth Book of Tasteless Lists
The Mammoth Book of Terror
The Mammoth Book of The West
The Mammoth Book of The World's Greatest Chess Games
The Mammoth Book of True Crime (revised)
The Mammoth Book of True War Stories
The Mammoth Book of Unsolved Crimes
The Mammoth Book of War Diaries and Letters
The Mammoth Encyclopedia of The Unsolved

THE MAMMOTH BOOK OF

Special
Forces

True Stories of the Fighting Elite Behind Enemy Lines

Edited by Jon E. Lewis

CARROLL & GRAF PUBLISHERS
New York

Carroll & Graf Publishers
An imprint of Avalon Publishing Group, Inc.
245 W. 17th Street
NY 10011
www.carrollandgraf.com

AVALON
publishing group incorporated

First published in the UK by Robinson,
an imprint of Constable & Robinson Ltd 2004

First Carroll & Graf edition 2004

ISBN 0-7867-1427-1

Printed and bound in the EU

'. . . *grant that we, the chosen members of the Special Air Service regiment may, by our works and our ways, dare all to win . . .*'

SAS regimental prayer

Contents

Introduction

*"Special Operations are defined as operations conducted
by specially trained, equipped and organized Department
of Defense forces against strategic or tactical targets in
pursuit of national military, political, economic or psychological objectives. These operations may be conducted
during periods of peace or hostilities. They may support
conventional operations, or they may be undertaken
independently when the use of conventional forces . . .
is inappropriate."*

United States Operations Command,
A Special Operations Primer, 1996

W HEN ALL IS said and done, the brutal business of war
comes in only two forms. There is the formalized
engagement between large regular formations, with their
strict uniforms and stricter hierarchies. And then there is
the shadowy mission of the irregular, small-scale unit, with
its unorthodox tactics and its unusual weapons.

There have been unconventional forces since the fires of
war were first stoked. After all, what did Odysseus do but
use "specially trained, equipped and organized" forces to
gain entry into Troy by concealing them inside the Wooden
Horse? (Incidentally, Odysseus' *ruse de guerre* provided the
blueprint for all manner of special force operations undertaken in disguise, including the Allied commando attack on
St Nazaire in 1942 and Otto Skorzeny's Operation Griffin
in 1944.) Think too, of Rogers' Rangers from the French
and Indian War of 1756, the British agents who played "the
Great Game" in central Asia against the Russians in the

early nineteenth century and John Singelton Mosby's Confederate Cavalry Raiders from the Civil War.

Modern special forces date to the First World War, and the attempts by the Allies and the central powers to break the military deadlock on the Western Front. One strategem of the Allies was to raise an irregular Arab army under Colonel T.E. Lawrence; this was to foment trouble against the Turks and so draw off Central Power resources from the main show (see Appendix I). The Germans, meanwhile, sought to break through the Allied trenches on the Western Front by creating and training special *Strosstruppen*. These "shock troops" caused mayhem during the Michael Offensive of 1918 until Allied might overcame them.

The Germans might have lost the Great War but they saw clearly that the future of warfare lay with hard-hitting mobile formations, be they of men or machinery. Hitler liked special forces, for they had around them the aura of the "superman" so beloved of Nazi philosophy. It was no coincidence, then, that the Second World War opened with a German special forces operation – a simulated attack on the German frontier that provided the Führer with the pretext to invade Poland. No surprise either, that the 1940 German invasion of the Low Countries included a dazzling airborne assault on the Belgian fortress of Eben Emael by the Koch Assault Detachment that still causes military historians to gape.

Whereas the Germans had become revolutionaries in warfare, the military establishments of the major Allied powers had long been overtaken by a glacial conservatism. The result: in 1939 the major Allied nations were entirely bereft of special forces.

Despite the late start, special forces soon proliferated amongst the Second World War allies. With the increasing complexity of warfare, specialization was an inevitability. With no early prospect of a major offensive against the Germans or Japanese, morale-boosting raids by a small elite were too much of a temptation. Moreover, the sheer scale of the frontline – which stretched around Europe, North Africa and the Far East – simply invited clandestine "behind the lines" missions of reconnaissance and sabotage.

The other allure of special forces was that, for a relatively small commitment of men and means, they might achieve a big, even strategically important result. In North Africa the SAS, which began with 70 soldiers, destroyed 300 Axis aircraft on the ground in North Africa. The demolition of the dry-dock at St Nazaire denied the German navy use of a major facility in the Battle of the Atlantic. In 1943 Royal Navy "frogmen" crippled the German heavy-battleship *Tirpitz*. A year later, Norwegian Commandos of the Special Operations Executive (SOE) destroyed the heavy-water plant at Vermok, thus frustrating the Nazis' development of the atomic bomb.

Success bred expansion, and special forces proliferated, to the extent that they sometimes had to compete for men and for missions.

Even so, cometh the peace of 1945, special forces units were shut down almost everywhere. Why? The top brass had long been distrustful of the "mobs for the jobs". Special forces were too independent and too prone to creaming off the best personnel and kit from regular formations. "Expensive, wasteful and unnecessary" was the complaint of Field Marshal Slim. So special forces were disbanded.

The face of war after 1945 was not the titanic clash of arms between the Soviet Bloc and the West expected by the general staffs, but a rash of savage little wars in colonial places: Malaysia, Oman, Vietnam, Algeria, the Congo . . . In these wars, conventional forces were often of little use. But who better to fight guerillas than highly trained, cherry-picked, superbly equipped "guerillas" of the special forces?

There was another stimulus to the rebirth of the special forces: the spread of terrorism from the 1950s onwards, particularly that emanating from the Middle East. Indeed, with the decline in Communist meddling in the Third World, the main burden of the special forces' mission has become anti- and counter-terrorism.

Fighting "shadow wars" in ex-colonial countries and counter-terrorist operations does not exhaust the capability of contemporary special forces. VIP protection, intelligence gathering, reconnaissance, training forces from foreign nations, even humanitarian assistance have all fallen into the special forces' brief. In short, special forces have come to have utility across the whole range of conflict, which is why they are the favourites of politicians. Special forces enable politicians to secure their designs with risk to few compatriots. The electorate like it – the sight of bodybags being flown home, as in Vietnam and the recent war in Iraq, is a distinct vote loser.

The enthusiasm of politicians for special forces has ensured that special forces have escaped the financial cut backs suffered by conventional military services. Indeed, most special units since the end of the Cold War, have seen their budgets grow. So too their responsibilities. "Send for the SAS", "Send for the SEALs" has become almost a knee-jerk response by the politicos at the the first whiff of trouble.

The overuse and misuse of special forces has caused unease amongst the special forces themselves, particularly when, as in Afghanistan and (more recently) Iraq, they have been used as an entirely conventional service. Not only is this against the *raison d'etre* of the special forces, it does little for the morale and the improvement of the conventional units themselves.

In the following pages, by contrast, the special forces are seen doing what they do, and have done, best: conducting operations behind enemy lines.

After all, even as vociferous a critic of special forces as Field Marshal Slim agreed that, "There is, however, one kind of special unit which should be retained – that designed to be employed in small parties, usually behind the enemy [lines] on tasks beyond the normal scope of warfare in the field".

From Arabia in 1916 to Iraq in 2003, these are the men and missions which put the "special" in special forces.

VICTOR TWO

Peter "Yorky" Crossland

Although 22 SAS was put on standby within hours of Saddam Hussein sending his armour into Kuwait on 2 August 1990, long months passed before any role was found for the Regiment. That General "Stormin' Norman" Schwarzkopf, the American in command of the Coalition ground forces gathered to evict Saddam from Kuwait, was no friend of special units hardly helped; reputedly Schwarzkopf met a contingent of US Special Forces in the Gulf with the greeting: "I remember you guys from Vietnam . . . you couldn't do your job there, and you didn't do your job in Panama. What makes you think you can do your job here?"

But 22 SAS did have one friend in a high place: the only Briton on Schwarzkopf's planning staff, CENTCOM, was Lieutenant General Peter de la Billiere – a former commander of the SAS. After toying with the idea of having the SAS rescue the hostages taken by Saddam to military installations as "human shields", de la Billiere scheduled the SAS to cut roads and cause diversions in the enemy rear at the beginning of the Coalition offensive. This was set for 29 January 1991.

The Regiment, therefore, was as surprised as most other people when, at 2 a.m. on 17 January, Apache helicopters from the US Army's 101st Airborne Division destroyed Iraqi radar installations, creating safe corridors down which hundreds of Allied aircraft and Tomahawk Cruise missiles flew to bombard targets in Iraq. So overwhelming was the Coalition's aerial onslaught that within twenty-four hours the Iraqi air force was all but wiped out and Saddam's communications system heavily mauled.

Saddam did manage one defiant gesture. On the second night of the campaign he launched Scud missiles at targets in Saudi Arabia and Israel. The Scud was an outdated Soviet surface-to-surface missile; of the six which crashed into Israel, none caused any injury. Yet the Scud was political dynamite; if Israel responded militarily to the Iraqi Scud attacks the fragile Coalition, which contained several Arab members, would be blown apart, for no Arab nation could be seen to side with the "Zionists" against another Arab nation, even Saddam's Iraq. Frantic diplomacy by the Coalition managed to persuade Israel from taking immediate punitive action. Batteries of Patriot ground-to-air missiles were dispatched to Tel Aviv, Jerusalem and Haifa. The Coalition diverted 30 per cent of its air effort to hunting the Scuds and their mobile missile launchers – but in the vastness of the Iraqi desert all too often the air strike arrived to find the Scud fired and the launcher hidden beyond detection. Asked by the media on 19 January about the "Scud menace" even the preternaturally upbeat Schwarzkopf could only lament that the "picture is unclear" and that seeking Scuds in the desert was akin to searching for proverbial pins in haystacks.

If the C-in-C found the picture unclear, his British number one saw, with perfect clarity, that 22 SAS were the mob for the job of destroying Iraq's Scuds and remaining military communications systems. De la Billiere signalled 22 SAS that "all SAS effort should be directed against Scuds". That very same day, 19 January, the 300 troopers from A, B and D squadrons gathered in the Gulf were rushed 1,500 km from their holding area to a forward mounting base just inside the Saudi border with Western Iraq.

The Regiment decided on two principal means of dealing with the Scud menace. It would insert into Iraq covert 8-man static patrols to watch Main Supply Routes (MSRs) and report on the movement of Scud traffic; the famous "Bravo Two Zero" was one such road-watch *team. The other arm of SAS attack against the Scuds was the deployment of four mobile fighting columns, two each from A and D Squadrons. It escaped no-one's notice that the SAS was thus deployed to do what it had been born to do – fight deep in the desert behind enemy lines.*

Peter "Yorky" Crossland (a pseudonym) was a member of Alpha Three Zero, one of A Squadron's fighting columns. Thirty troopers strong, Alpha Three Zero rode into war on eight Land Rover 110s, most armed with a Browning .5 heavy machine gun, plus assorted GPMGs, 40mm grenade launchers, and Milan anti-tank weapons. A Mercedes Unimog carried the bulk of the stores; the column also boasted two motorcycle outriders. In total Alpha Three Zero spent six weeks behind Iraqi lines Scud-hunting. They were also ordered to destroy a massive microwave communications centre, a few kilometres outside Baghdad, which was the hub of Iraqi Scud operations.

The target was code-named Victor Two.

W E PATROLLED ANOTHER couple of hundred metres before we saw the target. This was our first sight of the position that we had come to destroy. Once more I started to observe with the spyglass, noticing that there was a large black sheet draped over the entry position. I informed Brian but he wasn't interested and merely told me to get a move on. Then I heard the sound of a large vehicle and at the same time the view in my spyglass blacked out. To my complete surprise there was a bus heading directly towards us. I immediately dropped to the ground, taking cover behind a small sand bank. Turning, I noticed all the others diving for cover too. Brian just stood there and said, "You're a windy bastard! Right, you and Slugger get back to the rest of the group and tell them to bring the vehicles up here."

As Slugger and I set off I said, "That lunatic is going to get us fucking killed."

Slugger agreed. "Yes, I know, mate. We're just going to

have to be very careful – get the job done and then get the fuck out of here as quickly as possible."

We quickly briefed the guys, then returned to where Brian was waiting. He was surrounded by a whole group of men: one burst of enemy fire would have taken most of them out. What the hell was going on? It turned out that he had got all the assault team together and was giving them a bollocking. We stood there in total amazement. He then proceeded to give us another change of plan. The problem was that not everybody was totally aware of the changes, and this proved to be very dangerous.

I was now ordered to go with Paul, acting as the cover party. There was a truck parked to the right of the target which would serve as our position. It proved to be a fuel tanker with bowser attached to the rear. When Paul and I arrived, everything seemed peaceful. As we watched the demolition party move off towards the target, our luck seemed to be holding and my feeling of apprehension disappeared. Suddenly I was feeling excited.

I recall noticing that the fire support group were not yet in position, and thought that we should therefore not attack the target yet although by this stage I wasn't sure whether their orders had been changed.

As the assault group closed on the target I moved round the truck, dropping to one knee near the bowser. Paul knelt alongside me. It was deathly quiet. I watched the remainder of the assault group move alongside the perimeter wall, covering them as they disappeared beneath the black tarpaulin sheet that served as a doorway. They had been gone for just a few seconds when suddenly I heard a noise from the truck. Paul heard it too and looked questioningly at me.

Very quietly he whispered, "What the fuck was that?"

I moved slowly forwards, heading towards the cab. More movement, and definitely a mumbling noise. "Shit. There's someone in there!"

Paul put his hand on the lever and tried to open the door. It would open only a fraction, and then we realised that it was tied with a piece of string. Paul moved away from the door and I stepped forwards and grabbed it, pulling hard so that the string broke. The door burst open to reveal a boy who, although in uniform, could have been no older than sixteen. In the brightness of the starlight I could see the whites of his eyes, his cheeks and short dark hair. My brain took a mental snapshot of him. In the same instant I pushed my rifle into the boy's chest, shaking my head in an attempt to indicate that he should keep quiet. Then I realised that there was another man in the cab.

The boy started to move backwards, pushing himself deeper into the seat. His voice was squealing in Arabic, "No. No. No!" I had one last try at keeping him quiet, but the boy was scared shitless. Then he made a move for his rifle, which lay beneath him. We moved in unison: his hand gripped the stock of his rifle as I pushed my rifle hard into his chest. We both knew what was going to happen next. Our eyes locked, and he registered my decision to kill him. For a split second everything around me disappeared. I could not see or hear anything except this young boy. Then I pulled the trigger and blew him away. Even as the bullets ripped into his chest his head was shaking and pleading. But it was all in vain.

As my two rounds punched hard through his chest at point blank range a burst of rapid fire flew over my shoulder into the cab. Paul had opened fire. Instinctively I peeled away to the left, realising after firing my second round that my weapon had a stoppage. The noise from Paul's automatic rifle was unbelievable as the rounds ripped through the bodies of the two Iraqis and the opposite cab door. Instantly enemy fire started coming from every direction. Several Russian-made SU22 anti-aircraft guns added their contribution. By comparison our weapons seemed puny, and even the Milans failed to be heard; nevertheless we laid it down thick and heavy. There was no point in being quiet any more, since we were now well compromised. Luckily at this point none of the fire was very effective, but the volume was tremendous. Red and green tracer rounds buzzed around like little hornets, ricocheting off the ground and deflecting in every direction. But from the direction of the incoming fire it was obvious that the enemy didn't have a clue where we were.

Realising that the demolition party would be coming out

through the wall at any moment, I ran to the back of the truck and shouted for Paul to follow. The first thing I saw was two of our guys taking up position slightly forward of another truck just left of the target. Next moment a figure jumped out of a truck on to one of the guys. I found out later that it was my best mate Des, who had been ambushed by an Iraqi soldier. Like the two whom Paul and I had shot, he had been asleep in the cab. The pair of them struggled for a moment, then the Iraqi broke free and ran like hell towards the burne line. I took a bead with my rifle on the running man, but he was crossing open ground with the fire support group immediately behind him. I could see no weapon, and was unsure if he was a soldier or a civilian. I held my fire and the man disappeared into the dark.

Inside the target compound, the demolition teams quickly fitted the charges. Stealth bombers had already done a good job and inflicted severe damage on the control centre. Our guys had just finished fitting the charges to all four legs of the microwave tower when the noise of small arms fire alerted them. On Slugger's command the four men fired off their grip switches, timing the explosive to detonate in one minute and thirty seconds. Then the assault team prepared to leave. Ben led them out, covered by Alistair. Quickly they checked the entrance area. Although there were no Iraqis in sight the tracer rounds were zipping by, blocking their exit. If they tried to make a break for it, the enemy would cut them down. On the other hand, in just over a minute there was going to be one hell of an explosion and the huge tower would come crashing down on top of them. With no alternative the assault group burst out, running like mad for cover. Luckily no one was hit.

I watched as the guys ran from the entrance point, rapidly heading back towards the burne and the protection of the support wagons. It was time for Paul and me to join them. We both ran, ducking and weaving towards the vehicles. As we approached them I yelled out, "Yorky and Paul coming in from the left," just to make sure they knew who it was. As we dived in behind the nearest wagon, a massive explosion ripped through the air. Although we had all been expecting it, the shock wave blast felt like a tornado. Three of the four demolition charges had gone off on time, and the large tower slowly buckled to one side and collapsed. The grating sound of metal on metal rose out of the dust.

The explosion caused the enemy fire to become more intense, but it was still not very effective. Not wanting to wait for the Iraqis to get their act together, we quickly slotted into our exit formation. I was near the front and recognised Brian, Ian, Slugger and Matt all in front of me. We were just approaching our three wagons when I noticed several silhouettes moving on top of the burne.

"Who the fuck's that lot on the burne?" someone else asked.

"It's okay, they're civvies."

Wrong. The silhouettes opened fire on us. Slugger dropped to the floor as the vortex of a high velocity round passed through his trouser leg. His immediate reaction was that he had been hit, but luckily the round itself never touched him. By this time Matt, Ian and I had reached the side of the Mark 9 wagon and quickly put the vehicle between the enemy and ourselves. To my left the roar of an engine made me notice that one of our wagons was taking off. However, at that moment I had other things on my mind.

Matt and Ian stood by the truck tailgate and poured some fire down on the enemy. I jumped up on the wagon and shouted for Leslie, who was sitting behind the Mark 19, to fire, indicating with my hand the direction of the enemy. But Leslie just grabbed the weapon and fired blindly into space, totally in the wrong direction.

"Fucking idiot." I grabbed hold of the weapon and turned it towards the enemy on the burne. "There! There!" I screamed at him over the noise.

Eventually he got a grip and started to engage the enemy. The rounds that Leslie had originally fired had gone off in the direction of our main fire support group. One of the guys later reported coming under fire from a number of what he thought were light mortars. I jumped off the truck and joined Matt and Ian at the rear, from where all three of us fired for all we were worth towards the enemy position.

By this time the amount of incoming fire was quite intense, but we tried desperately to stand our ground. Looking to my left, I saw more of our lads putting fire down towards the enemy.

"Where's Brian?" I shouted.

"He's fucked off in a wagon."

Then I recalled hearing one of our vehicles start up and drive off. As we came under fire Brian had dived on to the front of the nearest truck and screamed to the driver, "Get the fuck out of here!" One or two other men had managed to jump on the back as it drove way into the darkness, leaving the rest of us behind.

There was an incredible amount of confusion at this stage. However, most of the guys were capable of taking control of the situation. When the enemy fire increased, and our main fire support group had still not re-appeared, it was generally decided to move our position. Frank, who was driving the Mark 19, slowly moved the wagon away from the burne. He had some bottle, driving directly into the line of enemy fire. I shall never know how he managed not to get hit. Nor was he the only hero. The two guys who were operating the MIRA, which was mounted high on the vehicle roll-bar, stood up in the wagon directing fire throughout the battle. With enemy fire ranging all around, these two stood their ground. One of them, Barry, took a direct hit on the Milan missile that was right next to his head. Battle really is a proving ground, and Victor Two was no exception.

The red and green hornets were everywhere, dancing in the amazing fireworks display that only war can create. The crack and thump of a thousand rounds whistled all around us. Tracer rounds flew past at incredible speed, then stopped suddenly as they hit a hard surface. I heard zip, zip, zip as hot lead buzzed my arms, my legs and my head.

Amid this chaos the fire support group were fighting desperately to extract themselves. At the time they were unaware of the real situation, thinking that some of us were still on the target. Communications had gone down just when we needed them most, which meant that neither group knew what the other was doing and had been engaging anything that looked as if it might be sheltering an Iraqi soldier. Permanent buildings, Portakabins and vehicles all littered the area, burning brightly if they had been set on fire.

Throughout all this there was still time to laugh. One of the guys, Charlie, said he had spotted an Iraqi having a shit just before the fire-fight started. He could clearly see the guy through the infra-red sight attached to the GPMG. He engaged him more out of fun than in any attempt to kill him, and later explained in great detail how he had shot short bursts after the retreating Iraqi while he was still trying to pull his trousers up. Another guy, Sam, had spotted an Iraqi firing from inside one of the Portakabins, and decided to take the whole building out with a 66mm rocket. He shouted at another guy to use his 66mm. After assembling the weapon the guy aimed it from a distance of no more than 30 metres and pressed the tit. The rocket screamed away but missed the Portakabin by some two metres. Everyone, including a number of Iraqis, watched in amazement as the rocket disappeared into the night.

We had started pulling back from the burne and gone about 200 metres when the enemy fire found us once more. The bullets buzzed around like flies homing in on a piece of meat. There was a great deal of confusion as we retreated. I remember about eight of us running at the side of the one remaining wagon. The other two had gone, although we didn't know where, and we were just following their last known direction. I remember hanging on to the side of the wagon for protection when all of a sudden a massive amount of incoming fire barely missed the top of it. I looked round at my old mate Des and shook my head; we both knew it was getting very dodgy.

Next thing I knew, Mel was next to me and saying, "This is a load of fucking shit!"

I just looked at him and said, "Well, you're one of the headsheds, Mel. You sort it out – it's what they pay you for!" With this I jumped off the vehicle. There was no way I was going to listen to Mel mouth off.

It felt as if we had been running for ages, although in reality we had probably covered no more than a kilometre or so. We stopped abruptly, as one of the guys said he could see two vehicles to our front and was sure they were ours. As we got closer we discovered that it was Brian's gang, which included Paul and some four or five more. It was obvious that the other guys had been either driving or commanding their vehicles, when Brian had jumped aboard and ordered them "to get the fuck out of here".

We formed up in all-round defence, preparing the wagons for a quick getaway if necessary. I thought that one of the vehicle commanders might take control, but it didn't happen. There were a number of junior NCOs who could have taken control, but this would probably have caused even more problems. We started talking in whispers, checking on who had made it back and who was still missing. Brian must have thought we were talking about him, for next minute he shouted out, "Shut the fuck up, all of you." At this point he tried to make a command decision. "Right, we're getting the fuck out of here!"

In unison some ten voices shouted back, "What about the fire support group?"

"They can make their own fucking way back."

"Bollocks. We're not leaving." The majority decision was to wait for the rest of the guys. Brian tried to bully his authority on the rest, but by this time we had had enough. I thought back to his briefing and the declaration: "We don't leave anybody behind."

It was around this time that I thought we were not going to make it. If the Iraqis followed, most of us would be forced to go on foot. I started to prepare myself mentally for a spot of E and E (escape and evasion). When we were all together our fighting had strength; split, as we were, I was starting to feel vulnerable.

Suddenly Barry, who was still manning the MIRA, shouted out, "I can see some vehicles coming towards us. I think they're ours! Yes, it's the fire support group." Ben, who was riding the only bike during the Victor Two assault, shot off into the darkness to make contact and bring them safely in. This action was to win him a Military Medal after the war. Bru opened up on his radio, also trying to contact them. Finally he succeeded, relaying our position precisely. Then someone thought of what seemed to him a good idea, "I'll switch on my infra-red firefly." This is a small, torch-like object which emits a very strong blue flashing light and is used as a distress beacon. Nobody got the chance to stop him. As the strobe light went on it instantly attracted the enemy fire, and high velocity rounds started pouring into our position.

"Switch it off! Switch it off!" the guys screamed as we all dived for cover. He had only been doing his best, but to recall this young man fumbling about trying to turn the confounded thing off would bring a smile to my face for years to come. Two minutes later the fire support group drove up, all of them alive and kicking. But a single look told you they had fought one hell of a battle. Best of all, Pat was back. Thank goodness for someone with a cool head and clear thoughts.

As soon as he arrived Pat took control, ordering everyone to mount up and prepare to move. He turned to Dave on the MIRA and requested, "Find me a way through this position." Then, checking the original Satnav location where Alistair had left the bike, he pointed his arm in front. "Find me a hole in that direction!"

"There are enemy slit trenches all over the place along that route," shouted Dave.

"Bring all the guns to bear in that direction – we're going to punch a lane through." With that the column moved forwards, our guns cutting down any resistance. The enemy were still firing to our rear but nothing much was coming our way, and even if it did nothing was going to stop us. For an hour we ran the gauntlet of Iraqi soldiers before disappearing once more into the empty darkness of the desert.

HECKLER & KOCH MP5

Founded by former Mauser employees in 1947, the Heckler & Koch company produce several weapons beloved of the world's special forces, but none more so than the MP5 sub-machine gun. When 22 SAS stormed the Iranian Embassy in London in 1981, it was the MP5 that the assault teams toted.

Utilizing a closed bolt system, the MP5 is arguably the most accurate, reliable and compact SMG in production. It has three differing modes of fire – single shot, three-round burst and fully automatic – is available with fixed or telescopic stocks. There are a number of variants for clandestine, counter-terrorist operations, among them the 12.7-inch shortened version, the MP5K, used by SAS undercover teams in Northern Ireland.

As well as Britain's SAS, special operations units from fifty other nations count upon the MP5.

URGENT FURY

Ian Padden

A pinprick in the expanse of the Caribbean, the island of Grenada jumped onto the front pages of the world's newspapers in October 1983 when its government was overthrown by socialist rebels. The CIA detected the hand of nearby Cuba and persuaded Washington DC that the stability of the US's watery backyard was threatened. To restore the island to its rightful government, the US launched an invasion – code-named Urgent Fury – which involved numerous US special forces, each with their own mission. Prime among the special units were 1st and 2nd Ranger Battalions of the 75th Infantry. The exploits of the Rangers in Grenada are detailed below.

Formed in 1974 to "conduct special military operations in support of the policies and objectives of the USA", as well as to "be the most proficient infantry [unit] in the world", the Ranger battalions comprise 600 personnel, all airborne qualified, all of them already professional soldiers from within the ranks of the US Army. Ranger selection is rigororous, and takes fifty-eight days to complete. Only 50 per cent of candidates pass and receive the coveted Ranger black beret.

The first Rangers in US history were formed by Major Robert Rogers in 1763 (see pp. 28–35), and various incarnations have followed over the centuries at the dictates of Mars. Today's Rangers trace a direct line of descent to the six Ranger battalions raised by the US in the Second World War, and which saw action over the globe from North Africa to the Pacific but most famously on D-Day 1944 in Normandy, when the 2nd Ranger Battalion under Lieutenant Colonel James Rudder (hence "Rudder's Rangers") destroyed the German gun emplacement on Pointe Du Hoc and the 5th Ranger Battalion was ordered to "lead the way" off the hell of Omaha Beach.

They did. The Rangers remained part of the US Army until they were disbanded at the end of the Korean war, only to be revived as a long-range reconnaissance unit for the conflict in Vietnam. Along with other special forces they fell out of favour post-Vietnam, but the escalating conflagration in the Middle East reminded the Department of the Army that crack units, ready for action any time and any place, are not a luxury for a modern nation. They are a prerequisite. And so the Rangers were born again in 1974 as the 1st and 2nd Ranger Battalions of the 75th Infantry. And so the Rangers were dispatched to Grenada in October 1983.

WHEN THE CALL went out to the Rangers to report immediately for a routine Emergency Deployment Readiness Exercise there was no panic, just haste. Thoughts of beating the time it took to deploy for the last exercise were foremost in most Rangers' minds.

However, it was not just the weight of their combat packs that changed when claymore mines, fragmentation grenades, mortar shells, and live ammunition were issued – their attitudes also changed when they realized that this "exercise" was going to be real combat.

Grenada? Where the hell is Grenada?

That question was asked by many a Ranger. The briefings quickly revealed the answer, and the map of the tiny island nation in the Caribbean became the focus of attention for one of the modern world's most elite fighting forces.

What's the terrain like? What's the weather like? Who are we fighting? How many of them are there? What sort of weapons do they have? Is it a jungle? How high are the mountains? Are there any tanks? What about aircraft?

These were but a few of the hundreds of questions that the harried intelligence officers had to face. What was even worse was that they had to answer them as well as they could, and they had to provide maps, photographs, enemy strength, equipment, etc. But they managed to do it in the short time they had available.

It can be safely said that under such circumstances no intelligence officer is ever satisfied with the information he gives out, and no field commander is ever fully satisfied with what he receives. There is always one silly little question that the soldier wants to know for which there is no answer, and that is the question that niggles him. If he had the answer, he probably wouldn't feel much better anyway; perhaps it's just having something to worry about that's important – anything, as long as it distracts him and keeps his mind off the actual start of the battle.

The fully armed and loaded Rangers could smell the kerosene fuel from the turboprop engines of the squat-looking C-130s as they marched toward them. They had boarded these aircraft many times before. They knew exactly where to put their feet on the ramp, where all the hand-holds were on the framework inside, where the uncomfortable spots were – it was almost second nature to them. As they boarded this time, everything seemed normal and familiar – with one exception. This time they were really being carried into battle and, apart from a handful of senior officers and NCOs, none of the Rangers had ever been in action before.

As the clamor and clatter of the loading in the great round bellies of the C-130s settled down, the engines were started and the doors were closed. The pilots eased the throttles forward, and the aircraft moved slowly toward the end of the take-off runway. The Ranger-laden C-130s were joined in the night skies by two similar aircraft. These were the AC-130 Spectre gunships of the Special Warfare unit of the U.S. Air Force that were to act as escorts and provide support for the Rangers.

The Spectres are perhaps the most heavily armed aircraft of their size in the world. With heavy calibre machine guns and cannons, they can lay down an incredible barrage of fire over a wide area of ground. Or, they can simply direct their fire to one specific spot, almost like a jet of water from a fire tender. In fact, the resemblance is such that the expression "hose the place down" is actually used when these "battleships of the air" are called to attack a specific target area. From an infantryman's point of view, watching the AC-130 Spectres in action is incredibly reassuring and quite awesome. That is, of course, if it's on your side. The thought of being on the receiving end of one of these aerial monsters is just not a subject to dwell upon.

To the pilots of the C-130 troop carriers, and the Rangers on board, it was comforting to know that the Spectres were available to go in before them and make a "hosing run."

There were two separate flights of aircraft carrying the Rangers. The lead flight of five contained the 1st Battalion, and the second flight of five carried the 2nd Battalion. Each C-130 held about fifty fully armed and equipped men, and there was very little room to spare.

For most of the flight very little was said by the individual Rangers; it was a time for personal thoughts – concerns about being ready for what was to come and hopes that the first exposure to hostile fire could be met without too much fear. Very few battle-tested warriors will deny that fear exists; they have experienced it repeatedly, and they manage it as best they can under the circumstances of the time. They know the meaning of fear, and they also know that, to a greater or lesser degree, it will always be there. It manifests itself in so many different ways with each individual, and it varies in intensity in an equally diverse manner. Repeated exposure helps, inasmuch as it gives a reserve of experience to draw on; that reserve simply permits better self management, and that is really about all that can be hoped for, because the fear will always be there.

Extensive military training, by virtue of its repetitive nature, is designed to ensure that soldiers will react automatically and responsively when under fire. This relieves the pressure and lessens the risk of error caused by fear. Again and again the battle-seasoned will tell the inexperienced, "Do it exactly as you have been taught in training.

Don't try and think when you don't have the time. Do it the way you were trained!"

The Rangers had spent years in training for what lay ahead and, as the aircraft hummed and droned through the night, most of the inexperienced Rangers must have realized that now was the time to fall back and rely on that training. The handful of experienced Rangers already knew that it had to be that way – they, too, had fears similar to those of their inexperienced colleagues. Their experience gave them a slight advantage. They had some idea what to expect, but it also put them at a disadvantage since their knowledge gave them access to a different set of fears. It was a "no win" situation between the tried and untried, and fear would always be slightly ahead.

The landing zone was the 9,100-foot-long runway at Point Saline on the southern tip of the island, and the flight carrying the 1st Battalion was to land first and secure the runway. Approximately fifteen minutes later the flight carrying the 2nd Battalion would arrive to help consolidate the situation, and from there both battalions would move on to other assigned objectives.

As the first aircraft approached the airfield, a hail of fire came up from four ZU-23-2 Soviet-built anti-aircraft guns situated on a hill overlooking the airfield. They were joined by an assortment of 12.7-mm cannons and heavy caliber machine guns. The 23-mm double barreled ZU guns were known as they had shown up on reconnaissance reports, but the intensity of the other fire power was somewhat unexpected. An initial pass of the runway revealed that large stakes had been driven into the surface along its length, and it was obvious that any attempt at a landing would meet with disaster. The enemy had obviously been expecting such an assault and had effectively denied the Rangers the use of the runway.

The second plan of attack immediately went into action – an extremely low-level parachute landing. Lieutenant Colonel Wes Taylor, commander of the 1st Battalion, and Lieutenant Colonel Ralph Hagler, commander of the 2nd Battalion, had carefully planned for such a contingency; but they had been hoping they would not have to do it since a parachute assault from 500 feet had never been attempted by U.S. troops in any war. Normal operational jumps were done from 1,200 feet, and that was low enough for most. Jumps from 500 feet had only been done by individual special agents during previous armed conflicts when they were being dropped behind enemy lines. It had never been done with battalion strength troops in full battle order.

If intelligence information was correct, the powerful antiaircraft guns could depress their barrels down to 600 feet; hence Taylor and Hagler decided to take the chance and commit to 500 feet. The pilots of the C-130s agreed to it, and their colleagues in the Spectres were set to conduct one of their famous hose jobs in support of the operation.

To the Rangers in the bellies of the 130s, life was not that simple – with less than fifteen minutes to go, they had to change from an "air land" mode to an "air drop" mode. Added to that, they were informed that their transports would not land after them, so they had to take everything with them. Apart from their weapons, each man would now have to jump with a rucksack that weighed over a hundred pounds.

Rearranging and repacking equipment in preparation for an air drop at the last minute, when everything had been carefully packed for a normal landing, was an absolute nightmare. To have committed to memory the exact position of all of life's little necessities for the upcoming battle, and then to have to rearrange them at the last moment, was annoying, confusing, and, to put it mildly, a pain in the neck.

Before most realized it, the doors were being opened and the C-130s were established on their drop run. The Rangers knew that when the first man went out the door, there was no time to think – everyone had to get out as quickly as possible. The drop window was very small, and it would only take some thirty seconds – probably less, with all the weight they were carrying – to get to the ground from 500 feet on the T-10 parachute. There was another niggling doubt in the minds of some – the thought of the parachute not opening. Normally it was not much of a concern as there was a reserve parachute to work with, but not this time.

There was no place to put it, and, in any case, even if it were worn, at 500 feet it could not be deployed in time.

As the jump doors were opened there was a roar of rushing air, and experience immediately told the men that the noise was much louder than usual, which could only mean that the aircraft were going in much faster than normal. That indeed was the case. If it had been an exercise, there would have been a no-jump situation; but this was not a practice, this was the proverbial *it*!

In the cockpit, the pilots' life was not easy. The crucial thing was to get the aircraft in the correct position over the drop zone – the drop height was so low that they had to fly right down the target line. There was absolutely no room for error. The sky was beginning to fill with flack, which did not help matters; and if the pilots did not get the lumbering 130s lined up correctly, they could not instruct the jumpmaster to release the Rangers. Then it would almost certainly be a catastrophe.

The pilots' problems were compounded by the fact that there was a strong wind – they estimated 20 knots – and it was raining heavily, thereby causing acute visual problems. None of this was helped by the fact that the runway drop zone was bordered by the sea on one side and hills on the other side. To have the aircraft out of position would mean the Rangers would fall into the sea, or hit the ground very quickly – either way it would be a disaster. They just had to get it right, to hell with everything else. When they got into position at the right height, the Rangers would have to go out that door, regardless of the altitude or speed of the 130. Another contributing factor was the temperature, which was over ninety degrees – that meant that the aircraft were handling more sluggishly than the normal aircraft drop speed of 120–130 knots. In order to be able to maneuver their machines with any reasonable degree of precision, the speed had to be kept up around 150 knots.

The experienced Rangers and the jumpmasters were aware of the problem, and they made only one statement, "Get us in the exact position at as slow a speed as you possibly can. We'll take it from there." The pilots struggled, with adrenalin running high, and they gave

the Rangers the exact position, with the speed at a savage
150 knots.

When the green light came on, the heavily loaded Rangers spilled out the two doors on either side of the aircraft. The air slammed into them like a freight train, and it snatched and tore at the deploying parachutes. Most were happy to be out the door as the weight of their packs had been almost unbearable when they were standing in the aircraft. But the speed at which they had come out, combined with their excessive weight, resulted in vicious jerks on the harness assemblies when the parachutes deployed. It left most of the Rangers gasping for breath, and those who had not followed the golden prejump rule of tightening the harness until it hurt suffered the added discomfort of the straps tightening quite sharply and suddenly around a rather delicate area of the groin.

However, even that could be tolerated somewhat, now that the fearsome weight of the rucksacks and equipment was off their legs. There was no time to dwell upon such pleasures because the ground – as well as rifle and machine-gun fire – was coming up quickly.

In the cockpits of the 130s the pilots were carefully watching what they were doing. It took just twenty-one seconds for all the Rangers to get out of all the aircraft, which was a brilliantly coordinated effort on the part of both the pilots and the Rangers. A few aircraft emptied in less than twenty seconds, which meant that the aircraft became about 20,000 pounds lighter in the same amount of time. That tremendous weight loss, in such a short period of time, caused the aircraft to want to leap upward into the thunderstorm of flack overhead, and the pilots had to be very careful not to allow that to happen.

Before the empty C-130s had pulled away to safety, the Rangers were hauling down on their canopy lines as they fought to get a half-decent landing in the 20-knot wind. There was no thought of a graceful landing, just a safe one. Out of almost 600 Rangers, there were only two real misfortunes – Sp4 Harold Hagen broke his leg, and one unfortunate Ranger, who had the softest landing of all, managed to find the sea and, fortunately, survived.

The success of the landing was an absolute testimony to the skill of the men and their training – the safety margins for practice jumps are no more than 130 knots aircraft speed, a minimum altitude of 1,200 feet, and a maximum wind component of 13 knots. Apart from the fact that all those limits had to be exceeded, the weight of equipment carried by each man was incredible. Lieutenant Raymond Thomas, a platoon leader, "fell" out the door with an M-60 machine gun, an M-16 rifle, a .45 pistol, 1,000 rounds of 7.62-mm ammunition, enough fragmentation grenades to last him a week, an undisclosed amount of 5.56-mm and .45 ammunition, and finally his own personal equipment and rations – including two canteens full of water! All accounts seem to indicate that Lieutenant Thomas was one of the majority.

It was 0630 hours when the 1st Battalion landed on the east end of the airfield; at the same time, the 2nd Battalion was dropping onto the west end. Once on the ground the Rangers went into action against much more stiff opposition than the intelligence officers had predicted, but it appears that the enemy defenders became very confused when the Rangers started to land all around them. The confusion served the Rangers well, and the opposition in the immediate vicinity of the airfield was cleaned out very quickly. Most of the Cuban and Grenadian militiamen seemingly took one look at the charging Rangers and immediately fled the area.

That was not exactly the case with the enemy troops who were dug in on the hill overlooking the airfield. They were putting up a little more fight, and the Rangers promptly called in the eager AC-130 Spectres and a few navy "fast movers." The air force liaison officers who had jumped with the Rangers went to work and directed the aerial assault. First the Spectres moved in. They resembled giant mythical dragons as they lumbered out of the sky, literally vomiting fire onto the enemy positions in the form of 20-mm cannon shells. Working with them, in complete contrast, were the Navy A-6s and A-7s that came screaming in at high speed from the aircraft carrier, USS *Independence*.

The Rangers then stormed up the hill and drove the remaining enemy off. In doing so, they captured hundreds of brand-new Soviet-made weapons, much to their surprise. As the hill was being taken, an enterprising Ranger found some steam rollers and adroitly "hot wire" started one. He then proceeded to drive down the runway smashing the stakes the Cubans had hastily driven in to prevent the aircraft from landing.

Meanwhile, other Rangers had cleared the Cubans away from the St. George's Medical School campus, which was by the airport, and had the American and foreign students who were there under their protection by 0850 hours.

By 1000 hours the runway was clear for aircraft to land, and the airlift of two battalions of the 82nd Airborne began. There were still a few of the enemy around. They would keep fighting as long as they were dug in; but the Rangers were in the open. However, as soon as the Rangers started to apply pressure, they either ran away or gave up.

The captured Cuban soldiers and the Grenadian Militiamen had conflicting stories to tell. The Grenadians maintained that they had done no shooting – it had been the Cubans. The Cubans, in turn, claimed it had been the Grenadians. It seems that they were not quite as united as they should have been, but the Rangers knew the truth – both groups were lying.

By early afternoon the area within a few miles around the airfield was fairly well cleared out, and both Ranger battalions started to reassemble in the airport area. The Cubans chose this moment to launch a counterattack in three Soviet-built armored personnel carriers. The Rangers filled the Cubans' vehicles with 90-mm recoilless rifle shells, and the Spectres got in on the act and utterly pulverized the hapless personnel carriers with 20-mm cannon fire. As if that wasn't enough, the Navy A-7 Corsairs threw in their two-cents worth and strafed what was left. Those enemies who were fortunate enough to live tried to make a break for it, but it was a waste of time as they were neatly picked off by the Rangers themselves. Sure it was overkill; but it put the message across, and that's what the whole thing was all about.

By late afternoon the airport area was completely secure, and the Rangers dug in and slept in the rain. Colonel Hagler of the 2nd Battalion commented that the rain was no problem, and added, "I've never seen a rusty Ranger."

The following day – Wednesday, October 26 – the 2nd Battalion set about the rescue and evacuation of the remaining 233 students at the St. George's Medical School at Grand Anse. The students were all in a beachside building about the size of a small hotel, and about sixty heavily armed Cubans had dug themselves in around the building. Navy CH-46 helicopters flew in close with 150 Rangers on board. About 100 of the Rangers attacked the entrenched Cubans while the remainder raced into the building, evacuated the students while the firefight was going on, and led them to giant Marine-crewed HH-53 helicopters, which had been brought in behind the Rangers to lift the students out. The complete operation took just twenty-six minutes, and the students – over sixty per HH-53 – were flown immediately to the Point Saline airfield. It was a classic Ranger raid.

The Rangers continued to clear up pockets of resistance with heavy fighting in some areas but, generally speaking, they had no real difficulties.

On their third day on the island – Thursday, October 27 – the Rangers were given their final mission. The Edgemont training area was reported to have some thirty Soviet advisors and 400 Cuban troops well entrenched and prepared to put up a fight. The Rangers were told it was almost a suicide mission, but an assault must be made. Three rifle companies of the 2nd Battalion were sent in, and the lead party, aboard Blackhawk helicopters provided by the 82nd Airborne, immediately ran into trouble.

It appears that the pilot of the lead helicopter was shot through the arm, and the helicopter went out of control. It then crashed into another Blackhawk, dragging it to the ground. A third machine was maneuvering nearby and crashed into a building while trying to avoid the stricken pair. Three Rangers were killed in the crashes, becoming the first fatalities the battalions had suffered since they had landed on the island. A further fifteen were injured, some quite badly, but the remaining Rangers succeeded in taking the training area with minimal effort. The Rangers camped in the Edgemont compound overnight, keeping it secure until the Marine HH-53 helicopters came in to sling load the wrecked Blackhawks out the next morning.

That same evening, October 28, at 1819 hours, Rangers of the 1st Battalion were flown off the island for redeployment in the States. By 1539 hours the following day, the last of the Rangers was taken off the island.

Their missions had been completed in an exemplary manner – in the true tradition of the battalions of Darby's Rangers of World War II.

The 1st and 2nd Battalions of the United States Rangers had demonstrated to their leaders, their nation, and to the rest of the world, that they were not just Rangers in name – they were Rangers in deed.

When their time came they were ready. They responded to the order which was first given some forty years ago – "Rangers, lead the way!"

ROGERS' RANGERS

The modern US Rangers trace their antecedents to 1756, when frontiersman Major Robert Rogers raised and trained nine companies of colonists to fight a stealthy hit-and-run war against the French and Indians. The Rangers' most effective, and most famous raid, occurred in 1759, when, after three weeks of marching, they mounted a surprise attack on the Indian fort of St Francis, deep inside French-held territory. More than 200 braves were killed, and St Francis fort was burned to the ground.

Rogers' Rangers were disbanded in 1763, with the close of the French and Indian War. Yet time has done little to diminish Rogers' achievement or vision. Indeed, the Plan of Discipline he composed for his newly formed Rangers reads like a blueprint for a twenty-first century special force:

Major Robert Rogers's Plan of Discipline

I. All Rangers are to be subject to the rules and articles of war; to appear at roll-call every evening on their own parade, equipped, each with a firelock, sixty rounds of powder and ball, and a hatchet, at which time an officer from each company is to inspect the same, to see they are in order, so as to be ready on any emergency to march at a minute's warning; and before they are dismissed the necessary guards are to be draughted, and scouts for the next day appointed.

II. Whenever you are ordered out to the enemy's forts or frontiers for discoveries, if your number be small, march in a single file, keeping at such a distance from each other as to prevent one shot from killing two men, sending one man, or more, forward, and the like on each side, at the distance of twenty yards from the main body, if the ground you march over will admit of it, to give the signal to the officer of the approach of an enemy, and of their number, etc.

III. If you march over marshes or soft ground, change your position, and march abreast of each other, to prevent the enemy from tracking you (as they would do if you marched in a single file) till you get over such ground, and then resume your former order, and march till it is quite dark before you encamp, which do, if possible, on a piece of ground that may afford your sentries the advantage of seeing or hearing the enemy at some considerable distance, keeping one-half of your whole party awake alternately through the night.

IV. Some time before you come to the place you would reconnoitre, make a stand, and send one or two men, in whom you can confide, to look out the best ground for making your observations.

V. If you have the good fortune to take any prisoners, keep them separate, till they are examined, and in your return take a different route from that in which you went out, then you may the better discover any party in your rear, and have an opportunity, if their strength be superior to yours, to alter your course, or disperse, as circumstances may require.

VI. If you march in a large body of three or four hundred, with a design to attack the enemy, divide your party into three columns, each headed by a proper officer, and let these columns march in single files, the columns to the right and left keeping at twenty yards distance or more from that of the center, if the ground will admit, and let proper guards be kept in the front and rear, and suitable flanking parties at a due distance as before directed, with orders to halt on all eminences, to take a view of the surrounding ground, to prevent your being ambuscaded, and to notify the approach or retreat of the enemy, that proper dispositions may be made for attacking, defending, etc. And if the enemy approach in your front on level ground, form a front of your three columns or main body with the advanced guard, keeping out your flanking parties, as if you were marching under the command of trusty officers, to prevent the enemy from pressing hard on either of your wings, or surrounding you, which is the usual method of the savages, if their number will admit of it, and be careful likewise to support and strengthen your rear guard.

VII. If you are obliged to receive the enemy's fire, fall, or squat down, till it is over, then rise and discharge at them. If their main body is equal to yours, extend yourselves occasionally; but if superior, be careful to support and strengthen your flanking parties, to make them equal with theirs, that if possible you may repulse them to their main body, in which case push upon them with the greatest resolution, with equal force in each flank and in the center, observing to keep at a due distance from each other, and advance from tree to tree, with one half of the party before the other ten or twelve yards. If the enemy push upon you, let your front line fire and fall down, and then let your rear advance thro' them and do the like, by which time those who before were in front will be ready to discharge again, and repeat the same alternately, as occasion shall require; by this means you will keep up such a constant fire, that the enemy will not be able easily to break your order, or gain your ground.

VIII. If you oblige the enemy to retreat, be careful, in your pursuit of them, to keep out your flanking parties, and to prevent them from gaining eminences, or rising grounds, in which case they would perhaps be able to rally and repulse you in their turn.

IX. If you are obliged to retreat, let the front of your whole party fire and fall back, till the rear hath done the same, making for the best ground you can; by this means you will oblige the enemy to pursue you, if they do it at all, in the face of constant fire.

X. If the enemy is so superior that you are in danger of being surrounded by them, let the whole body disperse, and every one take a different road to the place of rendezvous appointed for the evening, which must every morning be altered and fixed for the evening ensuing, in order to bring the whole party, or as many of them as possible together, after any separation that may happen in the day; but if you should happen to be actually surrounded, form yourselves into a square, or, if in the woods, a circle is best, and, if possible, make a stand till the darkness of the night favours your escape.

XI. If your rear is attacked, the main body and flankers must face about to the right or left, as occasion shall require, and form themselves to oppose the enemy, as before directed; and the same method must be observed, if attacked in either of your flanks, by which means you will always make a rear of one of your flank guards.

XII. If you determine to rally after a retreat, in order to make a fresh stand against the enemy, by all means endeavour to do it on the most rising ground you come at, which will give you greatly the advantage in point of situation, and enable you to repulse superior numbers.

XIII. In general, when pushed upon the enemy, reserve your fire till they approach very near, which will then put them into the greater surprise and consternation, and give you an opportunity of rushing upon them with your hatchets and cutlasses to the better advantage.

XIV. When you encamp at night, fix your sentries in such a manner as not to be relieved from the main body till morning, profound secrecy and silence being often of the last importance in these cases. Each sentry, therefore, should consist of six men, two of whom must be constantly alert, and when relieved by their fellows, it should be done without noise; and in case those on duty see or hear anything which alarms them, they are not to speak, but one of them is silently to retreat, and acquaint the commanding officer thereof, that proper dispositions may be made; and all occasional sentries should be fixed in like manner.

XV. At first dawn of day, awake your whole detachment; that being the time when savages choose to fall upon their enemies, you should by all means be in readiness to receive them.

XVI. If the enemy should be discovered by your detachments in the morning, and their numbers are superior to yours, and victory doubtful, you should not attack them till the evening, as then they will not know your numbers, and if you are repulsed, your retreat will be favoured by the darkness of the night.

XVII. Before you leave your encampment, send out small parties to scout round it, to see if there be any appearance or track of an enemy that might have been near you during the night.

XVIII. When you stop for refreshment, choose some spring or rivulet if you can, and dispose your party so as not to be surprised, posting proper guards and sentries at a due distance, and let a small party waylay the path you came in, lest the enemy should be pursuing.

XIX. If, in your return, you have to cross rivers, avoid the usual fords as much as possible, lest the enemy should have discovered, and be there expecting you.

XX. If you have to pass by lakes, keep some distance from the edge of the water, lest, in case of an ambuscade or an attack from the enemy, when in that situation, your retreat should be cut off.

XXI. If the enemy pursues your rear, take a full circle till you come to your own tracks, and there form an ambush to receive them, and give them the first fire.

XXII. When you return from a scout, and come near our forts, avoid the usual roads, and avenues thereto, lest the enemy should have headed you, and lay in ambush to receive you, when almost exhausted with fatigue.

XXIII. When you pursue any party that has been near our forts or encampments, follow not directly in their tracks, lest you should be discovered by their rear guards, who, at such a time, would be most alert; but endeavor, by a different route to head and meet them in some narrow pass, or lay in ambush to receive them when and where they least expect it.

XXIV. If you are to embark in canoes, battoes, or otherwise, by water, choose the evening for the time of your embarkation, as you will then have the whole night before you, to pass undiscovered by any parties of the enemy, on hills or other places, which command a prospect of the lake or river you are upon.

XXV. In paddling or rowing, give orders that the boat or canoe next the sternmost, wait for her, and the third for the second, and the fourth for the third, and so on, to prevent separation, and that you may be ready to assist each other on any emergency.

XXVI. Appoint one man in each boat to look out for fires, on adjacent shores, from the numbers and size of which you may form some judgment of the number that kindled them, and whether you are able to attack them or not.

XXVII. If you find the enemy encamped near the banks of a river, or lake, which you imagine they will attempt to cross for their security upon being attacked, leave a detachment of your party on the opposite shore to receive them, while, with the remainder, you surprise them, having them between you and the lake or river.

XXVIII. If you cannot satisfy yourself as to the enemy's number and strength, from their fire, etc., conceal your boats at some distance, and ascertain their number by a reconnoitering party, when they embark, or march, in the morning, marking the course they steer, etc., when you may pursue, ambush, and attack them, or let them pass, as prudence shall direct you. In general, however, that you may not be discovered by the enemy on the lakes and rivers at a great distance, it is safest to lay by, with your boats and party concealed all day, without noise or show, and to pursue your intended route by night; and whether you go by land or water, give out parole and countersigns, in order to know one another in the dark, and likewise appoint a station for every man to repair to, in case of any accident that may separate you.

Such in general are the rules to be observed in the Ranging service; there are, however, a thousand occurrences and circumstances which may happen, that will make it necessary, in some measure; to depart from them, and to put other arts and stratagems in practice; in which cases every man's reason and judgment must be his guide, according to the particular situation and nature of things; and that he may do this to advantage, he should keep in mind a maxim never to be departed from by a commander, viz.: to preserve a firmness and presence of mind on every occasion.

COCKLESHELL HEROES

Patrick Pringle

*The famous raid on shipping at Bordeaux in December
1942 was carried out by a Royal Marines unit with the
long-winded cover name of Royal Marines Boom Patrol
Detachment (RMBPD). Its members passed into military legend as "the cockleshell heroes".*

S OMETHING HAD TO be done about the German ships at
 Bordeaux. They were sailing regularly to and from
Japan. They were running the Allied blockade, taking
out prototypes of German weapons and equipment – and
bringing back rubber and other raw materials vital in war.
Either the ships should be destroyed in the harbour, or the
port itself would have to be made unusable.

Easier said than done. The RAF could have bombed
Bordeaux, but it would have meant killing a lot of French
civilians. Could the Navy bombard the port, then? That
was out of the question. Bordeaux was beautifully protected
by nature, 62 miles of river and estuary separating it from
the Atlantic Ocean. Therefore the only possibility was a
combined operation.

The harbour approaches were well guarded by the Germans, so a powerful force would be required. Estimates
were drawn up at Combined Operations Headquarters.
There would have to be a large force of warships and
transports, with strong air support, and not less than
50,000 troops.

That also was out of the question. Neither the men nor

the equipment could be spared in the desperate days of July 1942.

Then Major Hasler offered to do the job with three canoes and six Marines.

The last man out of Norway in 1940, Hasler had been messing about in small boats since the age of twelve, when he and a school-friend had built their own canoe. He had joined the Royal Marines at eighteen, and was twenty-eight in 1942. Recently he had made himself an expert – in theory – on methods of attacking enemy ships in harbour by stealth. He was looking for a chance to translate his expertise into practice when he heard about the problem of Bordeaux.

A year earlier Hasler had worked out a scheme on paper for attacking ships with canoes and underwater swimmers. Combined Ops HQ had turned the idea down as being too far-fetched. When the first Italian frogmen proved it was nothing of the kind, Hasler's rejected paper was read a second time. In January 1942 he was posted to experimental duties. He taught himself underwater swimming with oxygen breathing apparatus, and studied the technique of attaching limpet-like magnetic mines to enemy ships. He experimented with many small powered underwater boats of both British and Italian design, but finally settled for a canoe.

It was a special kind of canoe called a cockle. Basically it was just a rubberized fabric skin stretched tightly over a wooden frame. That was too fragile for Hasler's purpose. He needed a canoe with a flat, rigid bottom that could be dragged over a stony beach without damaging the skin. It also had to be sturdy enough to be lifted and carried with a heavy load without breaking its back. As no such canoe existed, Hasler consulted a boat-designer, Fred Goatley. Together they produced a collapsible two-man canoe that could do all Hasler asked. It was awarded the official name of Cockle Mark II.

Hasler's next task was more difficult. He had to persuade Combined Ops HQ to let him form a Royal Marine unit to use the products of his experiments. After the usual fight against authority he was allowed to form the new unit on

July 6. A call was put out to the Marines for volunteers for hazardous service. Few who answered the call had any experience of handling small boats, and some could not even swim. Such deficiencies did not worry Hasler. Those things could be taught. The qualifications he looked for were courage and daring, guts and determination, intelligence and self-reliance. He wanted men who would obey orders but who rejected the old precept, which was still being hammered into recruits in 1942, that Servicemen were "not paid to think".

The new unit of thirty-four men, all ranks, was put through a fierce training programme by its commanding officer. They were soon carrying out mock raids with apparent success. After ten weeks Hasler was asking for a real operation. Then he was told about the problem of Bordeaux.

It took him just twenty-four hours to draft an outline plan. He proposed to raid the port with six men, including himself, in three canoes. The only help he wanted was transport to the mouth of the Gironde estuary. He asked for a submarine because it could get closer inshore, although it was far from ideal for launching the canoes.

His plan was approved in all except one detail. Vice-Admiral Lord Louis Mountbatten, Chief of Combined Ops, ordered that Major Hasler himself was not to take part in the raid.

"Why not?" asked Hasler.

"Because you are too valuable to lose, and it is unlikely that anyone will return from this raid."

"In that case I must go. I cannot command a unit like this without sharing its dangers."

In front of Hasler, Mountbatten asked the opinion of the other senior officers at Combined Operations HQ. Almost all of them said Hasler ought not to go.

"I agree with them," Mountbatten told Hasler. "It's against my better judgment that I'm going to let you go."

Mountbatten made one change in his plans. He increased the number of canoes to six.

"In case of accidents," he said.

So Hasler had to pick a team of twelve. Actually thirteen

boarded the submarine. Norman Colley, the thirteenth, travelled as reserve.

They sailed from the Firth of Clyde aboard the submarine *Tuna* on November 30, 1942. The men did not know where they were going until they were under way. Then Hasler told them the plan.

"We shall be dropped in the dark about ten miles from the light-house on the Pointe de Grave." He sketched a map on the black-board. "That is at the entrance to the Gironde estuary. We paddle up, following the coast on our starboard. It's about sixty miles to Bordeaux. We shall move at night only, lying up on the bank during the day."

He went on to tell them about tides and likely lying-up places, and then described their targets and the probable harbour defences. He asked if there were any questions. Sergeant Wallace, the senior NCO, asked the obvious one.

"How do we get back?"

"We don't," Hasler answered bluntly. "There is no return transport to take us home. After the attack we shall split up, and the crew of each canoe will try to make its own way overland to neutral Spain. The French escape organization will help us if it can."

He paused to let that sink in.

"Does anyone want to withdraw from the operation?" he asked.

They all shook their heads.

"Good. Anyway," said Hasler, "it's much less dangerous than a bayonet charge."

He was wrong about that.

The canoes were launched in the Bay of Biscay shortly before 8 p.m. on December 7. One of them fouled a sharp corner as she went up the submarine's torpedo hatch, tearing a long slit in her fabric side. Hasler inspected the damage.

"You can't come in this," he told the crew of the canoe, Marines Ellery and Fisher. "Bad luck."

Their blackened faces were glum as the boat went back down the hatch. For them, as for Norman Colley, the operation was over. These three were to return home safely on the *Tuna*.

The other five canoes were launched on a rolling sea. Their heavy loads of explosive made them low in the water. The night was moonless by their choice, unpleasantly cloudless and starry by accident. A German trawler was patrolling nearby. Another danger was a minefield laid by the RAF. The French coast was a vague shadow in the distance – until suddenly the searchlights shone out across the sea. At the same time the trawler turned towards the *Tuna*. She had been plotted on the German radar.

The submarine vanished. Ten men paddled five canoes silently towards the entrance to the Gironde. It was bitterly cold. Hasler's own canoe, *Catfish*, leaked slightly. Marine Sparks, his No. 2, had to bail out every hour.

The five canoes kept close together while Hasler set the course. He followed the coast towards the north-west. For three hours everything was according to plan. The swell built up to rollers when they went over a sandbank, but they were far enough from the shore to be out of trouble. The flood tide helped them along. They had got off to a wonderful start.

Suddenly Hasler pricked up his ears. He heard a sound of water roaring ahead. The flood tide became stronger, the roaring louder. It sounded like surf breaking on rocks. Impossible – the coast was a mile and a half to starboard. But there were breakers ahead. Hasler saw the white froth and knew it was not so wonderful now. They were running towards a tide-race, a hazard that was not marked on his chart.

Hasler had sailed small boats through tide-races years before, off notorious spots like Start Point and Portland Bill. The others had not. He had trained them in handling a canoe in rough water, but they had never known anything as rough as this.

He gave them brief instructions, and then each canoe was paddled head-on into the surge and swirl. Waves broke over them, and the violence of the sea flung them about as they strove with their paddles to hold their course.

It was hard going for Hasler, so he could imagine the ordeal the others went through. When he reached calmer water he turned to watch for the other canoes.

One . . . two . . . three.

That was all. *Coalfish* was missing. Sergeant Wallace and Marine Ewart had not come through.

Hasler ordered a search. Sparks uttered the cry of a seagull, the unit's signal-call. No answer. No sign of the canoe, although its buoyancy bags would have kept it afloat. No sign of the crew, although they were wearing life-jackets.

Sergeant Wallace, the man from Dublin who had asked how they would get back after the operation, had disappeared.

"We'll have to go on," ordered Hasler.

The others, already cold, wet, and exhausted, were still fighting against the powerful tide. Their spirits were grim, no longer buoyant, as they turned their backs on the tide-race.

They paddled between the coast and the little island of Cordouan. Now they could see the silhouette of the lighthouse on Pointe de Grave. Hasler was pleased to see the light was not burning. Then he was horrified to hear more breakers roaring ahead. Another tide-race. Worse than the first.

In they went, paddling desperately to keep the bows head-on, while great rollers buffeted and hurled them about.

Through the roaring Hasler heard a shout and then a splash. When he came through and turned he saw the canoe *Conger* had capsized. Her crew, Corporal Sheard and Marine Moffat, were in the water but clinging to their boat.

Hasler examined the canoe. She was swamped, and bailing was impossible in that heavy sea. Beach it and then bail it? Hasler dismissed the thought. It would mean almost certain capture on that stretch of coast. Besides, it was already 2.30 a.m. To make matters worse, the lighthouse on Pointe de Grave suddenly blazed out.

Hasler made up his mind quickly.

"Sparks, try to scuttle *Conger*," he ordered. "Sheard, hang on to my stern. Moffat, on to *Cuttlefish*. We'll tow you round Pointe de Grave and then in to the shore as far as we can. After that you'll have to swim for it."

Sparks slashed at the canoe with his clasp knife. As she was heavily loaded she might sink. Her crew obeyed Hasler. They knew he was running into danger to try to save them. They also knew – and he knew – that it would still be a hard swim to the shore. Even if they reached it they would be too exhausted to go on. They could only hope to land in a deserted and sheltered spot where they could lie up and get their strength back.

Catfish and *Cuttlefish* were slowed down to a speed of one knot as they paddled on with Sheard and Moffat in tow. The search-light made them all feel naked and exposed. They expected to hear the guns start up any moment. Instead they heard what was almost as bad – the now familiar roaring of yet another tide-race ahead.

"Hold on," Hasler told the two men in the water.

Sheard was a small, tough Devonian, Moffat a big tough fellow from Belfast and Yorkshire. Both needed all their toughness as they were plunged into the foaming, roaring, swirling of the third tide-race.

Almost unbelievably, they all came through.

At last they were off the Pointe de Grave, and the tide carried them round and into the Gironde estuary.

After an hour in the water Sheard and Moffat were still hanging on. Hasler wanted to take them farther, to get clear of the port of Le Verdon. But now the tide was pulling him straight towards the jetty, and he could not fight against it with Sheard's extra weight. *Cuttlefish* was having the same trouble with Moffat.

"I'm sorry, we'll have to leave you here," Hasler whispered.

Sheard and Moffat thanked him for taking them so far. Then they dropped off and swam towards the shore. At least it was not far, and they were both still wearing fully inflated life-jackets. But they would have little chance of escape, and if they were captured pressure would be put on them for information.

Moffat never reached the shore. His body was found ten days later, washed up seventy miles away.

Sheard was never heard of again.

Catfish, Cuttlefish, and *Crayfish,* the remaining three canoes, paddled hard across the current to get away from the jetty. Then they had another unpleasant surprise. Three or four small destroyers were anchored off the jetty, blocking their course.

And the tide was too strong for them to paddle round the ships.

"We'll have to go between the destroyers and the jetty," Hasler said to Lieutenant Mackinnon of *Cuttlefish,* his second-in-command. "One at a time. We'll meet the other end. I'll go first, you last."

Hasler and Sparks crouched and used single paddles, holding them low to avoid making a sound. The channel was only a few hundred yards wide. They saw a signal lamp on a destroyer start signalling to the jetty and waited every second for a searchlight to pick them out. But they got through.

Crayfish followed safely. The two canoes waited for *Cuttlefish.* Mackinnon, once a clerk in a Glasgow coal merchant's office, had risen from the ranks. Marine Conway, his No. 2, was a former milk roundsman of twenty. That night had proved them a superb crew, Hasler reflected as he waited for them.

But they did not come. Once the men waiting thought they heard faint shouts, and replied with a soft seagull's cry. No answer. Hasler dared not wait any longer. He had to find a good hide-out before daybreak.

Mountbatten had been right in sending six canoes. There were only two left now, and they were still a long way from their target.

Crayfish was commanded by Corporal Laver, a quiet young Regular who had joined the Marines shortly before the war. His No. 2, Marine Mills, a high-spirited boy of twenty, had worked in a sports store at Kettering before joining the corps.

The two canoes paddled on up the Garonne river, fol-

lowing the bank. At half past six they tried to land. A line of
stakes planted in the river-bed held them off. They paddled
on for another hour, and then grounded on a sandy beach.
After more than eleven hours of paddling, during which
they had covered twenty-six land-miles, they hardly had
the strength to drag up their canoes and carry them into
some sparse scrub.

It was a poor hiding-place, as they soon discovered.
Shortly after daybreak about a dozen French fishermen
came in. They were joined on the beach by their wives.
Fires were lit, and the women began cooking a meal.
Excited chatter and gestures made it clear that the Marines
had been seen.

Hasler went out into the open.

"Good morning," he said in his broken French. "We are
British soldiers – friends. Please do not tell anyone you have
seen us."

The men and their wives were frightened. They feared
Hasler was a German trying to trap them. They told him
they would promise nothing.

The four Marines ate their rations and took turns to
sleep.

Barely ten miles away two of their comrades were also
sleeping, but in unhappier circumstances.

Sergeant Wallace and Marine Ewart, in *Coalfish*, had
survived the first tide-race, and had paddled on alone. They
had gone through the other two tide-races – only to capsize
off the Pointe de Grave. They had swum ashore and were
taken prisoner, in a state of exhaustion.

While Wallace and Ewart slept, the Germans did some
salvage work. They picked up maps and limpet mines and
finally found the wrecked canoe. An alert was given. The
area was searched.

As Wallace and Ewart were both wearing uniform, they
were entitled to be treated as prisoners-of-war. They were
also entitled to refuse to answer questions. Unfortunately
Germans in 1942 were less civilized than their ancestors the
Huns.

The German High Command ordered that the two

prisoners should be questioned "with no methods barred" but with the promise that if they talked freely their lives would be spared and they would be treated well. Whatever the results of this interrogation, the order continued, they were both to be executed.

Wallace and Ewart could not have been less talkative.

The alert was cancelled, and the Germans published a short communique: "On December 8," it announced, "a small British sabotage squad was engaged at the mouth of the Garonne river and finished off in combat."

The communiqué was given out on the German radio. At Combined Ops HQ in London it was taken to mean that Hasler's whole party had been destroyed.

On December 8, at dusk, one of Hasler's little party gave the alarm. "Look out! Germans!"

They all looked, and saw what appeared like a line of about fifty men, advancing towards them from the river. They drew their pistols and checked their fighting knives. Hasler picked up his Sten gun.

"The French have betrayed us, then," said Mills bitterly.

They stood waiting. The Germans seemed to be coming on very slowly. No, they had stopped. Then Hasler laughed.

"They're not Germans," he said. "They're just bits of wood!"

It was the line of stakes that had been facing them all through the day.

They had to wait for the flood stream, and it was midnight when they floated the two canoes again. They paddled hard for six hours, covering another twenty-five land miles. Once they were nearly run down by a convoy of six or seven ships coming up from astern, bound for Bordeaux.

"More targets for us," said Sparks when the danger had passed.

They found a much better hide-out for their second day in the estuary, and were not disturbed by any fishermen or their wives. They prepared to set off early to catch the flood tide. While they were carrying the canoes back to the river, a Frenchman came down from a nearby farm.

Again Hasler spoke openly, and asked him not to betray them.

"Come to my house and have a drink," the farmer invited with a friendly smile.

Hasler said they were in a hurry. The Frenchman pressed them.

"Whatever you are doing, a drink will do you good."

"We have to hurry," repeated Hasler. "We'll take you up on it after the war."

The Frenchman agreed with a grin, and promised to say nothing. They set off again.

There were several islands to negotiate that night, and they had to hole up among them during the six hours of ebb tide. It was nearly 3 a.m. when the flood tide came again, and they paddled on to the last of the islands, the Ile de Cazeau. It was almost daybreak when they found a hide-out.

They could not have known that Mackinnon and Conway had holed up on the same island, a bare two or three miles away.

What had happened to *Cuttlefish* off Le Verdon was never discovered. Somehow Mackinnon and Conway had made their way past the anchored destroyers, and they had almost caught up *Catfish* and *Crayfish*. They were determined to attack at Bordeaux according to plan. The port was now only twelve miles away.

So six of the original party of twelve were still in the fight, and almost reunited, although none of them had any idea of that. Two more of their comrades were not far off, either. At four o'clock that morning, when the three canoes were approaching the Ile de Cazeau, Sergeant Wallace and Marine Ewart were taken to Bordeaux for interrogation by the German Security Police.

There is no record of what happened, but we can be sure the Germans tortured their prisoners. All the German Security Police were sadistic thugs, and they had been specifically ordered to use torture in this case. It is equally certain that they failed to get anything out of their prisoners. Wallace and Ewart even managed to convince their interrogators that they had been on their own.

On the evening of that day the two parties of Marines on the Ile de Cazeau made their separate preparations for the last lap of their voyage. They would probably have met again, but Mackinnon and Conway were unlucky. They had hardly launched *Cuttlefish* when she hit a submerged obstruction and was wrecked. They had to abandon the canoe and swim for the shore.

Bitterly disappointed, they set off overland for Spain. They were never to see the others again.

Catfish and *Crayfish* left the island shortly before 7 p.m. By 11 p.m. they had reached their last hide-out, a perfect spot among nine-foot reeds. Ahead they could see the lights of Bordeaux harbour, and even heard the rattle of cranes.

They stayed in their hide for the rest of the night and the next day.

"Sparks and I will work up the west bank of the main docks," Hasler told his companions. "Laver and Mills will try the east docks. If you don't find targets there, come back to the south basin and attack those two ships over there." They looked out through the reeds at a good-sized cargo ship and a cargo liner.

In the evening they had their last meal and then fused their limpet mines. Each canoe had eight. The whole process took more than an hour.

At 9 p.m. Hasler gave the order to start the time-fuses. The thumb screws were turned. A click indicated that the glass inside had broken, releasing the liquid acetone.

Whatever else happened, those mines were certain to explode in about nine hours' time.

At 9.15 p.m. they launched their canoes again and wished each other good luck. They did not expect to meet after the attack. The plan was for each crew to scuttle their canoe and escape on their own.

The harbour was brightly illuminated – much too brightly for the Marines. Hasler kept *Catfish* well away from the shore as he and Sparks paddled up to the main docks. After ninety minutes they rounded a bend and saw their targets lined up for them.

There were seven ships tied up along the west bank. Hasler and Sparks hugged their iron sides as they paddled up, using their prey as protection from the eyes of sentries and look-outs.

The first two ships, a tanker and a cargo-liner, were hardly worth their ammunition. If they had any mines left they would attack them on the way back. Next came a cargo ship, well worth their attention but difficult to reach because a tanker was moored alongside. The fifth was a large cargo ship, a perfect target. *Catfish* went in to attack just past her bows.

Now the moment had come it seemed so simple, just like the dummy runs on the training course. Hasler stowed his paddle. Sparks placed the magnetic holdfast on the ship's hull. Hasler attached a limpet mine to the placing rod, lowered it into the water, brought it up to the ship's hull. He felt it cling. He detached the placing rod, Sparks released the holdfast, and they paddled on.

They placed another limpet amidships, and a third near the stern. Hasler noticed real live limpets clinging to the ship's hull, too.

The last two ships were moored alongside each other. The outer one was a German naval craft the size of a frigate. She was not a great prize, but the enemy navy was always worth a strike. They made sure of a good one by fixing two limpets on the hull.

Just about this time, and barely a mile away, Sergeant Wallace and Marine Ewart were taken by lorry to a deserted sandpit in the middle of a forest, tied to two posts, and murdered by a firing party supplied by the German Navy. Thanks to their silence under torture, their comrades were striking at the targets at the very moment of their death.

After their attack on the German naval craft Hasler and Sparks had to turn their canoe round to go back downstream. This meant swinging out away from the doomed ship, leaving the protection of her hull for a few dangerous moments. They had almost completed the turn when a torch suddenly shone down on them from the deck.

They looked up and saw the silhouette of a sentry. He was holding the torch and looking down at them over the ship's rail.

They gave one more quiet push with their paddles and then crouched low and still as the canoe glided softly back towards the ship's side.

The torch followed them.

The tide, ebbing now, took them slowly downstream. They remained motionless as they heard the sentry clump along the deck, still keeping them in the beam of his torch.

They reached the stern, and shelter again. At a signal from Hasler, Sparks swiftly put out his holdfast and moored the canoe to the ship.

Why didn't the sentry shout, or shoot, or raise the alarm? Was he short-sighted? Hadn't he seen there were two men in a canoe? Or was their camouflage so good that he thought them a drifting log.

The sentry had stopped. He was standing above them again. He switched off his torch but did not walk away. They heard him shifting his feet. No doubt he was listening. How long should they wait?

The tide would not wait. Hasler signalled to Sparks to let go.

Still crouching, still not paddling, they sat motionless as the tide took the canoe gently down the river and at last out of sight.

They had three limpets left. Hasler wanted to put them on the big cargo ship protected by the tanker. Unable to get alongside, he decided to attack her first at the bows. He steered the canoe to a point between the two ships. They were about to go to work when Hasler suddenly noticed that the two ships were closing together.

He placed a hand on each hull and began to push the canoe back. Sparks quickly did the same. They got out just before the two ships nestled together. Another few seconds, and they would have been crushed.

They paddled on past the tanker, and placed two limpets

on the cargo ship's stern. They put their last limpet on the
tanker.

They shook hands, grinned, and paddled rapidly downstream. They had done their part of the job. Now they had
to try to escape.

Strangely high in the water now, they paddled their canoe
away from the harbour, past their last hide-out, past the
hide before the last, on the Ile de Cazeau. They paused in
midstream for a rest.

"Listen!"

The sound astern was faint but familiar. They laughed
and turned round to meet *Cuttlefish* coming down after
them. The other canoe was more cautious. Laver and Mills
stopped paddling and gave a soft seagull cry. Hasler replied
with a loud one in answer. *Cuttlefish* raced down to join
him.

"We found no targets in the east docks, so we did for
those two ships in the south basin," reported Laver. "We
stuck five limpets on one and three on the other."

"Nice work."

The two canoes paddled down together until nearly
daybreak. Then they parted – for the last time.

"Good luck."

"Good luck."

Two of them were to have good luck. The other two were
going to be murdered.

At seven o'clock that morning the first of the limpet mines
exploded. There was chaos in Bordeaux harbour as one ship
after another was holed and began to sink. The damage was
so great that the news of the attack was reported immediately to Hitler. He demanded furiously how it could have
happened. No one was able to reply. The Germans still did
not know what had hit them. They only knew it hurt. The
suggested expedition of warships, aircraft, and 50,000
troops could hardly have done better than the ten Marines
in five canoes.

The news of the success was received with satisfaction at
Combined Ops HQ, but without wholehearted jubilation.

It looked as if Mountbatten's forecast would prove right. On January 25, 1943 – more than six weeks after the attack – all ten raiders were officially reported missing.

A month later a coded message from a British woman in Switzerland said that Hasler and Sparks were safe and in the hands of the French Resistance. On April 1 they reached Gibraltar, after many more dangerous adventures and narrow escapes and much life-saving help from the French. Hasler was awarded the DSO, Sparks the DSM.

Laver and Mills were the unlucky pair. After only two days on land they were picked up by the French police, who handed them over to the German Security Police.

Mackinnon and Conway lasted longer. They had made some progress towards the Spanish frontier, with the aid of French civilians who risked their lives to help, before they were betrayed and also delivered to the German Security Police.

All four were entitled to proper treatment as prisoners-of-war. All four were executed, or rather murdered, probably in Paris on March 23, by orders of the German High Command.

HITLER'S COMMANDO ORDER

The six men of the Royal Marines Boom Detachment Patrol shot by the Germans after the Bordeaux raid were executed in accordance with Hitler's infamous Commando Order of 18 October 1942. Part of this read:

From now on all men operating against German troops in so-called Commando raids in Europe or in Africa are to be annihilated to the last man. This is to be carried out whether they be soldiers in uniform, or saboteurs, with or without arms; and whether fighting or seeking to escape; and it is equally immaterial whether they come into action from ships and aircraft, or whether they land by parachute. Even if these individuals on discovery make obvious their intention of giving themselves up as prisoners, no pardon is on any account to be given.

So controversial was the order, that General Jodl, Chief of the Operations Staff of the Oberkommando der Wehrmacht (German Armed Forces High Command), directed that: "This order is intended for Commanders only and is under no circumstances to fall into enemy hands."

Hundreds of Allied special forces soldiers would be executed under the terms of Hitler's edict by the war's end.

OPERATION STRUGGLE

T.J. Waldron & James Gleeson

The use of special forces under the water was pioneered by the Italians — their decidedly unmilitary reputation notwithstanding — whose 10th MAS Flotilla developed an electric underwater chariot to be ridden by frogmen as early as 1936. The chariot contained an explosive warhead — hence the chariot's popular soubriquet of "human torpedo" — which could be detached and clamped to enemy shipping by means of magnets — as the 10th MAS demonstrated with explosive effectiveness in September 1941 when they penetrated Gibraltar and blew up three British ships, and then in December when they sank the British battleships Valiant *and* Queen Elizabeth *at their moorings in Alexandria harbour.*

The Royal Navy decided to reply in kind, and began experimenting with a two-man chariot of the Italian-type, but also with a 48-foot-long midget submarine which carried an operational crew of four. It was "X craft" which sunk the German battleship Tirpitz. *How they did so is perhaps best described by the official citation.*

The King has approved the award of the Victoria Cross for valour to Lieutenant Basil Charles Godfrey Place, D.S.C., R.N., and Lieutenant Donald Cameron, R.N.R., the Commanding Officers of two of His Majesty's Midget Submarines X 6 and X 7, which on 22nd September 1943 carried out a most daring and successful attack on the German battleship *Tirpitz*, moored in the protected anchorage of Kaafjord, North Norway. To reach the anchorage necessitated the penetration of an enemy minefield and a passage of fifty miles up the fiord, known to be vigilantly patrolled by the enemy, and to be guarded by nets, gun defences and listening posts, this, after a passage of at least a thousand miles from base.

Having successfully eluded all these hazards and entered the fleet anchorage, Lieutenants Cameron and Place, with complete disregard for danger, worked their small craft past the close anti-submarine and torpedo nets surrounding the *Tirpitz* and from a position inside these nets, carried out a cool and determined attack.

Whilst they were still inside the nets, a fierce enemy counter attack by guns and depth charges developed which made their withdrawal impossible. Lieutenants Place and Cameron, therefore, scuttled their craft to prevent them from falling into the hands of the enemy. Before doing so, they took every measure to ensure the safety of their crews, the majority of whom, together with themselves, were subsequently taken prisoner.

In the course of this operation, these very small craft pressed home their attack to the full, in doing so accepting all the dangers inherent in such vessels, and facing every possible hazard which ingenuity could devise for the protection, in harbour, of vitally important fleet units. The courage, endurance, and utter contempt for danger in the immediate face of the enemy shown by Lieutenants Cameron and Place during this determined and successful attack were supreme.

His Majesty has also approved the appointment to the Distinguished Service Order of Sub-Lt. Robert Aitken, R.N.V.R., Sub-Lt. Haddon Kendall, R.N.V.R., and Sub-Lt. John Thornton Lorimer, R.N.V.R., and the award of the Conspicuous Gallantry Medal to Engine Room Artificer, Fourth Class, Edmund Goddard for their gallantry, skill and daring during the successful attack on the *Tirpitz*.

Epic attacks by the Royal Navy's "X craft", however, were not limited to the war in Europe.

Perhaps the most outstanding incident in this form of warfare in the Far East was the epic "Operation Struggle" carried out by XE I, commanded by Lt. J. E. Smart, M.B.E., R.N.V.R., and XE 3, which was commanded by Lt. Ian Fraser, D.S.C., R.N.R. Just after 06.00 hrs. on 30th July 1945, the tiny XE 3 was on tow of *Stygian*, her large parent submarine, both craft had stopped and the sea was calm. The change-over of crews was made by dinghy carrying four men at a time. The only defects found by the operational crew on taking over XE 3 from the passage crew were a bent and damaged induction and the loss of the telephone bell connection on the periscope guard which had been ripped off while under tow and consequently ditched.

In his report to the Commander-in-Chief British Pacific Fleet, the Captain of the Submarine Flotilla said this about the outward passage:

This was carried out in good weather, and both craft were taken to the scene of operations without a hitch. The failure of the telephone communication was entirely due to the improvised tow which was necessary due to the provision of "S" class submarines which are not fitted for towing. This failure did not, however, affect the operation, owing, partly to the good weather conditions experienced, and partly on account of the good drill on the part of both towing and towed submarines.

The passage crews of both craft did their jobs splendidly. It is not often realised how big a part these men play in the success of an operation. Towing at high speed is far from being an easy or even a particularly safe job, and it is very far from being a comfortable one. It calls for a high degree of alertness under trying conditions for several days at a time. In addition it calls for constant attention to the vital routine duties of mopping up moisture, testing, and if necessary, repairing every item of equipment in the craft. To a considerable extent the success of an operation depends upon the condition in which the craft is turned over to the operational crew. In no sense of the word are the "X" craft passage crews "Maintenance Crews."

The best analogy that can be given is that they correspond to a diving watch in a large submarine (except for the fact that they are continuously on watch for days, without a break) and like the diving watch of a big submarine, they are relieved when the crew goes to action stations. That both craft were turned over to the operational crews in perfect condition reflects the highest credit on the passage Commanding Officers and their crews.

The co-operation afforded by the towing submarine was of a high order, and both craft were slipped considerably nearer to Singapore than the ordered slipping position. This shows excellent judgment on the part of Lts. Clarabut and Kent, and was of material assistance in shortening the operation.

XE 3 was slipped in position 036 degrees Horsborough Light about 23.00 hrs. on the night of 30th July and she went on her lonely way with her course set 240 degrees at five knots. Engine Room Artificer Reed was at the helm, Sub-Lt. Smith, from New Zealand at the controls, Leading-Seaman Magennis in the control room, and Lt. Fraser, the C.O., on the casing above the water navigating through a minefield. The night was cloudy, although the moon was up, and positions were very difficult to obtain. The same course was maintained until 00.34 hrs. on 31st July, which was "D" day for the operation, when it was altered to 260 degrees.

There were plenty of positions of channel buoys supplied by our intelligence on the briefing, but unfortunately none of them was lit, and during the whole of the run in on the surface not a single buoy was sighted. They felt their way along in the dark until 01.28 hrs. when the course was altered to 224 degrees because Fraser intended to run for about three and a half miles on this course before altering again to 279 degrees and passing between the widest space of certain projected listening posts.

About ten minutes later a very dubious land fix was obtained which put the craft in a position 223 degrees Po Mungging 3.6 miles, so course was once more altered, this time to 218 degrees. An accurate four-point fix taken about fifteen minutes later confirmed their course, the position being 223 degrees Po Mungging 5 miles. At seventeen minutes past two, course was once more altered to 279 degrees, the engine was stopped and they crept forward on batteries past the listening posts. After another half an hour they were fixed in position 129.5 degrees Johore Hill 8.3 miles. XE 3 then went ahead on engine at 4.5 knots on a course 280 degrees.

Lt. Fraser was still sitting on the casing when, just after 03.00 hrs. he sighted what appeared to be a channel buoy. They closed to within fifty yards and found out that it was a fishing boat. A hurried alteration of course was ordered and XE 3 sheered off. Apparently she was not seen, which was extremely fortunate since she was up moon of the fishing boat.

At 04.20 hrs. two ships were sighted. They looked like a large tanker and an escorting motor-launch, and as they appeared to be closing at high speed, the "X" craft dived, and remained silent on the bottom for twenty minutes when she surfaced with very low buoyancy. Unfortunately there was no warning of this dive and the Log was damaged when XE 3 bottomed. When the "X" craft surfaced again it was found that the two ships were still on the same bearing but they looked a lot closer, so once again the craft dived and she proceeded on a course of 360 degrees until the sounding machine indicated that the Johore Shoal was being crossed just to the Westward of the buoy.

With depth being held at thirty feet, the small craft wormed her way up Johore Strait. Course was altered at 05.10 hrs. to 325 degrees, and a little later they went off on another leg of 312 degrees. At 06.00 hrs. the Commanding Officer, First Lieutenant, and E.R.A. took benzadrine tablets in order to ward off sleep, but these had no effect for some considerable time, in fact, twenty-five minutes later the First Lieutenant fell asleep while on the planes for about half an hour. The Commanding Officer maintained depth by moving two feet fore and aft in the centre of the control room as required. By 07.00 hrs. it was estimated that the boom was approximately half a mile ahead and once again XE 3 was bottomed awaiting daylight. The Commanding Officer got down to a sleep at this time, and slept until 07.30 hrs. By 07.45 hrs. the benzadrine had taken full effect and the morale of the whole crew went up a 100 per cent. Leading-Seaman Magennis, the "X" craft diver, had been asleep in the engine room since 05.00 hrs. Reid, the E.R.A., who had also taken benzadrine, did not require to sleep.

XE 3 proceeded at a depth of ten feet on a course of 312 degrees at eight o'clock in the morning. Eight minutes later a periscope fix was obtained which showed that the craft was three and a half miles from the boom. Since they were farther from the boom than had been estimated, the Commanding Officer ordered an increase in speed. From this point onwards, until the target was reached, XE 3 cut along at the increased speed, except for the duration of periscope searches. At 10.30 hrs. in a flat, calm, oily sea the midget submarine passed through the boom which appeared to be a ramshackle affair with a permanently open gate. They spotted a trawler, presumably the gate vessel anchored on the east side of the gate. This vessel was passed with due caution in case it was fitted with submarine detection gear. It was estimated that since it took the "X" craft over four and half hours from the Johore Shoal buoy to the boom, a distance of six miles at 970 revolutions, that a tidal stream of some one and three quarter knots was setting against XE 3. The boom gate was estimated to be about three hundred yards wide.

They carried out the navigation of the Johore Strait without a great deal of difficulty. The only shipping encountered was a small drifter which was moving in the same direction. They noticed a damaged train-ferry, apparently she had a broken back, lying anchored, or beached, in Serrangoon harbour. Because of the fact that the water was absolutely calm they found that it was only possible to make very hasty periscope observations. In his report, Fraser mentioned this fact and added his regrets that in consequence very little navigational intelligence could be obtained. He mentioned, however, that all lights and buoys that he saw were in position as shown on Admiralty charts. They found that the sounding machine was of the greatest value as an aid to navigation, more particularly on the run out when the motor was running full ahead the periscope was raised only four times to check position all the way from the target to the boom.

The target, which was the heavy cruiser *Takao* of the Japanese Imperial Navy, was sighted at 12.50 hrs. and there was great excitement among the crew as the news was passed to them. Course was altered as necessary to close and commence a run in from thirty degrees on her starboard bow. They found that the *Takao* was extremely well camouflaged against the land but she had been easily distinguishable during the first looks when she had a background of sea. In one good look round before starting the run in the only vessels they saw in the stream were some sort of destroyer escort and a few small vessels. Fraser had a last look during the run in, and as he himself said, "I was very upset to see a motor cutter filled to the gunwales with Japanese liberty men only about thirty yards from my periscope." A somewhat disconcerting moment as may well be imagined.

It was 14.08 hrs. when the first run in to attack was started with the point of aim "A" turret on the target. Fifteen minutes later XE 3 was taken deep to twenty-two feet, and during the next twelve minutes she bumped her way along the bottom of the Johore Strait at depths varying from twenty-two feet to twelve feet; at 14.42 hrs. she brought up with a resounding thump against a solid object which they presumed was the *Takao*. The depth as shown on the gauge was fifteen feet. This situation was not very promising because the water at this point was very clear, and had the diver been put out he would have had very great difficulty in dragging the limpet mines along the casing of the "X" craft to the bottom of the target without being seen. They then tried desperately to alter course so as to bring XE 3 alongside parallel to the *Takao*. When they tried to move, however, they found that the craft was held fast. Eventually, after nearly ten minutes of frantic motor movements, she staggered up the side of the hole into which she had fallen, and reached some form of daylight and relief again at a minimum depth of fourteen feet.

Having shaken themselves clear they altered course to north and commenced a run out prior to a second attack. By this time it was getting really late and it was decided that the only thing left to do was to bottom crawl with a point of aim on the forward funnel of the target until XE 3 fell into the 24-foot patch under *Takao*'s midships' portion and then to drop off the cargo there. The second run in to attack was started just after 15.00 hours on the same course, aiming for the funnel, and after more bottom scraping with a minimum depth of seventeen feet, XE 3 was settled with a depth of twenty-two feet showing on the after gauge, right under the very centre of the target.

The next part of this tricky operation had to be carried out by Leading-Seaman Magennis. Making sure his oxygen breathing apparatus was working correctly he closed the water-tight doors and flooded the escape compartment, and made his exit. In all, he placed six limpets in two clusters of three, forty-five feet apart on the filthy bottom of the *Takao*, which was covered by several years growth of seaweed and barnacles which had to be scraped off before the limpets would stick. Three of the counter mining pins jammed and Magennis was unable to remove them. He was caused some anxiety too by a leaky reducer connection which was sending bubbles up to the surface. Had anyone on board noticed them they would immediately have become suspicious. Another difficulty was the fact that the *Takao* had an angular bottom, up which the limpets were inclined to run. He overcame this by anchoring the limpets together by their holdfasts, two on one side and one on the other side of the keel. The diver returned to the submarine just after 16.00 hrs.

Magennis, who is a softly spoken Irishman, said this of that part of the operation. "My first impression was, how murky the water was. The bottom of the target resembled something like an underwater jungle, and I had to clear a patch of undergrowth and barnacles off six places in order to make sure that the magnetic limpets would stick on. Getting them on was quite like my old training days, when I had stuck many dummies under our own ship. It took me about three quarters of an hour altogether before I got back to the midget sub."

Just after the diver had returned, the port and starboard cargoes of fused high explosives were slipped. The port cargo cleared at once but the starboard carrier stuck and by no effort from the inside could it be cleared. With this flooded, which gave XE 3 very negative buoyancy, speed was increased to full ahead until the craft had dragged herself some thirty feet or so from the target. Here is an extract from Lt. Fraser's report showing what happened after this:

It now became necessary that a diver would have to leave the craft, which was lying at seventeen feet, and try to clear the carrier from the outside. This was a very dangerous mission, as bubbles were certain to be caused when the W & D upper lid was opened (the W & D upper lid is the upper lid of the escape hatch), and at that time, had anyone been looking, it was almost certain that XE 3 could be seen only a few feet from the surface in clear water. Leading-Seaman Magennis, who was exhausted after his previous dive, volunteered at once to do this, showing great courage and determination and complete disregard for unknown dangers in the face of the enemy. He went on oxygen again at 16.25 hrs., and made his exit to the casing with a large spanner in his hand. After seven minutes he managed, by much banging at the carrier and levering at the release pins, to get the carrier away, and at 16.39 hrs. he entered the W & D.

Magennis himself had very little to say about his own effort in this hazardous situation. "When we found that the side charge had flooded and jammed, Lt. Fraser immediately volunteered to go out and clear same – but knowing it was my job, I went out and did same."

So – at long last XE 3 was ready to start her run back to the boom. Unfortunately, her difficulties were not yet over. On the way out it was discovered that owing to the extreme freshness of the water, a trim could not be maintained by using the internal trimming tanks, and it was necessary partly to blow main ballast. Maintaining trim was most difficult at all times because the density of the water was continually changing. In fact, just after 17.00 hrs., XE 3 actually broke surface for about six seconds when only about a mile from the *Takao*. So – with some misgivings, they fought their way to the boom. At 19.00 hrs. a high-revving motor-boat passed immediately overhead. Lt Fraser says of this incident, "An observer – had he been there – would have seen a complete 'X' craft crew standing or sitting with their fingers in their ears waiting for a bang. Luckily there was no such thing, and the boom was reached and passed at 19.49 hrs. without further incident."

At the boom, course was altered. From 20.30 hrs. onwards XE 3 was kept at thirty feet until at 21.00 hrs. she surfaced and proceeded on engine, passing a few yards off Johore Shoal buoy. They sighted a large junk about half a mile away in the half light; they also saw a small craft away to starboard which they thought at first was XE 1 but which eventually proved to be a small sailing boat. At 23.30 hrs. watch was set for *Stygian*, the parent submarine, and she was called up on R/T every hour and half hour. At 23.45 hrs., after a further alteration of course, the green light from *Stygian* was seen ahead as expected. *Stygian* and XE 3 retired until after 03.30 hrs., when crews were changed and tow passed.

Lt. Fraser, Commanding Officer of XE 3, finished his report on the operation like this:

I consider that the two greatest contributions to the success of this operation were the resourcefulness and hard work of the passage crew, who after a very depressing start, and with bad trim, struggled for two days mending leaks and minor defects and who, on turning the craft over to the operational crew, produced a boat without a single defect of any sort that would impair the fighting efficiency of the craft. Also to the Commanding Officer and Ship's Company of H.M. Submarine *Stygian*, who fed us like lords, and provided for us in every way.

A number of unforeseen difficulties beset Lt. Smart in XE 1 right from the very start, and his approach was, in consequence, delayed. When the Captain of the Submarine Flotilla put in his report of the whole operation to the Commander-in-Chief of the British Pacific Fleet, he said that Lt. Smart decided, in view of the lateness of the hour, not to place limpets because he found it impossible to get his craft actually underneath the cruiser. His form of attack, therefore, was to manœuvre the "X" craft alongside, and underneath the overhang of the target's hull, and then to drop off his explosive charges. In his own report, Lt. Smart criticised himself because he did not press home his attack on the target to which he had been assigned, and switched to the cruiser allocated to XE 3. But, on the other hand, in the absence of intelligence on the time the boom would close, it had been accepted that it would probably shut at sunset. In this case, because of the delays encountered, Lt. Smart was faced with the prospect of being caught inside the boom if he had pressed on to his own target. To be caught inside the boom after the explosion would, in the words of the Flotilla Captain, "have been most unpleasant, and probably fatal."

The Flotilla Captain went on to say, "It was most unlikely that a diver would be able to cut through the net in the dark. A further consideration was the possibility of capture due to being unable to get out of the boom and the consequent 'blowing of the gaff' which would have jeopardised future operations. It is also to be remarked," continued the Flotilla Captain, "that although Lt. Smart thought XE 3 was in all probability astern of him, he had to face the possibility of her having carried out her attack on time. In this event there would be considerable risk of the movements of XE I round the target operating the disturbance fuse of XE 3's charge and blowing him to pieces. This risk Lt. Smart accepted. His decisions are considered to have been sound, and to have shown cool and calculated balance between the various risks involved."

XE I was further unfortunate in that she was not picked up on the night she was due to be met by her parent submarine, *Spark*, and had to wait around until the following night when contact was made successfully. The reason for this delay was that the communication apparatus carried by *Spark* worked on a comparatively narrow beam, and consequently the two craft missed each other.

The net result of the operation was that the bottom was blown out of the cruiser.

Announcing the award of the Victoria Cross to Lt. Fraser and Leading-Seaman Magennis, the citation states:

The courage and determination of Lt. Fraser are beyond all praise. Any man not possessed of his relentless determination to achieve his objective in full, regardless of all the consequences, would have dropped his charges alongside the target instead of persisting until he had forced his submarine right under the cruiser.

Referring to Leading-Seaman Magennis, the citation says this:

A lesser man would have been content to place a few limpets and then to return to the craft. Magennis, however, persisted until he had placed his full outfit before returning to the craft in an exhausted condition. Magennis displayed very great courage and devotion to duty and complete disregard for his own safety.

Further awards made to the crew of XE 3 were the D.S.C. to Sub-Lt. W. J. L. Smith, of Christchurch, New Zealand, and E.R.A. Reed, of Grimsby, who was awarded the C.G.M. The report says this:

Throughout the whole of this dangerous operation Sub-Lt. Smith, as First Lieutenant of the craft, and Reed, as Engine Room Artificer, remained at the controls of the submarine for the sixteen and a half hours that she was dived. Their skill in handling the craft and controlling her through the hazards of the eighty-mile trip contributed largely to the success of the operation.

The C.O. of XE I, Lt. Smart, was awarded the D.S.O. About his part the report has this to say:

Like XE 3, Lt. Smart, also left the believed safe channels during his long approach up the Singapore Straits, and entered mined waters to avoid suspected hydrophone posts. XE 1 had for a target a heavy cruiser of the "Nachi" class berthed about two miles beyond the *Takao*, but she was delayed in her attack owing to several encounters with enemy surface craft, and instead of passing the boom ahead of XE 3 as planned, actually passed it ninety minutes later. This robbed Lt. Smart of the necessary margin of time to reach his target and withdraw before dark, so he accordingly decided to attack the *Takao*. Unable to get his craft under the target, and not knowing whether XE 3 had already laid her charges, Lt. Smart and his crew risked being killed by the detonation of XE 3's charges in order to lay alongside and drop their charges. Lt. Smart displayed great courage throughout this hazardous operation which involved the same great dangers as those faced by XE 3.

Digressing for a moment from the more serious aspect of some of these desperate enterprises, there is a story told by a submarine coxswain about a gallant, very well-known, and

much-decorated Submarine Commander. When he was
operating in the tropics he would allow his crew over the
side for a swim sometimes, having first sent out a petty
officer to row around in a dinghy to keep a look-out for
sharks. On this occasion the lads were disporting themselves happily, under the benevolent eye of their Captain on
the conning-tower of the submarine, while the P.O. sculled
up and down in the blazing sun about a hundred yards away
from the parent craft. Suddenly the Captain spied the
triangular fin of a shark cutting through the water –
"Shark!" he yelled at the pitch of his lungs – local records
for the Australian Crawl went by the board as the men
safely made the ship, leaving the ocean to the sinister grey
shape of the shark, and the perspiring figure of the Petty
Officer pulling for the submarine. The Captain hailed the
P.O. and pointing to the shark, he yelled, "There he is !"
The Petty Officer, who was armed with nothing more
offensive than his two oars, rested on them for a moment,
turned his head and replied, "What do you want me to do,
sir – strangle the bloody thing?"

These men often made light of the dangers they faced –
but the dangers were very real.

There was one item of equipment carried by British underwater operators in the Far East which is perhaps of particular interest; it was known amongst them as a "Siamese
Blood Chit," and consisted of a white silk square with a
Union Jack in the middle, surrounded by writing in various
oriental languages, and the translation of the message it
carried was as follows: – "I am a British Naval Officer who
has been engaged in operations against the Japanese. If I am
captured, I cannot continue to fight against the Japanese so
I appeal to you to hide me and provide me with food until I
can rejoin our forces. If you will help me by giving me food
and hiding me in safety until our armies arrive in Malaya,
you will earn the gratitude of my government who will give
you a big reward and I am authorised to give you a chit to
this effect."

These silk squares were designed to be folded and carried
in a pocket, to be displayed – should the need arise. Tony

Eldridge and Sydney Woollcott carried one each in a pocket of the diving suits when they carried out a chariot attack on Japanese shipping in Phuket harbour. Fortunately they had no occasion to use them. These two had stuck together since their training days in Scotland; Eldridge was now a Sub-Lieutenant, and Woollcott a Petty Officer. Here is Eldridge's report on the operation which was to sink Japanese supply ships:

H.M.S. *Trenchant* dived at dawn on the 28th October and proceeded close inshore to make a reconnaissance of Phuket. This passage into Phuket was uneventful excepting for reports from the Asdic Officer that we were running into a minefield. This, however, we skirted and found ourselves four and a half miles off the harbour. We then did a periscope reconnaissance of the targets and found that they were both lying very close together. All the chariot crews were able to have a look at the targets and the surrounding landmarks, which proved to be quite useful afterwards.

As the sea was absolutely dead calm, and a clear night seemed most probable, the Captain of H.M.S. *Trenchant* decided he would not be able to drop us off as close as he had expected. H.M.S. *Trenchant* surfaced south of Goh Dorkmai at about 19.00 hrs. It was a perfect night with a brilliant moon. Chariot drivers then went on to the bridge and had another reconnaissance of the harbour entrance. Although the visibility was good from the point of view of finding the target, and eventually homing the submarine, we were not a little concerned about the possibility of being sighted in the vicinity of the target.

After a very large supper, we started to dress at 21.00 hrs. We should have been hotter and more uncomfortable in our diving dresses while waiting for zero hour had it not been for the submarine crew who had let rubber piping from a louvre vent into our facepieces. Zero hour, 22.10 hrs. "Open fore-hatch — up divers." By the time we were comfortably seated in our machines and the Captain was ready to trim down, our protosorb canisters were almost glowing with heat through breathing out of water.

Our final instructions were from the Navigation Officer, who came down on to the saddle tanks and gave us our course – North 65 West for six and a half miles entering Phuket harbour, South 75 East for seven miles retreating from Phuket harbour. By 22.15 hrs. the launching had been completed without a hitch.

I had been on my course for approximately ten minutes when I was signalled by my Number Two (Petty Officer Woollcott) who told me he could get no oxygen from the machine and was only breathing from the one three-hour bottle attached to his bag. We then went alongside the submarine again and reported the distressing news, which, in the ordinary course of events, would have scrubbed out the attack. It was suggested to Petty Officer Woollcott that he should carry out the long run-in on air. This was immediately agreed to, which in my opinion was a most courageous decision, knowing that should we have to dive hurriedly he would have been drowned.

Having left the submarine for the second time we had been on our course for approximately twenty minutes when my Number Two informed me that he was O.K. and his oxygen valve from the machine bottle set was working. We proceeded to trim down. Having acquired perfect trim we carried on towards the harbour entrance in third speed. We tried fourth speed to make up for the time that had been lost at the start of the run, but found that the following sea lifted the stern clear of the water. We reverted to third speed again and held this all the way in. The lighthouse on Goh Tapou Noi Island was visible all the way. The target became visible when about one and a half miles away. I started making long dives in second speed when about one and a half miles from the harbour entrance, because of the particularly bright moon. The water was very clear indeed, and I estimated the temperature as eighty-seven degrees Fahrenheit. We probably passed through a few freshwater patches as I continually found myself dropping suddenly from eighteen feet to thirty feet without any apparent reason. I dived for the final time on a compass course when five hundred yards from the target.

After what seemed to be a very long time, we finally passed under what we thought must be the bows, because of the narrow beam, and proceeded to go out on the other side and for some unknown reason dropped to thirty-five feet. I did not blow main ballast and, having regained a trim, started to come in on the port side at about twenty-two feet. When I was under the shadow of the target I blew main ballast, the time being 00.30 hrs. on the 29th. The jackstay protected us as we came up on to the bottom, and Number Two got out and went forward. Finding the head not near enough to the bilge keel he signalled me to come forward slightly. As soon as I moved the main motor, the jackstay held in the barnacles and folded over backwards, leaving me cramped over to one side bearing off with my hands against the most shocking ship's bottom I have ever been on. However, under the circumstances I was really quite comfortable, seeing that I could at least breathe. To bring the head up so as to help Number Two affix it, I moved the battery aft. He then proceeded to fix the explosive head with two clips on to the bilge keel. Number Two worked incredibly fast, he had secured the head and set the clock by 00.45 hrs. As soon as he had secured the head Number Two returned to the machine, we both shook hands over the cockpit, and proceeded to make our escape.

Number Two could not get into the machine until we were clear of the ship's bottom, but clung on to the side until we were about twenty-five yards away on our return course. Approximately forty yards from the target I received signal four, to surface, from my Number Two. Well knowing that there must be some very good reason to come up, I did so about fifty yards from the ship. I proceeded to leave the harbour on the surface at slow speed, trusting that I would not be seen, which fortunately was the case. A few minutes later my Number Two signalled me that he was O.K. and breathing comfortably once more. Without delay we dived away for approximately twenty-five minutes. (Apparently Number Two's complaint had been that, during the time he was working on the ship's bottom, one side of his oxygen bag had come adrift and his breathing became restricted owing to a kink in his breathing tube). When well clear of the harbour entrance, we surfaced, blew main ballast, and proceeded in fourth speed steering for Goh Dorkmai. This was quite a comfortable trip, even though we had a slight ahead swell. I flashed the arranged signal three times on the way out and finally saw the welcome sight of a "T" boat silhouette.

On coming alongside the submarine I was received with a fearful flashing of red lights, apparently because they thought we were going past. Petty Officer Smith on the second machine had just come back alongside and was being taken inboard. My Number Two and myself were then lugged inboard in a great hurry because of an Asdic report of an M.T.B. in the vicinity. This prevented us from salving any gear, torches, etc., from the machine, or from removing the battery vent. Both machines' comp. tanks were flooded and main ballast was vented, thus sending them to the bottom for ever.

After the divers had undressed, the inevitable discussion on the run ensued, and we waited up to hear the two explosions. H.M.S. *Trenchant* dived at 05.00 hrs. and manoeuvred into position about four and a half to five miles off the harbour, keeping a periscope watch for the explosions. The periscope had just been lowered when the first explosion was heard, so unfortunately we missed the effect. At 06.32 hrs. the Captain was having a look-see through the periscope when the second head went off. It was rather amusing that four people looked through the periscope before the noise of the explosion reached the submarine. I personally saw water, smoke, and pieces of wreckage fly into the air about twice the height of the masts. It appeared that a large portion of the starboard side just aft of midships was torn out. It immediately heeled over to starboard and settled down by the stern. The bows were soon high out of the water with the rounded underside showing. All this noise did not bring out any surface patrol vessels but one aircraft arrived and circled round for an hour.

Captain Fell said this about the circumstances in which the underwater operations under his command were carried out in the Pacific:

When H.M.S. *Bonaventure* left Rothesay for the Pacific with her six XE craft, the Pacific war was at its height. By the time we arrived eight weeks later the whole scene changed. We were kept three weeks in Trinidad doing "hot weather" exercises, and at Pearl Harbour were told that Admiral Nimitz no longer wanted us. Morale fell with a bang, but some hope remained, as we were told to proceed to Manus in the Admiralty Islands. Before we got there we were diverted south to Brisbane and arrived with our tails right down, in black despair. I flew to see Admiral Fraser in Sydney and he ordered me to discuss with Admiral Daniel, in Melbourne, a use for the ship in the "Fleet Train". He also reluctantly allowed me to fly north to the Philippines to have one final talk with the U.S. Naval Authorities about an operation. This flight was a "rugged" affair but ended four days later in Subic Bay (P.I.) with the U.S. Submarine Admiral, James Fife. We sat on his verandah drinking cups of coffee, and he listened for hours while I used every argument I could think of for making use of us.

At the end he showed the most astonishing grasp of what I had said, and in words that somehow softened the blow, and making his reasons seem so sane, he explained that we were too late. Our friendship began there, and the more I saw of this man in the next months strengthened my feelings that I had met the most sincere, the straightest and ablest of men. Before America entered the war, James Fife spent his time in England and was frequently on hazardous patrols in British submarines. He understood, honoured and admired our great Navy, but he was big enough to see its limitations and to fight to prevent them occurring in the U.S. Submarine Service. In England, our own Submarine Service saw, loved and gained much from James Fife.

When I returned to Sydney, exhausted and dispirited, I reported to Admiral Fraser. He was sympathetic, but could offer no hope, then by the merest chance meeting with a friend of Admiral Fife's, I learnt of the need to cut the telegraphic communications between Malaya, China and Japan.

I saw the C.-in-C. at once, flew back to my ship at Brisbane, took her to a hidden anchorage in the Great Barrier Reef, and proved that a submarine cable could be located and cut by an "X" craft, at the cost, unhappily, of the lives of two of the bravest gentlemen it has been my privilege to meet and serve with. I then flew north to New Guinea and the Philippines and was met by Admiral Fife, glowing with enthusiasm. His staff were put to work on plans, and time was found in his harassed and over-crowded life to help, advise and direct our efforts.

We now started to practise on a disused cable, deeply bedded in coraline growth and primeval mud. This meant another trip to Australia and back, hitch-hiking in any plane that was going my way. The long 4,000 miles took me to islands full of fighting, and others which were untouched, save where airstrips had been hacked from the jungle.

In all, disappointments, planning, training, final trials took nearly two months, and without Admiral Fife's help, our C.-in-C's. faith in us, and the loyalty, energy and courage of the whole of 14 Submarine Flotilla, Fraser, Westmacott, Shean and Smart would never have sailed on their magnificent operations.

There is much to be written about James Fife, and much more will be heard of him in the future. His name need only be mentioned to the U.S. Navy today, to have them turn to you, their faces alight with admiration.

I know I am very proud to have served under him, and to have flown his flag in H.M.S. *Bonaventure* for the two most exciting weeks of my life.

It is perhaps fitting that the last tribute to the deathless courage of these men should come from enemy sources – from the implacable Japanese.

In September 1944, twenty-three underwater operators set out for Singapore harbour to sink Japanese shipping. Something went wrong – the alarm was given. They attacked a motor-boat full of Japanese soldiers which spotted them, and captured the boat, but, by then, escape was out of the question. They destroyed their equipment so that it should not fall into the hands of the Japanese. They were hunted day and night from island to island. They fought with the weapons they had captured, and they fell one by one. In the end, nine of them were surprised and captured, the tenth set out to try and sail to Australia in a tiny craft. He was captured when his canoe was stranded on fishing net stakes near far-off Timor. One of the prisoners died in captivity. The remaining nine were then court-martialled, and each after a formal trial convicted and ceremoniously beheaded. This is what the prosecuting officer said at the court-martial:

With such fine determination they infiltrated into a Japanese area. We do not hesitate to call them real heroes of a forlorn hope. It has been fortunate for us that their intention was frustrated, half-way, but when we fathom their intention, and share their feelings, we cannot but spare a tear for them. When the deed is so heroic, its sublime spirit must be respected and its success or failure becomes a secondary matter. The last moment of a hero must be dramatic – in these circumstances I consider that a death sentence should be given to each of the accused.

Their demeanour at their execution was such that Major-General Otsuka, at a staff conference of the 7th Japanese Army, reported on the patriotism, enterprise and sublime end of these men, which he said should be taken as a model by the Japanese. Only by bracing up their own spirits in emulation could Japan hope to win the war. Three weeks later, however, the Japanese surrendered.

THE DROP

Baron von der Heydte

It was not only underwater operations that the Italians pioneered (see p. 53–74); as early as 1927 they experimented with the delivery of soldiers to the battlefield by parachute. A decade later, the Red Army of Russia perfected parachuting to the degree whereby they could drop, during a war game, an entire regiment of parachutists from specially adapted transport aircraft.

For all his moral and military madnesses, Hitler was no dullard in his appreciation of new tactics in warfare. In 1938 Hitler had General Kurt Student, a fighter ace of appointed Inspector of Parachute Troops; soon afterwards, Student was given command of the first parachute division, 7 Flieger. The division provided minor parachute units for the invasion of Norway and Holland, but in May 1941 it was allotted a role in history – the first mass parachute operation in time of war. The target was Crete.

To Operation Merkur *(Mercury), the invasion of Crete, the Germans committed massive resources – some 15,000 paratroops from 7th Airborne itself, plus a follow-up force of 8,500 mountain troops, and 700 motorcyclists from 5th Armoured Division. To transport and protect the* Sprung nach Kreta *the Luftwaffe provided 539 Ju-52 transports, 100 DS 230 gliders and hundreds of Stuka dive-bombers and other aircraft. Against this invasion from the sky, the Allies could muster no aircraft and 30,000 troops of whom the majority were kitless, exhausted refugees from the calamitous campaign against the Germans on the Greek mainland.*

Everything seemed to favour Student and the 7th Airborne. Yet, in truth, their assault was compromised before the men emplaned. Cryptologists at Britain's Code and Cipher School at Bletchley had decoded Luftwaffe Enigma messages, and knew where and when the invasion would come. The result was a bloodbath. At Maleme airstrip, the 7th Airborne's main drop zone, the parachutists were pot-shotted as they drifted slowly down to earth; one company of 3rd Battalion, 1st Assault Regiment, sustained 112 fatalities from a drop of 126 men in the early hours of the invasion on 20 May. Even in the less well defended sectors of the island the Germans encountered death among the olive groves, as Baron von der Heydte, commander of 3rd Battalion of the 3rd Parachute Regiment, found to the cost of his men.

I WAS ROUSED BY my adjutant and started awake, still drowsy, to hear a roar of engines growing louder and louder, as if coming from a great distance. It took me a moment or two to remember where I was and what lay before me.

"We are nearing Crete, sir."

I got up and moved towards the open door, beside which the dispatcher, whose duty it was to see that all final preparations for the jump were ready, was seated. Our 'plane was poised steady in the air, almost as though motionless. Looking out, beyond the silver-grey wing with its black cross marking, I could see our target – still small, like a cliff rising out of the glittering sea to meet us – the island of Crete.

Slowly, infinitely slowly, like the last drops wrung from a drying well, the minutes passed. Again and again I glanced stealthily at my wristwatch. There is nothing so awful, so exhausting, as this waiting for the moment of a jump. In vain I tried to compel myself to be calm and patient. A strange unrest had also gripped most of those who were flying with me. Each man attempted to overcome it in his own manner. Some told each other jokes which they had heard a thousand times before, others talked of their plans for after the war, and two or three – Willi Riese among them – stared silently ahead as if all that was happening around them was no concern of theirs. Did Riese, I wonder, have any presentiment of what was awaiting him in Crete? Scarcely able to bear it any longer, I stepped once again to the open door. We were just flying over the beaches. The thin strip of surf, which looked from above like a glinting white ribbon, separated the blue waters from the yellow-green of the shore. The mountains reared up before us, and the 'planes approaching them looked like giant birds trying to reach their eyries in the rocks.

We were still flying inland as if to run against a dark mountainside. It seemed almost as though we could touch the steep slopes upon which trees and solitary buildings appeared like toys. Then our left wing dipped and we swung away from the mountain and the 'plane started to circle; but soon we straightened out again, and at that moment there came the pilot's order, "Prepare to jump!"

Everyone rose and started to fasten his hook to the static line which ran down the centre of the body of the 'plane. And while we stood there, securing our hooks, we noticed that we were losing height, and the pressure of air became hard, almost painful, to the ear.

Next came the order, "Ready to jump!"

In two strides I was at the door, my men pressing close behind me, and grasped the supports on either side of it. The slipstream clutched at my cheeks, and I felt as though they were fluttering like small flags in the wind.

Suddenly, a lot of little white clouds appeared from nowhere and stood poised in the air about us. They looked harmless enough, like puffs of cottonwool, for the roar of the 'plane's engines had drowned the sound of the ack-ack shells' detonation.

Below me was the village of Alikianou. I could see people in the streets staring up at us, others running away and disappearing into doorways. The shadows of our 'planes swept like ghostly hands over the sun-drenched white houses, while behind the village there gleamed a large mirror – the reservoir – with single coloured parachutes, like autumn leaves, drifting down towards it.

Our 'plane slowed down. The moment had come. "Go!"

I pushed with hands and feet, throwing my arms forward as if trying to clutch the black cross on the wing. And then the slipstream caught me, and I was swirling through space with the air roaring in my ears. A sudden jerk upon the webbing, a pressure on the chest which knocked the breath out of my lungs, and then – I looked upwards and saw, spread above me, the wide-open, motley hood of my parachute. In relation to this giant umbrella I felt small and insignificant. It was like descending in a lift. . . . No – not a lift. Only someone who has experienced a parachute jump can know this wonderful feeling of being suspended in mid-air, this weightlessness independent of the earth. For a moment I enjoyed this silent suspension which followed the St. Vitus's dance, then I looked around. To the right and left of me parachutes were hanging in the air – an infinite number of them, it seemed. And then I glanced downwards and received a shock which almost made my heart stop. It seemed that I was drifting with increasing speed towards a large reservoir which lay below me like the open mouth of a beast of prey. The waters of the reservoir loomed black and menacing, nor was there any breath of wind to urge me a little aside that I might escape drowning in the abyss. When I had marched to the front in September 1939 I had been prepared to die at some time during the war, but I had thought only of a soldier's death in battle. Could it possibly have been my destiny to be drowned in a reservoir?

The size of this reservoir grew ever larger, and I was coming nearer and nearer to it. I tried to conceive some means of escape. I tried to pray. But it was no use. I was left with only fear, fear, fear. Then suddenly there came a rough jerk. The drifting, the falling had ceased. I was down to earth again – or, at least, I was connected with the earth.

My parachute had been caught in a fig-tree growing beside the reservoir, and I was hanging by my harness over the water's edge. I unbuckled the harness, dropped, and found myself on solid ground again, all alive. Nothing else could happen to me now, I reckoned. Anyone could come and I would fight him and show him how strong I was and how much I treasured life. I do not know if babies have any feelings when they arrive in the world from their mothers' wombs, but, if they do, theirs would be precisely the same sensation as that experienced by parachutists when they have landed after a jump.

I looked about me. It was curious, I thought, for although I had seen parachutes on every side during the drop, I was now apparently alone, absolutely alone. I could see no soldiers anywhere, nor even any movement beyond the hundreds of parachutes still hanging in the air and the aeroplanes which had dropped them now heading back towards the mainland.

The reservoir beside which I had landed lay in an olive-grove. To my right, as I had reckoned from the air, was the road from Alikianou to Canea. On that road, near a cluster of white houses, my battalion staff should have assembled. And there, at least, I should meet some of my men. The cluster of houses had been marked by our reconnaissance as a British supply-dump. Yet a guide-book to Crete, which I had bought in Athens, described the same buildings as a prison. At all events, I had given orders to No. 1 Company to occupy these buildings and at the same time to con-solidate the battalion's dropping-ground.

It was remarkably quiet, almost peaceful, in the olive grove where I was standing. Apart from the drone of the homing aeroplanes, there was no sound – no human voice, nor even a rifle-shot.

It is a strange feeling to be dropped suddenly into an alien land with orders to conquer it. Every tree, every bush, every blade of grass holds its secret. One feels more like an explorer going out to meet unknown perils than a soldier seeking his enemy.

Mechanically I glanced at my wrist-watch. It showed exactly 7.15–7.15 a.m. on May 20th, 1941. A radiant summer's morning. In an atmosphere untroubled by the smallest breeze the apparent movement of the heat-haze, which glittered and vibrated as if a myriad ghosts were dancing before my eyes, served further to increase the sensation of eeriness.

Briefly I took my bearings and walked rapidly, as though fleeing from something incomprehensible, in the direction where I expected to find the road. A few hundred yards farther on I saw a hedge of cacti and agaves ahead of me, so I hurried forward, forced my way through the hedge, and found myself standing on a deserted, dusty white highway. I could see a whitewashed wall showing through the trees a few hundred yards away. That, I reckoned, would be the prison – and a great feeling of relief came over me. Now I knew where I was. Over there I would meet German soldiers with whom I could speak and who would help me to overcome these invisible perils.

The uncanny quietness persisted, and still the only sound to fill the morning air was the even throb of aeroplane engines overhead. My battalion, I assumed, must completely have landed by now, for only in the far distance, probably over Alikianou where the Engineer Battalion was supposed to drop, were parachutes still drifting earthwards.

More like a tramp than a soldier at war I walked along the road towards the white wall before me. And now, as the last of the aircraft turned north towards base, the sound of engines grew fainter and fainter, more and more distant. Somewhere on the high ground ahead of me, to the left of the road, where the village of Galatas was situated, a machine-gun started stuttering. Another answered, followed by rifle-shots. Part of the 2nd Battalion must have contacted the enemy. I registered this fact appreciatively, yet practically without concern, for I was not responsible for what happened over there. Then suddenly, from the mountains behind me, there came a screech of engines – not the ponderous roar of a transport 'plane, but a sound more like a siren – followed by a fierce crackle of machine-gun fire. Automatically I hurled myself into the ditch – a deep, concrete ditch bordering a large field of corn – and at that moment a German fighter with all guns blazing swept over within a few feet of where I lay. A stream of bullets threw up fountains of dust on the road, and ricochets sang away into the distance. Then, as suddenly as it had appeared, the apparition passed. The fighter pulled up high and disap-

peared over the olive groves in the direction of what I took
to be Canea. So the first shots to be aimed at me during this
attack had been fired by one of my own countrymen! No
one could have thought of laying out identification signals
so soon after landing, and the fighter-pilot, whose task it
was to support our attack, had obviously never imagined
that this lackadaisical figure wandering in such unmilitary
fashion down the centre of the road could possibly have
been the commanding officer of a German battalion.

Breathless with fright, I stayed for a moment or two in
the ditch. And it was while I was still trying to pull myself
together that a fresh terror assailed me: I heard, very close
to where I lay, a rustling sound in the tall corn, as though
someone were dragging himself along the ground. I held
my breath and felt for the revolver in the pocket of my
jumping-suit; but, before I could pull it out, a pair of brown
gloves had parted the corn-plants a few yards away from me
and, very cautiously, a German helmet made its appearance. Its owner was one of my sergeants, who also – but
much more prudently than I – wished to make his way
towards the white walls of the prison.

The great iron gates of the prison were wide open. From
each corner of the squat, white building sub-machine-
gunners of my battalion were covering the road; but within
the courtyard the atmosphere was rather of manœuvres
than of war. Laughing and joking, the men were helping
themselves from a wheelbarrow laden with invitingly-red
oranges. They were in the highest of spirits: the jump was
over, the landing had succeeded, and it seemed that the
worst was already behind them. Psychologists may ponder
whence that sense of power and courage is derived once a
parachutist has gained terra firma after a successful jump. It
is a sensation almost of intoxication. He feels himself a
match for any man and ready to take on anything that comes
along.

My staff, meanwhile, had all reported present: the adjutant, orderly officer, intelligence officer, wireless section,
and signals group. Messengers had already arrived from all
four companies stating that, with the exception of one

platoon belonging to No. 1 Company, of which there was still no report, they had been accurately dropped. So far only No. 1 Company had made any contact with the enemy. After a brief exchange of shots in an olive grove on the road to Canea, south-east of the prison, the enemy had withdrawn. The 3rd Battalion, on the other hand, appeared to be heavily engaged on the heights which rose to the south of the prison. The sound of machine-gun fire, which came particularly from the direction of Galatas, became progressively more intense and was punctuated by the dull explosions of grenades, the staccato rap of automatics, and the detonations of ack-ack and field-gun shells.

While a wireless set in a corner of the courtyard tried to establish radio contact with our four companies, I sat down on a step and wrote my first battle-orders after the landing. So preoccupied, in fact, was I with formulating these orders that I scarcely noticed the arrival of an extraordinary group which, when I had put my signature to the paper and looked upwards, I saw standing before me: three of my soldiers were having a violent argument with four convicts. Unable to understand what the Greeks wanted, my men had brought them to me. But I was as much in the dark as they. The convicts shouted, gesticulated, threw their hands into the air. But why? My men had seized them at the gates as they were making a bid for their long-lost freedom. I could only assume that they were now protesting their innocence and asserting their right to go free, but the fact that I was able to recite the first ten verses of Homer's *Odyssey* without fault did not help me in the least to understand them. I was practically at my wits' end when unexpected help arrived in the shape of another convict, who had been watching these proceedings. Stepping forward, he bowed elegantly, announced himself as a Mr. Constantopoulos, and asked me in perfect German if he might be permitted to act as interpreter.

Once he had made it clear to his countrymen that it would not be in their best interests to venture on to the field of battle, I asked him about himself.

He was a merchant, he said, and had lived for a long time in Germany.

"And what brings you here?" I asked him.

"*Herr Offizier*," he replied, "being a German, you could not understand this; but in the Levant a merchant must choose between cheating and being cheated. And you know that nobody likes to be cheated."

When my companies had acknowledged receipt of my orders by radio, I ordered my staff and the remainder of the fourth company to follow me across the road. With five paces between each man, we moved carefully on through an olive grove. There was no sign of my companies, and we felt as though we were all alone in this valley. The sounds of battle on the high ground to our left seemed nearer than before, and continued with undiminished fury. Then, suddenly, a machine-gun barked very close in front of us. It was answered by another – possibly a Bren gun. Three or four hand-grenades exploded, and some ricochets whistled through the air quite close to us. We stopped involuntarily. I tried to see ahead, but, despite the olive-trees being equidistantly spaced, their trunks did not permit a wide field of vision.

As suddenly as the shooting in front of us had started, it stopped, and the same lifeless silence surrounded us. It was an eerie feeling, and we were almost relieved to hear the sounds of fighting on the heights of Galatas, which were at least a token that we were not entirely alone in this hostile world. The gnarled, crippled olive-trees around us looked like deformed and evil beings, laughing and mocking us as if to say: "Go on farther, right ahead, you alien intruders! And the farther you go, the farther you advance towards your destruction!"

We were all drenched with perspiration, partly due to the humidity and heat of the island's atmosphere, partly due to the excitement, suppressed fear, and the presentiment of danger, and partly because by some brain-wave of the planners we were wearing the same sort of clothing as had been worn by German parachutists only six weeks previously when jumping over Narvik, close to the Arctic Circle.

We had not gone a hundred yards when a machine-gun barked in front of us, though this time it seemed a little farther away. Single rifle-shots whipped through the air around us. But still we could see nothing.

"What the devil's going on?" I thought, and decided to try to find out for myself. Leaving my men in the olive grove, I set off with a few orderlies and a wireless section in the direction in which I supposed lay the barren heights towards which No. 2 Company was heading. It was essential, I felt, that I should reach some point of vantage where I could see what was happening. We crossed the Cladiso rivulet, which followed the road along the valley, and made our way quickly, zig-zagging and keeping well apart from each other, up the slope. Half-way up there stood a cottage, behind which our men had laid out an air identification signal. Despite the fact, however, that the signal had been placed on the side hidden from the enemy, they had somehow spotted it, and as we ran gasping up the slope a number of small-calibre shells, such as those I had heard earlier in the morning, landed all around the hut. We rushed forward and took cover, awaiting the next volley. But it never came.

In almost peaceful silence, the sun-drenched slope and the little cottage lay before us. I gave the signal to advance, and we jumped up. And then, suddenly, we saw a movement near the cottage, and a figure emerged. Was it one of our men?

No, the man looked like a peasant. He came towards us, slowly and laboriously, as though he were carrying a heavy load. He was holding something in his hands, close to his body.

I called to him. He stopped, hesitated as if about to turn and run away, then seemed to change his mind and continued walking towards us. What did he want? My men covered him with their automatics, ready to fire. He was a youth, scarcely more than fourteen years of age. His face was chalk-white, distorted with pain. And then we saw a terrible sight. His stomach had been ripped open by a shell-spinter; and what he was holding in his hands, what he was trying to press into himself, was his own bleeding mass of entrails. A mixture of pity and horror for the poor unfortunate seized me. I ordered one of my men to take him down to the medical section.

The cottage out of which he had come was empty and partially destroyed. The other inhabitants must have fled, leaving the boy behind on his own.

The view which I had gained by reaching the high ground was not very great. To the north and west lay fresh mountain ranges which we had been unable to see from the valley and of the existence of which I had not known. Up the most westerly of these peaks, which was just as barren as that upon which we were standing, a platoon of paratroopers was making an ascent. The spread-out line of men, moving slowly up the yellow-green slope, looked like ants crawling up a sand-pile. A dense screen of trees prevented my seeing into the valley on my left, where the sounds of fighting continued unabated. On the far side of the valley, where the thickly timbered slopes rose towards Galatas, the houses gleamed white among the dark green foliage and the church stood out against the deep blue sky of mid-morning.

We descended to the valley once more, and there I decided to set up temporary headquarters in a deep gully which ran along the bottom of the slope. The transmitter was tuned in, and we tried to establish contact with the other companies. The medical staff, which had remained at the prison to care for the first wounded, was sent for, and the battalion M.O. organized a field dressing station in the gully. I glanced at my watch. How quickly the time had passed. It was 10.30 a.m. – three hours since we had landed.

When the first reports arrived from the companies they were contradictory and obscure. While sections of the battalion, advancing westwards on the right flank along the high ground south of the valley, had met without any serious resistance from the enemy, the resistance in the valley itself had increased by the hour. The British seemed slowly to be establishing a line of defence. During the first hours the fighting had apparently consisted of single, disjointed actions, sudden, unexpected encounters, and mutual surprises; but now both sides were gradually organizing themselves for battle.

A scouting party from No. 2 Company enjoyed a surprising success during the initial advance. While approaching the Cladiso rivulet, it located two British guns in an olive grove to its left. The guns were trained on the prison, and the gunners, oblivious of the German advance, were standing by, awaiting the order to fire.

With the din of battle drowning the sound of their approach, the scouts cautiously worked their way up a steep slope under cover of dense undergrowth until they found themselves overlooking the gun positions from the top of a rocky acclivity. They could hear the British soldiers talking loudly as they made preparations to start firing.

The leader of the scout-party blew his whistle, and the men rushed forward, hurling a couple of grenades as they went. Taken unawares, the crew of the nearest gun fled for cover, and the gun was captured.

The scouting party did not manage to reach the second gun. Its crew, suddenly realizing the danger they were in, retaliated with rifles and automatics, forcing the Germans to take cover. While they fought desperately at such close quarters, a half-track vehicle, ignoring the German fire, drove up. The gun-crew broke cover, rushed to the gun, hitched it to the half-track, and hanging on to the back of it made good their escape. In their wake they left only two dead and a heap of ammunition.

The paratroops advanced farther, but had progressed only a short distance before they came under heavy fire from a solitary building, which in more peaceful times probably served as a roadhouse.

The gun! Some of the men hauled the gun-carriage round, a lance-corporal loaded it, sighted it on the house through the olive trees, and fired. The shot was a near miss, and the British nest replied with rapid fire. The next shot hit the roof.

Shouting, the paratroopers stormed forward. Only in the fiercest hand-to-hand fighting and by suffering losses themselves were they able to overcome the resistance of the British, and when finally the ruined house fell into their hands not one of the defenders remained unwounded.

The first prisoners were brought to my headquarters while a runner from the scouting party was excitedly reporting the capture of the gun and the lone house. They were about twenty Greek soldiers. Some of them looked sullen, making no attempt to conceal their hatred for us; others seemed frightened, as though sure that their hour had come. Since they spoke only Greek, we were unable to interrogate them, so I sent them back to the regimental staff, which had established its headquarters near the prison.

Bad news came from No. I Company, which was suffering losses and had apparently found itself in an unfavourable position opposite strong enemy elements. I decided to go and see at first-hand exactly what was going on.

Handing over command of battalion headquarters to my adjutant, I set off with my orderly to try to locate No. I Company. On our way we passed the gun and the shattered house which had been captured by our scouting party. As we neared the firing line, ricochetting bullets sang past our heads and a burst of machine-gun fire caused a spurt of dust to rise from the dry ground barely ten yards ahead of us. Then we saw some soldiers belonging to No. I Company. They were strung out in a shallow ditch which ran along the edge of an olive grove facing an open field. We ran the last few yards, threw ourselves down behind some trees, and slipped like seals into the ditch.

The company's position was far from satisfactory. Our men were pinned down by fire from at least two machine-guns, none of which had yet, been pin-pointed. The road to the left and the deep gully of the Cladiso were also obviously well covered by the British.

After a brief reconnaissance I sent a message by wireless asking for the mortar section attached to No. 4 Company to be brought up in readiness to go into action against the machine-gun nests as soon as they were located.

The mortar section, accompanied by the commander of No. 4 Company, was not long in arriving, and while the two mortars were being got into position I crawled forward with the company commander to recce the target area.

We had no luck, vainly scanning the olive grove opposite us and the high ground to our left through our binoculars. The British, on the other hand, must have had better eyesight than we, for a shower of bullets spattered the ground immediately in front of us. We wasted no time in crawling back under cover.

Securely pinned down by the enemy and unable to catch a sight of him, the company was obviously in a practically untenable position. Casualties mounted. There were cries for assistance on all sides. Someone was calling for stretcher-bearers. A man close by suddenly slumped over his weapon and lay still. Another, with ashen face, dragged himself back under cover of the olive trees to apply a field dressing to his wound.

Suddenly there came a deafening explosion and a shower of earth rose close behind us. British guns were laying down an artillery barrage on our position – and yet we still could not see them.

Once again, with extreme caution, I crawled forward to the edge of the ditch and scanned the terrain through my glasses. This time I had better luck. Beside a white house, visible through some dark shrubs on a slope to our left, I saw a distinct movement. Yes, no doubt about it, there were British soldiers there – several of them. Was it an observation post? I could not tell, but at any rate this was definitely something worth firing at. I called for the leader of the mortar section, and he crawled up to join me.

It was while I was pointing out the house to him that I saw the commander of No. 4 Company ducking across the road and following a ditch which led up the slope on the other side. Evidently he wanted to get a better view of the target from over there. I was annoyed: he had no business to go scouting on his own, albeit I understood only too well his desire to see something of the enemy. By word of mouth, which I could hear relayed from man to man all the way to the ditch from which he was observing, I sent a message ordering him to report back to me immediately.

The mortar section, meanwhile, had found the range of the white house, and I could see the section leader, oblivious to all else, standing up to observe the effect of his fire.

"Schmetsch!" I roared at him. "Get under cover!"

He looked at me, surprised. "But, sir," he called back, "I can see so much better like this."

As suddenly as the enemy's barrage had started, so it

ceased. Most of the shells had landed behind us in the olive grove or down by the Cladiso, and as far as I could ascertain they had caused no casualties among our men. The sudden relief from the constant crashing of shells was nevertheless a blessing indeed.

I kept the white house under observation through my glasses. Through the dust thrown up by the exploding mortar shells I saw dark shadows hastening back and forth, but after the third or fourth explosion I could detect no further movement.

Then, along the ditch, growing louder and louder, I heard a message being relayed from man to man. I tried to catch the precise words, hoping that my ears had deceived me; but there was no mistaking my orderly's words when he called: "Report to Battalion. Commander of No. 4 Company seriously wounded."

This was the very devil. I immediately sent word that the second-in-command of No. 4 Company should report to me, only to receive the reply a moment later, "Second-in-command No. 4 Company wounded."

Four men carried the commander of No. 4 Company down to the roadside, where they left him for the time being in the shelter of an agave hedge. The second-in-command, meanwhile, who had been hit high in the arm, leaped across the road cursing heartily and took cover while one of the soldiers dressed his wound.

Despite the enemy's fire, I had experienced no feeling of fear until now. I had been annoyed by the firing because it had pinned us down and stopped us advancing, but the thought that I might actually be hit had not struck me. Now, however, that I had seen one of my company commanders lying seriously wounded by the hedge and his second-in-command leaping with a blood-sodden sleeve across the road, I suddenly felt fear crawling into my heart. It literally crawled. I could feel it rising from my stomach towards my heart. It quickened the heartbeats, then seemed to stop them altogether. In vain I set my teeth to try and steady myself. I clutched the earth, pressing my body against it, seeking protection from it as a child would cling to its mother's breast.

And then the enemy artillery started up again. The shells were landing in the olive grove and shrapnel flew in all directions. I heard a voice behind me: "One of the mortars has had a direct hit, sir. There are two wounded."

We were certainly in a spot.

But one from which the Germans escaped. Poor communications and tactical mistakes by the Allied commanders on Crete – notably an unnecessary withdrawal from Maleme airfield – provided the Germans with a victory instead of a defeat. On 27 May the British and New Zealand forces on the island began evacuation; despite its own appalling losses in the Battle of Crete, the Royal Navy succeeded in taking off 18,000 troops. Of the rest of the Allied garrison, 12,000 became prisoners of war, and 2,000 were killed in the fighting.

Nonetheless, Crete was a disaster for the Germans too. Hitler, Student recalled, was "most displeased by the whole affair". Some 4,000 German troops, – including almost the entire airborne leadership – was killed in the Sprung nach Kreta. *"The days of the paratroopers are over," declared Hitler. And for the Germans, they were. Never again would the Third Reich organize a mass airborne drop.*

The Allies took a different conclusion away from Crete. They saw that it was the German style of parachute warfare that was flawed and not parachute operations per se. On Crete the Germans dropped their parachutists on top of the target. The Allies, in their most successful parachute operations, the invasions of Sicily and Normandy, landed their parachutists away from the target, and then had them move against it overland.

THE BATTERY AT MERVILLE

Hilary St George Saunders

D-Day 1944 was something of a festival for Allied special forces. SAS teams were dropped to cause havoc behind the German frontline, US UDT units – the forerunner of the SEALs – cleared obstacles on the beaches, Rangers attacked the gun battery at Pointe du Hoc and led the way off Omaha beach, commandos led the British seaborne assault, whilst the flanks of the invasion were protected by the American 82nd and 101st Airborne Divisions on the right, and the British 6th Airborne Division on the left. It was a unit of the 6th Airborne, the 9th Battalion of the Parachute Regiment, that was tasked with the destruction of a battery of 150mm guns at Merville. The elimination of the battery was vital, for its guns commanded the beaches designated for the seaborne landing of the British 3rd Division.

T O THE 9th Battalion had fallen the most dangerous mission of all, the destruction of the coastal battery near Merville. The Battalion was under the command of Lieutenant Colonel T.B.H. Otway, Royal Ulster Rifles. Otway received his orders on April 2nd and had therefore only two months to rehearse the operation for which he was allowed *carte blanche*. A spot in England at West Woodhay near Newbury, where conditions were very similar to those subsequently to be encountered in Normandy, was chosen. It was good agricultural land in full production, but Otway obtained the use of it in forty-eight hours, though to do so permission had to be obtained from no less than seven different ministries in Whitehall, a record which should surely stand to the credit of the Parachute Regiment. Here in a week the sappers built a scale model of the battery, its shape and dimensions being known to them from the air photographs available. Tubular scaffolding took the place of the guns. Not only was the actual objective itself reproduced, so also were the approaches to it. Four mechanical excavators and six large bulldozers, brought on tank transporters from as far away as Liverpool and Plymouth, worked night and day, "the hours of darkness being illuminated by the headlights of vehicles".

To keep the projected operation a profound secret was naturally of the highest importance, and very stringent measures were adopted. No one without a special pass signed by the commanding officer himself could make use of any road in the neighbourhood, and a number of attractive girls, specially briefed for the purpose, were introduced into the area with orders to extract all the information they could from the parachute troops. In this they failed utterly, though the whole plan was known to every officer and man, the only piece of knowledge withheld being the actual name and whereabouts of the battery. Such elaborate precautions interfered with the lives of the local inhabitants, most of whom took them in good part. "But a number, eager to maintain the rights of property, had to be pacified by drinks in the mess."

Rehearsals by day and night were frequent. Most were conducted with live ammunition, and continued until every one of the thirty-five officers and 600 other ranks composing the Battalion knew exactly what his part was and how to play it. On 31 May the Battalion was moved to Broadwell and briefed. The briefing lasted five days, and every man attending was required to submit to his immediate superior his own sketch, drawn from memory, of the position he was to occupy. In addition to the assault by the 9th Battalion three gliders, carrying volunteers from 9th Battalion and No. 591 Parachute Squadron, Royal Engineers, were to crash-land on the top of the battery, regarding which a large amount of information had been collected. The guns were said to be of 150-mm. calibre mounted in concrete emplacements twelve feet high and five feet deep facing northwest. The concrete itself was six feet six inches thick, and in addition earth twelve feet thick surrounded two of the casemates. Access to them was by means of steel doors. The strength of the garrison was thought to be 200 all ranks (it was in fact 130). The colonel commanding them was a newcomer, the previous occupant of the post having lost it through his love of the bottle. This had led him to indulge in many excesses of which the final and fatal was a ride on the switch-back merry-go-round at the local fair near Merville. As soon as he was well aboard one of the cars, the local inhabitants bribed the owner of the switchback to keep it in continuous motion for as long as he could. For upwards of two hours the German colonel, deathly sick, was whirled up and down and round and round. When at last it stopped he was taken to his billet in a state of collapse.

To defend their guns the garrison disposed of several machine-guns and one dual-purpose 20-mm. gun. Some twenty weapon pits were plotted on the air photographs. Nor was this all: the position, which measured approximately 400 yards by 400 was surrounded by a cattle fence, and a minefield one hundred yards wide, bounded on its inner side by a concertina fence of barbed wire fifteen feet thick and five feet high. Isolated minefields had been laid across all likely approaches to the battery, and an anti-tank ditch, 400 yards long, dug on the west and north-west. If ever defenders could claim that they were holding an impregnable position, the garrison of the battery at Merville could surely do so. Around it on every side were open field and orchards, much scarred to the south by bomb craters, for Bomber Command had been very active and had attacked the battery more than once, scoring two direct hits on a casemate, neither of which had penetrated the concrete.

It was essential for the battery to be destroyed half an hour before the first assault craft touched down on the beaches. The nearest suitable dropping zone was 2,400 yards away, and the earliest moment at which the advance party of the parachutists could jump was 00.20 hours. Were

the attack to be unsuccessful the battery was to be shelled
by the Navy. It was therefore decided that the attack should
begin at 04.30 hours, and the naval bombardment at 05.30
hours, thus leaving the battalion one hour to overrun the
position and be clear of it.

The plan of attack was elaborate and Otway divided his
force into eleven separate parties, each with a definite task.
Among them were the organization party at the rendezvous,
the battery reconnaissance party, a taping party of one
officer and eight other ranks to show the way, a breaching
company, an assault company, and a reserve company. To
these were added the glider assault party of three officers
and forty-seven other ranks of the Battalion and one officer
and seven other ranks of the 591st Parachute Squadron,
Royal Engineers. Each man wore a jumping smock with a
skull and crossbones marked in luminous paint on the left
breast. In addition, there were two sniping parties armed
with Bren guns and anti-tank rifles, and a diversion party,
two of whom could speak German (these were armed with
Piats and Bren guns), a firm base party to organize the spot
from which the Battalion was to launch the assault, and
finally what was known as the glider element, made up of
five gliders carrying special heavy equipment which included flame throwers, two six-pounder anti-tank guns and
three jeeps loaded with ammunition, scaling ladders, Bangalore torpedoes, and duralumin footbridges.

The plan was as follows. The rendezvous organization
and battery reconnaissance parties, ten strong, were to land
from an Albemarle, mark the dropping zone and reconnoitre a route to the battery through its defences. Between
00.30 hours and 00.40 hours a very heavy weight of 4,000-
pound bombs was to be dropped by a hundred Lancasters.
During the bombing the glider element carrying the special
equipment was to land as close as it could to the Battalion
rendezvous, and have unloaded their cargo in time for the
Battalion to make use of it when it dropped. The taping
party was also to land and, equipped with Polish mine
detectors, to clear three paths through the minefield. The
commander of the reconnaissance party was to meet the
Battalion at a cross-roads north-east of the village of Gon-

neville and lead it to the firm base which he had previously chosen, and which was to be about 300 yards outside the perimeter to the south-east. To cover the Battalion a company of the Canadian Parachute Battalion was detailed to be in readiness.

The assault itself was to be led by the breaching platoons, three in number, which formed the breaching company. Its task was to blow gaps in the wire, whereupon the reserve and assault companies following the tapes, were to dash through and to make straight for the battery, protected by two sniping parties. The main attack was to be delivered from the south-east with a demonstration against the gate facing north. The three gliders which were to crash on top of the battery were to be released at a height of 6,000 feet at 04.24 hours, one and a half minutes later a bugle was to sound reveille, whereupon mortars from the firm base would fire star shells to illuminate the target. At 04.28 hours the bugler would sound the "Fall-in", which would be the signal for all fire to cease. The first glider was to land at 04.30 hours, and the bugler would then blow "Lights out" to stop the firing of star shells.

Naval bombardment parties in touch with H.M.S. *Arethusa*, ordered to open fire on the battery at 05.30 hours if the assault failed, were to drop with the Battalion. As soon as the battery was captured, yellow flares were to be lit, and the Battalion would then move off to its firm base, reorganize and set out for the high ground on which stood the village of Le Plein, block the roads leading from Franceville Plage to Le Plein and seize a German headquarters at Salenelles.

Such was the objective and such was the plan for seizing it. It was explained yet again to every officer and man at the final briefing by the commanding officer. He was followed by the R.A.F. station commander who, having wished them all good luck, committed himself to the rash statement that his pilots had never missed a dropping zone or been late in reaching one. "It was lucky for him," records one who survived to write an account of what happened, "that there was no chance of any discussion on this point after the operation."

On the morning of 4 June the Reverend J. Gwinnett,
C.F., the Battalion's chaplain, conducted a drumhead service, at which a special Pegasus flag, made by the Women's
Voluntary Service at Oxford, was dedicated. It was offered
by the men of the Permanent Staff of the Transit Camp
who as a result of parachute operations were no longer fit
for action. Gwinnett's discourse, which was most moving,
was on the theme "Fear knocked at the door. Faith opened
it and there was nothing there." Gale was blunter. "The
Hun thinks," he said, "that only a bloody fool will go there.
That's why we're going."

The glider assault force and the rendezvous and reconnaissance parties took off from Brize Norton and Harwell,
the rest of the Battalion earlier at 23.10 hours. All went well
until four minutes from the dropping zone, when moderate
anti-aircraft fire was encountered. This was particularly
unfortunate, for many of the pilots, who were already
finding it hard to distinguish between the mouths of the
Orne and the Dives, began to take evasive action, to the
great peril and discomfort of their passengers. A man with
an eighty-pound load and a parachute on top of it cannot
climb quickly to his feet again if he has been thrown down
in the confined space of an aircraft's fuselage; and when the
green lights came on the men composing many of the sticks
were still rolling on the floor. As a result the Battalion,
instead of being dropped in a concentrated area, 1,900 yards
by 800, was spread over fifty square miles of Normandy,
one stick landing as far away as thirty miles from the
battery. On the other hand the battery reconnaissance
and rendezvous parties dropped at their correct time and
on the right spot. They at once set about laying out their
lights and signs, and the reconnaissance party moved in
darkness towards the battery, narrowly escaping elimination from the shower of 4,000-pound bombs dropped by
the Lancasters. Not one of them hit the target but a number
of cattle in the nearby fields were killed and wounded.

Otway himself, like many of his men, had been flung
untimely out of his Dakota as it was taking evasive action.
His knowledge of the locality, gained by the study of maps
and photographs, enabled him to recognize the spot on

which he was about to land: it was a German headquarters. He and two men, of whom one was his batman, fell into the garden beside it, and were at once fired at by the Germans inside who fortunately seem to have been armed with nothing more lethal than pistols. One of the parachutists silenced this fusillade by throwing a brick through the window, which the Germans evidently mistook for a grenade. Otway's batman fell through the glass roof of the greenhouse but was able to rejoin him at the rendezvous.

On reaching it Otway found a condition of affairs which might well have quelled a stouter heart. To quote from his staccato official report: "By 02.50 hours the battalion had grown to one hundred and fifty strong with twenty lengths of Bangalore torpedo. Each company was approximately thirty strong. Enough signals to carry on – no three-inch mortars – one machine-gun – one half of one sniping party – no six-pounder guns – no jeeps or trailers or any glider stores – no sappers – no field ambulance, but six unit medical orderlies – no mine detectors – one company commander missing. The commanding officer decided to advance immediately."

A Company was in the van, followed by Otway and such of his battalion headquarters as had arrived. Then came a small number of the diversion party, then thirty men of B Company with some Bangalore torpedoes. They were followed by twenty men of C Company, the battalion medical officer, and the medical orderlies. This small but very resolute force set out along country lanes and tracks bordered by high banks and thick hedges, on the other side of which could be seen the dim forms of apple trees heavily laden. They halted often to make sure by the light of the moon that they were moving in the right direction, and at one moment successfully slipped by a patrol of the enemy.

On the way to the firm base they met, as arranged, the battery reconnaissance party under Major G. Smith. They had cut the outer cattle fence, penetrated the minefield, and lain for half an hour beside the concertina wire, spotting the enemy's posts by listening to the talk and coughing of the sentries. During their approach to the minefield an enemy patrol had passed within two feet of the ditch in which they were crouching. They had in due course been joined by the taping party commanded by Major A.J. Parry. It had no tapes or mine detectors, but had marked the way through the minefield by scratching heel-marks in the dust. These tasks had been accomplished without a single casualty, though the officers and men employed on them had had to crawl forward on their hands and knees feeling for trip wires, of which several were encountered.

At 04.30 hours the Battalion reached the firm base where B Company was divided into two breaching teams, and A and C Companies were joined together into one assault force consisting of four parties, each of twelve men, one party for each gun of the battery. So far the enemy had made no sign, but hardly had Otway and his men reached their firm base when six enemy machine-guns, all outside the perimeter, opened fire, and four more from inside it. There was one Vickers machine-gun with the assault force, and this successfully silenced three of the German machine-guns on one flank, while the diversion party, now only six men under Sergeant Knight, performed a similar task to the right flank on their way to the main gate.

At this crucial moment two of the three gliders carrying the special assault party could be seen circling low over the battery, tracer from the 20-mm. guns pouring into them. The third glider had not arrived, for the tow-rope parted early, and it had had to land in England to the chagrin of its occupants. The two gliders which reached the battery were piloted by Staff Sergeants S.G. Bone and D.F. Kerr. Bone's glider, with Captain R. Gordon-Brown on board, had been severely strained in mid-Channel by the sudden opening of its parachute arrester gear. It and its tug, with Pilot Officer Garnett at the controls, had also been repeatedly hit by anti-aircraft fire, but this did not prevent the combination from circling the battery four times before the glider was released.

The plan for illuminating the battery with star shells had gone awry, for there were no shells or mortars from which to fire them, and Staff Sergeant Bone in consequence at first mistook the village of Merville for the battery. He turned away in time, but landed four miles from the

objective. All within disembarked unhurt and under Gordon-Brown presently reached Le Mesnil where they fought
for two days in defence of brigade headquarters and then
rejoined the Battalion. With them was the special flag made
by the Oxford Women's Voluntary Service. It was to
remain with the Battalion for the rest of the war and to
be carried in every action.

Staff Sergeant Kerr had better fortune. With four men
hit on board from anti-aircraft fire, and with his glider
beginning to smoulder, he prepared to land in a large field
200 yards from the casemates. The wheels had indeed
touched ground, when out of the darkness loomed a large
white board with the word "Minen" written on it and
decorated with a skull and crossbones. Pulling back the
control column, Kerr lifted the glider over the field and the
hedge and sunken road beyond. He then crash-landed in an
orchard some 200 yards east of the firm base. He and his
passengers, the wounded included, with Lieutenant A.
Pond at their head, stumbled out of the glider, which
had lost both wings and was on fire, and immediately
engaged a platoon of the 1st/736th Regiment of the
716th Division of the German Army. The ensuing fight
lasted four hours, but the Germans were never able to come
to the help of the battery's garrison.

Hardly had the occupants of the glider joined battle,
when Otway gave the signal for the gaps in the wire to be
blown. The assault parties then moved against the battery,
but slowly, for bomb craters, wire and mines strewed the
way. Nothing, however, could stop the indomitable troops
whose average age was twenty-one – most of them, be it
remembered, in action for the first time. In due course they
reached the guns and engaged in hand-to-hand combat with
the German gunners. These resisted stoutly until one of
them happened to catch sight of the badge on the battle
smock of a parachutist. "*Fallschirmjäger,*" he yelled,
whereupon he and his remaining comrades lost heart and
surrendered.

Three guns were destroyed by Gammon bombs; and one
by firing two shells at once through the barrel. The destruction was checked by Lieutenant M. Dowling, though

mortally wounded. The success signal was lit half an hour before H.M.S. *Arethusa* was due to begin the bombardment, and to make certain that their victory should be made known, Lieutenant J. Loring, the battalion signals officer, pulled a somewhat crumpled carrier pigeon from the blouse of his battledress and flung it into the air. It duly arrived in England a few hours later.

After withdrawing to the firm base, Otway found that he had about eighty men still on their feet. About thirty casualties were being treated in the battalion aid post, set up in a ruined barn close by. Twenty of them were stretcher cases. One officer had been killed and four wounded, and sixty-five other ranks killed, wounded or missing. The wounded were left with Captain H. Watts, the medical officer, and with a German doctor and two orderlies, who took good care of them.

Filled with triumph at an exploit which was of immeasurable aid to the seaborne invaders, the Battalion moved off to carry out its second task, the seizure of the high ground near Le Plein. They had not gone far before a Frenchman appeared and warned them that the little village of Hauger on their route was held by 200 of the enemy. It was now full daylight, and after seizing the crossroads in front of the village, Otway called a halt. The position to be attacked was a small château, loopholed for defence, and surrounded by a stone wall six feet high. It proved too strong to overrun, and the Battalion therefore took up a defensive position opposite it, where they were much annoyed by snipers but where they prevented the enemy from moving to the Orne. By then they were so thin on the ground that there had to be an interval of ten yards between each man.

It was presently discovered that the garrison of the château and the village were for the most part Russians compelled by the Germans to fight for them on the grounds, which they unfortunately believed, that if they fell into the hands of the Allies they would be shot as traitors. The position was eventually captured on the next day by commando troops.

Such were the deeds performed by the five battalions of

the Parachute Regiment, the 22nd Independent Company and the 1st Canadian Parachute Battalion on D-Day. The palm must be given to Otway and his gallant 9th, but every objective assigned had been taken by troops, hardly any of whom had been in action before. Unable to uphold a tradition which they did not possess, they could and did create one. Most praiseworthy of all perhaps, they had in twenty-four hours shewn themselves to be of the same stout breed as the men of the 1st Airborne Division.

BANDIT COUNTRY

Anthony Crockett

In May 1950, the 3rd Commando Brigade of the Royal Marines was ordered to Malaya, a British dominion, where a Communist insurgency was being fomented by the Malayan Races' Liberation Army (MRLA). Its name notwithstanding, the "Army" contained no Malays; it was recruited entirely from the large Chinese population in the peninsula, many of whom farmed "squats" at the edge of the jungle, from which they supplied the Communist terrorists, or "bandits", with aid. Consequently, the squats and their borders became one of the main arenas for RM Commando operations in Malaya.

Anthony Crockett was an officer with 42 Commando RM in Malaya.

A FEW WEEKS AFTER I took over command of A Troop an informer approached the police with information about the presence of four bandits in a certain area. They were not thought to be big fry, but probably Min Yuen. Their importance, however, lay in the fact that they were suspected to be an essential link in an intricate chain of supply which was handling food and ammunition. The area in which they were reported to be was not many miles from Ipoh. About half a mile from it there was a large resettlement village. To reach the place in day-light, troops would have to pass either through a rubber estate or through a district of extensive Chinese cultivation, in both of which the bandits would undoubtedly have established an efficient warning system.

Some distance away there was a large disused mining-pool which was, in places, very deep. After the Japanese surrender scattered dumps of weapons and ammunition were left all over Malaya, and not all of them were reported by the Japanese to the British military authorities. It was the custom to destroy much of this material when found, there being no further economical use for it. One of these dumps had been discovered a few years previously, but by that time there were no British troops available who were able to undertake the complicated task of destroying it. The police therefore had no choice but to deal with it as best they could. They transported its contents – aerial bombs and a few mortar bombs – to this pool and dumped them in the deepest section, hoping that the water would soon render them of no further use.

It was this ammunition which was now being secretly salvaged from the pool and carried many miles through old tin tailings and rubber estates deep into the jungle. The actual salvage and the porterage as far as the jungle edge was reputed to be carried out by the Min Yuen. There they were met by uniformed bandits with a team of Sakai who undertook the long haul far into the mountains, where rumour had it they had set up a large camp complete with school, hospital and an armoury. By this route also were supposed to go supplies of food, medicine and clothing. The disruption of this system, by knocking out the men who worked at its source, was therefore of some considerable importance.

The bandits were reported to be living in an area of belukar and overgrown rubber. On the western side of it ran the main road, a rubber estate and the railway. On the east it was bounded by a river which ran close by the railway at either end of the area. To the east of the river lay a wide expanse of Chinese smallholdings criss-crossed by small tracks and streams, and to the east of that again ran a dirt road leading to the resettlement village.

It was suspected that the small Min Yuen group carried out most of its work by night and lay up during the day. It was also probable that its outside contacts, who maybe worked in the rubber or nearby smallholdings, visited it during the daytime. This was therefore presumed to be the best period in which to make certain of finding them "at home".

We discussed the problem at length with the police and finally decided that, in spite of this, we would form up during the dark hours and start our search immediately it began to grow light. By choosing this time of the day we took a risk at hitting at thin air and finding that the birds had flown, but we also avoided most possibilities of our approach being discovered and reported.

For the operation I had at my disposal my own troop, Y Troop, half of S Troop and a number of police jungle squads. This may sound an abnormally large force to winkle out four men, but it should be realized that the country was very thick and that it was the easiest thing in the world for a man to lie low and let a search party walk almost over him, or to slip through a line of beaters who constantly were forced to lose visual touch with each other.

My plan, in brief, was to cover the line of the railway with a number of stops supplied by Y Troop and some jungle squads, and the line of the river with part of A Troop and some more police. I intended to sweep the wedge-shaped area, from its broad base at the northern end to the apex where the railway and the river joined forces again, with half of A Troop and half S Troop. Back-stops, provided by the police, were to be placed along the broad base of the wedge in case the bandits should try to break back through the searchers.

The whole success of the enterprise was likely to depend on the surprise it could achieve. It was essential to get everyone into their correct positions without giving away their presence. It was equally important that the timings should be so planned that each group was in place by the time the operation was due to start. This required much co-ordination, as the various components of the force had to come from different places and had to approach their respective areas from various directions. Due to the distance of the place from our various starting points, troops and police had to travel some of the way in vehicles.

Now the country, in any part of the world, is deadly quiet at night. In the East it is filled with a thousand local sounds, but over it all lies a blanket of silence. Through this the noise of the engines of military vehicles can be heard for miles. A bandit sentry, hearing the high-pitched whine of road convoys in the middle of the night, however far distant, could not but think it unusual for that hour and would be instantly on the alert for further developments. A long approach march was therefore necessary so that, even if the sounds of our transport were heard a long way off, they would not give any indication of the direction in which we were intending to go.

Here we ran into another difficulty. No one knew this particular area very well, and it was considered most inadvisable to carry out any form of reconnaissance of it beforehand for fear of attracting attention towards it. I did, however, manage to arrange a flight over the area in an Auster so that we appeared to be making an ordinary routine approach to Ipoh airport. In addition, the OSPC Ipoh, Nobby Clarke, was only too anxious to find an excuse for coming out with us, and volunteered to act as guide, claiming that he had once, some time ago, been to that very place. For the rest, we had to be content with a close study of some aerial photographs, which we knew, as a result of my flight, were rather out of date.

The afternoon before the operation I held a briefing meeting in A Troop camp. To it came all the officers and NCOs in the troops concerned, Nobby, and the police lieutenants who were to command the jungle squads. On a blackboard I had drawn a plan of the whole area. On this I explained what I proposed to do. In view of the fact that most sections of the force would be out of sight of each other, wireless communication was of great importance. An intricate system had to be evolved so that control of the operation would be effective and quick warning could be given of the direction taken by any bandits who might break cover. Careful arrangements had also to be made for the vehicle convoys. They were to start from various camps, for various destinations, and each had different distances to cover. It was even important to load the trucks with troops in a certain order, so that when we started to walk we approached our allotted areas in the right sequence. For the most part our way would lie along narrow footpaths, and it was essential that those who had the farthest to go should not be blocked by those who had to stop first. Confusion in the dark, whispering, the sounds of men and bits of equipment knocking against each other must be avoided, and there must be no question of one lot of men having to pass through another to get up to their positions.

Next morning, at some ungodly hour, we turned to. In A Troop our admirable cooks, who I doubt had been to bed at all, had breakfast ready for us. It was a moonless night, but the stars shone so brightly that there was no difficulty in walking about the darkened camp. The tenseness of excitement was in the air. There was a feeling that this time we were really on to something. Although there was no need for it, men talked to each other in undertones, and even the cooks in the galley did not seem to be throwing their pots and pans about with their usual air of careless abandon. Out trucks began to form up in a line on the road outside the camp, and presently the police arrived in theirs. The troop was fallen in, a last check made of weapons, ammunition and equipment and we "embussed".

When we started I was horrified by the noise. I knew that the engines of our vehicles were far from silent, but in the stillness of the night and to my (then) unduly sensitive ears I felt that we must be making a din which could be heard all over the State of Perak. It was fortunate for us that it was a bright night. Strict instructions had been passed that no lights whatever were to be used in the convoys. Even sidelights, when reflected on trees or the sides of road cuttings, can throw a glare upwards into the sky. We droned slowly through a dead world, where shadows threw deep gaps of blackness among the rubber trees and the starlight danced across the flat tin tailings like moonlight on the sea. We passed a tin mine and the cluster of huts which marked its labourers' lines, and every dog in the place came alive and barked their suspicion at us.

Presently we reached the T-junction. From there ran the dirt road which eventually led to the resettlement village. We climbed out of our trucks and sorted ourselves into our correct formations before setting off. Again a last-minute check of everything, while weapons were loaded and the signallers made certain that their sets were working properly.

Our route ran through old rubber – tall, gnarled trees, reaching upwards from high, tangled undergrowth – while the stars glowed from a sky of almost translucent blue-green, like light through a threadbare curtain. It was the world of Arthur Rackham, where the whorls of tree-trunks became faces and the twisted branches gnarled, arthritic hands. The night still lay deep amongst the trees.

It had not rained for a day or two, and the surface of the road was dusty. The deep ruts made by the lorries which moved the possessions of the squatters to the village were hard. Their knife-edges were traps for the unwary jungle boot, with its soft and yielding sole. But there was a cushion of soft dirt on the surface, and our feet made no noise. We plodded on in silence, a silence which seemed to add emphasis to the grimness of our purpose, while the trees, hostile and resentful, glowered at us from either side. At last we rounded a bend in the road. There in front of us, instead of the grey blur of trees, was a clear-cut chunk of starry sky. We were approaching the open country and the immediate area of the operation.

On the very edge of the rubber we halted. Nobby, with a small escort, went forward to find the footpath which led off westwards from the road towards the river. Presently a man came back to lead up the remainder of us. It began to grow darker and a light breeze blew up, bringing with it low, whispy clouds, which set strange shadows gliding eerily across the ground. In single file we started down the track. On either side lay Chinese vegetable gardens. It was a little hard not to imagine ourselves carrying out a nocturnal inspection of some council allotments. The track wound in and out between rows of beans, sometimes diving through patches of tapioca, with their high stalks and their large leaves almost shutting out the sky above our heads.

Sometimes it crossed small streams and now and again it split in two or three different directions. Then there would be a pause, while Nobby and his escort went forward to make quite certain that we kept to the right route. In the distance the line of the river was easy to distinguish by the dark strip of trees along its banks.

Gradually the long snake of men began to decrease in size as the various small parties broke off to take up their respective positions, and I was left with Nobby and our small headquarters – two signallers with their wireless sets, Peters my servant, and a few Chinese detectives. We established ourselves on the edge of the rubber, where there was a small clearing, from which a track led down to the river bank. The signallers got their sets working and started to take in reports from the stops and search parties as they came up on the air to say they were in position. So far, so good. We seemed to have arrived without arousing suspicion.

Near our headquarters was a Chinese squatter house – half human habitation and half pigsty – a ramshackle affair of wooden beams, grass roof and walls. From it had come sounds of life as soon as we appeared and we had carried out a quick investigation. It was inhabited all right – by a large sow, a litter of piglets, a very old man and a young girl. The pigs had been the first to waken, and it was not until we had gone right inside the shack that we noticed the two sleeping figures under a mosquito net. They looked scared, but we charged them to keep quiet and to stay where they were.

There was still half an hour or so until daylight, and we sat down to wait. This was always the worst time, although this period was essential. Allowance had to be made for some part of the force getting lost or going astray and therefore taking longer to get into its position than planned. We could not smoke, and the mosquitoes, which are always at their worst and most aggressive in rubber, had a field day at our expense. Very gradually the blue-black of the sky began to pale and the chill brilliance of the stars to fade. The silhouette of leaves and branches stood out, for a few moments, even more distinctly against a background of ever-lightening blue. Somewhere in the distance a cock crew. Suddenly it was morning.

I tapped the signal corporal on the shoulder and told him to broadcast "Start search now".

For the time being there was nothing to do in head-quarters except to wait impatiently for something to happen. The search party, strung out in a long line, moved forward at a snail's pace, with their weapons at the ready, trying to make no noise as they wrestled with the thick undergrowth. Along the river bank and overlooking the railway track groups of men lay hidden, the safety catches on their rifles pushed forward and their eyes glued on the ground in front of them for the slightest suspicion of a move, for a flash of black or khaki clothing, the quick scuttle of a human figure bent double in flight.

It was this moment that the old man and the young girl chose to break the tension. With a nervous, toothless smile he advanced towards us with a pile of small earthenware bowls in his hands. These he set out on a fallen tree beside us. The girl, in shapeless black tunic and trousers, followed, with downcast eyes, a teapot in a wicker holder in her hands. Behind her, as if to watch the fun, bumping and barging each other, trotted some of the piglets. The girl began to pour the tea into the bowls.

The calm was shattered by a sudden burst from a Sten. It was followed by the sharp report of a bursting grenade and then more firing. In a flash, old man, girl, and piglets had vanished. Nothing but a steaming bowl of pale gold liquid remained to prove that they had ever been there.

Then there was silence. Not a shout, not a shot, not a sound of movement.

I watched the face of the signal corporal, eager to catch in it the first sign that he was receiving a report over his wireless set. He was sitting with his back against a tree, his features expressionless and his body relaxed, idly doodling in the soft earth with his pencil. His calm detachment was infuriating.

Then he bent forward, straightened his headphones and began to write on the signal pad on his knee. I watched over his shoulder.

"Small camp for three or four found twenty yards in front of start line [of search]. One bandit killed. Two others broke back towards back-stops. Search continues."

I sent back "Well done", told the corporal to inform the other stations not on the net and then to stop transmitting. It was essential to keep the air clear for any other important messages, and this was not the time for general chit-chat.

It was at this moment that several excited police arrived with a badly-frightened Chinese held firmly by the arms. He was middle-aged, in a white shirt and khaki shorts. In one hand he clutched a toothbrush, a face flannel and a small pale-blue tin of Gibbs toothpowder. His captors reckoned he was a bandit. Just before the shooting had started he had appeared through the thick bamboo on the opposite side of the river and climbed down into the water. He was obviously terrified, and when three or four detectives all started to shout at him at once he was reduced to a complete state of dither. His story was a simple one. He was a tapper and owned a smallholding of rubber trees on the stretch of land between the railway and the river. He had a small hut there, where he had been living with his wife and children. He was in the process of being resettled and, in fact, his family had moved into their new home in the nearby resettlement village. He had been intending to join them in a day or two when he had finished moving all their belongings. He had just got up and had been going down to the river for his morning wash. He was not a bandit and had nothing to do with any bandits.

One of Nobby's Chinese, a man with an anti-bandit record of great personal courage and long experience, walked away from the group surrounding the suspect. He shook his head, and in Chinese said, "He's no bandit. I can tell at once. You can let him go."

I must admit that I had thought the same as soon as I set eyes on the man. In spite of the fear in his face he had an air of honesty and dignity; but I said nothing, realizing that I knew very little about such things, while I was surrounded by experts. A pair of handcuffs were produced and clapped on the man, and he was told to sit down against a tree. (Note: This man was later taken back to the police station after the operation was over, where his innocence was firmly established and he was allowed to return home. He was a lucky man. I feel certain that if he had emerged on to that river bank a few minutes later nothing could have saved him from being shot as he did so.)

For a time quiet reigned. The old man and the girl appeared from their house. A quick glance of recognition passed between them and the suspect. Then they behaved as if he was not there. The girl had brought the teapot with her. The old man carried a bowl of milk and another of sugar. We gratefully accepted the hot drink, the Chinese sucking theirs back with most audible relish. Then once again the stillness was blasted. A quick burst of automatic fire, excited shouts. Then a prolonged fusillade of Bren firing. The noise came from the vicinity of the start line. The old man and the girl repeated their vanishing act, and none too soon, for suddenly a shower of leaves descended on our heads and we realized that bullets were whistling through the trees above us.

Once again the wireless came to life: "Second bandit killed. No further bandits seen so far. Search continues. All ground fifty yards in front of start line cleared."

A few minutes later there was a loud shout to our right front, a rifle shot, and a sound of splashing in the river. Presently a bunch of excited police appeared from the direction of the river, hauling along with them a dripping young Chinese. He was squat and rubbery, with long, straight hair falling over his face, dressed in a black shirt and khaki shorts. Handcuffs were snapped on to his wrists and he was quickly frisked. The search produced nothing except his wallet, containing an identity card and a few dollars.

He was brought before Nobby and questioned. He stoutly denied he was a bandit and claimed that he was a tapper.

"Where is your tapping knife?" he was asked.

"I left it behind in the rubber," he replied.

"What were you doing down by the river?"

"I heard the shooting and wanted to get away."

"Do you live here?"

"No," and then mentioned where his home was.

"Then what were you doing here so early in the day?"

So the questioning went on, question following rapid question, while the man's eyes swept from one interrogator to the next and turned to the ground when he paused to measure his replies. There was obviously something fishy about him. His clothes, though none the better for being in the river and his rather rough handling, were clean. Now, there are two obvious signs by which a rubber tapper can be spotted at once. The first is the small, hooked knife, which is used for making incisions in the bark of the rubber tree, and which is generally worn on the waistbelt. The second is the mass of brown, latex stains which normally cover the front of his clothes.

Both these signs were conspicuous by their absence, and the detectives warmed to their questioning. The more they tried to nail the suspect down, the louder he protested his innocence and the harsher his replies became. There *was* something odd about him, although almost impossible to define. To me he was as obviously a bandit as the first man was not, although I could not tell why I felt so sure.

The interrogation went on for ages but, as it all took place in Chinese, meant nothing to me and, as it was causing far too much noise, I had it removed out of earshot. Meanwhile the search continued, its progress being reported at intervals over the air. The area was narrowing as the searchers moved steadily towards the narrow edge of the wedge. It seemed certain that if there were any more bandits around they would be cornered sooner or later.

Presently an excited Chinese detective inspector appeared. The young suspect had broken down under examination and confessed that he was a bandit. There had been four of them, he said, engaged, as we thought, on the supply route. The fourth man was sick, very sick. In fact he had beriberi. Had we found him yet? He would not be able to get very far, as he was so weak that he could not walk. In a perfect spate of confessions he admitted to knowing where two important food dumps were, and said that he would lead us to them straight away.

By this time the area was reported as having been searched from end to end. A small party was detached from the men lining the river and sent off with the captured bandit to locate the food dumps. He was as good as his word. One of them contained several hundredweight of food, mostly rice, so cunningly hidden that it was actually only a few yards from where a party of stops had been placed. The food was stored in sealed drums, which had been buried in the ground, covered with earth and concealed by pulling over them the branches of bushes and trailing vines.

There was still the fourth man to be found. It could only be a matter of time before he was captured, as the area was completely sealed. Anyhow, it was improbable that he could move very far in his weak state. I decided to start a fresh search for him and sent over from my side of the river a party to locate the small camp originally found and to work outwards from that. About twenty minutes later they found him. The original search must have passed right over him, for he was only a few yards from the camp. When the first contact was made he had crawled and then dragged himself away, until he had collapsed in the middle of some thick bushes. He could not stand up, let alone walk, and he had to be carried pick-a-back.

That was the end of the operation. There was nothing left to do except to send out orders for dealing with the food dumps, sort out the full story and return to our camps. The two bodies were brought in later. The first man, who had been caught in the camp itself, had thrown the grenade which we had heard, and had been shot as he threw it. The second man had then managed to break away and had doubled back towards the police, who had been positioned immediately behind the start line. They had spotted him and opened fire with everything they had. These had been the bullets which had come so uncomfortably near us. This had driven him forward again but, as he then found himself between the police and the searching line, he had tried to escape to the flank. He had been spotted by Y Troop along the railway line and had been shot down by Bren fire as he ran between two bits of cover.

Two rifles, a pistol and a hand-grenade were recovered, as well as a quantity of documents, mostly Communist propaganda pamphlets. One of the rifles was so riddled with bullet holes that, as it was handed to me to examine, it simply fell to pieces.

It was a measure of the rigid discipline and fear with which the Communists ruled even their fellows, and their almost utter isolation from free, day-to-day contacts that, while nearby there should have been a large food dump, one of their Min Yuen workers was suffering from an advanced degree of malnutrition. I saw quite a lot of that young man in later weeks. He was not yet seventeen, and when they had got him into hospital, he was so weak that the doctors would not let him be questioned by the police, even though his information might have been of immediate importance. When he grew stronger we were allowed to visit him, but he could not tell us much that we did not already know.

He was a case typical of many others. His home had been a squatter house a few miles outside Ipoh. He had worked in a cobbler's in the town, while his father had farmed his bit of land around the house. One evening, when he was at home, three Chinese had come to the back of the house and called him out. One was a man he had known slightly. The other two were strangers. They talked to him of poor wages and the big money being made by others at his expense. They told him how they and others were working to overthrow the Government, so that one day they would run the country for themselves. Further than that they had not gone. Before they disappeared they told him not to speak of their visit, to think over what they had said, and that they would be back again.

A few days later they returned. They went over the same ground again and then spoke of the pressing need of the Cause for young men. He would be well paid. Food and clothing would be provided for him and any money he was given would therefore be available to spend as he liked. He would be given a weapon and so thenceforth he would be strong. He would be in the forefront of the Liberation and early on the band-wagon. They did not threaten him, but there was something in their manner of talking which filled him with fear.

Frightened and undecided, he had no one to turn to for advice and only a limited intelligence with which to wrestle with this problem. It was finally his sister who turned the scales. Unbeknown to him, she had been enlisted into the Min Yuen. Already she was involved in the clandestine collection of "subscriptions", although none of her family was aware of this. She had either suspected or had been tipped off about her brother's predicament, and she took the matter up with him one day.

The next time the men came to his house the boy left with them. Since then he had never dared to go back. He had met his sister once. She had told him that their father knew where his son had gone.

"To me he is dead," the old man had said. "I will never wish to see him again. He is no longer my son."

Life had proved to be sadly different to the pictures painted so magnificently to him. He had been issued with no smart khaki uniform and, for a long time, he had been without a weapon. Finally he was given a hand-grenade. Its detonator was a home-made affair and he was more frightened of than grateful for it. He had lived always in hiding, in very temporary camps in the open, continually on the move and in fear of discovery. Several times he and the others with whom he was living had been almost cut off and surrounded by patrols. All this time his work had been confined to the lowly task of carrying supplies. In the many months since he had been enrolled he had in all never been paid more than a few dollars.

I never heard what happened to him in the end. He could not have been charged with the capital offence of carrying a weapon, as we found nothing with or near him although, on his own evidence, he had once possessed one. In any case, by law he was too young to pay for his offence with his life. It is unlikely that he has returned to his old way of life as a free man, for his former comrades would be the first to consider him a danger requiring immediate elimination.

Maybe his face still carries that deserted, puzzled look as he ponders over the realities of conquest and true liberty.

In May 1952 the Commando brigade was withdrawn from Malaya. Left behind were 221 "bandits" killed and captured.

EMERGENCY EXIT

Bernard Fergusson

Spring, 1942. The situation of the British Army in the Far East was perilous; it had been ejected by the Japanese from Burma, and India itself was threatened. Morale amongst the exhausted and emaciated troops was at rock bottom. To retake Burma – hold India even – the Commander-in-Chief India, General Sir Archibald Wavell, needed to pull something unorthodox out of the military cap. That something was Orde Wingate, who had served under Wavell in pre-war Palestine.

Born in 1903, Wingate was one of the most enigmatic officers in the British Army, insubordinate yet intolerant of criticism, manic depressive yet extraordinarily clear-headed about the theory and practice of guerilla warfare, which he had tasted in Palestine as a leader of the "Special Night Squads" against the Arabs.

Such a latterday T.E. Lawrence was exactly the magnetic, unconventional independent officer Wavell needed in Burma in 1942. Hastily promoted to Colonel, Wingate was given command of all commando operations behind Japanese lines in Burma. Aiding Wingate was Major Michael Calvert of the Bush Warfare School. Together Wingate and Calvert formulated the tactical concept of a Long Range Penetration Force which would be supplied on operations by air. This was an utterly novel idea in the Far East at the time. Moreover, Wingate considered that the Brigade should be composed of seven separate columns, each composed of about 400 men. The columns were small enough to be mobile and elusive, but could be combined to pack a real punch against specific Japanese targets.

Wingate named his force the Chindits after the "Chinthe", the mythical figure guarding Burmese temples. Their first mission was to infiltrate into Burma and attack the strategically important north-south railway and other targets. In mid-February 1943 the Chindit columns began crossing the River Chindwin. All the columns were assigned separate tasks; the job of Number 5 Column under Major Bernard Fergusson was to blow the railway bridge at Bongyaung. After a sharp engagement with Japanese forces, No. 5 Column dynamited the bridge on 6 March, Fergusson later recounting: "The flash illumined the whole hillside. It showed the men standing tense and waiting, the muleteeers with a good grip of their mules; and the brown of the path and the green of the trees preternaturally vivid. Then came the bang. The mules plunged and kicked, the hills for miles around rolled the noise of it about their hollows."

For good measure, No. 5 Column also blew the neighbouring gorge, blocking the line with tons of rock.

By now the Chindit columns were being sought relentlessly by the Japanese, who had finally understood that enemy was being supplied by air. There was other trouble for the Chindits; on crossing the Irrawaddy they found not jungle but an arid, open wasteland in which Japanese armour could operate. In Fergusson's words, the far side of the Irrawaddy "would seem to us a prison". Water and forage became scarcer, and air supplies, because of the greater distance involved, less reliable. Eventually, Wingate decided at the end of March that he had no option but to withdraw the columns. Fergusson's column, along with that led by Calvert, was appointed the rearguard. The Chindits were a thousand miles from home.

B RIGADE LED, and I resumed my old position as tail column except for the Burrif headquarters, to whom had been allotted the difficult task of obliterating our trail.

Brigade left at 1 a.m., and it was close on 3 a.m. before I saw the last man in front of me move off, and gave the word to march. We had all had a good rest; and had it not been for hunger (for we had to husband our scanty ration) we should have been in very good form.

Everything depended on our reaching Inywa without our turnabout being suspected; and our route therefore avoided all tracks. Wingate's uncanny instinct for cross-country marching – his sense of watersheds, good gradients, thinner jungle and so forth – was apparent even from my place far down the long procession. But it was a slow business, with frequent halts; and, with the knowledge of the Irrawaddy stretched like a barrier between ourselves and the free country beyond, the march was anything but exhilarating. Wingate had said himself that, once over the 'Waddy, we were seven-eighths out of the wood. Meanwhile, one was aware of its sinister breadth ahead of us, a malevolent ally, however passive, of the Japanese.

But the most depressing aspect of that miserable march was the slaughter of the mules. Were this to become known to the Japanese, our intention would be clear to them. Wingate had directed that they should be led off the track and slaughtered as opportunities occurred. They could not be shot on the hill-tops, for fear of the sound carrying; but every time we descended into a *chaung* half a dozen would be led away from the track we were making, their loads and saddlery concealed in the undergrowth, and six shots would ring out. Poor Bill Smyly, who had looked after them so wisely and well all the way from the banks of the Narain Nullah in the Central Provinces, to whom they were the light of his life, who had quarrelled with half the officers in the column on their behalf, who had not lost a single beast from avoidable causes – poor Bill Smyly marched that day with a white face, slipping away every now and then to dispatch a few more, and rejoining the column with tears on his cheeks.

Soon a message came back down the line that no more were to be shot; even although the places were chosen with some care, the sound was carrying up to the head of the procession, where the Brigadier was marching. The message said that they were to be slaughtered noiselessly. We had been using pistols instead of a rifle, in the hope that the noise would be lessened. Now we tried the ghastly experiment of cutting their throats; but the first operation sickened us all so much that I said we should try it no more. We had already disposed of sixteen animals since leaving the bivouac.

The Brigadier's orders, at the conference the previous afternoon, had been as follows. We were making for Inywa, where the Shweli enters the Irrawaddy. Leaving the Hehtin Chaung at 1 a.m. on the 27th, we hoped to make Inywa at 6 p.m. on the 28th, and to begin crossing that night. The proposed bivouac area for the night 27th-28th was the marshes of Chaungmido, where one of the other columns had reported finding water on the southward journey. If by chance the march was interrupted, the rendezvous was to be in the jungle one mile south of the village of Pyinlebin.

Once arrived at Inywa, there were to be tasks for each column. Burrif H.Q. were to help 8 Column collect boats from the lower reaches of the Shweli: 7 Column was to cross first and make a bridgehead on the west bank: Brigade Headquarters were to cross next: and 5 Column was to throw a screen all round the crossing area, to protect it while the rest of the brigade crossed. We were to be the rearguard, the place of honour; and to be the last over.

There was a very real possibility that, with the Japs lining both the Irrawaddy and the Shweli, we were already in the bag. All columns had reported their awareness of reinforcements moving up; we in No. 5 Column had learnt of it in the neighbourhood of Mogok and Myitson, and other people had similar tales. There was little one could do in the way of insurance; but two things I had already arranged. I had asked Gim Anderson and the Brigadier to make a note, in case I failed to reach India, that I recommended both Duncan and John for decoration for their sterling services; I had witnessed Gim write down their names, along with those of various N.C.O.s and men, in his notebook. Secondly, I enjoined on both Duncan and John that, in the event of their getting out alive and my failing to do so, they were to seek an audience with General Wavell in

Delhi, on my behalf; and to give him my views on the feasibility of this form of warfare. I made them repeat several times over the arguments which, even should the expedition finish in disaster, seemed to me irrefutable proof that such enterprises were worth while.

Mentally and physically, it was a horrid march. At one o'clock, soon after crossing a track running north and south, the first we had seen, Hosegood, the brigade intelligence officer, came back to meet me, and to say that we were going into a midday bivouac, moving off at about three. The spot chosen was the junction between the Hintha Chaung and one of its tributaries; there was a little water in pools. Hosegood settled me down half a mile short of brigade and a little later the Burrifs came in behind me. I ordered tea to be brewed up, and told John Fraser to have his men kill a mule, and distribute it for meat. Leaving Duncan to settle in the column, I went forward to see the Brigadier.

I found him eating some rice and raisins, and had ten minutes' talk with him; he was in good form and cheerful. I returned to the column, and had been back ten minutes when I heard some shooting on the hill above and behind me. I immediately sent out Philippe and Tommy Blow with their platoons and sent a runner to the Brigadier to say that I had done so. Colonel Wheeler came along, and said that one of his riflemen had been fired on while relieving nature a couple of hundred yards from the bivouac; he also had sent a party under Macpherson to investigate. It seemed to us that the patrol, or whatever it was, must have come along the north and south track which we had crossed shortly before we halted and either seen the smoke of our fires, or followed up our track, although a party of Burrifs had been systematically obliterating it, so far as possible.

A mounted officer came along the *chaung* from brigade with orders. Columns were to get on the move at once; brigade was already moving off. Five Column was to lay an ambush, and deal with any attempt to follow up. I asked for more details: I wasn't clear how to lay an ambush in an area which it was by no means certain the enemy would come through; but all he could say was that I was to lay an ambush: he had been given no details.

Leaving John Fraser again in charge, I went along to where I had last seen brigade, but they had gone. I saw Scotty: his column was held up by the tail of 7 Column, which was just vanishing in the wake of brigade, up the hill out of the *chaung*.

"Look here, Scotty," I said. "I'm not altogether clear what is wanted of me, but it is quite obvious you won't be away from here for nearly an hour yet. I can't help feeling the Jap is far more likely to nip round the flank and cut in on the procession than to follow up the tail. However, I'll stay here and attract as much attention as I can; and when you're clear I'll make tracks down the *chaung*, as prominently as I can, so that if the Japs have gone to bring up more men, they will follow down the *chaung* instead of up the hill. Will you explain all that to the Brigadier? I'm sure I'm doing the wrong thing, but it seems to me the most helpful thing I can do."

Scotty agreed, and I went back to the column. Philippe and Tommy were both back, but had nothing to report; Tommy was short of one section, under Corporal McGhie, which never turned up again. Wheeler came along, and said that Macpherson was also back, having seen nothing. Since the first exchange of shots, all had been silent. He agreed that the patrol had probably done its job in locating us, and had gone off to report; somebody claimed to have heard a motor-bicycle starting up, but this was by no means certain. I told Wheeler of the message I had sent to Wingate, and asked if he agreed; he pursed his lips, and said he wasn't sure, but that as I had sent the message I had better stick to what I had said to avoid confusion.

The Burrifs couldn't get clear until Scotty's column was clear, and it wasn't until after four that the last man disappeared up the hill. I sent a couple of platoons and some animals a few hundred yards along their track, and then reversed them: the idea was to make it look as if they had bivouacked on the far side of the *chaung* for their noon halt, and then come back to resume the march. At about half-past four, I started laying my false trail.

We marched down that *chaung* in the most disgraceful fashion. Moving six abreast, and chucking down litter on the scale of a paperchase, we fairly plastered the sand with footprints; Robinson Crusoe would have had three fits and a spasm if he had seen them. We had once again the old precarious feeling of the Pinlebu Road and the approach to Tigyaing: but, as Duncan said, it was rather fun being so deliberately naughty. According to the map, the hills closed in on the *chaung* till it became a dangerous defile, about a mile and a half south of Hintha village; then they opened out for good, and the *chaung* ran away north into the flat jungle plains stretching to the Shweli. Until we were through the jaws of the defile I was thoroughly apprehensive; but we got past them without incident about six o'clock.

I had resolved, and Duncan enthusiastically approved, to make a false bivouac just before dark; and this we did on the *chaung* a mile from the village. We lit enormous fires, which felt as though they could be seen from twenty miles away; and on these we brewed our tea. The meat from a mule which the Burrifs had been slaughtering when the scare occurred had unfortunately not been distributed: we had all had to go to action stations, and except for some eager and provident Burrifs nobody had picked up any meat at all. So the food problem was acute, and I allowed only a couple of biscuits to be eaten. We certainly shouldn't be able to have a supply drop until well beyond the Irrawaddy, and whatever success attended the crossing there were obviously lean days ahead.

As soon as it was dark, we stoked up the fires in the bivouac till they looked like Jubilee Night; we tied some mules to trees well away from each other, in the hopes that they would feel lonely and bray; we used our last few explosives in setting booby traps; and in addition we pulled the pins out of grenades and weighted them down with tempting articles of kit. Then, very quietly and cautiously, in contrast to our disgraceful behaviour heretofore, we stole away five or six hundred yards down the *chaung*, and, crowded together as never before, slept an uneasy sleep until three in the morning.

Hintha village was shown on the map as being about a mile away. It seemed to me probable that it was occupied. If the enemy had us under observation at all, Hintha would be a likely place to have a post. It lay on a track junction where one track ran east and west, and another north and south – the one we had crossed just before the unlucky bivouac; and the fact that there were few tracks or villages in the area enhanced its importance. My plan was to send the column straight on down the *chaung*, while I myself took two platoons into the village to see if there were Japs there, and, if there were, to hit them. This should attract to the neighbourhood any other Japs there might be about, and distract them from following up and harassing the main body. After my conversation with Wheeler, I wasn't at all sure that I had done the right thing the previous afternoon, but I thought that a scrap at Hintha might justify it. For the platoons to take part, I selected Philippe Stibbé's and Jim Harman's commandos, and put them at the head of the column.

The plan broke down because the *chaung* proved to be blocked with prickly bamboo, and reconnaissance disclosed no alternative route to the main track into the village. This was the north and south track already mentioned, which dropped down from the hills into the *chaung* just about where we had laid the false bivouac; from this point to the village it was wide enough to take a bullock-cart. I had no alternative but to take the whole column with me so far, until the bamboo gave place to decent jungle; there I would send off the column, and go on into the village with the two platoons.

I halted more than once to probe for a gap in the bamboo, but drew a blank every time. According to the map I still had half a mile to play with before reaching the village; but the time factor was worrying me, for it was now nearing four o'clock, and by six that night we had to be at Inywa, a distance of twenty miles. I went on a little farther down the track, and suddenly saw, a hundred yards ahead of me, the sloping roofs of houses, half a mile too soon.

They say that the mind plays curious tricks in moments of crisis, and I remember distinctly that the sloping roofs at that moment reminded me of the medieval roofs of the old town of Chinon, as I saw them one moonlight night from the terrace of the ruined castle, fifteen years before. I had stumbled right into the outskirts of the village. The path forked at my feet; one branch, the less used of the two, ran along the edge of the bamboo; the other ran straight on towards the houses. Between the two was low undergrowth over which it was just possible to see: I fancy it must have been *bizat*, a thick thornless bush six or seven feet high, very common on the site of deserted villages, or on cultivation which has been allowed to fall into disuse.

The moon was still low, and where the track was flanked with trees it had been very dark: but here, where it was open, one could get a good view of the sleeping houses, moonlit on the east but with deep shadows on the west side of each. It all seemed still and peaceful; no sentries were guarding the approach; and I began to think that we had been playing our bivouac drama to an empty house. I was worried at the column being jammed together on the track behind me, with no means of getting off it should, the village prove to be held. The men were very silent, fully realising how much depended on the next few minutes; the only noise came from the mules, as they shifted their feet and creaked their saddlery. I told Duncan to organise a resumed search for a way into the jungle from the track, while I went forward with Philippe Stibbé's platoon to investigate; I passed the word also for a couple of Karens to act as interpreters.

Without waiting for Philippe to complete his orders, I moved cautiously forward with Po Po Tou and Jameson. As we went, we saw over the *bizat* the reflection of a fire against one of the houses on the left. Seventy yards or so from the fork in the track, we came to a T-junction, flanked by houses, and with a small track only, between two large houses, continuing the line of that on which we were: we had obviously come on to the main east and west track.

The fire was about forty yards along to the left, in the compound of the second house. With a grenade in my right hand I walked quietly towards it. Round it, symmetrically, one of each side, sat four men. They looked so peaceful and innocent that I immediately concluded that they were Burmese; and in that tongue (of which my knowledge was limited to a few sentences) I asked, "What is the name of this village?"

The men on the far side looked up, and those on this side looked round: I was only three yards from them. They were Japs. Resisting a curious instinct which was prompting me to apologise for interrupting them, I pulled the pin out of my grenade, which had suddenly become sticky with sweat, and lobbed it – oh, so neatly – into the fire. I just caught the expression of absolute terror on their faces; they were making no attempt to move; and ran. It was a four-second grenade, and went off almost at once. I looked round when I heard it go, and they were all sprawling on the ground.

Back at the T-junction, Philippe had just arrived and was looking eager. I told him to get in at once with the bayonet and capture that end of the village. As I spoke, a man ran past me from the direction of the fire: I shot him in the side with my pistol, and he sprawled on the ground for a moment, but was up and away again in a flash.

Philippe lost no time, but as he reached the point on the track opposite the fire, light machine-guns opened up; he and his men had to go to ground, though not before they had spitted several men running out of the house beyond the fire. I called to Philippe to ask if he could get on, but he shouted back in a singularly calm voice:

"I don't think we can – it's pretty hot. I'm afraid I've been hit myself."

I told him to hand over to his platoon sergeant and to try the right flank, and they nipped into some houses on that side of the track; but by now another light machine-gun had opened up, and there were a good many bullets flying about. Duncan had come up by now, and as he arrived we heard movement from the house immediately to our left, a matter of ten yards. This was followed by two or three shots by our ears; Duncan hove a couple of grenades into it, and there were loud groans, which went on, diminuendo, to the end of the action, but no more shooting.

I was worried about the man who had run past me early on; it was obvious that he had gone to rouse other Japs at that end of the village. So I sent Peter Dorans down there with some men of column headquarters who suddenly appeared, to block that approach. Most of them came back almost immediately, and when I asked them what the hell they were playing at, they replied that Corporal Dorans had told them they were in the way; and, confiscating their grenades, had sent all of them back except two.

I went back down to the fork tracks, and got hold of Jim Harman. I told him that Philippe's platoon would keep the Japs in play from where they were, and that he was to take his platoon up the little track and catch the Japs in flank. There was still no news from the rear about any signs of a route into the jungle. I went back to Philippe and warned him what was going to happen, shouting across the same information to Sergeant Thornborrow over the way. Somewhere in the darkness we heard a motorcyclist trying to start up his machine.

Philippe was hit in the shoulder; not badly, but he had lost a good deal of blood. I was talking to him and Corporal Litherland, who had also been hit: the two of them were at the foot of a tree on the right of the track up which we had come, just at the junction. Suddenly there was a rush of Japs up the track from the right, where Peter Dorans was, and two or three grenades came flaming through the air: the Japs have a glowing fuse on their grenades, very useful in a night action to those at whom they are thrown. One rolled to within a few yards of me, and I flung myself down behind a dark shadow which I took to be a fold in the ground; I realised only too clearly as soon as I was down that it was nothing more substantial than the shadow of a tree in the moonlight. The thing went off, and I felt a hot, sharp pain in the bone of my hip. At that moment there was a series of loud explosions: Peter, from the ditch where he was lying, had rolled half a dozen grenades among the Japs. Where I had seen them dimly in the moonlight and shadows, there was now a heap of writhing bodies, into which Peter was emptying his rifle. There was no further attack from that side.

I hopped to my feet and was overjoyed to find I was all right and able to walk. But poor Philippe had been hit again, this time in the small of the back; so had Corporal Litherland, and a third man who had been groaning and was now dead.

Philippe could still walk, and I told him to go back out of the way down the column. He walked a couple of yards, said, "Blast, I've forgotten my pack," picked it up and went off. This was the last time I saw him. Litherland also, with some help, was able to walk down the track.

There came a burst of shooting and some grenades from the little track where Jim and the commandos had gone. Thornborrow and his men were firing occasional rounds when they thought they saw a target, but another effort to get forward brought more casualties. I went back to the fork to see how Jim had got on, and I found him already back.

"There was an LMG there," he said, "but we've knocked it out. I've been right up to the main track, and I believe we could get the animals through that way."

Alec Macdonald was beside me, and immediately said, "I'll have a look. Come on," and disappeared up the track. I had a feeling that, having failed on Peter Dorans' flank, the Japs would try and come in on the right, somewhere down the column; so I passed the word back to try and work a small flank guard into the jungle on that side if possible. Then I went back to the T-junction, and made arrangements to attract all the attention we could, so as to give Alec a free run. (I seemed to spend the whole action trotting up and down that seventy yards of track.)

There came another burst of fire from the little track, a mixture of LMG, tommy guns and grenades. The commando platoon alone in the column had tommy guns, which was one of the reasons I had selected them for the role. Their cheerful rattle, however, meant that the little track was no longer clear. I hurried back to the fork, and there found Denny Sharp.

"This is going to be no good," I said. "Denny, take all the animals you can find, go back to the *chaung* and see if you can get down it. We'll go on playing about here to keep their attention fixed; I'll try and join you farther down the *chaung*, but if I don't then you know the rendezvous. Keep away from Chaungmido, as we don't want to get brigade muddled up in this."

Back to the T-junction I went, and found on the right of the track the Burrif platoon. They had two or three casualties from "overs"; Jameson had one in the shoulder, and so did another splendid N.C.O., Nay Dun, whose name always made me think of a trout fly. I told John to take them back, but he must have sent them under Pam Heald, because he himself still remained with me at the end of the action.

Another casualty was Abdul the Damned. Somehow he had wandered up into the battle leading Duncan's horse: armouring being at a discount, Duncan had made him into his syce, and jolly good he had become. Abdul had a nasty wound in the shoulder and was weeping bitterly, howling like a child: the horse had also been hit in the shoulder, and could barely walk; Duncan shot it there and then.

The sound of shooting opened up where I had expected it; away back down the column, the flank attack was coming in. It was audibly beaten off, and I sent another message down the column warning them to look out for a repeat performance still farther down the line. Then a messenger arrived, and said:

"Captain Macdonald's killed, sir."

"Nonsense," I said. "How do you know?"

"Mr. Harman's back, sir. And he's badly wounded."

I went back to the fork. Jim was there, with blood streaming from a wound in his head, and his left arm held in his right hand. Alec had led the way down the track, with Jim following; then Sergeant Pester and then Pte. Fuller. They had met two LMGs, new ones, which had opened up. Alec had fallen instantly, calling out, "Go on in, Jim!" Jim had been hit in the head and shoulder, Pester was unhurt, Fuller killed. Jim and Pester between them had knocked out both guns, and the track was again clear. They had had a look at Alec on the way back, and he was dead.

I reckoned we had killed a good many Japs, one way and another, but it was nearly six o'clock and would soon be light; and what I dreaded more than anything else was the possibility of being caught in daylight on the track, with little, lithe Japs, unencumbered by packs or weariness, able to crawl under the bushes at ground level and snipe the guts out of us. There was no sign of any animals; Denny seemed to have got them back all right, but what, if any, luck he was

having at the *chaung* I didn't know. At that moment somebody (I think John Fraser) came up with the news that a
place had been found a couple of hundred yards back where
you could squeeze through the bamboo into a stretch of
disused paddy, beyond which there was open teak jungle.
This decided me. At this moment came the noise of the
"repeat performance" on the tail of the column which we
had been expecting. There was a couple of minutes of
shooting, then it too stopped.

"Well, what do we do now?" I said vaguely to John and
Duncan.

"Well, you'd better make your mind up, and bloody
quick too!" said Duncan affably.

"Get everybody in sight into the paddy," I said, "and
don't forget Thornborrow."

The paddy was as it had been described, and in the
growing light it was hard to see why we hadn't discovered
it earlier. It was a stretch of about a hundred yards long by
forty wide, opening off the track to the westward, towards
the *chaung*. And, greatest boon of all, beyond it, quite
clearly in the dim daylight, one could discern that the
jungle was teak – good, open teak, where you can move
in any direction at any pace you like, and yet be swallowed
up from view in less than a hundred yards.

"Now," I said to Duncan, "are we quite sure that everybody knows the rendezvous?"

"Absolutely," he said; and with that assurance I told
Brookes the bugler to blow on his "instrument," as he
always called it, the call known as "Second Dispersal," on
hearing which every group in the column was trained to
break off from the main body and make its way independently to the rendezvous. I waited for a moment, to reassure
myself that it was being acted on; and then joined my own
group as it went off confidently into the jungle on a north-
erly bearing.

Soon we came to the east and west track, put out stops to
prevent interruption, and crossed it rapidly in one wave.
We travelled about a mile, and then halted to take stock. It
was now about seven o'clock.

With me were Duncan and John, the bulk of column

headquarters, Tommy Blow and his platoon, Tommy Roberts and the bulk of the support platoon, Sergeant Thornborrow and the remnants of Philippe Stibbé's platoon. Missing from column headquarters were Sergeant-Major Cairns, Pepper the runner, Lance-Corporal Lee the column clerk, Foster and White the signallers and one or two others. Most of the men were accounted for somehow; Cairns had last been seen helping Denny with the animals; Foster, White and Lee were believed to have gone with the animals which carried their various bits of property; Pepper had been sent on a message. Duncan counted heads, and made us about sixty. We had two or three of Tommy Roberts's animals, which he had refrained from sending back with the others in case he was required to give mortar support. We also had one chestnut charger.

Abdul and I were the only two wounded, and Tommy Blow, who had been a member of the St. John Ambulance Brigade in civil life, was ordered by Duncan to have a look at us. There was a very small jagged hole just above my hip joint, bleeding mildly, on which he put a field dressing: it felt no worse than a kick in the football field. Abdul, on the other hand, had a really bad hole, and was in a good deal of pain. Tommy washed out the wound with sulphanilamide, of which he had a few tablets in his haversack, and put a dressing on: he also produced a sling, and made him put his arm in it. Then we pushed on: we had still nearly twenty miles to do, and eleven hours to do it in; there was no time to be lost.

We had a halt for tea sometime about midday; otherwise we marched all day. Once or twice people suggested that I should get on the charger, but I was obsessed by the idea that if I did my leg would get stiff; and anyway with a stout stick I got along very well. During the morning we got rid of all the animals except the charger, and buried their loads, leaving the mules at a place where they had water to drink and bamboo leaves to eat. The charger we kept, partly in case somebody passed out and had to be carried (everybody was pretty weak for lack of food by now) and partly because it would do for meat later. Mules are better eating than horses, but none of the support mules would do for riding, and as we had to get rid of their loads, to get rid of them as well quickened our speed across country considerably.

Early in the afternoon we found a column's track. It came in from the south-west, and headed pretty well the same direction as that in which we were going. It was fresh – not more than an hour or two old, and definitely British; so we followed it until just before dusk, when I dug my toes in and said I couldn't manage another yard. The map had proved as inaccurate this side of Hintha as it had while we were approaching the village; but we had little doubt that we were pretty well at the rendezvous, one mile south of Pyinlebin; or at all events not more than a half-mile out. During the last half-hour of daylight, we had seen some animal droppings which were still warm, and we knew we must have been gaining on whoever was making the track; so Duncan shoved on a bit, and came back with the welcome news that he had found the headquarters of the Burma Rifles, just going into bivouac, and had spoken to Colonel Wheeler. The Brigadier had ordered them to do just what we had been doing: to make misleading tracks off to the north-east.

I sent John Fraser to see them, to discuss what to do in the morning if there were still no signs of the brigade, and then tried to settle down for some sleep. Almost all the blankets had been lost; except for Philippe's platoon, they had all been carried on mules, and so were all with Denny Sharp. It was one of those nights of bitter cold which one occasionally gets in that otherwise warm climate, and no-body outside Philippe's platoon got much sleep. Duncan and I huddled together vainly for warmth, but tired as we were it was too cold for sleeping. We were anxious too, for John Fraser never came back: whether he had run into enemy or was just simply lost we could not tell, but when morning came, and brought no John, we were really anxious. We sent a patrol to the Burrif bivouac, but they had flitted.

Soon after seven there came the sound of firing over towards the Irrawaddy, and we girt up our loins and marched westward towards the sound of the guns. At nine o'clock we suddenly came to the edge of the jungle, and gazed out over a couple of miles of paddy to the river. Beyond it, the friendly hills of the Gangaw Range climbed steeply into the blue sky. The shooting had stopped, and the whole morning looked peaceful and Sabbatical. Two hundred yards out into the paddy was a small hovel, with one or two children playing outside it: Duncan and I went over and talked to the man and woman who from time to time we saw moving about their morning tasks.

Duncan had a very good head for languages, and had picked up a little Burmese. He bought some rice and asked about Japs. The man seemed vaguely reassuring, but we couldn't follow all he said. At that moment, down the track by which we had come appeared a Jemadar and half a dozen Karens of the Burma Rifles headquarters. The Jemadar, San Shwe Htoo, spoke good English, and we used him to interpret; but we got nothing of interest out of the man. I told San Shwe Htoo to warn him that he and his family and anybody else who might come to visit him were to keep to their house, and not move before nightfall: we should watch from the edge of the jungle to make sure these orders were obeyed.

San Shwe Htoo had orders to patrol to the village of Maugon, about a mile to the southward, on the bank of the river; at my request he gave me a man who knew where Colonel Wheeler and the rest of Burrif H.Q. were. With him as guide and Peter Dorans as escort, I set off to see Wheeler and discover what he proposed doing. I wasn't very spry on my legs, and it took the best part of an hour to get there. I found Wheeler cheerful but worried; like myself he had expected to find brigade where we bivouacked last night, but there was no sign of them. He had sent a patrol into Pyinlebin to confirm that we were where we meant to be, and then, when he heard the firing, he had done the same as myself and marched towards it.

John Fraser had joined him the night before, but had missed the track on the way back; and, after spending most of the night trying to find me, he had made his way back to the Burrifs, and marched with them this morning to their present location. He was now out with Macpherson on another effort to locate brigade headquarters, and to get orders. Wheeler and I had come to the same conclusion about the shooting that we had heard earlier: that the brigade's crossing had been opposed, and now, in all probability, had been abandoned. He promised to let me know the results of Macpherson's patrol, and I said I would stay where I was on the edge of the jungle until I heard from him further. Peter Buchanan the adjutant came back with me to see where I was, and to try his hand at getting further dope out of the man in the hovel. Wheeler asked me when I had last eaten, and when he heard the answer most nobly insisted on my accepting two squares of his last slab of chocolate.

When Peter Buchanan and I reached my bivouac, I was delighted to find Denny Sharp, Jim Harman and most of his commandos, Gerry Roberts and his platoon, Bill Edge, Pepper, Foster and White, all arrived in. They had had a longer march than we, having failed to get down the *chaung*, and having been compelled to go back up it the way we had come in, the previous evening. Once on the hill, they got away across country; but while climbing up it, two of the most precious mules of the whole string had tumbled over the cliff into the *chaung* below: one carried the wireless, and the other the ciphers. Lance-Corporal Lee had gone back down to recover the ciphers, and had not been seen since. They had heard, as they came away, the sound of explosions from the dummy bivouac, where some Nips presumably paid the price of their inquisitiveness. Otherwise they had not been interrupted. There had, however, been one more serious loss: while going through some elephant grass, their column had split in two, and the rear half had not caught them up again. Among those whom they had thus lost were Pam Heald and all the Burrifs, bar one rifleman, Maung Kyan; Bill Aird and some wounded; Sergeant-Major Cairns and the colour-serjeant; Willy Williamson and most of the support platoon; Bill Smyly and most of the Gurkhas.

Nobody had seen David Whitehead, and I was worried about him and Lance-Corporal Lee: about the others, I was pretty sure that they could look after themselves, and would turn up all right. But one piece of news they brought plunged us all into sorrow, and filled us at the same time with an admiration which will never diminish.

Philippe Stibbé had lost a great deal of blood by the time the dispersal was sounded, and had to be mounted on a pony. Bill Aird had had time to dress both his wounds; the second one looked as if it might be in the kidneys. To start with he had been with a party which had no other animals with it, and which was in a bad bit of country. Realising that he was slowing up the party, he had begged to be left behind. Those with him indignantly refused; but when, after another half-mile, his pony had been responsible for several more delays, he slipped from the saddle to the ground, and said, "Now you've jolly well got to leave me." Nor does the story end there; for a Burma rifleman, unwounded, cheerfully said he would stay with Philippe and look after him; and in spite of Philippe's vehement orders to the contrary, he did so. We believe that this was Rifleman Maung Tun, but have not been able to establish his identity beyond doubt. The Burrifs had always had a great affection for Philippe, and this noble story, with its double heroism, is the highest manifestation I have known of the comradeship between the British and Burman soldier.

At three o'clock John Fraser turned up. He and Macpherson had found brigade, and learned that the facts were as Wheeler and I had guessed them to be. Two platoons of 7 Column had got across before interruption occurred, and a fierce fire had opened on the near bank from the west side. Through glasses more Japanese had been seen along the bank, hurrying towards the crossing-place; and the bridgehead was not considered strong enough to hold them off. Jacksie Pickering had had an unpleasant time rowing a rubber boat about in the middle of the river under heavy fire; Scotty had had a bullet through his map-case as he stood on the near beach; the intelligence sergeant in brigade headquarters had been killed by a shot from the far side of the river. Reluctantly the Brigadier had called it off, and was now in bivouac near Pyinlebin, where he had not previously been: arriving late the night before, he had had to cut straight to Inywa, trusting to pick up the Burrifs and myself later.

John and Macpherson had both talked to the Brigadier, who had told them that his orders now were to split the whole brigade into small parties to make their way to India independently. These parties should not exceed forty in strength, since that was the maximum number which could comfortably feed on the country. He was arranging a supply drop for brigade headquarters and the Burma Rifles: had he known that I was in the area and had lost my wireless, he would have included me also. As it was, he would put in an indent for me for any place or time that I might choose.

John had also seen Gim Anderson, the brigade major, who told him that most of the missing elements of my column had joined up with Ken Gilkes and 7 Column. He knew that Pam and a lot of Burrifs were there, very worried about John; also Bill Aird, Bill Smyly and Willy Williamson, Cairns and the colour-sergeant. John was, of course, out of touch with me at that moment, and had no particular hope of finding me again: but instead of joining up with 7 Column, whose exact whereabouts at that moment were unknown, he decided to go back with Macpherson to the Burrifs and attach himself to them, as his parent unit, knowing that they might by now have got in touch with me again.

Added to all this, he brought a message for me from Wheeler. We had discussed that morning the possibility of joining forces and walking out together. With the increase in my strength from 70 to 120, of which Peter Buchanan had told him, he felt that together we should be too strong to live on the country; and as neither of us had a wireless, it was a case of living on the country or not living at all. However, since hearing Wingate's orders about breaking up into small parties, he was resolved to get moving as soon as he could, and was prepared to bequeath to me his interest in the brigade supply drop. He was proposing to move at five that evening.

I thought I would have one more try at finding brigade, and, in order to see Wheeler before he left, I made an immediate move. At Wheeler's bivouac, I found him ready to start, and had five minutes with him. He was going to try and cross the Shweli at a village called Seikngu; thence he would steer north and east to the Irrawaddy; thence north and west; and he hoped eventually to reach the Chindwin somewhere north of Homalin. He gave me a note to the Brigadier to hand in if I found him; and I remember it ended: "Hope to meet you in happier circumstances."

He asked if I could give him some money, and I had a whip round, which produced about 300 rupees. I could have given him much more, but my method of carrying the column's money was to issue so much to every man, and it took time to collect.

Facetiously we arranged to dine together in Calcutta, and as he marched off I called out to him, "Shall we start with cocktails or sherry?"

"I prefer sherry," he answered, in a mock-prim voice.

We had a little over an hour of daylight left, and we marched off towards the point in the woods where John had seen brigade. We failed to make it before dark by about a mile, so I halted for the night, impressing on the sentries that they must rouse us at the very second they became aware of impending dawn. They did so, and we hastened to the brigade bivouac area. We found the place, with the depressions in the grass where they had been sleeping; but they had gone, and, with the usual standard of junglecraft which under the eye of the Brigadier they always attained, they had not left a vestige of a trail. Brigade had gone, and with them our chance of a supply drop. We were free to make for India.

Of the 3,000 men Wingate led into Burma, only 2,182 returned. Many carped at the losses, but General Au-chinleck, who took over from Wavell and who unlike his predecessor was no great admirer of Wingate, observed that Chindits had brought a good return on the Army's investment. The results of the Chindit expedition were:

Our ability to re-enter Burma, and the inability of the Japanese to stop us was demonstrated to the Burmese.

The railway Mandalay-Myitkyina was put out of action for a period of four weeks and the Japanese were forced to use the longer and more limited L of C via Bhamo.

Between six and eight Japanese battalions were drawn off from any other operations which the Japanese may have contemplated; and the activities of 77 Indian Infantry Brigade may have prevented them continuing their advance beyond Sumprabum [i.e. to Fort Hertz].

Much valuable information, both as regards the topography of the country and conditions of life in occupied Burma, was gained.

The operations had a good morale effect on our own troops generally and on the public, both in India and abroad.

Auchinleck might also have added that Operation Long-cloth demonstrated the viability of air supply. There was also the effect on morale. For Wingate had showed conclusively that the Japanese could be beaten at their own game: jungle fighting.

RUNG SAT

Ian Padden

Commissioned by President John F. Kennedy on 1 January 1962 to "conduct Naval Special Warfare", the US Navy's Sea-Air-Land (SEAL) teams have their origins in the Underwater Demolitions Teams of World War, which cleared safe lanes through the German beach defences on D-Day 1944. During the Korean War Underwater Demolition Teams (UDTs) operating off the destroyer USS Horace A. Bass *raided the North Korean coast blowing bridges and tunnels, and undertook the reconnaissance for the amphibious landings at Inchon.*

Kennedy's SEALs themselves first saw service during the Cuban crisis in 1962. With the hotting up of the Vietnam war, it was inevitable that SEAL teams would be sent to South-East Asia, and the first SEAL platoons duly arrived in theatre in 1966. The SEALs took with them one of the most powerful arsenals of the day. It included: the M63A1 Stoner light machine gun, the M60 GPMG, and the M79 grenade launcher. SEALs also frequently carried the 9mm Smith and Wesson Mark 22 Model 0 silenced pistol, nicknamed the "hush puppy" since it was developed originally for silencing guard dogs. Combat knives such as the Ka-bar, Gerber and Randall were standard. "Tiger stripe" camouflage fatigues were preferred to the usual combat-issue green-leaf pattern, although many SEALs wore blue jeans since these best withstood the delta's fearsome mosquitoes.

B ETWEEN THE SPRAWLING, noisy city of Saigon and the South China Sea lies a river delta and mangrove swamp area that covers some 400 square miles of the earth's surface.

When viewed from the air, the collage of green could be described as beautiful. However, beneath the undulating canopy of green, the jungle is a dense, tangled mass of sweltering, soggy vegetation, with growing plants and trees fighting for life through the putrifying remains of dead fauna and flora.

Hundreds of rivers and streams feed into the area and then fan out to create the massive delta that stretches to the sea. Most of the area is affected by a four-foot tide that races in and out at speeds from three to four knots; and when the tide is out, the complete area is a mass of stinking, slimy mud that pops and crackles as though it were alive.

The jungle vegetation and the rotting, slimy ground it stands on are both repugnant and almost evil, and, as is the way of nature, creatures that inhabit such territory normally match their surroundings. This region is one of the exceptions to the rule – its inhabitants are infinitely more nasty and more repulsive than their surroundings.

There are alligators that eat anything; toothless pythons that hang from trees like Christmas decorations and have appetites similar to those of "over-toothed" alligators; large red ants whose poisonous bites leave an incredible burning sensation; jungle cats that scream and howl and whose eyes seem to glow in the dark; large rats; blood-sucking leeches; mosquitoes; poisonous snakes and a variety of other reptiles; "lung fish" that live in the slimy mud and gasp and sigh as though they might be human beings; strange-looking birds that attack without warning; and bats that are reputed to suck blood. There are many other creatures and insects, most of which appear to have a perverse sense about them, to the extent that not even the words *mean* and *evil* are adequate to describe them.

Perhaps it is the creatures that are attracted to the environment, and not the environment that develops the character of the creatures. Perhaps it makes no difference; the result would probably still be the same: the Rung Sat –

the jungle delta and mangrove swamp between Saigon and the South China Sea.

The area was a veritable nightmare for the average human being – including the fanatical Vietcong, the guerilla soldiers of the North Vietnamese leader Ho Chi Min. However, by early 1966, they had established themselves in the "better areas" of the Rung Sat and were conducting operations against Saigon and the surrounding area, particularly against the extensive river traffic that transported South Vietnam's vital food supplies.

Early in 1966, SEAL Team One was in operation in what was officially termed the "Rung Sat Special Zone." This Vietcong lair required special attention, and, as none of the Regular South Vietnamese Army units would go anywhere near the area, the SEALs were given the job.

At first the SEALs spent months conducting reconnaissance patrols in the worst possible areas of the zone, namely those regions surrounding the better areas that the Vietcong were using as base camps and supply dumps.

When the months of incredible reconnaissance work were completed, with the SEALs often sitting for hours within fifty feet of the enemy, it was decided that the time had come to let the enemy know that there were other creatures in the abysmal jungle – other than its natural inhabitants – that they should be afraid of.

A unit called Detachment Golf of SEAL Team One operated almost exclusively in the Rung Sat. During the later stages of the conflict in Vietnam, captured enemy documents revealed that not only were the Vietcong afraid to go where the SEALs went, but they were terrified of the "wild animals" of Detachment Golf. This fact had previously been stated by some Hoi Chanh (Vietcong defectors), and it had confirmed what the SEALs had hoped for – that they would be the terrorists of the Rung Sat, not the Vietcong.

One team from Detachment Golf had been given information that a pagoda in the middle of the jungle was being used to store weapons, and the men set out to destroy it.

Using one of their specialized boats, a heavily armed small platoon of twelve men, led by a lieutenant and a chief petty officer, navigated their way up the river toward a landing point that was near the pagoda.

As they rounded a bend in the river, close to where they were intending to land, they spotted six men wearing the type of black pajamas that were the favored uniform of the Vietcong. The men were armed with rifles, and, on seeing the SEAL boat, they started running toward a small hut a little way from the water's edge.

The experienced SEALs (the average age of the men in this platoon was twenty-eight), who were not known for wasting ammunition by shooting at the enemy when they were not at close range, held their fire and waited for their lieutenant to call the action. As he ordered the boat to head for the bank, the Vietcong started shooting from inside the hut. The lieutenant turned to a seaman carrying a 57-mm recoilless rifle and casually requested that the man put a round in the roof of the hut. The seaman nodded, sighted the weapon from the moving boat, and squeezed the firing handle. The weapon responded with a deep cracking sound, and a "soft target" high-explosive round embedded itself in the roof and exploded.

When the enemy continued to fire, the lieutenant called for a round in the window. Another crack from the 57 and a round whistled in through the window. With a shrug of his shoulders the lieutenant called for a shot in the door, and the gunner simply complied – it was his day to be on target. Another round through the now empty door caused the building to explode. The enemy fire stopped.

As the SEALs scrambled ashore, they saw a large group of the enemy appear a little farther along the river bank, and a tremendous firefight ensued. The first six men they had shot were the rearguard of a battalion of Vietcong who were on their way to collect arms from the pagoda.

The SEALs, despite the fact that they were heavily outnumbered, steadily advanced through the jungle toward the enemy and continued to pick them off. After about half an hour, the lieutenant called off the chase – to pursue the enemy any further would just increase the possibility of his platoon being ambushed.

Returning to the boat, they collected spare ammunition and set out through the jungle toward the pagoda.

After about three hours of working their way quietly through the dense jungle, the scout signaled the men to halt. Everyone watched the scout's hand signals, a system of communication devised by the SEALs to eliminate the necessity for talking. He had located a group of about 20 of the enemy coming toward the platoon; they were carrying arms and ammunition and had obviously come from the pagoda. The SEALs quickly set up an ambush line and waited patiently.

Fifteen minutes later they heard the quick chatter of the approaching Vietcong, and their hands tightened on their weapons. As the leading enemy came into view, the 57-mm rifle opened the ambush, with the first round instantly killing the leading pair of Vietcong. Four more of the enemy died within seconds from a hail of fire put up by the rest of the platoon, and the remainder of the enemy dropped their loads and dispersed into the jungle.

As a result of the ambush, the lieutenant decided that to continue toward the pagoda would not be a good idea. The enemy at the pagoda would definitely have heard the ambush and would either be waiting for them or preparing patrols to search for them.

He had the chief petty officer take an accurate compass reading, something which he could not trust himself to do as he had numerous pieces of shrapnel from previous missions still embedded in his body, and they could seriously affect the sensitive navigation compass. There were others in the platoon who had the same problem; their colleagues just would not trust them to take compass readings.

He kept the platoon heading south into one of the worst areas of the mangrove swamps; the chances were that even if the enemy troops located their trail, they would not follow them into the festering swamp.

They were wading through a fetid, swamp channel just before dark when a gunner's mate became temporarily stuck in the soggy bottom below. As he quietly started to work his legs free, he saw an old log floating in his direction; but experience told him that it was not a log. He quietly and quickly signaled to his nearest colleague. The trapped gunner's mate removed the magazine from his M-16 and silently ejected the round from the chamber of the barrel. The seaman he had signaled was quickly wading toward him and had followed his example. When the alligator had drifted within three feet of him, the gunner's mate hit it squarely between the eyes with the butt of the M-16. As the great gnarled beast swung his head upward and to one side, the butt of the seaman's weapon caught him on top of his right eye. With a great flurry of thrashing and continuing blows from the two SEALs, the surprised beast withdrew. The gunner's mate nodded his thanks and was about to ask for assistance to get his legs unstuck when he suddenly realized he was free. As the two men waded to the bank, they saw the remainder of the platoon standing there quietly laughing.

Shortly afterward the scout found a clump of mangroves that were above the muddy waters, and the lieutenant signaled that they would use it as a harbor for the night.

Sentries were posted as the remainder of the platoon found places to settle down, all close to one another. For the next few hours, they listened intently to the strange sounds of the jungle swamp. They were sounds that this group of SEALs was very familiar with, but the SEALs could take no chances with the cunning enemy. There was just a possibility that the enemy would follow.

When the jungle settled into its night-time noises, so did those SEALs who were not on sentry duty. There was no eating, talking, or smoking. Most of the men ate little or nothing while they were on patrol in the Rung Sat, although they all carried food in the form of special Emergency Ration Packs.

Before dawn the team was on the move again, slowly working its way back through the swamps in the direction of the pagoda.

By 1000 hours the men had silently crept within fifty feet of the building, but could see no movement. They remained in their positions without moving for the next three hours; they just watched and listened for anything that would indicate they were walking into a trap. The chief petty officer half lay, half crouched, alongside a large tree, and he had a good view of the pagoda; the lieutenant was about fifteen feet away to his left, and he, too, was watching the building and its approaches. About fifteen feet behind them were a gunner's mate and a boatswain's mate; both were in a position to watch the rear and part of the flanks.

They had been waiting for about twenty minutes, and their ears were well accustomed to the sounds around them, when a strange noise was heard. The chief petty officer heard it first and could not quite determine where it was coming from. It was not the sound of a human; he could easily distinguish any human movement from that of an animal. As he looked at the boatswain's mate, he noticed that the man's eyes were looking above his head, and he was signaling the chief not to move. The boatswain's mate was slowly pulling out the razor-sharp knife that the chief had seen him use like a surgeon on numerous occasions. He also knew that the man could throw the knife more accurately than most men could shoot, so whatever it was that was above him would probably get a surprise.

The chief found out what it was a few moments later when a huge form came into view a few feet from his head. It was the body of a massive python, and it slid slowly down onto the ground beside the chief. The SEALs who saw the creature, including the lieutenant, swore it was at least thirty feet long. The chief just said it was big. The monster python, however, did not move when it landed on the ground beside the chief; it sat there with its head not two feet from his face and just stared at him.

For the next two and a half hours, the staring contest continued. The chief swore he blinked normally; the others swore he didn't blink the entire period. Finally, the massive reptile decided to end the contest and slowly moved away, passing very close to the horrified gunner's mate. The chief later stated that pythons had quite pretty faces. No one argued; they now considered him an expert in the subject.

When the python had left, the lieutenant signaled the

platoon to move toward the pagoda. A careful search showed that the place was empty and well booby trapped. The SEALs added a few booby traps of their own before leaving and heading back toward the river where they had first encountered the enemy.

They were almost half way to the river when their scout was seen moving quickly back toward them. He explained that a group of Vietcong – approximately fifty strong – were strung out in an ambush line ahead and were well concealed. The lieutenant and the chief worked out a counterambush plan that would require the SEALs to take the enemy by surprise on the west or right flank.

After an hour of very careful maneuvering, they came up behind about fifteen of the enemy huddled in a tight group over two machine guns; four Vietcong manned the guns, and the remainder were armed with automatic weapons. One of the SEALs, a semiprofessional baseball player before he entered the Navy, moved a little farther to the rear and quietly hurled a grenade far to the front and toward the east flank of the ambush line.

The sound of the falling grenade caused a burst of fire from the east flank, and when it exploded, the SEALs opened up from behind the enemy machine gunners.

In the fierce firefight that followed, eleven of the enemy were killed and the remainder fled, except one, who had been knocked unconscious by the butt of an M-16 that had driven off the alligator. The man was now bound and gagged, and thrown over the shoulder of one of the gunners mates as the SEALs quickly left the area.

It was now too dangerous to remain in the area. The enemy troops had been surprised too many times and had taken a beating – they would start searching in force very shortly. The lieutenant broke his radio silence and called for an exfiltration by helicopter. He gave his status as "a SEAL platoon plus one bundle," a signal to the intelligence officers that he had a Vietcong prisoner.

About an hour later, a giant CH47 helicopter escorted by six Huey gunships arrived at the exfiltration point, and the SEALs with their now conscious, but bewildered, bundle were quickly lifted out.

One of the SEALs who had never had a nickname in his entire life now had one – he was for evermore known as The Python.

Since Vietnam, SEAL teams have served in Panama, Grenada, and both Gulf Wars. A refinement to SEAL organization came in 1980 with the formation of SEAL Team 6, which consists of 100 selected volunteers from the other SEAL teams. SEAL Team 6 are the SEALs' counter-terrorist specialists.

THE COLOMBIAN JOB

Gaz Hunter

Since the early 1990s, 22 SAS has trained and advised anti-narcotics police in Colombia, the global centre of the hard-drugs trade. One of the first SAS teams sent out was commanded by Staff Sergeant Gaz Hunter (a pseudonym) of B Squadron.

WE PICKED UP our weapons and ran to the waiting Hueys, a dozen men to each one. Tucked in close behind one another, the helis took off, dropped their noses, and snaked out low over the jungle, weaving constantly in case of ground fire. Climbing steeply to get out of small-arms range we turned south. The Hueys had 7.62mm M-60D machine-guns mounted on pintles in their port-side doors, one to each helicopter. A thin layer of high cloud blocked the sun and as we climbed it grew bitterly cold. I shivered inside my DPM combat gear. It was our third week in Colombia. We were way down in the south of the country now, with a different regional command group. Our mission was to seek and destroy the local cartel's main airstrip and processing centre. Acting on information received, we were hoping to catch them with their next shipment ready to go.

After twenty minutes airborne, we came on a small coca plantation, several acres across, with a small hut at its heart: the captain in charge told one of his men to note it for future attention. The coca bushes were planted in neat rows, a few feet apart, in land that had been slashed and burned out of the jungle. This little farm was a good sign: it meant we were probably getting near one of the cartel's main operational nodes. Sure enough, we saw a second, larger, coca plantation below us almost at once.

We plunged down to tree-top height. The captain turned in his seat and waved at me. "Danger area," he said.

I nodded enthusiastically. "Great." I locked and loaded. I had that tight feeling you get when there's the chance of a contact, half fear, half anticipation.

A broad river appeared below us, gleaming like a mirror in the light. The pilot dropped the helicopter right down on to it. Now we were below tree-top height, flying very fast and very low, skimming the surface of the water. There was a massive sensation of ground-rush, the brilliant green walls of the jungle flashing past in a blur on either side. The thump and clatter of the Huey grew louder still, echoing back up off the river, the machine bucking and yawing in the low-level turbulence.

We shot out over a small mud village. The captain shouted something I couldn't hear. He pointed at the ground. We looped into a tight turn, and set down hard on a scrubby little football pitch. You can go just about anywhere in Colombia and never be more than a click from a kick-about pitch. The policemen bundled out, trotted over to a nearby hut and squeezed inside. I took a good look around, then followed them. Obviously we weren't going to be staying long: the pilot was still turning and burning. When I reached the door of the shack I found the men arguing over a map. Gradually the locals from the village wandered up, in singletons and small groups, to have a look at the strangers who had landed from the sky.

"Is it usual for helicopters to come this way?" I asked the captain.

"Oh, no," he assured me. "It's very unusual."

Christ, I thought, another sneak attack. After about ten minutes of map-wrangling we took off, flying back up the river we had just been following. Then the pilot turned the machine back on to its original heading, coming back down over the water for the second time. This was bad operational practice and, with the map business, it meant only one thing: we were lost. We started circling. "It's here somewhere," the captain shouted. It was his job to pin down the location before we got airborne. He hadn't bothered doing his staff-work.

But I still had the feeling this was going to be our lucky day.

We were dead low, clipping the tops of the trees. I wasn't the only one there with that feeling in my gut: the door-gunner cocked and made ready. I grinned at the policeman opposite. Like me, I could tell he wanted to get out there and do the job. Then, suddenly, there was the airfield, right below us, a scrubby rectangle blown out of the virgin jungle. Someone shouted, "Armed men! On the ground." The captain looked at us, giving us the thumbs down. Oh, no, I thought, you're not backing out of this one now. I tapped the stock of the Armalite with the heel of my palm, giving him some teeth and pointing down at the strip. "Let's go get them," I shouted. He looked at the door-gunner. The gunner waggled the barrel of the M-60 up and down and nodded vigorously. He, too, was raring to go.

The Huey bucked and lurched. I wondered if we had been hit. There had been no thumps, but I was acutely conscious of the fuel-cells under the floor of the cabin: 844 litres of high-octane aviation fuel. "Incoming!" the pilot screamed. Through the door I could see bright orange tracer floating up at us from the edges of the trees. Everyone went very quiet. I tapped the gunner on the shoulder and pointed at the flashes. "*Si*," he said. We were within range. He squinted briefly along his sights. The gun roared as he opened up.

I couldn't hear or see the captain giving any commands. "Down!" I signalled to the pilot. "Get us down! Lower!" He pushed on the Huey's collective and we screamed in along the edge of the field. Our gunner hosed down the tree line, M-60 hammering. Glancing back out of the door, I saw the second gunship swoop in behind us, spraying the other side of the strip. There was a hot smell of cordite, and big brass cartridge cases flying everywhere. Fumes whipped around the cabin and back out into the slipstream.

I could feel my heart pumping hard and my blood

running. There was the deafening noise of the M-60 and the rotors, the smell of hot engine oil and gunsmoke. Everything was bright and pin-sharp.

We peeled off out of the attack, but our own pilot turned the wrong way, putting us directly into the path of any ricochets from the following Huey, and stopping our own gun from bearing on the target. I shouted at him and pointed, but he looked blank. We turned sharply at the end of the strip and came back in for a second pass. I couldn't see any return fire from the ground now. We shot back along the runway again, then banged down hard at its northernmost end. In a second we were all out and down, firing into the trees where we had last seen the muzzle flashes. There was no return fire. After one short burst of three I quit firing to save ammo.

We started pepper-potting: one man forward, down, observe and fire, next man forward, down, observe and fire, the first on his feet again making a short zigzag dash forward. Matt's group in the second Huey had landed right behind us. The police started running along a narrow track to our left, spearing its way into the dense jungle. There was only enough room for them to run in single file. Against all my instincts and training, I followed. There wasn't much choice. At once we came under fire from the trees to our left. I could hear rounds slapping and whacking into the surrounding bush, the heavier thud of the tree-strikes.

I had closed right up on the leaders of our group. I got down on one knee and waited. A burst of fire came in close to my position, the bullets whistling through the under-growth, the air pressure parting the leaves, and buzzing past like huge wasps. Another burst rapped into the trees just above my head: *Thwock! Thwock! Thwock!* The fat punching sound in the dense, moist wood was exactly like that of a round going into a human body. One bullet came right out of the other side of an atap palm directly in front of me: a huge chunk splintered out towards my face. I ducked aside. There was the high-pitched *ping!* of a ricochet, and I saw yellow-orange muzzle flash in among the dark green. I could tell where that one had come from. I swivelled slightly, took aim at the blue haze in the bush, and blasted back, firing controlled double-taps, moving the Armalite in a slow arc to cover the location.

At my back, Matt was firing at the same spot. There was a high-pitched scream as someone made a hit. At that it was up and on. The jungle ahead of us suddenly opened up: I saw a clearing with some buildings dead in the centre. The policemen swept up and around these shacks, then stopped.

"Clear through, clear through," I yelled in Spanish. "Follow on and fire!" The men had regrouped at the far edge of the clearing. They stood there, looking pleased with themselves, instead of going in pursuit. As far as they were concerned, the job was done. I thought we had just started. I could still hear the distant sounds of cartel gunmen crashing off into the jungle. "They're running away," I said. "Let's get after them and finish the job."

"No, no," called the captain, lighting a cigarette. "They've gone now."

I looked around. All over the clearing and in atap-covered lean-tos around the central hut there were big fifty-gallon oil drums, filled with a mixture of fermenting coca leaves and petrol. The smell was putrid, rank and disgusting in the hot air. Boxes and crates of chemicals, sulphuric acid, acetone and the rest, all stacked ready for use, lay next to what looked like a huge washing-machine. Some of the police had started searching, and there was a sudden shout. They had found three drugs workers cowering under the beds in a long wooden accommodation hut. They dragged these men out by the scruff of the neck and began to interrogate them, shouting in their faces and slapping them.

The rest of us got busy destroying the processing plant. There was too much equipment and cocaine paste to ship out on the helicopters, so we made a big pile of it, doused it in fuel, and burned it. Next we carried all the chemicals into the huts, threw in anything else lying around that looked like it might be useful, and set fire to them. There were cracks and whizzes as it went up, and sharp snaps from the blazing wood. Columns of oily smoke billowed up into the air. We backed off and stood for a while, watching the firework display. Some of these labs, the really big ones, can produce as much as $1 billion a month in refined cocaine. This outfit wasn't quite in that league, but it was a start, the best drugs-enforcement effort I'd seen yet.

The captain came up and told us we were going off to hit another, even bigger, drugs camp: they had extracted its location from the prisoners. I decided there wasn't all that much wrong with our leader's commitment, it was just the lazy, haphazard way he went about things. We mounted up in the Hueys again.

With directions from the captured men, we were over the next target in no time. From the air, we saw that the strip was pockmarked with deep holes, as though it had been deliberately cratered. The Huey shimmied in, lifted its nose and we jumped off its skids from the hover. Fanning out, we skirmished around the main house. A woman with a small child on her hip came out, waving her arm and shouting abuse. The police charged past her and arrested a man inside.

After slapping this man across the face a few times, they rushed off across the airfield like a pack of dogs. The prisoner had told them something. Watching the tree line, I followed them across. Hidden in the tall growth were four huge metal barrels lined up in a row. They were filled to the brim with semi-refined coca paste. Bingo! We had found one of the major shipment points for the local operation. Alongside these barrels were dozens of wooden planks, which at first was a bit puzzling. Then I realized they went over the craters in the runway, so that the shipment planes could land. The craters were deliberate, designed to make us think that the strip was disused.

We were inspecting these finds when I heard two shots from the other end of the field. Two or three of the policemen had remained down there with the prisoner. It might be that they were trying to scare more information out of him. Or it might be something else. We made a new bonfire out of everything we could find, including the planks, set it alight, and went back to join the rest of the team.

The prisoner was on his knees. They had his hands tied behind his back, and they were really laying into him, slapping, punching and kicking. When they saw us, they stopped, stood him up and dusted him off. Things seemed to calm down a bit.

There was another shout, this time from the nearby riverbank. Someone had found a second cache of semi-processed cocaine, about eight drums of it, hidden near a small creek leading down into the river. Following this inlet back towards the camp, we found two rubber boats with powerful outboards carefully hidden in among the undergrowth: getaway craft. From the air, we had missed them. We poured petrol over them and left them blazing.

When I got back, the police were jumpy, scared looking. The prisoner had been talking. He was white and his mouth was running blood. "This is a very bad place," said the captain encouragingly. "Many narco-terrorists here."

The Hueys, which had been standing off at a safe distance, came whopping back in for the pick-up. "This is a big find," I said. "Why not use it? They'll be back to see what the damage is. Leave an OP in for a few days – say, three or four men. Let them watch what happens. If they do come back we'll extract the OP covertly, come back in with the Hueys, only this time we'll land clear and work our way in. Surround the bastards. Then we'll catch them all, just when they think they've got rid of us." The captain smiled back at me, shaking his head.

As we finished talking, there was a loud bang from the rainforest and I turned with the Armalite up. Low velocity, I thought. Pistol round. Four policemen came out of the trees and started climbing into the helis. Last I'd heard, the man we'd caught was coming back to base with us for further questioning. "Where's the prisoner?" I asked.

"He was small fry," replied the captain. "They've let him go."

ONE NIGHT IN THE AEGEAN

John Lodwick

The inspiration for Alistair Maclean's classic war novel
The Guns of Navarone, *the Special Boat Squadron was
a 1941 marriage of the SAS's D Squadron and the
Commando Boat Sections. Led by Major the Earl Jellicoe, the SBS served in the Mediterranean and the
Adriatic, but it was the Aegean which proved its happiest
hunting ground. Never more than 250 strong, the SBS
tied down 18,000 German troops with its hit-and-sail
actions.*

*The SBS, it might be said, was unconventional in
every sense. There was little formal discipline, the German MP 38/40 was the weapon of choice, and uniform
was whatever came to hand. As John Lodwick, an SBS
member recalled in his memoir of the SBS's war in the
Aegean,* The Filibusters, *the insouciance of the SBS
extended into combat itself, epitomized by an exploit of
Lieutenant David Clark on the occupied island of Simi.*

IN APPEARANCE, DAVID Clark was fair and juvenile. His
attitude was casual in the extreme, and many people who
were deceived by his appearance were plunged deeper in
their deception by his apparent vagueness.

For David Clark was, indeed, vague. He never wrote an
operarional report unless ordered to do so, and, normally,
the most that could be dragged from him was that it had all
been most awfully unpleasant, that such and such a number
of Germans had been killed, and that there had been some

trouble or other at a telegraph station. "We blew it up in the end, didn't we, Sergeant Miller?" "Yes, sir. You laid the charges yourself, if you remember."

The interrogator would be puzzled. From other members of the patrol he had received definite information that they had been ambushed after finishing the job. He would mention this fact.

"Oh, you mean those stray *shots* . . ." David Clark would say. "A couple of Germans tried to knock off Mr. Clark," supplemented Miller, "we killed them."

Something of this kind occurred in Simi. David Clark found his way to a German billet, and pushed the door open gently with his foot. The Germans were playing cards. David Clark spoke their language.

"It would all be so much *easier* if you would just raise your hands," he said.

The Germans do not appear to have agreed with him. An *unter-offizier* put *his* hand in his pocket and pulled out a Lüger. First he shot out the lights, then he shot at David Clark. This bullet struck David's carbine, wrecking it. David and Miller withdrew and threw grenades through the window into the room until all noise had ceased. There were about ten men in the room. "Such a *tiring* walk back," was David's comment. "People *would* keep on firing at us."

Yet the SBS's casualness was deceptive; its training at Ahlit in Palestine was extensive and gruelling. Few special forces were better prepared. Or more competent.
Here Lodwick recounts another episode of SBS elan in the Aegean, the raid on the Cyclades islands.

On all the outlying members of that group, the Germans maintained small garrisons, who consisted for the most part of young naval ratings, entrusted with a shipping watch. They also possessed radio transmitters with which to report the movement of hostile air and surface craft. Brigadier Turnbull's plan, which was approved in early April 1944, was no less than the liquidation of these posts on a single night.

Sutherland's squadron was mobilized for this task. My patrol was given Mikonos, in many ways the easiest of the group to attack.

Lassen, with his own patrol, and Keith Balsillie's under his command, was to attack Santorini. Nobby Clarke was to visit first Ios and then Amorgos, where the enemy had recently re-established themselves.

These raids were successful, the various garrisons either being taken alive or liquidated, their radio sets destroyed, and the German information service paralysed for a long period to come.

Before the war, Mikonos was a tourist resort, deriving considerable prosperity from the Delphic ruins on nearby Delos. Its buildings were in consequence more modern and their sanitation more advanced than in those encountered throughout the Dodecanese. Mikonos is well populated. We landed on a dark night in conditions of secrecy, but not many hours had elapsed before the news of our arrival had spread. That day chanced to be a Sunday, the eve of the Greek National Festival of St. George. By ten o'clock in the morning I was receiving deputations who had come considerable distances in order to welcome us. The men, stiff in their festive clothes, with starched collars, saluted with dim memories of military service . . . the women, perched primly on mule back, gazed at us solemnly and threw flowers. It was all very touching. We were the first Allied troops to visit Mikonos since the declaration of war.

It goes without saying that everybody knew of the arrival of the *Inglesi* with the exception of the Germans. There were nine Germans on Mikonos. Seven lived in the best villa in the town. Two were stationed in a lighthouse some distance away. Throughout the day their movements were reported to us. The Germans, it seemed, were getting drunk.

Next morning, at first light, we attacked the villa. Simultaneously, three young Greeks, who had volunteered to work for us, were sent up to the lighthouse to dispose of the two men there.

The German sentry at the villa was shot at once by Rifleman Lynch. The villa was then rushed, but the occupants had had time to collect their wits. They barricaded themselves in a single room, whilst one of their number threw grenades down the stairs at us. We now sent for the mayor of the town. This man spoke German and had a German wife. He was brought to the garden wall and told to order the garrison to surrender. The Germans made no reply. Although unable to stand up in their room without drawing a volley of shots, they could hear aircraft overhead and shrewdly guessed them to be friendly. They began to fire Very lights in the hope of attracting attention. The aircraft, which were, in fact, Junkers, escorting a convoy, did not see the Very lights.

The young Greeks now arrived with the two prisoners from the lighthouse. I took one of these prisoners to the garden wall and ordered him to tell his comrades that unless they surrendered immediately we would burn the house down with the aid of a dump of petrol in its grounds. This was a bluff, for it would have taken us the entire day to place that petrol in position. The Germans, however, had no means of knowing this. They surrendered immediately. The villa was delivered over to the exultant civilian population, who looted it efficiently. British and Germans adjourned to a local hotel for lunch.

On the first floor of the Bank of Athens, in Santorini town, was a billet containing forty-eight Italians and twenty Germans. There were other targets on Santorini but Lassen reserved this one for himself. He took with him Stefan Casulli and twelve men. Despite many sentries and police dogs, surprise was achieved. The billet, from which exit was impossible, became a death trap for its occupants. "There was," wrote Lassen, "a grand mix-up in the dark."

He is too modest. In point of fact, Lassen, accompanied by Sergeant Nicholson, walked from room to room. They paid the greatest attention to detail. First, Nicholson would kick the door open . . . then Lassen would throw two grenades inside . . . then Nicholson, firing his Bren from the hip, would spray the walls and corners . . . finally,

Lassen, with his pistol, would deal with any remaining signs of life.

Next day, of all the enemy in this billet, only four Germans and six Italians were seen by the townspeople.

Unhappily, this massacre, although almost complete, was not achieved without loss. Stefan Casulli . . . standing *in* a doorway instead of to one side of it . . . was shot through the chest. He died immediately. His companion, Sergeant Kingston, a medical orderly, received a bullet in the stomach, from which wound he succumbed on the following day. Marine Trafford and Guardsman Harris – the latter Bill Blyth's batman – were slightly wounded by the sentries outside the billet. They forgot their pain in the pleasure of watching four fear-crazed Italians jumping through the windows from a height of forty feet.

Two other attacks were taking place in Santorini at the same time as Lassen's. Sergeant B. Henderson, a physical training instructor, familiarly known as "The Brown Body" in consequence of his nudist tendencies, was sent to investigate the house occupied by the German commander and his orderly. Not unnaturally, Henderson now heard what he described as "the murmur of voices issuing from the rear of the house".

He dashed round just in time to find the German officer making an undignified escape through the back streets.

Keith Balsillie was fulfilling his mission thoroughly. Keith was fortunate in having with him on this job Corporal Karl Kahane, a fluent German speaker. Led by Kahane, the party entered the first German billet. They found a man asleep in bed.

"For you, my friend," said Kahane, "the war is over. Now be a good fellow . . . get dressed and lead us to your comrades."

The German was so persuaded by the logic of Kahane's remarks – which admittedly were supported by considerable firepower – that he immediately conducted Balsillie to a second house. Here, three more Germans were found asleep in bed. These Germans also allowed themselves to be convinced and the procession, now swollen in numbers, moved on to a third house, where yet another trio of

Germans were found asleep in bed. Here, at least, there was a little variety, for two of the Germans were in bed together. Only one German now remained in the area and he, hearing of the fate of his comrades, tamely presented himself of his own accord. Balsillie prepared the radio station for demolition and withdrew to contact Lassen.

Nest day, as might be expected, there was considerable air activity over the island. Santorini is crescent-shaped, the spawn of that extinct volcano which affords its deep harbour moderate shelter. There is very little cover in Santorini and had the defending ground forces not been virtually exterminated, things might have gone badly for Lassen. Fortunately the enemy command in the larger island of Melos seem to have thought that the island had been captured. They did not appear with reinforcements for over forty-eight hours. Lassen was able to collect his scattered forces and to evacuate in comfort.

Subsequent events in Santorini throw interesting sidelights on the mentality of both Germans and Greeks. The Germans gave Stefan Casulli and Kingston a funeral with full military honours. On the same day they issued a proclamation demanding the names of those who had helped the British. Six Greeks, including the mayor of a village, presented themselves voluntarily. They were shot.

We must now turn to the third leg of this most successful experiment in concerted attack. Nobby Clarke and his patrol, accompanied by Captain McClelland, a Civil Affairs Officer, had landed in Ios on 25th April. As on the other two islands, the Germans here were careless in the extreme . . . a state of affairs which must be attributed to the enemy's practice of censoring all news of our raids, with the result that all who had not actually suffered were unaware of the disasters that might come with the night.

Corporal Holmes, sent with a small party to collect three of the garrison was unable to make the capture. The Germans, when approached, seized a number of children and held these unfortunate little creatures in front of them to cover their withdrawal.

Nobby Clarke, with Pomford and McClelland, was more fortunate. Forcing their way into a house, they surprised two Germans who were undressing. These men were more courageous than their comrades. Refusing to surrender, they attacked the invaders with bare hands and were killed. A third German, who was visiting his mistress in another part of the town, was captured as he was about to get into bed with her. This man was most disconsolate. Had he known that his mistress, herself, had supplied the information concerning his whereabouts, he might have been more disconsolate still.

Nobby Clarke marched his captives along the quay. Presently, footsteps were heard. Two men were seen approaching. When challenged, they opened fire. The British replied with grenades but the intruders succeeded in getting behind a house. Covered by the house they escaped to the hills.

Unperturbed by this setback, Clarke proceeded with the business of the evening. He blew up the telegraph and cable stations and detonated a dump of 75 mm shells. In the harbour he sank one caïque and unloaded the food from a second, for distribution to the civilian population. On the following day he requested the mayor to send a messenger to the surviving Germans with orders that they report to him immediately, under pain of being hunted down without mercy. The credulous Germans, who might easily have remained hidden, surrendered half an hour later.

Clarke then sailed for Amorgos, where he was joined by Flying Officer Macris and five men of the Greek Sacred Squadron. There were ten Germans now on Amorgos, all living in a house in the chief town. That night the house was surrounded and fire opened upon it by two Bren guns. Macris and another Greek climbed up some trellis work and tossed grenades into various rooms. At a blast from Clarke's whistle, firing ceased and the Germans were invited to surrender. Instead of capitulating they made a sortie with arms in their hands. Eight of them were killed as they reached the open; the remaining pair escaped to the hills.

Thus concluded forty-eight hours of British intervention in the Cyclades. Casualties suffered by the enemy were 41 killed, 27 wounded and 19 made prisoner. S.B.S. losses in the three operations were two killed and three slightly wounded, of a total expeditionary strength of thirty-nine men.

The list of stores and equipment of all kinds lost by the enemy I need not enumerate.

The immediate result of these raids was the distribution of large garrisons of German mountain troops throughout the Cyclades. Sutherland, however, remained sceptical as to the ability of the enemy to defend even his own living quarters against determined infiltration. To prove his point, he dispatched Lassen and thirteen men to Paros, a large island lying only seventy miles from Athens. An air landing strip had recently been completed on Paros. Workmen of the Todt organization still slept in tents along its fringe.

Lassen, as was his custom, divided his party into small groups, each with a separate target. The main attack failed – the alarm being given almost at once by some unusually alert sentries – but the subsidiary expeditions were in each case successful. Private Perkins, accompanied by a Greek officer penetrated into one house to discover a German officer standing uncertainly in pyjamas and holding a Lüger.

"Hands up," said Perkins, who spoke good German, "everything is finished for you."

The German officer does not appear to have believed this. He replied with an incredulous "*Wass?*" and a shot. The Greek killed him. In the next room the pair found and killed three private soldiers.

Sergeant Nicholson and Marine Williams, detailed to capture a second German officer, discovered their quarry hiding behind a door, clad in a flowered dressing-gown. He accompanied them without fuss. Several other German occupants of the house hid beneath beds and inside cupboards. They hoped to avoid capture. Nicholson and Williams who were perfectly well aware of the number of people in the house made no attempt to search it. Withdrawing, they threw phosphorus and fragmentation grenades through all the windows. Three of the men hidden were killed.

So, incidentally, was Nicholson's prisoner, hit first in the neck by one of his own snipers and subsequently in the chest by a grenade explosion. Nicholson, who had wasted several perfectly good field dressings and mouthfuls of brandy in an endeavour to save the man, returned sadly to the rendezvous.

A strange, plump, freckled, kilted figure now enters the story. It is that of Captain Douglas Stobie, a very early member of the Special Air Service, who had had the misfortune to break a leg in Tunisia, in consequence of which disaster he had been invalided home. He arrived back now, bringing with him a tommy gun, the largest biceps and calf measurements in the Middle East, and a huge file of papers, apparently the result of some disagreement with the Army Pay Office. Stobie, it seemed, had not received his servant allowance or some such emolument for the period of his convalescence in the United Kingdom. He was determined that justice should be done to him. Briefed to accompany Nobby Clarke on a raid in Naxos, he took his file with him. During the intervals of planning and fighting, Stobie composed letters of complaint.

The Naxos operation was most successful. This was the first island in which guerrillas were encountered and their assistance was invaluable. Clarke and Stobie found Naxos well guarded and in a state of considerable alertness following the raid on Paros. They decided to devote their attention to a single German garrison of one officer and seventeen men. The three houses in which this group lived were surrounded and progressively demolished by large explosive charges. All the Germans became casualties, though Clarke was obliged to leave the wounded behind, owing to the approach of an enemy relief column.

The final operations of Sutherland's squadron, prior to handing over to Lapraik, are of minor importance. Sutherland himself, who had been chafing at base for weeks, was now finally able to get out and, with a motley force, penetrated deep into the Cyclades, sinking a caïque in Siphnos and capturing a stray German on the same island.

Harold Chevalier, also with a scratch force, accompanied a naval patrol travelling north. Caïques of all sizes were stopped and searched in the waters between Samos and

Chios. Eventually patience was rewarded by the appearance of a ship which could be commandeered with a clear conscience. The four Germans on board her were made prisoners.

Throughout this whole period, the naval liaison work, under Commander John Campbell, R.N.R., was of a very high order. Motor launches carrying S.B.S. parties never hesitated to go close inshore, lay off – some times for hours – within shouting distance of enemy observation posts and, in more than one case, re-embarked personnel under the immediate threat of air attack.

CITADEL

Otto Skorzeny

A junior Waffen SS officer serving in Berlin, Otto Skorzeny became Chief of Germany's Special Troops by sheer chance; when Hitler's order to create a German equivalent of the British Army's commandos was circulated within Army High Command someone remembered a university acquaintance who might pass as leader of the new unit. And so Otto Skorzeny was plucked from behind his desk and brevetted Chief of Special Troops. He was also promoted to captain.

Inadvertently, the German Army had picked a natural-born commando for the job. Physically imposing – he was six feet four inches, with a duelling scar from ear to chin – Skorzeny also had the singular mental attribute necessary for commando deeds: audacity. Within six months of his appointment, Skorzeny and his special troops brought off the most improbable feat of the war so far – the rescue of Mussolini from his mountain prison at Gran Sasso. A year later, September 1944, Hitler asked Skorzeny to do the impossible once again.

A T THE CONFERENCE on the third day, I was told to remain behind. The Führer had also asked Keitel, Jodl, Ribbentrop and Himmler not to go. We sat at the same round table in the corner. Hitler gave a short dissertation on the situation in the south-east. He said that the front on the Hungarian border had just been stabilized and must be maintained there at all costs. In the vast bulge there

were more than a million German troops, who would be lost
for good if there was a sudden collapse. "We have received
secret reports," he said, "that the head of the Hungarian
state, Admiral Horthy, is attempting to get in touch with
our enemies with a view to a separate peace. It would mean
the loss of our armies. He is approaching both the Western
powers and the Russians. He is even prepared to throw
himself on the mercy of the Kremlin.

"You, Skorzeny," he continued, "must be prepared to
seize the Citadel of Budapest by force, if he betrays his
alliance with us. The General Staff is thinking of a *coup de
main* with parachute or glider troops. The command of the
whole operation in that city has been entrusted to the new
Corps Commander, General Kleemann. You are under his
orders for this affair, but must push ahead at once with your
preparations, as the Corps staff is still being got together."

It was in these words that Adolf Hitler put his audacious
plan before his little audience. He continued: "To make it
easier for you to cope with any difficulties in getting your
force together, you will receive from me written orders and
wide powers." Colonel-General Jodl then read out a list of
the units placed under my orders. It included one parachute
battalion from the Luftwaffe, 600 Parachute Battalion of
the Waffen SS, and one motorized infantry battalion
formed from members of the Officer Cadet Training
School at Wiener-Neustadt. Two sections of gliders had
been notified and given movement orders. "An aircraft
from the FHQ transportation pool will be placed at your
disposal for the duration of the operation," added General
Jodl.

Adolf Hitler went on to discuss with Ribbentrop the
reports just received from the German Embassy in Budapest, which were to the effect that the situation was very
strained and the Hungarian government was showing itself
far from well disposed towards its Axis partner.

The written order was handed over to me after it had
been signed and the party went their different ways. With
the words "I rely on you and your men", the Führer left the
room.

I remained behind alone and when I read what was

written on the paper, I was more than amazed at the possibilities it offered. It was a sheet of so-called state paper, with an eagle and swastika in gold at the top left-hand corner and underneath the words "Der Führer und Reichskanzler" in old-fashioned script. This document (which was lost during the troubles of 1945, or to be more accurate, stolen with the rest of my belongings) was more or less in these terms:

"Sturmbannführer Skorzeny is carrying out a personal and highly confidential order of the highest importance. I order all political and military authorities everywhere to give him all the help he needs and comply with his wishes."

At the foot was the signature – by now a very shaky signature – of the head of the German state. I may say that I had to produce the document on only one rather unimportant occasion.

After reading my orders – it was already 2 a.m. – I still had work to do. Two days previously I had taken the precaution of warning the "Mitte" commando, formerly SS Infantry Battalion 502, to be ready for action. I knew that, even at this late hour, Captain von Foelkersam would still be expecting a call from me, so I promptly got through to Friedenthal. "Hallo, Foelkersam. I've just received an important new assignment! Get out your pencil and write down: The 1st company at full strength will emplane at Gatow airfield at 8 a.m. today. Treble ammunition supply and don't forget explosives for four pioneer detachments. Emergency rations for six days. Lieutenant Hunke will be in command. Our destination is known to the commander of Ju Flight 52. I'm leaving here by air as early as possible and will land before ten at the aerodrome of the Heinkel works at Oranienburg. Meet me there. Two hours later you, Radl and Ostafel will fly on with me. Any questions? Password 'take it easy!' as before."

Having got things going at Friedenthal, I decided on "Panzerfaust" as the code word for the new operation. Then I recollected that I had not informed Friedenthal accordingly and made good the omission by telegraph.

Then I remembered that I had gliders at my disposal, and also parachute troops. But how could the General Staff be thinking of parachute or glider landings on the Citadel? I knew my Budapest pretty well.

The only possible landing place in the city was the big open space known as the "Field of Blood". But if the Hungarians were hostile, this area would be completely commanded from the Citadel, not to mention the other three sides, and our fellows would be shot to pieces before they could assemble. I should not be able to put down more than a handful of special troops there, and then only if the situation at the time permitted.

Following our flight to Vienna, Foelkersam, Ostafel and I drove on straight to Wiener-Neustadt from Aspern. Radl was to contact the Intelligence Headquarters as further news might have come through. In Wiener-Neustadt we reported at the old "Kriegsakademie", which had traditions going back to the time of Maria Theresa. In the lofty corridors the portraits of former commandants gazed down upon us. The commandant in office, Colonel H., had been told of our coming. When I explained what was afoot, he was most anxious to lead the battalion himself, and I had some trouble in convincing him that, in view of his seniority, it would hardly be appropriate. But he refused to be denied the opportunity of participating as a freelance.

Then the battalion commander selected, a major, and the company commanders were called in. They were all old-front fighters, who had been transferred as instructors to the Akademie. Meanwhile, all the suitable cadets had been assembled in the court. There were nearly a thousand of them. When I passed down the ranks to familiarize myself with my new command, I could almost have jumped for joy. Germany would find it hard to produce such a hand-picked selection, I thought. Battalions of that calibre were almost non-existent. I felt proud to be leading such men and something of my feelings must have been betrayed in the short speech I made to them: "You have, no doubt, heard my name from your officers and many of you will remember the Italian affair. But don't think that I'm merely taking you on another adventure. It will be a serious and perhaps bloody business and the stake is high. You and I will do our duty together, and as we believe in our cause we will do what we set out to do and thereby serve our country and our people."

The SS parachute battalion had also arrived in the vicinity of Vienna, and both officers and men made a good impression. I had a feeling, however, that I must keep them well in hand, as they seemed only too prone to act on their own – a procedure which could well endanger the success of the whole expedition! What shape it would take I then had no idea. I could not even tell how the situation in Hungary would develop.

After arriving in Budapest it was three days before we had settled the motorization and equipment problems, and then I felt it was time I had a look round the city myself. The papers for a certain "Dr. Wolff", a gentleman of about my size, were soon produced. I slipped into comfortable civilian clothes, an acquaintance gave me an introduction to a friend in the city and I was ready to start.

The friend, a businessman, gave us the sort of welcome of which only Hungarians are capable. His hospitality extended to placing his whole house, and the butler and cook, at my disposal. I almost blush to say that I had never lived so luxuriously as in these three weeks – and in the fifth year of the war too! Our host would have been positively insulted if we had not done full justice to his menus.

My Corps Commander had also arrived in Budapest. He had his work cut out to get together an effective staff and train his troops to the requisite standard. I lent him Foelkersam and Ostafel to work with the Corps staff. The first thing was to devise a plan to alert all the troops in and around the city, so that they would be ready for action at any moment. It was essential that all railways, stations, post offices and other transport and communication centres should always be in German hands.

Our Intelligence had ascertained that Niklas von Horthy, the son of the head of the state, had had a secret meeting with some delegates from Tito, with a view to getting in touch with the Russian High Command and opening negotiations for a separate peace. FHQ had obviously been accurately informed on the matter. The fact that Tito should be used seemed to me quite incomprehensible.

How was it possible for the Protector of Hungary to seek the good offices of her mortal enemy, Yugoslavia? What sort of fate could he expect for himself and his country?

I suggested to the top men of our Intelligence Service that an attempt should be made to introduce one of our agents into the negotiations. In this we were successful. A Croat managed to be well received, both by the Yugoslav delegates and Niklas von Horthy himself, and to win the confidence of both parties, and we thus learned that there was to be a meeting with old Horthy himself, one night in the immediate future. This was a shock, as it was not in our interests that the head of the state should be personally involved in the affair. But I felt that this was a headache for the Intelligence people and the Security Police. I had plenty of troubles of my own.

Every time I visited the Citadel, ostensibly to see the Air Attaché, German Ambassador or Corps Commander, I became more and more worried as to how we should tackle this natural fortress. Though my original instructions on the point were not too clear, I could not see how we could prevent the defection of the Hungarian government by anything less than an operation against the whole government quarter and the Citadel. Any such action must be preceded by some hostile act against Germany. It could only be a swift answer to such an act.

Foelkersam was therefore instructed to make a most careful study of all available plans of the city and supplement his knowledge with minute inspections of the streets and buildings. The result of his labours was full of surprises. There was a labyrinth of passages under the Citadel – a nasty "snag" for us.

The "alert" plan, which had now been worked out, provided that I and the detachment under my command should effect a military occupation of the Citadel. I had abandoned the idea of a glider or parachute landing altogether.

It was now time for my troops to come to Budapest. The GOC Corps insisted that there should be no further delay. They left Vienna about the beginning of October, and took up their quarters in the suburbs.

In the first week of October, SS Obergruppenführer Bach-Zelevski also came to Budapest. He had been sent by the FHQ to take charge of all proceedings in the city. Having come from Warsaw, where he had just put down the rising of the Polish Underground, he took care to let us know at our conferences that he was a "strong man". He told us he was determined to be as ruthless as he had been in Warsaw. He had even brought a 65 cm mortar with him, a weapon which had only been brought into play twice before – at the sieges of Sebastopol and Warsaw.

I considered his methods unnecessarily brutal, and said that we would attain our ends better and quicker in other and less objectionable ways. Operation Panzerfaust could succeed without the help of the famous mortar. Many of the officers seemed impressed by Bach-Zelevski's intervention and almost afraid of him, but I disregarded his bad manners, stuck to my point of view and got it accepted.

I could not understand why fifteen or twenty officers should be present at conferences when the alert plan was discussed. It seemed to me that the Hungarian government was bound to hear of them and act accordingly. We received a very alarming report from our Intelligence that General M., commanding the Hungarian Army in the Carpathians, was personally engaged in direct negotiations with the Russians. Of course that information was transmitted to FHQ, but it issued no definite orders as to what counter-measures should be taken. Conference followed conference.

On the night of the 10th October, there was a meeting between Horthy junior and the Yugoslav delegates. The German police were warned in advance, but took no action. The next meeting was to take place on Sunday, the 15th, in the vicinity of the Danube quay. Just before the 15th, FHQ sent General Wenck to Budapest with orders to take command if necessary and issue such orders as he thought fit. The Security Police were determined to take action at the first opportunity and arrest the Protector's son and the Yugoslav delegates. The codeword "Mouse" was chosen for this operation, owing to Niklas's nickname, "Nicky", being mistaken for Micky. The association with "Micky Mouse" was obvious.

The adoption of this plan by the police was based on the supposition that the Protector, to avoid the public exposure of his son, would mend his ways and abandon the plan for a separate peace.

General Winkelman had asked me to have a company of my men ready for that afternoon. He said that he knew that Niklas von Horthy's previous meetings had been guarded by Honved troops. If he was right, I could see that my men were considered in the light of a counterblast. I agreed on condition that I myself should decide how and when they should intervene.

On the Saturday, I received an urgent telegram from Berlin, ordering me, to my sorrow, to send Radl back to Berlin. He was very annoyed, but of course complied.

The 15th October was a bright Sunday. The streets were empty at the time appointed for the rendezvous. My company was in a side street in covered trucks. Captain von Foelkersam kept me in touch with them, as obviously I could not show myself in uniform that day. If I was to appear on the stage, so to speak, I must be inconspicuous. My driver and another man, both Luftwaffe personnel, were taking the air on a seat in the little garden which occupied most of the square. I drove up in my own car shortly before the meeting began. When I entered the square, I noticed a Hungarian military lorry and a private car, which was presumably Horthy's, stationed in front of the building of which we had been told. It took me no time to make up my mind and park my own car right in the path of these vehicles, so that they could not get away in a hurry.

The floor above the offices in this building had been occupied the day before by policemen, who had taken lodgings nearby. Others were to enter it from the street about 10.10 p.m., and make the arrests.

Three Honved officers were sitting in the covered lorry, but could not be seen from the street. Two others were lounging on benches in the gardens. I was standing by my car, pretending to be fiddling with the engine, when the curtain rose on the drama.

The first German policeman had hardly entered the building when there was a burst of machine-pistol fire from the lorry, and the second fell to the ground with a wound in the stomach. The two other Hungarian officers came running out of the gardens, firing their revolvers. I had just time to take cover behind my car when its open door was drilled. Things were getting really hot! Honved soldiers appeared at the windows and on the balconies of houses. The moment the first shots rang out, my driver and his companion rushed up to me, assuming that I had been hit. The driver was shot through the thigh, but could still walk. I gave the agreed signal to my detachment, and we three defended ourselves with our weapons as best we could against the rain of fire from the enemy. It was a most uncomfortable situation, though it only lasted a few minutes.

By then my car was not much more than a sieve. Bullets ricocheting from walls passed unpleasantly near and we could only put our noses out of cover for long enough to have potshots at the enemy and keep them at least 10 to 15 metres away.

Then I heard my men running out of the side street in our direction. Foelkersam had taken the situation in at a glance and posted the first section at the corner of the square, while the others swept through the gardens and began firing at the house-fronts. My first assailants now withdrew to the shelter of a nearby house, which was occupied by Hungarians in some strength. I observed that these men were lining up for an assault and quick thinking inspired us to hurl a number of grenades in the doorway, thereby bringing down the door and some marble slabs, which temporarily blocked the entrance.

With that the fighting ceased. It may have lasted five minutes.

Our policemen now came down from the upper floor, bringing four prisoners with them. The two Hungarians, "Micky Mouse" and his comrade Bornemisza, were bundled into one of our trucks. To conceal their identity, our fellows had tried to roll them up in carpets, with only partial success, I observed, noting the effort required to get the refractory prisoners into the vehicle.

The lorry moved off and my company withdrew. I was

anxious to avoid further scuffles, which were only too likely when the enemy recovered from his surprise. Fortunately, our retirement passed without further incident.

Some instinct prompted me to follow the truck. Another car and driver were available for me. Barely a hundred metres from the square, under the Elizabeth bridge, I saw three Honved companies approaching at the double. If they got any nearer, they could easily find themselves involved in a mix-up with my men – an eventuality I was determined to prevent at all costs. Time must be gained somehow, but bluff was my only resource. I told my driver to pull up, and ran towards the officer who appeared to be in command. "Halt your men quick!" I yelled. "There's a hell of a mix-up going on up there! No one knows what's happening! You'd better find out for yourself first!"

The trick came off. The troops halted and the officer seemed undecided what to do. It was lucky for me that he knew some German, as otherwise he might not have understood me. The short pause was vital from my point of view. By now, my own men must have got away in their trucks. "I must get on!" I called to the Hungarian officer, jumped into my car and made for the aerodrome. When I arrived, the two Hungarians were in a plane, and two minutes later they were on their way to Vienna.

My next destination was Corps Headquarters, in a hotel at the top of a hill. Here I met General Wenck. We were all wondering what would happen now. It was known that the Hungarians had been taking military precautions at the Citadel for some days. The garrison had been reinforced and it was said that some of the streets had been mined.

About midday, a call came through from the German Embassy, lodged in a small palace on the Citadel. The Military Attaché told us that the Citadel was now being officially occupied by Honved troops, and the gates and roads were closed to traffic. He had tried to get away himself, but had been turned back. Shortly afterwards, the telephone wires must have been cut, as we could not get through. The German establishments, of which there were several, were practically isolated.

Just before 2 o'clock, we were told to stand by for a

special announcement on the Hungarian wireless. A message from the Regent, Admiral Horthy, came through: "Hungary has concluded a separate peace with Russia!" Now we knew where we were. Our counter-measures must be carried out at once.

Orders for the execution of Operation Panzerfaust were also issued. I thought them premature, and asked that it should be postponed for a few hours, and that the immediate reply to the Hungarian action should be to draw a cordon of German troops round the Citadel. This job was assigned to the 22nd SS Division. The occupation by German troops of the railway stations and other important buildings passed off without incident in the afternoon.

A general was dispatched to the Hungarian GHQ at the front. Unfortunately, he arrived too late. General M. and some of his officers and secretaries had already gone over to the Russians. It surprised us greatly that his action, and the Hungarian wireless announcement, did not have such a serious effect on the Hungarian troops as might have been expected. Generally speaking, they remained where they were and few of the officers followed the example of their commander-in-chief. But it was essential that there should be no delay in preventing the Hungarian War Ministry from following up with an order to capitulate.

At a conference late in the afternoon, it was decided that Operation Panzerfaust should be carried out early in the morning of the 16th. The slight postponement suited me well, as I could put it to good use. I fixed on 6 a.m. for zero-hour, as I considered surprise essential and the early hours were best from that point of view. Foelkersam and I pored for hours over the plan of the Citadel which we had made, and our ideas of the coming action began to assume definite shape.

I projected a concentric assault, which should yet have a focal point in the centre, which I intended to be a detachment approaching from Vienna Street. The factor of surprise would be of greatest effect at that point. I hoped to rush the Vienna gate with little resistance and without too much noise, and suddenly emerge in the square facing the

Citadel. A rapid decision should follow automatically. If we could quickly force our way into the presumed centre of the Hungarian resistance, the action would soon be over, with a minimum of casualties on both sides.

We then instructed our units in their specific tasks. We had been allotted one company of Panther and one of Goliath tanks. Incidentally, these little Goliath tanks were a recent addition to German armament. They were radio-controlled, low, handy affairs, with caterpillar tracks and a big explosive charge in the bows. They could prove very useful in breaking down any barricades or gates.

The battalion of the Wiener-Neustadt Kriegsakademie was to attack through the gardens on the southern slope of the Citadel – no small undertaking, as we knew that these gardens had been converted into a complex of trenches, machine-gun emplacements and anti-aircraft gun positions. Its function was to beat down resistance and facilitate the occupation of the castle.

A platoon of the "Mitte" Battalion, reinforced by two Panthers, would attack the western side with the object of forcing one of the entrances at the back, while a platoon of the 600 SS Parachute Battalion made its way into the chain-bridge tunnel passing under the Citadel, cleared out the subterranean passages and reached the ministries of War and Home Affairs above. The rest of the "Mitte" unit, the bulk of the SS parachute battalion, six Panthers and the Goliath company, were to be available for my *coup de main*. The Luftwaffe parachute battalion would be kept in reserve for emergencies.

The orders for the individual assignments were carefully worked out, and about midnight my troops were in position behind the cordon drawn by the 22nd Division.

The streets had worn their usual appearance all day, as the civil population did not seem to have noticed the activities of either the Hungarian or German troops. The coffee houses were full as ever, and did not empty until a very late hour. The news from the stations was equally reassuring; supply trains were coming from Germany and passing through to the front in the ordinary way.

Just after midnight, a high-ranking officer of the Hun-

garian War Ministry presented himself at Corps Headquarters. He had come by some route unknown to us,
and said that he was authorized by his Minister to negotiate.
We replied that there could be no negotiations until the
Regent's proclamation was withdrawn, and also that it was
an unfriendly act to hold the members of the embassy and
other German organizations prisoner in the Citadel. At my
suggestion, the Hungarians were given until 6 a.m. to
decide whether they would remove the mines and barricades in Vienna Street leading to the German Embassy.
That time was fixed with a view to my design for a surprise
attack on the Citadel with a minimum of bloodshed.

About 3 a.m., I went to my command post at the foot of
the Citadel and summoned all my officers. The night was
very dark and we had to use our torches when examining
our sketch plans. There were a few details to be cleared up,
though my officers had worked hard and familiarized
themselves thoroughly with the ground. My second-in-
command produced some coffee, which was very welcome
on such a nerve-racking occasion.

Meanwhile, I had made my final decision on the procedure to be adopted. We must simply march up the hill to the
Citadel and do our best to give the impression that nothing
unusual was afoot. The men must stay in their trucks. I
knew that my order to that effect was taking a big risk, as
they would be defenceless for the first few moments if the
convoy was attacked, but I had no option if I wanted a quick
end to any scuffle. I informed my battalion commanders of
my plans and assured them that if it succeeded they could
count on speedy help from the Citadel.

I assembled my column and told the officers that as soon
as the Vienna Gate had been passed it must split in two and
proceed at full speed by two parallel roads to the Citadel
square. The company and platoon commanders were given
strict instructions as to the use of their arms. They were not
to reply to casual shots in their direction, and must do
everything in their power to arrive at the rendezvous without firing themselves. The watchword must be: "The
Hungarians are not our enemies."

Just before 5.30 a.m., when it was beginning to get light,

I took my place in my truck at the head of the column. Behind me, I had two Panthers, followed by a platoon of the Goliath company, and the rest of the unit in their trucks. Automatics were set at safety. Most of the men had slumped in their seats and were enjoying a quiet nap. They had the hardened warriors' gift of snatching a bit of sleep when a really tough job lay ahead.

I took the precaution of sending my second-in-command to Corps Headquarters, to ascertain whether there had been any change in the situation, but the answer was in the negative, so zero hour was adhered to.

In my truck I had Foelkersam and Ostafel, as well as five NCOs who had been in the Gran Sasso show. I considered them my personal assault group. Each was armed with a machine-pistol, a few hand grenades, and the new *panzerfaust* (bazooka). We were wondering what the Hungarian tanks in the Citadel would do. If necessary our tanks and *panzerfausts* would have to look after them.

At one minute before 6 o'clock, I waved my arm as the signal to switch on. Then I stood up in my truck and pointed upwards several times, whereupon we started off, rather slowly, as it was uphill. I could only hope that none of our vehicles struck a mine, which would have blocked our advance and upset our plan. The Vienna Gate emerged out of the half-light – the way was open! A few Hungarian soldiers stared curiously at us. We were soon at the top. "Gradually accelerate," I whispered to my driver.

On our right was a Honved barracks. "Nasty if we get fired on from the flank," murmured Foelkersam at my side. There were two machine-guns behind sandbags in front of the barracks, but nothing happened. No sound could be heard but the rumble of the Panthers behind.

I chose the side street on the right in which the German Embassy was situated. We could now travel at a good pace without losing the rest of the column. The tanks were doing a good 35 to 40 kilometres to the hour, and at length the Citadel was not more than a thousand metres away and a substantial part of our task had been accomplished.

Now the great detached mass of the War Ministry appeared to the left, and we heard the distant sound of two heavy explosions. Our men must have forced their way through the tunnel. The critical moment was at hand. We were past the War Ministry and in the square in a flash. Three Hungarian tanks faced us, but as we drew level the leading one tilted its gun skywards as a signal that they would not fire.

A barricade of stones had been placed in front of the gate of the Citadel. I told my driver to draw aside and signalled to the leading Panther to charge it. We left our truck and ran behind, while the barricade collapsed under the weight of the 30-ton monster, which continued its irresistible thrust. Levelling its long gun-barrel at the centre of the courtyard, it found itself faced with a battery of six anti-tank guns.

We leaped over the debris of the barricade and burst through the shattered gate. A colonel of the guard got out his revolver to stop us, but Foelkersam knocked it out of his hand. On our right was what appeared to be the main entrance, and we took it at the run, almost colliding with a Honved officer, whom I ordered to lead us straight to the Commandant. He immediately complied, and at his side we rushed up the broad staircase, not failing to notice the elegant red carpet.

On reaching the first floor we turned left into a corridor, and I left one of my men behind to cover us. The officer pointed to a door and we went into a small ante-room where a table had been drawn up to the open window and a man was lying on it firing a machine-gun into the courtyard. Holzer, a short, stocky NCO, clasped the gun in his arms and flung it out of the window. The gunner was so surprised that he fell off the table.

I saw a door on my right, knocked and walked straight in. A Honved Major-General got up and came towards me. "Are you the Commandant?" I asked. "You must surrender the Citadel at once! If you don't, you will be responsible for any bloodshed. You must decide immediately!" As we could hear shots outside, including bursts of machine-gun fire, I added: "You can see that any resistance is hopeless. I have already occupied the Citadel." I was speaking the truth, as I was quite certain that the "Mitte" Battalion, led by the redoubtable Lieutenant Hunke, was just behind me and must have seized all the strategic points.

The Hungarian Major-General was not long in making up his mind: "I surrender the Citadel and will order the ceasefire at once." We shook hands and soon arranged that a Hungarian officer and one of ours should inform the troops fighting in the Citadel gardens of the ceasefire. After ten minutes had passed, no noise of battle could be heard.

Accompanied, at my request, by two Hungarian majors to serve as interpreters, I went along the corridor to have a look round. We came to the rooms adjoining the Regent's reception room. I was astonished to find that he was not there and learned that he had left shortly before six o'clock. It transpired later that he had been escorted by General Pfeffer-Wildenbruch, of the Waffen SS, to the latter's residence on the Citadel hill. His family had previously taken refuge with the Papal Nuncio. The presence of Horthy would have made no difference to our plans, which were not concerned with him personally, but confined to controlling the seat of government.

While we were looking out of the window over the so-called "Meadow of Blood", a few bullets whistled past. Hunke subsequently explained that it had proved impossible to notify the ceasefire to some of the Hungarian posts on the Danube side of the Citadel gardens. Two rounds from a *panzerfaust* soon convinced them that it would be wiser to abandon resistance.

The whole operation had not taken more than half an hour. Peace returned to the city and the citizens in the vicinity could turnover and go to sleep again. I rang up Corps Headquarters on a special line and could almost hear the sigh of relief at the other end. Apparently they had considered the success of my *coup* as somewhat problematic.

Shortly afterwards, the reports came in from the War Ministry (where alone, there had been a short, sharp action), and the Ministry for Home Affairs, and one by one the commanders of the different groups turned up to relate their experiences. Our casualties had been agreeably low, not more than four killed and about twelve wounded. The only serious fighting had been in the gardens. I asked the Commandant about the Hungarian casualties and was told that they amounted to three killed and fifteen wounded. It was a great satisfaction that the operation had not resulted in serious losses on both sides.

We made the Hungarian other ranks surrender their arms and stack them in the courtyard, but I allowed all officers to retain their revolvers and then invited them to meet me in one of the assembly rooms of the building. I made a short speech, reminding them that there had been no war between Germany and Hungary for centuries and that we had always been loyal allies. I went on to say that even now there was no reason for strife. What everyone wanted was a new Europe, but that could only come into being if Germany was saved.

My Austrian accent certainly reinforced the impression made by my words, to judge by the warmth with which each of the Hungarian officers shook hands with me. In the afternoon they marched back to their barracks with their men and next day took the oath of allegiance to the new government at the War Ministry.

Corps HQ had ordered that I and my troops should remain in occupation of the Citadel until further orders. In the evening, I gave a dinner to all my officers in one of the salons. My guests included the commandant of the Kriegsakademie at Wiener-Neustadt, who was highly delighted that his "eagles", as he called his cadets, had given such a good account of themselves.

The head of the new Hungarian government came to pay his respects and thank me on its behalf. I replied that I was thankful that the action had been so brief and damage to the splendid buildings had been avoided. I shuddered to think what a mess the 65 cm mortar of ruthless Herr Bach-Zelevski would have made of them. We agreed that there should be a state funeral for the Hungarian and German dead, the arrangements being left to the government. I welcomed the idea as calculated to put an end to any ill-feeling between the two nations.

Skorzeny was soon back in action. During the German Ardennes offensive of December 1944, he organized "American brigades" of disguised Germans to cause havoc behind US lines. Eisenhower was a prisoner in his own HQ for a week.

This ruse de guerre later caused Skorzeny to be charged with war crimes by the victorious Allies. At one stage, it looked as though Skorzeny would hang, until the British war hero, Wing Commander Yeo Thomas, revealed that the British had "fought in enemy uniform" as a matter of course. Skorzeny was duly acquitted.

On release from captivity, Skorzeny emigrated to Spain where he reverted to his pre-war occupation, engineering. He died in 1975.

THE PASS OF LA MOLINA

Hilary St George Saunders

*Formed in 1942 from volunteers from the Royal Marines
Division, the Royal Marine Commandos received their
blooding at Dieppe, where they sustained nearly 100
casualties from an embarkation strength of 370. Despite
the Dieppe disaster and the issue of a green beret (judged
effeminate), the Royal Marine Commandos were possessed by an unquenchable self-confidence. It was well
placed. Few special force units during the Second World
War fought as valiantly as did the RM Commandos at
La Molina in 1943.*

THE GULF OF Salerno embraces more beauty than most
parts of the world, and civilization has known its
shores since the sixth century BC. Sands line its shallow
curve from the honey-coloured temple of Paestum in the
south-east to the city of Salerno in the north-west. Beyond,
crowded between steep hills and the sea, lies Vietri, and
beside it the little cove of Marina. The mountains – they are
just too large to be called hills – run from east to west and
cut off Salerno Bay from the plain of Naples. A defile called
La Molina winds through them, carrying the shortest road
between Naples and Salerno. It was these hills, White
Cross Hills, Hospital Hill, Castle Hill, and the little villages
nestling in their sides – Pigoletti, La Molina, and Dragone –
which were to be the scene of the fiercest fighting.

The Gulf of Salerno had been chosen for the main assault
upon Italy because it provided landing beaches of sufficient

width and length to put ashore a whole army, and was just
within extreme range for fighter aircraft based on Sicily.
Eisenhower was playing for high stakes; nothing less than
the city of Rome. If the Eternal City fell, the whole of Italy
might fall; and as the Allied plenipotentiaries signed the
armistice with Badoglio's representatives in an almond
grove at Cassibile, not far from where Durnford-Slater
and his men had landed to destroy the coastal battery, it
seemed that the bold stroke must succeed. Italy was out of
the war, and her General Staff, true to Cavour's principle of
sacred egoism, were hastening to the aid of the victors. The
plan was, therefore, this: the Fifth Army, consisting of the
US VI Corps on the right and the British X Corps on the
left, were to make an assault landing in the Bay of Salerno,
and thrusting ahead as fast as they could, to capture the
great port of Naples.

To aid the advance of X Corps, it was decided that
Commando troops should be landed at Marina with orders
to destroy the coast defence batteries there situated and
thus prevent their fire from sweeping the western half of the
Bay of Salerno. They were also to push inland, seize the
defile of La Molina through which, as has been said, the
shortest road to Naples runs, and hold it until the 46th
Division reached them and passed through. At the same
time three battalions of American Rangers, of which one
had been trained by Vaughan at Achnacarry, and of which
two were to be commanded by Colonel Bill Darby, an old
and trusted friend of the Commandos, were to land seven
miles west of Marina at the little fishing village of Maiori,
and thence to move inland and seize the defile of Nocera
through which also X Corps must pass. Were the plan to
succeed, the 46th Division, issuing from the hills at the
points seized by the Commandos and the Rangers, would
burst upon the plain and arrive at the outskirts of Naples
three or four days after it had come ashore.

The units to which the task of silencing the coastal
batteries and seizing the defile of La Molina was entrusted
were No. 2 Commando now under Jack Churchill, 338
strong, and No. 41 (Royal Marine) Commando under
Lumsden, 400 strong. With them went Laycock, his

G.S.O.I., Tom Churchill, the brother of Jack, and Randolph Churchill, son of the Prime Minister. The Commandos were to have the help of one troop of 6-pounder anti-tank guns and one American 4.2-inch mortar company. They could also call for the support from the guns of a destroyer, H.M.S. *Blackmoor*, and from those belonging to the 71st Regiment of Field Artillery of the 46th Division.

It was decided to land in four waves, the first composed of 210, all ranks, of No. 2 Commando, in five assault craft. They would deal with the battery at Marina and secure the beachhead. The remainder of the force, No. 41 (Royal Marine) Commando and Brigade Headquarters, would then land. They would push on at once to seize the defile at La Molina, despatching two Troops to clear the town of Vietri on the way. In the meantime two Troops of No. 2 Commando would seize the western approaches of Salerno. The third wave, which were to be taken ashore by the assault craft which had put the first wave on the beach, was to consist of the rest of No. 2 Commando, and the fourth wave would be made up of the 6-pounder anti-tank gun troop and the tank landing craft carrying the American mortar company. Such were the plans worked out in the École Moderne in Algiers by Laycock and his staff, who had flown thither from Sicily.

When at Palermo the two Commandos carried out a brigade exercise with the 128th Brigade commanded by Brigadier James, V.C., its object being to rehearse those who were to take part in the forthcoming assault. "This exercise had one great merit," records Tom Churchill, "it was carried out without the issue of a single piece of paper." Co-operation was good, and it was with high hopes that the Commandos boarded the *Prince Albert*, and No. 41 (Royal Marine) Commando the infantry landing craft, and put out to sea early on the 8th September.

The passage was calm. At about 21.00 hours on the 9th the convoy was bombed without effect. Just before the bombers appeared, the news of the Italian armistice was announced on the wireless and gave rise to much speculation. Some thought that they would be met on the beach by the local mayor with a reception committee and a brass band. Others took a different view.

At 02.15 hours the convoy reached the assault area and both Commandos began their landing according to plan. The first wave of No. 2 Commando landed unopposed on the beach at Marina exactly at H-hour (03.30 hours). One troop formed a beachhead and the rest, under Jack Churchill, moved at once to the high ground overlooking the beach on which the battery was situated. It was found to be undefended, and half a dozen men were made prisoner. No. 41 (Royal Marine) Commando and Brigade Headquarters landed ten minutes after No. 2 Commando against minor opposition and moved off according to the plan, some to Vietri and the majority to the defile of La Molina. Vietri provided no resistance, but the garrison of pill boxes in the narrow valley leading north towards La Molina, and a Mark IV German tank at a road bend, sought to resist the advance. The tank was at once attacked by the leading troop which killed the crew who were outside the tank, and the Commando pushed on.

Behind them the rest of No. 2 Commando with Brigade Headquarters moved into Vietri and established themselves in a German barracks "which bore all the signs of a hasty evacuation". Over everything was "that characteristic German smell . . . which pervades any house or room which they have occupied". Laycock, with Tom Churchill and his liaison officer, Philip Dunne, who had carried out the successful raid on the Twin Pimples from Tobruk, went forward to get into contact with Jack Churchill and his Commando. It was still dark but the sky was alight with white Very lights and the air full of challenges "as small parties of Commando soldiers passed each other carrying up ammunition and stores from the beach". On the way to the Commando, Brigade Headquarters ran into a German patrol. "Suddenly out of the road in front an enormous Hun rose up, muttering," says Tom Churchill. "In a flash, Baldwin, who was just in front of me, dropping him with two bullets in his stomach." His comrades were accounted for by a scratch team of signallers and batmen, but not before the Brigadier had had the satisfaction of firing his pistol. Jack Churchill produced a captured German Order dated only five days before, prophesying very accurately the manner in which the Commando would come ashore at Vietri. There followed detailed orders for dealing with the assault and, had the German garrison obeyed them, it must have cost No. 2 Commando very dear.

The rising sun shone down upon the yellow, pink, and white houses of Vietri village and on the green copper dome of the church. The place is remarkable for two viaducts which traverse the mouth of the defile; one is a modern construction, the other Roman work. No. 41 (Royal Marine) Commando seized them, after destroying a German tank, but for some days the Germans covered both with machine-gun fire. They then pushed on to the pass of La Molina.

In accordance with the plan, two troops of No. 2 Commando under Captain the Duke of Wellington and Captain Patric Henderson, were then sent by the Brigadier into the northern outskirts of Salerno. They soon reported the presence of enemy tanks in the town. Henderson ensconced himself at the window of a house with a Piat, and after waiting for a few minutes put two bombs into a German tank and jammed its turret.

The hours slipped by and presently came news that the 138th Brigade had successfully landed immediately to the south of Salerno but was held up on its eastern outskirts. About this time a wireless message was received at Laycock's headquarters ordering a counter-attack to retake Vietri at all cost. The Divisional Commander was informed that the village had never been lost, and it later transpired that the crews of the landing craft, when making their second trip to shore, had come under mortar fire. They abandoned the unloading of the Commandos' heavy kit which they had on board, and reported that the village was in the hands of the Germans. This faintheartedness was the cause of hardship and much discomfort to the Commandos, who might well have run short of food and ammunition, had not the stout-hearted maintenance parties on the main beaches been able to maintain supplies of both. That afternoon mortar fire fell upon Vietri and also upon La Molina.

A few British tanks arrived, but advanced no further than
La Molina, and presently withdrew through Vietri towards
Salerno.

By then Laycock and his officers at Brigade Headquarters were beginning to suspect that the situation on the
main beaches was not as satisfactory as it might be, and the
suspicion became a certainty when the Divisional Commander paid them a visit and told them to expect a delay in
their relief because severe opposition had been encountered at most of the main landing points. It was also
increasing hour by hour in the tall hills seized by the
two Commandos. Vietri was presently under fairly heavy
mortar fire. One of the bombs burst in the street just
outside Brigade Headquarters and grievously wounded
an Italian family. "It was a poignant sight to see Commando soldiers, grimed with battle, tenderly carrying to
the aid post three young Italian girls aged sixteen or
seventeen, their gay cotton frocks stained with blood from
serious abdominal wounds. They died later and their
relatives quietly carried them away."

In an effort to quell this mortar and machine-gun fire the
steep wooded slopes were searched with counter-fire, but
without much success. An officer of No. 41 (Royal Marine)
Commando went out to reconnoitre and was made prisoner.
For two hours he was held in an enemy observation post
skilfully concealed by the thick shrubs, until those manning
it withdrew for the night, taking him with them. On reaching a rocky patch, the Royal Marine officer, a ballet dancer
in peacetime, broke away and covered some twenty-five
yards in a series of huge bounds, making for cover. He was
hit in the leg, but was able to limp back to our lines when
darkness had fallen.

With nightfall came better news. A squadron of the 44th
Reconnaissance Regiment, part of the 138th Brigade, arrived. They had passed through Salerno with the help of
the two troops of No. 2 Commando still hanging on in its
western outskirts. Hopes were high that evening that the
next day would see the 46th Division streaming northwards
towards Naples.

The night of the 9th/10th September passed quietly. At

dawn the Reconnaissance Squadron reported the enemy to
be strongly entrenched across the pass. Some of his positions overlooked those held by No. 41 (Royal Marine)
Commando, which had laid mines on the road to thwart
any sudden move against them by German tanks now in
some force on the other side of the pass. The Reconnaissance Squadron was soon compelled to withdraw to Salerno, and Brigadier James arrived about breakfast time with
the news that the enemy were pressing him hard.

Shortly afterwards a heavy machine-gun team of Germans were seen moving near to the summit of the great hill
above Vietri. "They looked very sinister," says Tom
Churchill, "as they climbed round the cliff . . . and it
was obvious that unless we knocked them out they were
going to make our position untenable." Jack Churchill,
from the roof of his headquarters, was able to direct the fire
of Lieutenant Brunswick's 3-inch mortars upon them, and
the American mortar detachment also took a hand. Presently the Brigadier, looking through his field-glasses, "had
the satisfactory experience of seeing a Hun blown into the
air and crash to earth, a sprawling mass of arms and legs".
Most of the team, including its officer, an Austrian, were
killed or captured. Such an incident could not be ignored
and two troops from the reserve of half No. 2 Commando,
clambered up the precipitous slopes for 1300 feet and
established themselves near the top of the hill, where they
held on, though supplied only with the greatest difficulty.

Since matters were going so ill on the main beaches, the
battle remained stationary, and for the Commando in their
precarious positions upon the steep slopes above the sea this
meant that it had to be fought in a perpendicular rather than
a horizontal plane. The situation, though they did not know
it, was becoming critical; X Corps was struggling desperately to maintain itself. The appeals of Laycock, therefore,
for more troops so as to establish in this precipitous and
terraced land pickets a hundred yards apart – the only
certain method of preventing the infiltration of the enemy
– had to be disregarded. A company of Royal Engineers
was, however, sent to act as infantry support.

Throughout the morning of the 10th the Royal Marines

withstood repeated attempts to break through their positions in the defile. A few Germans slipped round their flank
but could accomplish little now that two troops of No. 2
Commando were in position on the hill above Vietri. On the
left, upon the hill where stands the village of Dragone, the
situation was relatively quiet, and the Troop of No. 2
Commando holding the position there had made contact
with the American Rangers who, it will be remembered,
had landed at Maiori. At 14.00 hours the Divisional General himself appeared and congratulated the Commandos
on the tenacity with which they were holding their positions. Half an hour later shells began to fall heavily on the
Royal Marine Commando, and a direct hit on headquarters
wounded Lumsden, its commanding officer, and his signals
officer, and put all the wireless sets out of action. Major J.R.
Edwards, the second-in-command, took over command.

Shortly before 17.00 hours on that day of blazing sunshine, A Troop of No. 41 (Royal Marine) Commando,
which had borne the brunt of the fight in the morning,
was once more heavily attacked, but was saved from anni-
hilation by Q Troop, which delivered a counter-attack
supported by a machine-gun most gallantly carried forward
by Sergeant D.C. Bullock and four men. The sergeant was
killed and the four men wounded, yet they set up their gun
and opened fire. But the left flank of the Commando was
still in a precarious position and it was realized that steps
would have to be taken to improve the situation before
darkness fell. Another appeal was therefore made to the
138th Brigade, and in response the 6th Lincolnshire Regiment arrived. Since its men did not know the ground, an
attack was carried out by No. 3 Troop of No. 2 Commando,
whose positions were taken over by a company of the
Lincolnshires. A section of tanks gave support and covering
fire; and, with great dash and determination, the Troop
secured a ridge to the left of the position which was thus
made secure. The counter-attack was completely successful.

Once more the night passed quietly. On the next day
reinforcements, but not reliefs, arrived in the persons of
two companies of the King's Own Yorkshire Light Infan-

try. They took up a position behind the all-important ridge on the left flank, and a Troop of No. 2 Commando went up to help No. 41 (Royal Marine) Commando hold on south of La Molina. The day passed without incident, and at dusk the welcome news arrived that the Commandos were to be relieved and to go into reserve in the narrow stretch of shore between Vietri and Salerno. The relief was completed by midnight.

Hopes that they had now played their part and could therefore be withdrawn dwindled soon after the morning of 12th September broke above that green but far from pleasant land. The enemy began a series of attacks of which the object was obviously to retake Salerno and then Vietri. They were held, but with nothing to spare, and at 08.30 hours the Commandos were moving once more back to their old positions after a rest of – for most of them – less than eight hours. No. 41 (Royal Marine) Commando again held the valley south of La Molina and the hills to the right of it, and No. 2 Commando occupied the hills immediately to the north of Vietri. By now the effect of casualties was beginning to be felt, and the Commandos were thinner on the ground. No. 41 (Royal Marine) Commando had lost eleven officers and seventy-four other ranks, No. 2 Commando one officer and thirty-three other ranks. There were, therefore, but 619 officers and men, all told, to hold this vital position. The 138th Brigade had no reserves but could still produce artillery and mortar fire. Naval support which had proved invaluable in checking the numerous German counter-attacks, was no longer available.

Fortunately the German attacks died away by mid-morning, and the rest of 12th September passed uneventfully. At dawn the next day the enemy made a supreme effort. A heavy barrage of mortar and artillery fire was put down on No. 2 Commando, and an attack launched against its centre and both flanks. The two forward troops were at that time out of touch with headquarters, and the two troops on the right soon lost their leaders. It seemed that the steep hill of Dragone was being overrun. The enemy were past the village and were firing on the rear of the main position.

Captain Brian Lees (Royal Army Medical Corps), the medical officer, had established his regimental aid post in a small stone hut near Commando headquarters which, owing to the speed of the enemy's advance, had had to withdraw in haste. The doctor was attending some twenty wounded at the time and did not notice what had happened. Having finished his immediate work on those in the post, he went to the door and, looking out, saw two German soldiers twenty yards away with their backs to him. He shut the door quickly and broke this unwelcome news to the medical orderlies but said nothing to his patients. He remained there unmolested and undetected until four hours later the Commandos returned, having won back the ground by a successful counter-attack.

That day saw the climax of the battle. For some time it seemed that the German thrust must penetrate the tenacious guard of the Commandos. They were clinging to the monstrously steep hillside with no prospect of reinforcements, and with nothing behind them but the village and sea. Nothing, except the guns. They belonged to the 71st Field Regiment of the Royal Artillery and were most ably directed by Lieutenant Shingleton. Their fire checked the enemy. Jack Churchill, with a soldier's eye, saw his opportunity and took it. At the critical moment he launched a counter-attack with one troop of No. 41 (Royal Marine) Commando and one troop of No. 2 Commando, the only reserves available. It was gallantly led by Major Richard Lawrie, who fell at the head of his men. His place was at once taken by Captain the Duke of Wellington, who with Major Edwards, led the charge and drove the enemy out of their positions. By noon they were retiring behind a smoke screen.

This counter-attack on Dragone hill proved decisive, and the mauled Germans retreated to the Pass. They had no further stomach for a fight with the gallant remnants of the two Commandos. Remnants was indeed the word, for 117 more men had fallen, 45 of No. 41 (Royal Marine) Commando and 72 of No. 2. Among them, in addition to Major Lawrie, were the three Troop leaders, Captain R. Broome, Captain F. Mason, and Lieutenant A. Brunswick.

The Commandos could do no more; but no more was necessary.

That night they were withdrawn and billeted a bare mile from the front line, in houses on the cliff road running between Vietri and Salerno. The houses, however, nestled beneath the steep cliff and no fire could be brought to bear upon them. The men passed the hours watching the German batteries of multiple mortars pitch as many as forty-eight bombs at a time into the harbour of Salerno, thus preventing the Navy from using the port and interfering with, but not putting a stop to, the Commando bathing parties. At night in the bright moonlight small patrols of Germans still penetrated into Salerno and opened fire upon anyone seen moving in the streets. Sentries were posted "in the shadows of the porches and up at the windows" of the billets, and the resting Commandos remained undisturbed. No. 41 (Royal Marine) Commando received a reinforcement of forty-eight men; and one officer and fourteen other ranks of No. 2 Commando, missing from a patrol, reached the Commando, having slipped through the lines of the enemy. These unexpected arrivals put fresh heart into the weary men. Unknown to them, the climax of the main battle, to which they had contributed so much, was at hand, for the enemy were making that day, the 14th, a supreme effort to fling the Allies into the sea.

Twenty-four hours' rest was little enough, but it sufficed, and the late afternoon of the 15th found them ready to respond to an order which was to take them away from Vietri and La Molina, scene of their stubborn defence, to the village of Mercatello, two and a half miles to the southwest, whence they were to deliver an equally stubborn attack on the other side of Salerno. Here they came under the orders of the 167th Brigade, whose brigadier was facing a perilous situation immediately to the north-east. The country inland from the flat meadows and marshes behind the sand of the beaches, becomes steeper and three prominent hills overlooked the Allied positions. A narrow winding lane runs from Mercatello towards them till it reaches Pigoletti, some three miles away. Like La Molina, this village is dominated by two steep hills, and to the east a high, nameless crag, soon to be christened Forty-One Commando Hill, frowns down upon the road. Pigoletti itself lies in a small valley beyond which is a ridge running north-east to south-west and connecting two high points; the one to the north-east was soon known as the Pimple, the one to the south-west as Whitecross Hill. The enemy were in possession of the village of Pigoletti and the three hills. These, said the Brigadier, and the village, had to be re-captured at any cost.

No. 41 (Royal Marine) Commando advanced immedi-ately to the attack of the hill to which it was soon to give its name. It was captured with the loss of one man killed and two wounded. The Commando consolidated its position, and no counter-attack developed. This was the one occasion throughout the fierce Salerno battle that a Commando found the task entrusted to it easier to perform than had been expected.

While No. 41 was thus engaged, No. 2 Commando prepared to advance up a thickly wooded valley inter-spersed with vines growing along steep terraces at the end of which stood the village of Pigoletti. At 18.30 hours, an hour after No. 41 had begun their attack, they moved off in six columns. The night was dark, for the moon was not yet up, and each troop shouted "Commando, Commando!" every five minutes. This shouting and the noise made by the men and the rattle of Tommy-gun fire unnerved the enemy.

At the head of the Commando was their colonel, Jack Churchill, sword in hand. He was on the right flank with No. 6 Troop under Lieutenant J.E.C. Nicholl, which, more fortunate than the others, had found a road leading to the objective. The Troop in consequence advanced faster than the rest, and Churchill with Corporal Fussell outdistanced everyone. The two men moved silently forward till, a short distance to their right, they heard the sound of digging. Churchill halted the Troop, and finding a footpath leading straight uphill to Pigoletti, thus cutting off a bend, went on alone with the corporal. Entering the village street they heard no sound save the chink of spades and picks, but presently in an archway giving on to a courtyard they saw the glow of a cigarette. Churchill crept along the wall till he could see the outlines of two German sentries, of whom one was smoking. As he made to attack, an Italian approached and asked the Germans to come in for a drink. The three men made off across the courtyard; the minutes passed and presently the sentries were heard coming back. As they reached the archway they were met by a fierce man in British battledress brandishing a sword and shouting *"Hände hoch!"* They obeyed with trembling haste, and Churchill was about to give them further orders when he perceived a large German mortar in the middle of the courtyard with, round it, its crew sleeping. "Come here, corporal," whispered Churchill into the night, and when Fussell came up, ordered him to keep the two sentries covered with his Tommy gun. Churchill then advanced upon the crew of the mortar, now beginning to stir, and, adopting the tactics that had already been so successful, demanded their surrender at the sword point. Fuddled with sleep and fear ten of them raised their hands. They were at once covered by Corporal Fussell and his Tommy gun, and Churchill, hastening back, led No. 6 Troop into the village. He then chose one of his prisoners and, taking him with him, visited each German sentry in turn. When challenged, the prisoner gave the password, Churchill flourished his sword, and the sentry surrendered. This process was repeated until Mad Jack had collected between thirty and forty prisoners and captured a regimental aid post intact. He ordered the Germans to carry their arms, their wounded, their mortar, and their ammunition back down the road to Mercatello. They trudged off, too occupied with heavy loads or too bemused to attempt resistance. For his deed that night Churchill was admitted to the Distinguished Service Order. When subsequently the Divisional General asked him why he carried a sword, he replied in his shrill voice: "In my opinion, sir, any officer who goes into action without his sword is improperly dressed."

No. 4 Troop took thirty-five prisoners in very similar circumstances, having had to advance over very difficult country full of "pits and holes" to do so. Like his colonel, Captain Hemming, their commander, was well in advance with his batman. They reached a belt of dark trees, and hearing a voice speaking German, Hemming shouted "*Hände Hoch!*" the only German words he knew. The German came forward and surrendered, together with three of his comrades. Delighted by this unexpected good fortune, Hemming was about to return to his troop when a fourth German ran out with his hands up, followed by a fifth and a sixth, until within a very short space of time he was surrounded by thirty-five of the enemy. They were all talking at once and all trying to press their individual surrender upon him. Hemming shouted for reinforcements and began removing the Germans' steel helmets. His troop came up and all was well.

The prisoners said later that the noise made by No. 2 Commando as it went shouting through the darkness and the vines was so great that it seemed to them that at least a division was upon them. Altogether in this triumphant action No. 2 Commando captured 136 prisoners, more at that date than the whole 46th Division had been able to send to their cages.

In accordance with orders, the Commando, having swept the valley, returned to its start line at midnight. But for the brave, as for the wicked, there is no rest. They were immediately given the order "about turn". Since no other troops were available, they were now required not only to hold Pigoletti, but also to seize the hill behind upon which the Germans had established a number of strong points.

The moon had now risen, and in its light they made their way to the outskirts of the village. Here the Germans began to show fight, but the little place was stormed and the Commando got in touch with their comrades of the Royal Marines on the right. Captain the Duke of Wellington then led two troops towards the second objective, the Pimple. He was met almost at once with withering machine-gun fire and a hail of grenades and was killed, together with many of his men. "He had fought like a lion," said one who was with him at the time, "through all those bitter days," and had worthily sustained a great name. The survivors fell back to the village. Courage alone could not take the hill.

The next morning both Commandos were much galled by the fire of 88-mm guns. To maintain supplies was very difficult, for much of the way was under fire. The most urgent call was for oil to maintain the automatic weapons and rifles in good working order, and is an indication of the spirit of the Commando and of the unceasing use to which they put their weapons.

In the afternoon it was decided that No. 41 (Royal Marine) Commando should make a night attack upon the Pimple, to start at 02.00 hours on the morning of 17th September. The men were very exhausted, but as determined as ever. When forming up in silence, Marine Blake of P Troop was suddenly seen to beat his chest and throw himself violently to the ground, while there issued from him an odd ringing sound. It came from a large and decorative alarm clock which he had found in Salerno and lodged in the blouse of his battledress.

As they were about to move off, heavy artillery fire fell upon the Commando. Major Edwards, in command, fell mortally wounded, and many of his men suffered a like fate. What heightened the catastrophe was that the fire came not from the enemy but from our own guns which had mistaken their target. In fairness to the gunners it must be recorded that, having just arrived in the area, only one of their batteries had had time to register. This terrible mistake proved fatal to success, though one troop succeeded in reaching the top of the Pimple, driving the enemy from it and occupying it. There they remained until 10.00 hours on the 17th, when the six of them who were left were withdrawn under cover of a smoke screen.

By now both Commandos were much exhausted; but help was at hand. The British and American mortar detachments, which had been with them at Vietri and La Molina arrived from that area and at once put down a heavy barrage upon the Germans. At first it was returned, but gradually the enemy's fire decreased. So matters stood for another twenty-four hours, during which a second and equally unsuccessful attack was made on the Pimple, this time by an infantry brigade. Not until the 19th did it fall into our hands, when it was occupied without a fight and found to be strewn with dead Germans. By then the two Commandos had at last been relieved.

The battle of Salerno was a grievous, glorious fight. At one time so critical had been the situation that the ships of the Royal Navy were put at fifteen minutes' notice to re-embark the troops. It was on the 16th September that matters finally turned in favour of the Allies, and three days later Goebbels was writing bitterly in his diary that "what the (German) Army did at Salerno was an outstanding scandal." In saying this he was unjust. The Germans had fought most stoutly. They had been vanquished in the end by the gallantry of the whole Fifth Army, and no units shone more brightly than No. 2 Commando and No. 41 (Royal Marine) Commando.

First at La Molina and Vietri, and then at Pigoletti they had stood firm when the situation was desperate and their own condition one of extreme fatigue, and they had conquered. "Such is their spirit," wrote the General Officer Commanding the 46th Division afterwards, "that it triumphed over all weakness of the flesh, and they got to close quarters with marked – and indeed awful – effect upon the Boche." The price paid was high: 367 killed, wounded, or missing, or 48 per cent of the 738 officers and men who had landed at Marina. Those who survived returned to Sicily. Those who did not found honoured graves upon the battlefield.

> Cowards die many times before their deaths;
> The valiant never taste of death but once.

Of course, by the time of La Molina, the Royal Marine Commandos' green beret was a source of pride not embarrassment. After Italy, the much expanded Royal Marine Commandos were committed to, among other campaigns, Normandy, Holland, the Adriatic, Germany and Burma.

Unlike most wartime special forces, the RM Commandos survived the outbreak of peace. Indeed, from 1945 onwards all Royal Marines, with the exception of the

RM Band Service, have been trained as commandos. Presently, the RM operational units comprise Nos 40, 42 and 45 Commando groups, each containing some 650 men. There is also a signal squadron, a raiding squadron, a logistics regiment, and an air defence troop.

THE LOFOTEN RAID

Evan John

*June 1940. France had fallen and the threat of invasion
hung palpably over Britain itself.*

*Most British minds were concentrated on defence. Not
that of Lieutenant Colonel Dudley Clarke (Royal Artillery), however. Recalling the guerilla campaign of the
Spanish against Napoleon and T.E. Lawrence's Arab
Revolt in Palestine, Clarke convinced the Chief of the
Imperial General Staff that small bands of highly
trained men could and should strike offensively at the
enemy. The CIGS, in his turn, convinced Churchill of
the commando concept. Churchill himself ordered that a
special department at the War Office, Section M09, was
created to deal with Clarke's scheme. Clarke himself was
its first leader.*

*Clarke's immediate problem, of where to find the men
for his new force, was easily solved. Ten independent
companies had been raised earlier in the year to fight the
Germans in Norway; it was from these independent
companies that Nos 1 and 2 Commandos were formed,
whilst other commando units were formed from volunteers
throughout the Army.*

*The honour of undertaking the first British commando
action of the war went to No. 11 Commando, under
Major Ronnie Todd. This took place on 23/24 June
1940, only days after the Commandos had been founded.
No. 11 Commando had little training, little equipment
(they had to borrow Tommy guns and beach landing
craft) and absolutely no idea of what to expect when they
landed in the Le Touquet-Boulogne area of occupied*

*France. They went anyway. The damage inflicted by No.
11 Commando was negligible – but the effect on British
morale was enormous. No. 11 Commando showed that the
bulldog still had bite. The Commandos were overwhelmed
with applications to join.*

*The next commando raid, on Guernsey, was a fiasco,
causing even Churchill – a keen convert to the commando
concept – to order, "Let there be no more Guernseys!" It
was at this juncture that M09 decided that the Nazis
should be dealt a definite blow rather than a pin-prick.
Accordingly a mass commando raid was ordered. The
target was the Lofoten Islands, Norway, from where the
Germans imported the bulk of the fish oil they used to
manufacture glycerine, a vital ingredient in explosives.
Leading the raid, codenamed Operation Claymore, in
March 1941 was Brigadier J.C. Haydon; with him went
52 Royal Engineers, 500 commandos, and a unit of
Norwegian soldiers. Among the Commandos was Bom-
bardier Evan John who described the raid in a extended
letter of running commentary to his wife.*

SUNDAY

S TILL MILD, and not very rough.
    We were told all about it last night. The objective is
two towns in the Lofoten Islands, Stamsund in Vestvagöy
and Svolvaer in Ostvagöy. Our unit is for the latter, our
platoon is to land on a strip of islets across the harbour from
the main town (3,000 inhabitants) and our job, principally,
is to blow up a Cod Liver factory (presumably because it is
in competition with some influential London firm!). We
also have to search for local quislings and invite recruits for
Norwegian Navy and Merchant Marine. Incidentally we
kill or (if possible) capture any German occupying troops.
    If our secret has been reasonably well kept, the latter
should be very few, and the whole business should be rather
a tame little jaunt. If they have had a day or more's warning,
it might be pretty good hell.

As I said somewhere earlier in this interminable letter, I think we made a fairly clear get-away from Riccarton, leaving its inhabitants in resentful ignorance of our destination. I'd trust *nobody* to keep his mouth shut. One man with us hadn't set foot on land for half an hour (for the first time since leaving Dunbeath), before he started telling a soldier there that we were going to attack Norway. The said soldier was one of a party due for leave this week, so that *he* could go home and tell everyone in England. I expect they'll get their leave stopped or delayed: our man is being put on fatigue in the cook's galley and not allowed to land for the show.

Some parties are definitely going to distribute coffee, food and clothes to the good people of Svolvaer, but I wonder if that will altogether atone for our blowing up the factory that is presumably their livelihood, throwing many of them out of work and spoiling the cod liver market, which may be the principal support of the fisher-folk all along that coast.

Let us hope they will be sufficiently philosophic or patriotic to say "*Krig er Krig*" – War is War – and not blame the brutal English too much. But I'd like to hear Lord Haw-Haw on bloody Churchill starving Norway of her innocent trade, and babies of their cod liver oil!

My Norwegian sailor is emphatic – perhaps a trifle too emphatic – about all Norway being enthusiastically anti-German and groaning under the yoke of a few quislings. I hope he's right.

Our orders include the (if possible) release of the British Vice-Consul and the (if possible) capture of a German University Professor at present making a lecture tour of the Lofotens!

A propos – I wonder what Lord Haw-Haw has said, or will have to say, about our occupation of Iceland. I'm afraid he'd say that it is likely to last longer than the War, and that our dear allies the Danes can say good-bye to it for good. A hundred years ago, our dear allies the Dutch (whose country was overrun by Napoleon as Denmark is now by Hitler) had to say good-bye to several of their colonies when peace came again. I've just been telling Major Talbot on deck an

amusing story in that connection: it has left a queer re-
minder of itself in the Hymn Book. Have you ever wondered why the otherwise metrical hymn contains the most
un-metrical couplet?:

> What though the spicy breezes
> Blow soft o'er Ceylòn's isle?

Well, I can tell you. When Napoleon, as aforesaid, overran
Holland, we took the opportunity to occupy the whole
Dutch Empire – Java, Sumatra, the Cape, Ceylon, etc.
While we were in occupation, the hymnographer wrote:

> What though the spicy breezes
> Blow soft o'er Java's isle?

which, as your musical ear will tell you, makes perfect
scansion. Peace came, and (since their riches were not
yet discovered) we handed Java and Sumatra back to the
Dutch. We *did* not hand back the Cape or Ceylon: Ceylon
was too convenient an annexe to India. Then there was a
new edition of *Hymns Ancient and Modern*. The editors
naturally asked the question: "Should Englishmen, even
when worshipping the God who created all things, be asked
to sing about an island that is no longer within the limits of
the British Empire?" And they (also naturally) answered:
"Perish the thought!" So, in defiance of metre, the line was
altered to:

> Blows soft o'er CeyLON's isle?

I wonder whether there will be a similar tale to tell of
Iceland.

No, I am not a Little Englander, a cynic, or a vilifier of
my own country, which, with all her faults, remains the
greatest and best country in this sorry world. I merely try to
see things as they are, and (I fear) must always be. For it *is* a
very sorry world, and Imperialism is one of its sorriest
phenomena. But no one will be more pleased than I if a new
and more enlightened Treaty of Versailles returns Iceland

to the Danes, and even Cyprus to the Greeks.

As you know, I study Thucydides, admire his view of politics, and his unhesitating acceptance of the fact that men in the mass, men organised into states and empires, behave in a robberish way that would make man the individual blush: and I doubt if things have essentially altered since Thucydides described the Imperialism of Athens – or Isaiah that of the Assyrians! Christianity, for all the immense changes it has made, hardly seems to have modified the great game of International Grab. And I'm quite sure that "Progress" as worshipped by H.G. Wells & Co. is quite incapable of doing so.

Just had a refreshing talk with Major Talbot, who prides himself (quite rightly) on the "Security"* of this expedition. I told him that the night before we moved from Riccarton I went down to get really authentic information from official sources – i.e., from the barmaid of the Berwick Arms – about where we were going next day. She beckoned me close and whispered in my ear: "As a matter of fact, I *do* know exactly what's happening. You are going to Dover."

The Major also talked about the general policy of the expedition, the not entering of private houses, the leaving of compensation for all damage done, etc.

It is a relief, as you can imagine, to be on a venture planned on these sort of lines. Would you believe that some of the men are grumbling at our taking food and clothes to Norwegians? "Why shouldn't *we* have them?" they ask. The answer is double and should, one would say, be decisive.

1. Because the giving of them to Norwegians is part of a policy that may shorten the War by months.

2. Because you men have so much food and so many clothes and "comforts" that you waste and throw them away by the bucketful.

Major Talbot says he is a little afraid that the Nazis may shoot a woman or two in our wake, photograph the results and publish the pictures as evidence of English atrocities. I hope he is exaggerating, or taking a newspaper view of Nazi

---

* That is the Army term for what normal people call "Secrecy".

methods. It could be only guesswork. But what a world we live in, where such guesses are made in anticipation!

I am told I missed a wonderful display of "Northern Lights" last night. I must hope for a repetition to-night.

It has been rather lovely for part of to-day. Deep blue water, bright blue sky, and clear sunlight. We are going a goodish speed but not rolling or pitching a quarter as much as we did yesterday.

I had a beastly dream last night – that I was reading a telegram to say that you had been badly injured in an air-raid and were hoping I could come and see you in a London hospital. It is a good thing I am not superstitious, and that my contempt for psycho-analysis doesn't extend to disbelief in its most obvious proposition – that suppressed anxieties become the realities of dreamtime.

It is somehow rather flattering, as well as comforting to go out on deck and see our escort of men-o'-war humming along around us. But I haven't seen a seal yet!

MONDAY 12 NOON

To-morrow is the day of landing. The time 06.45, three-quarters of an hour before Arctic dawn. They are serving out the rifle ammunition now, the grenades (which are filthy dangerous things) not till the last moment.

I don't feel at all Arctic, having missed my seals and my Northern Lights. It is now misty and drizzly outside (which is what we want – aeroplanes being our chief and perhaps only danger). But is often as misty and drizzly in England, and it is no colder than I've known it often there.

Now I must get my ammunition.

5.30

Last daylight before attack. Last daylit preparations. Sailors tapping and testing davits. Colonel Elström is inspecting Norskers with their *ruksaks* full of soap, cigarettes, coffee, etc. His *Inspektjon* interrupts a conversation I was having with a very nice middle-aged Norwegian, and also a game of chess I was playing with my handsome young sailor. I jot down the state of the game, and try to tell him, in faltering and inaccurate Norsk, the story of the two French officers in Napoleon's army: they began a game of chess in Moscow in 1812; it was interrupted by the order to retreat from the burning city; one of them wrote down the state of the game on the back of an old envelope, saying, "We'll finish it when we meet again"; they didn't meet again till after the Retreat (and what a Retreat! Close on half a million souls dying of wounds, hunger, frostbite or drowning in the Beresine); but they did run across each other in a Berlin café next spring, and one of them pulled out his old envelope, reset the game, and insisted on finishing it. I tell my Norwegian that we shall do the same, but after our Advance, in some kaffe-hus in Oslo.

Unfortunately, I have already spoilt the whole business. I have lost the bit of paper on which I wrote the position down!

It also occurs to me that if there are to be explosions to-morrow, and Norwegian civilians to be moved out of the danger zone, I had better know the Norsk way of saying: "For your own safety." A sailor supplies it. "For din egen sikkerhet," if I'm spelling it right. I like "sikker" for "safe" or "sure". It reminds me of Bruce's "make siccar".

It is clearing up a little. Fresher, but not at all cold. Things begin to get exciting.

Well, we've all been waiting for this since last August and now it's come, we are all glad. Maybe it's a good thing that our first venture is likely to be a tame one. And perhaps it won't be! Too excited and interested to be at all frightened.

Overnight shave and wash – cold water, Arctic Circle, but no discomfort. Feel very fit. Must now say good night.

I am getting too fond of this unconscionably long letter to like the prospect of having to destroy it on the altar of "Security". I may have to. If I don't, here it is – the record of gradual approach to possible battle as felt by one who has never yet seen a man die, never even seen a dead man.

Of course I'm not taking it ashore. We're not allowed to

take any written papers ashore, for fear of death or capture. But I am taking ashore my Army Book 156 (blank) in case I get a few moments to scribble something down.

TUESDAY 5.15 (SCRIBBLED IN BOAT)

It is just light enough to write. We are packed sardine-wise and half asleep, being embarked in more than enough time. It is calm and clear twilight. In spite of the latitude, season of the year and early morning hour. I don't need gloves, though in an open boat at sea!

We are beginning to move in earnest. I can see nothing except a saxe-blue sky, a gull, and occasionally the mast-heads of the man-of-war leading us.

Some spray coming in which is cold!

Whole silhouette of man-of-war. She is slowing down and we are passing her. I have seldom seen anything so dramatic and beautiful – every spar and rope clean-cut against the blue, every man standing rigid and motionless at his gun or instrument.

ON LAND SVOLVAER

Bang-banging everywhere. Presumably demolition, plus (?) men-o'-war sinking German trawlers.

A perfectly lovely morning. Beautiful little mountain peaks, pink in sunlight, round a rather picturesque little town.

8.00 A.M. (for address, see reverse side of page.)

Guarding half-wrecked office.

Sapper has put one charge of explosive on safe and made a hole in it. But safe still resists and he has gone for more H.E. We don't want sappers so much as burglars!

No Germans this side of water. Must be dead or captured t'other side, because crowd is parading with Norwegian flag, cheering, etc.

09.00 A.M.

The safe is being a b—y nuisance. I don't know the Norsk for sledge-hammer so have drawn this for a Norwegian,

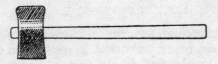

and made him produce required sledge-hammer to batter door.

Meanwhile the sapper is prizing it with a whale-harpoon harpoon head!

10.00

Safe open. Little of interest. £5 worth of notes and coppers – to be returned to firm. Fine blaze in adjoining factory and yard.

We have captured one German soldier, a nasty-looking little twerp in a green uniform; he is smiling sheepishly and seems rather pleased to be captured. Officer has taken camera from him and is photographing fire.

Large crowd of Norsk children collecting. Much fraternisation.

It *has* been very tame. Little danger now unless from air, or torpedo on return.

12.00

Back on S.S. *Domino* with many recruits for Norsk army and navy in England, 100–200 prisoners, mainly sailors, but one flying officer and some soldiers. All objectives achieved. One casualty on our side – an officer has wounded himself with his own revolver. So it has been a mere tea party for us, and all the heroics look a little silly.

4.00

All, or nearly all, is over. Norway is invisible to the left (PORT!). The last of the Lofotens sliding past on the right (STARBOARD!), looking like gigantic fairy icebergs in the evening sun.

When I say "nearly all" there are still torpedoes and (for an hour or two of daylight still) aeroplanes. *Apropos* of the latter, I've just had a nasty false alarm. I had been handing back the last of our ammunition to the powder magazine through a manhole in the floor; round me some men were engaged on the very ticklish business of extracting fuses from hand grenades, on an extremely crowded mess deck. I had barely left it to go above when I heard a loud explosion and rushed back, expecting to find the place a shambles. They were still quietly un-fusing grenades and the bang was one of our anti-aircraft guns firing at a single German plane.

This has now vanished, and the sky is clear.

Speaking of crowded mess decks – we were not too badly off on the voyage out, better than on the *Ludo*. We have now a lot of prisoners (the officers, naval and air force, looking like ridiculous stiff caricatures of Nazis, in impossibly starched uniforms), soldiers, airmen, the rest German mercantile marine and Norsk quislingites. We have also some 100 Norsk recruits for the loyal navy and army. We are turned off our mess deck to make room for the prisoners; are supposed to eat (50 of us) where another 50 men were and are still eating, and to sleep in a passage entrance to the officers' mess. No other solution, and no one to blame, except the prisoners for letting themselves be caught!

Well, it has been far and away the most interesting, lively and instructive half-day of my whole life. I can hardly believe it is only this morning, admittedly early this morning, that we were looking up at that gloriously silhouetted warship and then gliding silently into the still unsuspecting harbour of Svolvaer. I only wish I had had time to scribble down some more impressions on the spot. Of two main pictures in my mind one is of that rather pokey but pleasant little office where I had to search for papers and get into the safe (I wish I could describe to you the lovely old photos on the wall, the super-Ibsen leading characters who founded the cod liver oil factory in eighteen-umpty-eight, and grew real Tirpitz side-whiskers while doing so: their monumental dignity was much disturbed by the sapper's operations with H.E., which cracked all their glass and jumped their gilt frames askew). The other is of the yards outside, the rows and tiers of hop-poles for drying out fish, and the factory itself, with odd bits of its machinery suddenly jumping skywards, twisting and swooping down again, as the sappers did their various explosions. I could not help feeling sorry for the *Maskinist* (Engineer, as we should say) who stood by with a very glum face, while his nurslings leapt through holes in the roof and clattered down many yards away; he, too, was pure Ibsen in all but costume – minor character, shall we say, in Act II of a hitherto undiscovered tragedy by the Master, entitled DEMOLIT-JON? Or shall I go back to my first impression of all, when I and two privates jumped out of the boat, scrambled up snow in the pink dawn and ran into the warehouse where Norwegian fishermen were slowly and deliberately piling fish? They stared at us, ox-like, for some minutes. I wondered if they were going to do any of the obvious things – shout, or go to a telephone, or cheer us, or curse us, or pack up and go home. They did the one thing I didn't expect. They continued to stare for some minutes, as though wondering who these odd creatures in khaki fancy dress could be; then they began slowly and deliberately to pile fish again.

The Lofotens raid was an unmitigated success. The fish-oil factories were devastated, eleven merchant ships were sunk, 216 prisoners were taken, and scores of Norwegian volunteers brought back to Britain to fight for the Allied cause.

STORM IN THE FJORD

Graeme Cook

Such was the success of the Lofotens raid of March 1941 (see preceding chaper), that British commandos determined to strike at another target in occupied Norway: the island of Vaagso. This time, however, the target was known to be heavily defended.

The codename for the Vaagso attack was "Archery". It was appropriate, for at Vaagso – even more than the Lofotens – the newly minted British Commandos hit the bullseye. Few commando raids have had such a profound effect on the course of a war, or on the practice of special warfare itself.

T HE ISLAND OF Vaagso lies at the mouth of the long, narrow Nordfjord, which cuts inland for 70 miles from the North Sea and is one of the most splendid and breathtaking of all the Norwegian fjords. It resembles a slender finger of water, pointing in from the wild North Sea deep inland between towering granite cliffs which rise almost sheer from the water's edge. The water of the fjord is placid and calm, in sharp contrast to the often wild and tempestuous sea that separates Britain from Norway. The immediate countryside along the reaches of the fjords has a rugged and majestic beauty which overawes those who have had the good fortune to witness its splendour. Before the outbreak of the Second World War thousands of tourists plied the still, calm waters in a variety of craft, drinking in the splendour of that fjord.

With the coming of the Second World War and the eventual fall of Norway to the Germans, the fjords which punctuate the rugged coastline of Norway took on a new importance. They provided the German Navy with a vital haven for its ships. The hundreds of islands dotted along the coastline made an ideal screen for the German merchant ships which slipped between them and the mainland to ferry the vital supplies of fish-oil to Germany out of sight of the British fleet which virtually ruled the waves in the North Sea. These German freighters and tankers could sail these inshore waters with almost complete impunity, free from the danger of submarine attack, for the bed of these inshore waters was rugged and hazardous and almost unnavigable by underwater craft.

At strategic points along the coast there were heavy German batteries, which could play havoc with British ships if they penetrated those inshore waters and tried to stop the trafficking of these enemy ships. There was therefore only one other way of effectively cutting off Hitler's supplies of fish-oil, and that was to cut it off at source, attacking and destroying the factories where it was produced.

To launch an amphibious attack on the Vaagso area was a formidable proposition by any standards. Unlike the Lofotens, Vaagso was heavily defended and garrisoned by 150 infantry troops, 100 men of the labour corps and around 50 sailors of the German Navy. On the tiny island of Maaloy, which lay opposite the town of South Vaagso in the stretch of water known as Ulvesund, there was a battery of four guns which covered Vaagsfjord, as well as a searchlight and an anti-aircraft gun. The guns were 12.5 cm cannon which had been captured from the French during the German invasion in the West. Covering the northern entrance to Ulvesund was a mobile battery of 105 mm guns based at the town of Halsoer. They were used to give cover to German ships forming up there. To add further hazard to any would-be attackers, there were armed German trawlers which escorted shipping through the narrow stretches of water between the island of Vaagso and the mainland.

Just south of the town of South Vaagso itself was an

infantry strongpoint which consisted of batteries of automatic weapons stoutly protected by barbed wire entanglements. The Germans had sited this particular battery very well, positioning it on the top of a low cliff which fell sheer to the water.

But perhaps the major menace for the commandos was the threat of attack from the air. The enemy had three airfields within striking distance of Vaagso. They were at Herdla, Stavanger and Trondheim, but aircraft operating from the latter two airfields would have to refuel at Herdla if they were to operate successfully over Vaagso.

Unlike the raid on the Lofotens, the attackers were to be faced with formidable opposition if they were to achieve their objective, which was to blow up the fish-oil factories, destroy the enemy garrison, sink as much shipping as possible and round up more quislings, capture enemy code books and documents and bring Norwegian volunteers back to Britain.

Because of the variety of aims laid down for the raid, and in particular the weight and type of opposition likely to be encountered, it was obvious to the planners that all three services would have to be involved. Indeed this would be the first truly combined operation where the army, navy and air force would each have to play a vital role.

Since there would be a heavy naval and army commitment in the raid, it was decided to appoint joint force commanders to co-ordinate the efforts of the participating land and sea forces. To lead the naval contingent, Mountbatten appointed Rear Admiral Harold Burrough, a naval officer noted for his ability to remain absolutely calm in the heat of the fiercest actions. The man chosen as Burrough's counterpart was Brigadier Haydon, who would draw his commandos from the Special Service Brigade.

Haydon had already proved his skill as a commander during the raid on the Lofotens, but now his keen eye for detail in planning and an ability to handle men was to be tested to the limit. Haydon had first won fame and distinction in 1940 for the part he played in arranging the escape of the Dutch royal family and senior members of the Netherlands government from Holland. As a result of the success of this mission he was admitted to the Distinguished Service Order.

Haydon reasoned that to pull off the Vaagso raid successfully he would need one full Commando and elements of some others to carry out the assault. This in itself gave him a problem. He knew that all the commandos were up to the task but he was fully aware that those who would have to be left out would not take kindly to their exclusion. Nevertheless the choice had to be made and after due deliberation he selected No. 3 Commando, under John Durnford-Slater's command, and No. 2 Commando to provide the major support elements.

Among the men of the commandos there was a tremendous loyalty to their individual groups; it was therefore with considerable pride that Durnford-Slater heard of Haydon's decision to use his Commando, and he launched himself into the herculean task of pre-raid preparation with vigour and enthusiasm.

No. 3 Commando had among it some of the cream of all the special service forces. When Durnford-Slater had picked his officers he had done so with caution, taking careful note of their individual qualities. It is as well that he did, for when the testing time came, as will be seen when they "hit the beach" at Vaagso, they were to show that they were made of the right stuff. They possessed the exceptional qualities of courage and individuality which are vital to the success of any commando operation.

Durnford-Slater's second-in-command was to be Major Jack Churchill, MC, a military eccentric of the sort who, during the war years, enriched the British Army with their volatile characteristics and gave it a quality found in no other army in the world. Even by that time Churchill, nicknamed "Mad Jack" because of his eccentricities, had made a name for himself. He had the habit of going to war with a weird assortment of weapons, not the least of which was a set of bagpipes on which he would play a prelude to the battle, doubtless inspiring his men but giving the German enemy a rude awakening. Among his arsenal of weapons he was known to arm himself with was a crossbow with which he would attempt to "bag" a German or two. But in the truest tradition of the British warrior, Churchill chose a mighty broad-hilted claymore as his constant companion in battle.

Churchill won the Military Cross during the British Army's retreat to Dunkirk. He is said to have arrived in the town on a bike, puffing and panting after a hair-raising ride, clutching his crossbow.

The story is told that later in the war "Mad Jack" captured more than thirty Germans in a single night by frightening the life out of them. He would creep up on them in the darkness, then leap out of cover brandishing his claymore and yelling "Hände hoch!" He presented a fearsome sight, screaming at the height of his voice and wielding his sword, bringing them to instant surrender. The Germans must have thought that some demon from the depths of hell had been cast upon them. His action that night won him admission to the Distinguished Service Order. He was both courageous and completely unpredictable, which made him a force to be reckoned with as far as the enemy was concerned.

No. 3 Commando's signals officer was Lieutenant Charley Head, a close and old friend of Durnford-Slater's, who was renowned as one of the greatest "scroungers" in the British Army, a considerable asset to any unit. Charley Head hailed from Cornwall and was a tall, outstanding man who was to show great courage at Vaagso.

The oldest officer in Durnford-Slater's staff was Captain "Slinger" Martin who looked after the mountain of administrative work that allowed the Commando to operate smoothly. He was a veteran of the First World War in which he had served as a trooper in the 9th Lancers, eventually rising to the rank of Quartermaster. By all the rules of the game he should have been too old to serve with the Commando but Martin did not allow a problem like age to stand in his way. His regiment was due to set sail for the Middle East when he learned that No. 3 Commando was being formed, so he got the army medical authorities to declare him too old to serve abroad; he then applied to join the commandos and was accepted. In due course he was to see more combat than many of his younger comrades.

No. 3 Commando's adjutant was Captain Alan Small-
man, a regular officer from the RASC, and the medical
officer was Captain S.D. Corry who made up the headquarters staff. Then there were the troop commanders
whose job it was to lead the individual troops which went
to make up the fighting units of the commando.

The six troops were commanded by: Captain Bill Bradley
(1 Troop), Lieutenant Bob Clement (2 Troop), Captain
John Giles (3 Troop), Captain "Algy" Forrester (4 Troop),
Captain "Sandy" Ronald (5 Troop) and Captain Peter
Young who, when he retired from the army in 1959, became
head of the Military History Department at the Royal
Military Academy, Sandhurst, and a noted military histor-
ian. Young was among the first of the officers to join the
Commando when it was formed in 1940.

In their own individual ways these men had the qualities
of leadership which drew from their men unswerving loyalty. The story is told of John Giles who once brought his
troop back to camp after an extremely long forced march on
a particularly hot summer's day. The main gate to the camp
was only a stone's throw from the pier which jutted out into
the water and both to test their obedience and also cool the
men off, he gave them a "left wheel" order as they approached the gates and they marched straight into the water
in perfect formation . . . with Giles at their head. Once in
the water he yelled a quick "column right" and swimming
at the regulation distance they struck out for the shore.
Such was the loyalty and devotion of the men to the officers
who led them.

In addition to the British Commandos taking part in the
raid there was to be a detachment of soldiers of the free
Norwegian army under the command of Martin Linge, a
young Norwegian who fought valiantly during the German
conquest of Norway and had escaped to England, determined to continue the fight against the Nazis who were
occupying his country.

As with any raid, if it were to stand any chance of
success, the need for detail and accurate planning was
vital, and the planners took great pains to provide for
every eventuality. The attacking commando force was

divided into five groups, each with its own targets and responsibilities.

Group One was made up of No. Two Troop, under the command of Lieutenant Clement, who was given the task of clearing the Germans from the southernmost tip of Vaagso island and wrecking a heavy gun, which intelligence reported was in that area and could prove troublesome to the main body of the raiders. This operation completed, Group One was to make its way north up the coastal road towards South Vaagso to give support to the commandos operating there.

Group Two, under the command of Durnford-Slater, would land just below South Vaagso. It would consist of Captain Bradley's No. One Troop which would be responsible for the main demolition work in the town, and Giles and Forrester's Three and Four Troops as fighting units; they would sweep through the town and wreck as many installations, factories and any other targets as they found worthwhile.

Group Three would be under the command of "Mad Jack" Churchill and consisted of Captain Ronald's No. Five Troop and Young's No. Six Troop. Their job would be to launch an assault against the island of Maaloy which stood only a stone's throw from South Vaagso. Their main objective would be to silence the batteries of guns on the island and wipe out the German troops there.

Group Four would be comprised of men "borrowed" from No. 2 Commando, and they would be held back as a floating reserve to sweep into action when and where they were needed.

The last Group, Five, was made up of more men of No. 2 Commando who would land from the destroyer *Oribi* on the west shore of Ulvesund between North and South Vaagso and there set up a road block to prevent enemy reinforcements reaching the main target area at South Vaagso.

In every sense of the expression this was to be a "combined operation", with each element relying upon the other for the success of the particular part it had to play in the attack. The naval commitment to the operation was to be considerable and vital. Haydon and Burrough's headquar-

ters was to be on board the cruiser *Kenya*, and the entire
force was to be escorted and supported by four ships from
the Royal Navy's 17th Destroyer Flotilla. They were *Onslow*, *Oribi*, *Offa* and *Chiddingfold*. The bulk of the commando forces would be landed from the infantry landing
ships *Prince Leopold* and *Prince Charles*, both of which were
converted Belgian cross-channel steamers.

One other ship was to take part in the operation, the
submarine *Tuna*. She would lie in wait off the coast for the
convoy of ships and act as a navigational beacon pointing
the way for the convoy into the fjord. The part this submarine was to play was absolutely vital. It was essential that
the force of ships make an absolutely accurate landfall, to
maintain the element of surprise and to avoid having to
fumble its way around the coastline looking for the entrance
to the fjord. Nothing was more calculated to wreak disaster
than for the commandos to find themselves at the wrong
point on the coast. Only a few weeks earlier a commando
raid on the Norwegian coast had had to be called off at the
eleventh hour as the ships were approaching the coast
because the naval navigating officer was unsure of his
bearings and was unwilling to guarantee their exact position. The success or failure of a raid depended entirely upon
hitting the beach at the right spot.

Because of the threat of attack from the air, the Royal Air
Force was to wage war in the sky, warding off enemy
aircraft which could easily pin down the attacking commandos, as well as bombing the beach with smoke bombs to
screen the landings from the defenders. But the RAF was
faced with a major problem. Their crack fighters, the
Spitfires and the Hurricanes, did not have the range to
operate from Britain over Vaagso. These were the only
aircraft which were a true match for the German Mes-
serschmitt fighters, so whatever the RAF chose to send over
other than these would be faced with stiff opposition. The
RAF chose to use Beaufighters and Blenheims to give air
cover to the attackers and Hampden bombers and more
Blenheims to carry out the bombing missions.

Briefly this was the plan of attack, though at that time,
the beginning of December 1941, the majority of the

commandos who were to take part in the raid knew nothing of it. They soon guessed however that there was something in the wind when all leave for the month was cancelled. Barrack room speculation was rife when the order came to kit up and embark on the two infantry landing craft at Gourock.

The *Prince Leopold* and the *Prince Charles* steamed out of Gourock on 13 December and sailed to Scapa Flow. With Christmas not far off and the prospect of a raid just around the corner there was a considerable air of jubilation on board the two ships as they sailed up the west coast of Scotland and dropped anchor in the sanctuary of Scapa Flow. Once they were there an intensive training programme got under way, each man being briefed on his particular part in the raid. Briefing was intensive, everything being rehearsed time and time again until each man knew his role by heart. Casualties are inevitable in any operation of this kind and every contingency, like the loss of a troop commander or an NCO and what would happen then, was covered. Day and night the commandos studied maps and photographs of the landing areas until these were imprinted indelibly on their minds. Not only did each man know what he was supposed to do, he also had to know what the other troops would be up to.

The RAF flew reconnaissance missions over Vaagso, taking photographs and dashing back with them to give the planners information which might indicate a strengthening of enemy defences or the arrival of ships which might prove obstacles. All of this information, together with that received from secret agents in Norway, was sifted through thoroughly so that the master minds could get an up-to-date picture of what was happening in the target area.

The day of departure drew near and the assembled force had a last-minute visitor who arrived to see them on their way. It was Mountbatten himself who addressed the assembled commandos, giving them words of encouragement which ended with a memorable foreword to the raid.

"One last thing," he said. "When my ship, the destroyer *Kelly*, went down off Crete early this year, the Germans machine-gunned the survivors in the water. There's absolutely no need to treat them gently on my account! Good luck to all of you." With these words of inspiration ringing in their ears the commandos set sail from Scapa Flow on the first leg of their journey to Norway. Their destination was Sullom Voe, a small naval base in the Shetlands where they were to lie in wait until the following day before making the crossing to Norway.

Operation Archery, as the raid had been codenamed, was underway, but the commandos got a foretaste of what was to come when the seven ships of the little fleet immediately ran into fearsome weather with turbulent seas which smashed mercilessly down on the ships. The ships' plates groaned as the heavy seas dashed against them, relentlessly trying to tear them apart. Even the seasoned sailors on board the ships found themselves suffering from the effects of the fierce seas which tossed the ships about on the waves.

So violent was the wind whipped up by a Force 8 gale that the ships heeled over alarmingly, seeming as if they would sink. The infantry landing ships were in a particularly precarious position since they were carrying landing craft on deck which tended to make them top heavy, making their chances of turning over even greater. Below decks the commandos were suffering the rigours of seasickness.

On board the *Prince Charles* Commander Fell, the captain, witnessed an astonishing phenomenon. He saw a writing table move up and down the wall, seemingly under its own volition. It was as if some occult force was at work and was all the more staggering since the desk was actually bolted to the forward bulkhead. But Fell was not a man who could be scared by the possible existence of some spiritual presence on his ship. He discovered after close examination that the movement of the table was the result of the extreme pressure of the sea on the ship's plates and that this pressure was squeezing the ship and forcing the table to ride up and down the wall.

The ferocity of the seas was such that the convoy had to reduce speed and it was not until dawn that the storm finally calmed, but nevertheless the seas were still temperamental. During the night they had played havoc with the ships, particularly the two assault ships which were by then leaking badly. Indeed the *Prince Charles* had shipped about 120 tons of water and four of its cabins had been flooded.

It was not until noon on Christmas Day that the ships steamed into Sullom Voe, considerably the worse for wear after their voyage. The two infantry landing ships had suffered damage and men got frantically to work to repair the damage in the shelter of the islands. But outside the sanctuary of the Shetland Islands the storm still raged and the weathermen predicted that it would last for yet another eighteen hours. It was decided therefore to postpone the raid for twenty-four hours. They could not take the chance of sustaining further damage from a storm which had already buckled and twisted the guard rails on the two commando carrying ships.

The delay had two beneficial effects: it allowed the commandos to recover from the terrible seasickness they had suffered during the voyage and gave the repair parties time to do the job completely and properly. The day of the attack was now set for Saturday, 27 December, and it was with a sense of relief that every one of the commandos greeted the news. The postponement had yet another advantage. It allowed everyone to eat his Christmas dinner in the peace of Sullom Voe though the festivities were overshadowed by the thoughts of the impending raid. That night the men slept well but the following day dawned with the storm still raging and it continued to do so all morning.

While the commandos and sailors alike waited patiently for the word to go, another raid was taking place as scheduled on the Lofotens. Operation Anklet which was intended to take place at the same time as Archery was already underway, and this in itself gave everyone cause for concern. The plan had been for the Archery Operation to draw the bulk of the Luftwaffe's aircraft away from the Anklet attack on the Lofotens, since Anklet was taking place without air cover. As it happened, Anklet went without a hitch and the operation was a success.

Then, in the afternoon, the weather forecasters predicted that the high winds would fade within a few hours. That was all the commanders wanted to know. At four o'clock that same afternoon, the anchor chains on the waiting ships rattled and clanged as the anchors were drawn up from the sea bed; the convoy steamed out of Sullom Voe with *Kenya* leading the way into the storm, followed by *Chiddingfold* and the infantry landing ships which were flanked by the other destroyers. At first the two infantry ships suffered from the still heavy seas with the *Prince Leopold* shipping water, but soon, as the forecasters had predicted, the wind subsided, though it was not until just after midnight that the storm finally blew itself out and the seas calmed. Throughout the turbulent crossing the fleet navigator had been constantly on the bridge checking and re-checking their position. The first part of the operation depended entirely on the accuracy of his calculations.

Some of the commandos had suffered a second bout of seasickness but now, with the water calm, this subsided and they settled down to rest, leaving the work to the Royal Navy. Then at 5 a.m. they had breakfast as the ships crept nearer to the Norwegian coast.

The time dragged by as the ships nosed through the water. Then the asdic operator on board *Kenya* picked up a submarine contact and reported to the bridge. Lookouts scanned the surface of the water ahead of the ship and there before them lay the *Tuna* in position and waiting for them. They were bang on target. The fleet navigator had taken them right across the North Sea through the teeth of a storm to the exact position at the mouth of the fjord . . . and they were only *one minute* late! This was a truly magnificent piece of navigation considering the conditions through which they had travelled.

The little fleet of ships slipped silently past the submarine which lay with its conning tower peeping just above the surface of the water and then, with their engines throbbing their monotonous tone, they slid into the mouth of the fjord whose mountainous walls seemed to crowd in on them. As the bows of the ships sliced through the icy water the men who waited silently on board heard the first dull tones of approaching aircraft. High above them the Hampden bombers of the RAF were droning in on their targets. From the aircraft the crews could just make out the little fleet of ships in the fjord.

As they swept across the towering mountains towards Rugsundo, their first target, the pilots opened their bomb doors exposing the clusters of bombs neatly hung in the bomb bays. Bomb-aimers peered into their bomb sights with their fingers poised over the release buttons. Through the intercom their staccato instructions were passed to the pilots who altered course to bring their aircraft on target. Then one by one the shout came, "Bombs away!" and the black cigar-shaped missiles hurtled earthwards with an ominous whistle which built up into a deafening crescendo of sound before the bombs crashed into the ground, erupting into fiery balls of debris.

From the ground the anti-aircraft batteries on Vaagso, Maaloy and Rugsundo burst into life, hurtling a murderous barrage of flak and bullets into the air in a bid to bring down the attacking bombers. Through the concentrated barrage of fire the Hampdens drove on, intent on striking their targets while multi-coloured tracer bullets laced through the air, drawing a crazy cobweb pattern on the dark sky.

The German defenders were taken completely by surprise, but had it not been for a curious chain of events the attacking commandos might have found themselves facing a hot reception.

When the convoy of British ships had first crept into the fjord the Germans were already going about their daily routine. In a hut on the island of Maaloy, a group of soldiers were intently listening to a NCO giving them a lecture on "How To Behave In The Presence of an Officer". The commander of the gun battery on Maaloy was a plump, ageing captain called Butziger who was given to oversleeping. True to form he had risen late from bed that morning and since there was nothing urgent requiring his attention, he went about his shaving routine at a leisurely pace. While Butziger shaved, his orderly polished the commander's jackboots. But while Butziger soaped up his face and the orderly brought the jackboots to a handsome shine, a lookout on the island of Husevaagso thought he detected a movement on the water in the fjord far below. He slipped into the hut behind him, brought out a pair of binoculars and raised them to his eyes. It was still quite dark, but nevertheless he could make out the shape of a ship which looked like a blacked-out destroyer nosing its way farther and slowly into the fjord. Quickly he returned to the hut and telephoned the battery commander's quarters on Maaloy.

The telephone on the table where the orderly was busy polishing his commander's boots jangled into life, but since his hands were covered with black polish the orderly paused before answering it and wiped his hands clean before stretching out to lift the receiver. As he did so, however, the ringing stopped and he did not give the call another thought.

But if the orderly was unconcerned by the urgency of the call the lookout on Husevaagso was mystified. Why had they not answered? He pondered for a while and then decided to ring the harbour-captain's office in South Vaagso to see if he could raise a reply from there, but when he did so he was informed that there was nothing to worry about, all was well. A German convoy was expected that morning and although they appeared to be a little ahead of schedule, there was no cause for concern.

"But these are not merchant ships," the lookout protested. "They are warships and they are completely blacked out." But the clerk in the harbour-captain's office was not to be convinced.

"Are you still celebrating Christmas?" he asked sarcastically. "Take care you don't get caught drunk on duty." Then he hung up on the bewildered lookout. But the man was nothing if not determined. He jotted down a brief message on a piece of paper and handed it to the signaller inside the lookout hut. It read:

"Unidentified warships entering fjord."

Obediently, the signaller flashed the message to the German naval signal station on Maaloy where it was received by signalman Van Soest who was on duty there at the time. After receiving the signal he flashed an acknowledgement then laid down his lamp. One would have thought that his next move would be to alert the gun battery which was positioned not 100 yards away from the signal station. Instead he hurried down to the waterside and jumped into a boat, then proceeded to row as fast as he could across the narrow stretch of water to the harbour-captain's office. While Van Soest rowed furiously across the water the British warships were edging into position and the landing craft, packed with commandos, were being lowered from the *Prince Charles* and the *Prince Leopold* with the commandos crouched below the deck level. One by one the craft pulled away from their mother ships and made off on the long journey to their appointed target areas. Meanwhile, HMS *Kenya* manoeuvred into position with her guns crews ready to open the initial bombardment.

The balloon was about to burst when Van Soest arrived at the harbour-captain's office and gave him the message. The harbour-captain, Leutnant zur See Sebelin, read the message then asked:

"Did you notify the battery?" He could not believe his ears when the answer came:

"No, sir. After all, they are an *army* battery and this is a *naval* signal!" The well-regulated German mind had reacted true to form and had played right into the hands of the British attackers. Before Sebelin could voice his astonishment the building shook, and the two men leapt to their feet in fright. *Kenya*'s guns had flashed into action and the first salvo of shells rained down on the target area, beginning the softening up process which was to precede the commandos' attack. It was exactly 0848 hours. In a few seconds the island of Maaloy was enshrouded in smoke as shells pounded down on to it from *Kenya*'s guns.

The landing craft swept in to the shore and commandos watched in awe as the island became enveloped in smoke. On the tiny dot of land the shells rained down, shaking the entire island and blasting it with violent explosions while the barrage of fire continued relentlessly for nine minutes, during which time huts and barrack rooms disappeared without a trace under the weight of fire. In that short space of time *Kenya* fired almost 450 shells into the target area and the destroyers *Offa* and *Onslow* also opened up to add to the devastation.

Meanwhile the two columns of assault landing craft churned up the water as they dashed in towards their targets. The starboard column was to land on Maaloy and it pulled off to the right, heading for the tiny island which was still taking the full weight of the bombardment while the Hampdens continued to drop bombs on Rugsundo.

Durnford-Slater, who was in the port column heading for the landing point just below South Vaagso, stood head and shoulders above the rim of the landing craft, and fired off twenty red Very lights. This was the signal for the bombardment to cease and the aircraft to sweep in and drop their smoke floats to create a screen for the commandos' landing.

Within a very short space of time, the Hampdens were bearing down on the landing areas with their bomb doors open again. Meanwhile the landing craft fanned out into line abreast for the landing, while "Mad Jack" Churchill stood erect in the centre craft playing "The March of the Cameron Men" on his bagpipes! To the Sassenachs in the boats the wailing of the bagpipes seemed to drown the noise of the diving aircraft and machine-gun fire from the island defenders.

As the landing craft nosed into the target area the Hampdens swept across the island and dropped their smoke bombs, which hit the beach and instantly billowed great clouds of smoke. Under the dense screen the commandos poured ashore on to Maaloy and were instantly engulfed in the smoke. For a time at least the commandos dashed blindly ashore, unable to see more than a few feet amid the dense smoke and yelling to each other to locate their comrades.

In the van of the advancing commandos who had spread out into assault formation was "Mad Jack" brandishing his claymore above his head and yelling curses and damnation to all Germans as well as urging his men on into the fray.

With their tommy guns clenched firmly in their hands the commandos dashed through the smoke and out the other side to find a machine-gun nest right in front of them. Sitting at the gun were three Germans, but before they had time to open fire on the advancing commandos, two of them were riddled through by a burst of fire from Private Grigg's tommy gun. The third German, utterly terrified, instantly threw up his hands in surrender and was taken prisoner.

While Number Five Troop scurried around the island mopping up small pockets of resistance Number Six Troop made for the gun batteries, only to find that the first two guns they came across were deserted. This puzzled the attackers for they had expected them to be manned, but the place was without troops. Another section of Six Troop, led by Captain Peter Young, had a similar experience when it found the third gun. There were no Germans to be seen. Yet again, Five Troop discovered the fourth gun undefended. In less than eight minutes since the commandos had landed the main objectives, the four guns, had been taken without resistance. The commandos were puzzled. They knew perfectly well that there were Germans on the island . . . but where?

A few men were left to guard the guns, some of which had been completely destroyed by the bombardment, while the other commandos made off to deal with the other targets. They darted over the brow of the great mound that was the centre of Maaloy and saw the German barracks which had been hit by shells from the British ships' guns. But again there were no Germans. An eerie feeling came over the commandos. It was as if the island were haunted by the ghosts of the Germans who had been there. There was not an enemy soldier to be seen . . . not even a dead one, though there should have been for the barracks were ablaze.

Suddenly, as if from nowhere, a lone German bolted towards the commandos who were making their way towards the blazing barrack buildings. A split second later three shots rang out from commandos' guns and the German gasped, then crumpled to the ground. Moments later a hand-grenade exploded far off to the right. One of the commando sub-sections, led by Sergeant Connolly, had spotted two Germans crouching in a small wooden hut and peering out of the window. Private Durling yanked the pin out of a hand grenade and tossed it towards the hut, yelling a warning to the others as he did so. But one of the commandos who was slightly deaf failed to hear the warning and the grenade exploded, fragmenting in front of him. Luckily he was only slightly wounded. The grenade had failed to blow up the hut but two frightened Germans emerged with their arms in the air. The wounded commando took them down to the beach to be loaded on to the waiting craft to spend the remainder of the war in a prisoner-of-war camp in England.

There was, however, still something puzzling the commandos. Why should that German who had been shot run uphill apparently to no objective and right into the teeth of the commandos' fire? The answer suddenly dawned on them as they made their way farther down the hill. The German had been bolting for an air-raid shelter, the entrance to which was masked from the commandos' view by a downward curve in the hill.

Sergeant Herbert crept up to the entrance and peered round the doorway into a long tunnel which opened out into a room. There inside the room was a group of Germans. This, it appeared, was the main air-raid shelter for the gun battery and the Germans had been in there since the bombardment began, not realizing that the commandos had landed, and waiting there until they felt it was safe to emerge.

Herbert saw the group of Germans as a worthy prize; he pulled the pin out of a grenade and was just about to lob it inside when a shout came:

"It's all right, George, we've got the bastards!" Seconds later two commandos emerged from the air-raid shelter with a posse of Germans. They had entered the shelter unseen by Sergeant Herbert and had almost come to a sorry end. Among the fifteen prisoners captured in that air-raid shelter was Butziger, the battery commander. He, like the others, was destined to spend the remainder of the war in a POW camp.

The commandos continued to search the island for Germans and found them crouching under sheds and huddled in dugouts. They suffered a similar fate to the others and were shepherded down to the assault craft where they were kept under guard. They would later provide useful information for the intelligence service when they were interrogated back in Britain.

A group of commandos searching for more Germans almost tripped over a badly wounded German soldier who lay in their tracks. He was obviously dying in agony and his body was horribly mutilated. He had been one of those caught out in the open when the bombardment had started and had taken the full force of it. The German's body jerked in the death throes as he groaned in pain. The man was beyond help, so one of the commandos raised his rifle and fired a single shot into him. The German became still and the commandos moved on.

As they edged down the hill amid the boulders that were strewn all over the island, the commandos suddenly came under fire from the fjord. A German patrol boat had spotted them rummaging about the rocks and opened up at them. The commandos instantly let loose at the boat with rifle and machine-gun fire, but it was well out of range of their weapons although the retaliation was enough to send the boat scurrying away.

A few of the commandos darted into a cluster of buildings and surprised a German soldier who surrendered without a fight. Then they unearthed a frightened "comfort girl" whose function on Maaloy was to "entertain" the troops. The couple were led off to captivity.

Meanwhile other commandos were scouring the other buildings on the island trying to flush out more Germans. Among them were Captain Peter Young and Lance-Corporal Harper who rounded the corner of one building to find themselves face to face with two armed Germans. They instantly doubled back round the corner and held a hurried conference, deciding to leap out together and have a go at the two enemy soldiers.

Young was armed with a rifle with fixed bayonet and Harper with a tommy gun. Acting as one they leapt out from behind the corner and yelled "Hände hoch!" The German nearest to Young made a lunge for Young's bayonet and tried to take it from him, but Young pulled it back and loosed off a round as the German turned and tried to escape. The German's knees folded under him and he crumpled to the ground. At almost the same time the second German levelled his pistol to fire but was cut down by a burst of bullets from Harper's tommy gun. Hearing the commotion, Trooper Clark swept round the corner

and unleashed a volley of fire at the Germans, then leapt
back around the corner again, quickly followed by Young
and Clark. Then one of the commandos tossed a grenade
round the corner and after the debris from the violent
explosion had subsided, the two Germans lay dead on the
ground.

Only two more enemy soldiers were found and they
turned out to be sailors. They were discovered lying flat
underneath one of the huts, and they were so terrified that
nothing the commandos could do would persuade them to
come out. They were petrified with fright. At last, after all
sorts of threats and cajoling had been tried, a burly commando by the name of "Curly" Gimbert, slid under the hut
and hauled the pair of them out by the feet. Both of them
were visibly shaking with fright but they need not have
worried. Their future was to be a safe one . . . in a POW
camp.

The battle for Maaloy was over, or so it seemed. In less
than twenty minutes every German on the island had been
killed or captured and all the objectives taken. The island
was firmly in the hands of the British commandos and their
Norwegian comrades. The assault on Maaloy had been
thought by the men who planned the raid to be the most
difficult target to secure and the prospect of a bitter and
bloody battle had been foreseen. In fact it had been the
reverse. But the fight was not quite over. The armed patrol
boat lying off the north of the island opened fire on the
commandos once more, and two of them, Troopers Hannan
and Mappleback of Number Six Troop, thought of a novel
way of retaliating. Their own rifles and tommy guns were
useless against the armament of the patrol boat and they
were out of range, but they remembered that one of the
German guns which had been taken by the commandos was
still in working order, so they swung it round and began
loosing off shells at the trawler. Although neither of them
was a trained gunner they actually succeeded in scoring
some hits on it, but alas, these were not very effective since
neither of them knew anything about setting the fuses on
the shells. It was Sergeant Vincent who put them wise to
the technique of fuse-setting, but before they could use

their new-found weapon effectively, Major Churchill put a stop to their target practice.

Jack Churchill realized that the job he and his men had been sent to do on Maaloy was already done, so he sent a signal to Brigadier Haydon on board *Kenya* telling him that the island had been secured and awaited further instructions. They were quick to come. A small force of men was to be sent to destroy the Mortenes fish-oil factory at Deknepol on the far side of the Ulvesund fjord, so Churchill despatched Captain Ronald with a detachment of men to demolish the factory, and Ronald set off in a landing craft to this end. As it turned out, and as was expected, there were no Germans at the factory and the only sign of life at all was a Norwegian watchman who obliged Ronald and his men by advising them how best to go about blowing up the factory. Shortly afterwards the whole structure seemed to lift off the ground, then settle in a tangled, wrecked mess and slide into the fjord. Another objective had fallen to the commandos without so much as a shot being fired.

But if the battle for the island of Maaloy resembled something of a cake-walk, the attack on South Vaagso and its environs was to prove quite different. It was here that the bloodiest fighting of the day was to take place. The Germans on Maaloy had shown little willingness for a fight but their comrades across the narrow strip of water were to fight with a courage and determination which was to gain the admiration of even the commandos themselves.

The first British soldiers to land on the island of Vaagso proper were the men of Lieutenant Clement's Group One who, crammed into two landing craft, made a landing at Hollevik. Their first objective was a field gun which British Intelligence had reported was sited on a hill behind the village. Before they had gone very far up the rocky shore, however, a shot rang out from a nearby house and Lieutenants Risnes and O'Flaherty went to investigate. O'Flaherty dashed up to the front door, and finding it locked, proceeded unsuccessfully to try to kick it in, so he levelled his .45 pistol and blasted the lock out. As he threw open the door, he and Risnes caught sight of two Germans darting down a short flight of stairs. O'Flaherty loosed off a round, hitting one of them in the backside, but he struggled on and out by the back door where Lance-Corporal Gittens was waiting with tommy gun levelled. He sprayed both men with bullets and they sagged and dropped to the ground. They were both critically wounded and O'Flaherty ordered some of his men to take them to the boats for treatment.

Meanwhile Risnes had found a Norwegian civilian and questioned him about the presence of German troops and the gun position. According to the Norwegian, the two men who had been wounded were part of a ten-man marine detachment. The other eight men had gone to Vaagso for their breakfast and had not returned. As to the gun position, he knew of no such emplacement in that area. They searched the immediate district and found no sign of a gun. For once the intelligence reports had proved incorrect.

Clement then attempted to radio Durnford-Slater for instructions, but finding the radio out of order he sent a message to Haydon on board the *Kelly*. The message was relayed to Durnford-Slater who instructed Clement to proceed up the South Vaagso road and come into reserve in the town where bitter fighting was taking place.

All had not been going well for Durnford-Slater's Group Two. Disaster struck them as they were charging in towards the shore in the landing craft just south of the town. As they neared the shore the Hampdens roared in to drop their phosphorus smoke-bombs. But as one of them did so, the armed German trawler *Föhn*, which was lying off the north of Maaloy, caught one of the Hampdens in its gunsight and loosed off a fusillade of fire. The bullets ripped into the starboard engine which immediately caught fire, throwing the aircraft out of control. At that very instant, the bomb-aimer released the phosphorus smoke bomb.

In one of the landing craft Lieutenant Arthur Komrower glanced upwards and watched the 60-pound bomb floating down. To his horror he realized it was heading straight for his boat. Komrower yelled a warning to the troops huddled in the boat but it was too late. He dived over the bows of the boat as the bomb, suspended on its parachute, settled in the middle of the boat and ignited, horribly burning the men crowded in the boat. The phosphorus spewed out of the bomb covering everyone in the boat, killing many of them outright and fatally wounding many others.

An instant later the boat hit the beach and the coxswain, who was himself burned, lowered the ramp. By then, however, the searing phosphorus had ignited ammunition and exploding bullets zipped around the boat injuring more of the commandos, some of whom were desperately trying to escape from the hell on board.

Komrower's leap to safety enabled him to escape the fury of the phosphorus, but since he had dived in front of the boat it crunched down on his leg, pinning him down beneath it while the searing fluid spat out of the boat and the choking, oily smoke billowed from it. Luckily, Martin Linge caught sight of the trapped man, and completely disregarding the bullets that whistled and whined around him, he leapt into the water beside Komrower and eventually succeeded in pulling him free and dragging him to safety.

At the same time as this epic of courage was being enacted, the men from the other boats charged inshore amid the smoke while enemy machine guns opened up at them, luckily inflicting no casualties. The commandos had not gone far when they found themselves at the base of a steep cliff. This proved an obstacle, but at least it sheltered them from the enemy fire and gave them time to regroup and prepare for the scaling of the cliff.

Less than four minutes after touching down on the beach, the first of the men were spilling over the top of the cliff and dashing into the dense smoke which obscured them from the Germans who were by then firing blindly into the thick screen of smoke. Bullets flashed through the thick cloud of smoke but still the commandos charged on until they emerged from the other side of the screen. The troops fanned out towards their respective objectives, some to wipe out machine-gun nests. others to mop up pockets of resistance and yet more to carry out the industrial dirty work, demolishing some of the fish-oil factories and blowing up other vital objectives.

The toughest resistance was found in the town of South Vaagso itself. The German infantry fought with toughness and resolution. Many of them were veterans of the war in Western Europe and were hardened fighters who would not give in without a desperate struggle.

While the battle raged amongst the clusters of wooden buildings, the Norwegian civilians cowered in their cellars seeking whatever protection they could.

In little more than a quarter of an hour after hitting the beach, Number Three Troop's advance through the town was halted by a major obstacle. In a large house the Germans had set up a defensive position and they fought like demons. While Captain Giles and his men darted nearer the building they were sniped at from the windows by German soldiers positioned in the house.

The commandos dashed from cover to cover, loosing off bursts of fire at the house as they went and killing three of the enemy in the process. It was obvious to Giles that he had to wipe out the resistance in the house if he and his men were to proceed any further, and in a mad, wild dash he led his men to the house and crashed in through the front door.

The commandos ran through the corridors, throwing open the doors and tossing grenades into the rooms which were instantly blasted by thunderous explosions. The whole house shook to the crash of exploding missiles and finally, when all the Germans had been cleared from the house, Giles darted out the rear door in pursuit of some who had fled out the back. As he emerged from the door a German sniper lurking in the back garden shot him in the stomach and he fell to the ground dead. With that bullet the commandos had lost one of their most courageous leaders.

Only seconds after that, Lieutenant Mike Hall took a bullet in the left elbow, which left his arm dangling uselessly by his side. Two of his men tried to rescue him from the growing concentration of fire and both of them were killed in the process. Three Troop's advance slowly ground to a halt, but not far off Captain Algy Forrester was meeting with better success.

Forrester was a man of unconquerable will who believed in bold tactics, and he led his men right up the middle of the main road, screaming death and defiance to the Germans while the commandos hurled grenades into the enemy-held houses. Forrester, in the van of this mad rush, sprayed the houses with bullets from his tommy gun which he fired from the hip. While this desperate charge was taking place, Lieutenant Komrower, determined to see action in spite of his badly damaged leg, hobbled up the main street behind the commandos, using an improvised cane as a support.

At last Number Four Troop came across yet another German strongpoint, the Ulvesund Hotel in which Leutnant Sebelin had rallied some Germans around him and set up a defensive position, hell-bent on fighting to the last man. The big hotel was well defended and Forrester was quick to appreciate that it could be taken only by a frontal assault. Never a man to be deterred by strong opposition, he pulled the pin out of a hand grenade and charged forward. But just as he was about to heave it into the building, a German caught him in his sights, squeezed the trigger and Forrester fell on top of his grenade which exploded a second later, killing him instantly.

The only officer left in the troop was Martin Linge, the Norwegian commando. He summed up the situation immediately and took command, leading another assault on the hotel. The men dashed forward but as Linge raced for the front of the hotel he was caught in the chest by a German bullet and fell dead on to the snow-covered ground. The second attack failed and now Number Four Troop was without a leader.

In lesser men the loss of their leaders might have sparked off an inclination to give up. But not so with the commandos who were trained to take the initiative. Although only a corporal, "Knocker" White took command of the troop. The loss of his commanders had raised his hackles and now, in a blazing fury, he began to rap out orders to his comrades, some of whom actually outranked him.

"Knocker" ordered the men to reload their weapons. He was going to lead yet another attack on the hotel but just as he was about to do so, Sergeant Ramsey of Number One Troop appeared on the scene, bringing with him a three-inch mortar. None of his men was particularly expert with a mortar, which they had acquired just before leaving for the raid, but nevertheless they began pumping mortar bombs into the hotel. Ten of these dropped through the roof, exploding and setting the hotel alight. Soon the whole structure was ablaze and the commandos surged forward, hurling grenades through the windows and causing further havoc.

Just as the building was finally taken Durnford-Slater arrived and took stock of the situation. Reinforcements were urgently needed to combat the strong German resistance, and he ordered Captain Bradley and his troop to bring up every man he could spare. Meanwhile he went back to an improvised headquarters and radioed a report to Haydon on the *Kelly*. By then Churchill had contacted Haydon and told him that Maaloy was taken, and "Mad Jack" was now ordered to bring as many men as he could from Maaloy to South Vaagso to lend support to Durnford-Slater's attack.

Churchill despatched Peter Young and eighteen of his men to South Vaagso, and they landed near the town cemetery where they were greeted by Charley Head, the signals officer who led Young to the Colonel. Durnford-Slater quickly put Young in the picture, telling him that Number Six Troop's attack had lost most of its momentum in spite of the brilliant leadership of "Knocker" White. Luckily young O'Flaherty had brought up his men and he and the remnants of Six Troop were busy mopping up opposition in the warehouses along the waterfront while Number One Troop was busy with its demolition work, wrecking the fish-oil factories. To add weight to the attack, Haydon sent the floating reserve, which had been held back, into action and they were soon landing on the shoreline.

The battle along the water's edge raged furiously, with heavy losses on both sides: O'Flaherty was wounded in the shoulder. But this did not stop him from fighting on, and in spite of his wound he led his men on into the fray.

The commandos rushed at a storehouse with guns blazing and four Germans emerged with their hands in the air. Then suddenly shots rang out and Sergeant Hughes and Trooper Clarke were both wounded, Hughes so seriously that he later died. The commandos tried desperately to discover where the shooting was coming from but they could not pin down the sniper.

They huddled behind the storehouse and peered around its corner in a bid to catch sight of their assailant. Then one of the commandos spotted a German helmet bobbing about in the window of a nearby house and several of them opened up on it, shattering the frame. Instantly the helmet careered backwards and the shooting ceased. But again they came under fire from a red warehouse some fifty yards from where they were crouched. The warehouse had to be taken, so Peter Young leapt up out of cover and scrambled towards it over the open space between the storehouse and the warehouse. He had got only half-way across the open space when a German trooper appeared in the doorway and began throwing stick grenades at him.

The first grenade landed some ten yards away from Young and exploded, followed by yet another which erupted in roughly the same place. During this bombardment Young continued to run, firing from the hip as he charged, and at last he reached the wall of the building, miraculously unscathed. He found that he was hidden from the trooper by a huge wooden crate which lay against the wall between him and the German. Other commandos scurried in beside Young and they fumbled in their haversacks for Mills bombs, but while they did so another stick grenade was tossed out from the door and landed only a few feet away from where they were standing. The men stood gaping at the grenade, unable to move, waiting for it to explode, but for some inexplicable reason it did not.

More commandos joined Young and they then proceeded to pitch grenades at the door and into the building. After there were several explosions inside the warehouse, Young crept in and could see no sign of Germans alive or dead until two shots rang out and narrowly missed him. He leapt back out of the door, and after a hasty conference with his companions it was decided to set fire to the wooden structure and smoke the Germans out. But before they could set fire to the place Lieutenant O'Flaherty, sporting a borrowed tommy gun, and Trooper Sherington made a wild dash for the door only to be met by a hail of fire. Both men tumbled to the floor. O'Flaherty had been shot in the face. A bullet had shattered his jaw, passed through his palate and ripped out an eye but mercifully he was still alive and lay on the floor with Sherington lying wounded beside him. Showing almost unbelievable determination the two men managed to drag themselves out of the building and were rescued by their comrades, whereupon the commandos sprayed the walls of the building with petrol and set it alight. Meanwhile Lance-Corporal Fyson positioned himself outside the door with his Bren gun and waited. In a few short minutes the Germans began to stumble out of the warehouse and were cut down by bursts of fire from Fyson's Bren gun.

With the warehouse ablaze the commandos moved on and linked up with Captain Hooper's reserve forces, who joined them in the battle against the German snipers still creating havoc in the streets of South Vaagso. Meanwhile the demolition squads blasted their objectives to bits with cleverly placed bombs and the whole town rocked as the explosive charges blew up.

While the trail of destruction continued, the RAF were playing their part in the plan. Thirteen Blenheim bombers were launching an attack on the German airfield at Herdla with 250-pound bombs. Two of the British bombers came to grief after one had been hit by anti-aircraft fire and collided with the other. When the aircraft had finally completed their mission, Herdla airfield was pock-marked with craters and no longer capable of taking aircraft, denying the German fighters a refuelling base from which to operate over Vaagso.

The Royal Navy was at the same time creating havoc amongst the shipping in Ulvesund fjord. The 250-ton armed patrol boat *Föhn* which, it will be remembered, shot down the Hampden bomber with such disastrous results, had been in the fjord that morning to escort a convoy of three ships through the Ulvesund. After her attack on the Hampden, she dashed up the Ulvesund to escape the guns of the British warships, taking her charges with her. Leutnant zur See Lohr put up a gallant fight but the *Föhn*'s guns were no match for those of the *Onslow* and the *Oribi*. One of the German ships, the 100-ton *Eismeer*, did not have up enough steam to make a dash for it. The others tried but it soon became evident that escape was out of the question. The 2,200-ton *Norma* and the 3,000-ton *Reimer Etzard Fritzen* ran themselves aground on the rocky shore and the crews leapt off on to dry land. On board the *Föhn*, which was by then taking hits from *Onslow*'s guns, Lohr could see that the ship was doomed and he prepared to dump the ship's top secret code books over the side, but as he was about to do so he was killed outright by a shell. After a rifle battle with the *Föhn*'s crew, a boarding party scrambled aboard and found the code books.

The discovery of the code books was in itself justification for the entire raid. These code books were to give the intelligence service in Britain a wealth of information, including the radio call signs for every German ship in Norway and France as well as their challenges, countersigns and emergency signals. Furthermore, the Germans did not know that Lohr had failed to drop them into the depths of the fjord and had no reason to suspect that they were in British hands. The result was that they did not bother to alter the codes. Before long these books were to be used to fox the Germans during one of the commandos' greatest raids, that on St. Nazaire. This was without question the major intelligence find of the raid.

Two more German ships fell to the British destroyers' guns that day. They were the armed tug *Rechtenfleth* and the *Anita L M Russ*, both of which sailed down the Ulvesund, completely unaware of the battle that was raging round the bend in the fjord at South Vaagso. When they got round the headland they saw the destroyers and mistook them for German warships. Then the horrible truth dawned on their captains and they tried to make a run for it, running around in the process. The two craft were then destroyed by gunfire.

Meanwhile Captain Birney, who had been landed with his force of commandos from the destroyer *Oribi* just below North Vaagso, was putting his alloted plan into action. His mission was twofold. He had to blow up the coastal road and prevent reinforcements sweeping south to the battle area, and secondly find and take prisoner the local quisling leader Johan Setland.

Birney sent half of his men into North Vaagso to flush out the quisling and also put the telephone exchange out of action, while the others dealt with the demolition of the road. When a German patrol arrived in the town they found that the commandos had been and gone, so they received instructions to carry on down the coast road and attempt to discover what was happening at South Vaagso, since radio contact had been lost with that town. The German patrol ran headlong into Birney's commandos and two of the Germans were killed in the opening volleys of the battle.

The commandos detonated the explosives on the road and then began re-embarking on their destroyer under fire from the remaining Germans. Immediately the commandos were out of the line of fire of the destroyers' guns, *Onslow* and *Oribi* opened up at the shore, silencing the German guns.

With the arrival of the reinforcements in South Vaagso under the command of Hooper, the tide of battle turned in favour of the commandos and swift advances were made through the town as the British soldiers gained ground, sweeping aside the stiff German resistance. The ubiquitous Durnford-Slater was continuously in the van of the attack and at one point was leading a small group of men when a German sailor sprang out of a side street and lobbed a stick grenade at the Colonel, then instantly threw his hands in the air in surrender. At that Durnford-Slater leapt into a doorway as the grenade exploded and luckily escaped with only minor injuries, but both of the men who were immediately beside him were badly injured. Sergeant Mills, who was nearby, levelled his rifle at the German.

"*Nein! Nein!*" the German yelled.

"*Ja! Ja!*" Mills retorted and shot him dead.

The Colonel had seen it all and gave the sergeant a knowing look.

"Yeah, well, Mills, you shouldn't have done that." And with that they moved on.

Just before noon, Durnford-Slater held a conference of troop commanders in a garden. The fighting was all but over though there was still some demolition work to be done. He positioned a group of men in a well-appointed house with the task of repelling any counter-attack that the last of the Germans might launch while he detailed others to blow up the Firda factory. Not long afterwards the town trembled as the explosives were detonated.

By one o'clock the last major elements of resistance had been dealt with and re-embarkation began. Almost two hours later, the commandos were back on board their ships. The withdrawal had not, however, gone without incident. There were still a few determined Germans holed up on the outskirts of the town and they sniped at the commandos as they made for the boats. One of the snipers was flushed out and taken prisoner, the last one of the day.

While the ships regrouped and sailed away, the full extent of the success of the raid became apparent as stories were told and debriefing took place.

The scene the commandos left behind was one of devastation. Every single German on the island of Maaloy had been killed or captured and the batteries completely destroyed. Many of the factories which produced the precious fish-oil had either been blown up or burnt to the ground. A lighthouse, telephone exchanges and several warehouses suffered a similar fate, and even a German tank which had been in its garage at the time of the attack was wrecked beyond repair. In addition more than 15,000 tons of shipping had been sunk or destroyed.

The German prisoners captured by the commandos provided Intelligence with a great deal of valuable information, but the prize capture of the day was the package of code books.

The attack had cost the raiders dearly. They lost 20 killed and 57 wounded out of a total landing force of 525 men. Six of the dead commandos were buried at sea on the way home.

As the little fleet of ships ploughed through the waves of the North Sea, heading into the now setting sun, they twice came under air attack from German aircraft bent on vengeance after the raid, but neither attack succeeded in inflicting any damage and the aircraft were beaten off by escorting RAF planes.

The raid on Vaagso was an unqualified success but although the raiders brought back with them a host of civilian volunteers to swell the ranks of the Norwegian Army in Britain, the Norwegian Prime Minister in exile was far from pleased that the raid had taken place at all and voiced his feelings with these words:

> Who could be so blind as to delude himself that this effort could have done anything to shorten the ordeal of Norway? Undoubtedly the enemy has been annoyed by the very impudence of the operation lancing deep into the shoreline he sought to secure, but it could have only one result: the Germans will now strengthen their defences making the ultimate victory even harder to achieve than it would have been if the raid had never taken place.

True, the Germans did build up their defences in Norway, but in doing so they had to draw troops from other German-occupied areas, thus weakening them. Hitler came to the conclusion that Britain intended intensifying its raids and hopefully securing strongpoints down the Norwegian coast so as to harass German shipping and deny her the supplies that filtered down the coast through the narrow passages between the islands and the mainland to Germany. Indeed, because of the commando raids, Hitler even considered the possibility that the Allies might launch their major offensive across the North Sea. As it was, Britain and her allies had no intention of doing so and therefore the thousands of German reinforcements who poured into Norway were wasting their time.

By 1944 the German garrison in Norway was some 372,000 men strong, and it is interesting to consider what might have happened had they not been drawn from the defensive positions they held in France on Hitler's orders. The invasion forces who were later in the war to sweep ashore on the Normandy beaches might well have faced stiffer opposition with a catastrophic result.

So although the Norwegian Prime Minister had what seemed like reasonable objections to that raid, it can be seen that viewing the war effort as a whole, the raid was well conceived and justified.

THE ATTACK ON ROMMEL'S HQ

Richard Arnold

*The Second World War in North Africa would probably
have been over in spring 1941 had Hitler not dispatched
to the theatre Erwin Rommel. A former leader of the
Führer's escort battalion, Rommel had distinguished
himself as commander of 7th Panzer during the Battle
of France. It mattered little Rommel knew nothing about
desert warfare – as Hitler grasped better than many of his
staff, Rommel was a master of mobile operations. Within
six weeks of Rommel's arrival in the desert, the Afrika
Korps was on the counter-offensive. Within six months of
his arrival, the British had been rolled back to the
Egyptian frontier. Since all German success in North
Africa seemed to emanate from Rommel, his elimination
seemed, to British planners, a worthwhile gamble. The
special force selected for the attack on Rommel's HQ at
Sidi Rafaa (Beda Littoria), halfway between Tobruk
and Bengaz, was 11 Scottish Commando.*

INFORMATION HAD BEEN passed from Intelligence to the
Headquarters of the Eighth Army that Rommel used a
certain building as his base, and that he was there in person.
A bold plan was drawn up, involving the Scottish Commando under Geoffrey Keyes, now a Lieutenant Colonel,
in which six officers and fifty-three other ranks would land
from submarines behind the enemy lines, attack Rommel's
Headquarters and either kill or capture him.

The raiding party was under the command of Laycock,

whilst Keyes was in command of the actual party to attack Rommel's headquarters. The party, divided into two groups, was carried in H.M. Submarines *Torbay* and *Talisman*, and when the *Torbay* reached the chosen spot, it was guided in by the signalling of an electric torch. When the landing party got ashore – some of them being injured when boats capsized in the heavy swell – they saw that the figure flashing the torch was dressed in Arab clothes. It was a member of the famous Desert Reconnaissance Group, who had been dropped a few days in advance of the Commandos. Captain Haselden, an Intelligence Officer, for such was the "Arab", had already established a headquarters in a small ruin, and had a fire lit for the newcomers.

The detachment from the *Talisman* experienced even greater trouble in getting ashore. The weather was growing worse and most of the boats capsized. However, Laycock and seven others managed to reach dry land.

The plan of operations was for Laycock to form a bridgehead, while Keyes would lead a detachment to attack Rommel's H.Q. Another detachment under Lieutenant Cook would cut telephone and telegraph wires from the H.Q.

After a weary march through driving rain, trudging through heavy mud, ever on the watch for pro-German Arabs and enemy patrols, Keyes and his party eventually reached Rommel's H.Q. It was planned that the attack should take place at midnight on the 17th November, to coincide with the opening of General Auchinleck's attack along the front.

Presently the Assault Group reached the bottom of the 250-feet escarpment, at the top of which lay Rommel's house. Silently they clambered up, when suddenly a dog began to bark at their approach. They crouched motionless in the shadows. About a hundred yards away, to one side, the door of a hut opened and a stream of light spread towards them. They waited. They could hear the man shouting at the dog. Presently the door closed. They reached the top without further incident and Lieutenant Cook took his party to find the pylon from which the cables ran.

Keyes took his men on and after a short march reached some outhouses. Again they aroused a watchdog. An Italian in uniform came out of a hut and called to one of the Commando officers. An Arab appeared in the doorway of the hut behind the Italian.

"We are German troops on patrol," called back the Commando officer, Captain Campbell, in the best German he was able to muster, and as arrogantly as he could. Meanwhile, the troopers fingered the triggers of their guns, ready for action.

The Italian was satisfied and went back into his hut, and at that moment Keyes and an N.C.O. arrived back from a reconnaissance of the buildings.

Together Keyes and Captain Campbell ran up the steps of the house and pushed open the door.

A German officer stood there!

Keyes at once closed with the German, but the German grabbed hold of Keyes' tommy gun and started to fight for it. Neither Captain Campbell nor Sergeant Terry could get round the struggling pair. However, Captain Campbell shot the German with his .38 revolver, and presently they heard a man coming down stairs into the large hall in which the party found themselves.

Sergeant Terry opened fire with his tommy gun but the German turned and fled upstairs.

A light was seen to be coming from underneath a door, Keyes flung it open, and fired two or three shots into the room at the ten Germans they saw there. Then he swung the door to. The door opened outwards into the hall. Captain Campbell told Keyes to open the door while he pitched a grenade in. Keyes did so and shouted, "Well done," as he saw the grenade roll into the room.

At that moment, while the door was still open, the Germans opened fire and Keyes fell, struck just over the heart. Campbell pushed the door to, and the grenade went off with a terrific explosion. Together, Captain Campbell and Sergeant Terry carried Keyes outside, but he was dead. Unfortunately, Campbell was himself shot in the leg by one of our own commandos who mistook him for a German, and as it was impossible to evacuate him to the beach he had to be left behind. He was taken prisoner, and his wounded leg amputated later.

Geoffrey Keyes was awarded the Victoria Cross for his part in the exploit, and the Germans buried him with full military honours in the nearby cemetery.

Meanwhile Lieutenant Cook had successfully found his pylon, blown it up, and set off back to join Laycock some twenty-odd miles away. He was, however, captured and had to spend the remainder of the war as a prisoner.

Sergeant Terry took command of the raiding party and brought it back to Laycock, but when the submarine arrived, the weather was so bad that it could not be taken off. However, the Germans were getting nearer and nearer, and although Laycock and his men had chosen a good defensive position, it was soon obvious from the volume of fire the Germans were pouring on them that they would soon be overrun. Laycock therefore split the detachment up into small parties and they dashed across the open country, seeking the shelter of the inland hills.

After many adventures, including falling in with friendly tribesmen (other members of the detachments had been murdered by Arabs), after forty-one days of wandering in the desert Colonel Laycock and Sergeant Terry finally reached the British lines at Cyrene. They were the only members of the party to do so.

And after all these hazardous journeys, and the deaths of gallant soldiers, the attack on the headquarters of Rommel was found to have been in vain. General Rommel had never used the building as his headquarters, and at the time of the raid was with his troops in the frontline, awaiting General Auchinleck's offensive. Our Intelligence Service was at fault.

SAS BATTLE REPORT: THE TOBRUK & BENGHAZI RAID, 1942

Despite the failure of the attack on Rommel's HQ, the temp-tation to launch another special forces raid against a specta-cular target proved too much for Allied planners in North Africa. Ten months later, in September 1942, the SAS was

*committed to a simultaneous landward attack on both Tobruk
and Benghazi. A participant reported:*

Intention

The intention was to drive into TOBRUK in three of
the 3-ton lorries disguised as British Prisoners-of-
War, with a guard made up of the SIG party in
German uniform (increased in number by Lt MAC-
DONALD, Lt HARRISON and myself).

The lorries were to turn along the South side of the
harbour and drive to the Wadi near MARSA UMM
ES SCLAU. Here troops were to de-bus, and divide
into two parties. Lt-Col HASELDEN with the SIG,
RA detachments, Lt TAYLOR's section, Lt SILLI-
TO's section and Lt MACDONALD's section were
to take the small house and gun positions on the West
side of the bay. The remainder of the Squadron, under
Major CAMPBELL was to take the positions on the
East side. Success signals were to be fired by each
party on completion of task, and then Major CAMP-
BELL's party was to proceed two miles East to find
out if there were any guns there and to deal with them.
Unless it proved to be extremely simple for Lt-Col
HASELDEN's party to push on Eastwards and take
the AA positions there, they were to hold until the Coy
of A & S Highlanders and 1 Platoon RNF were landed
from MTBs in the bay.

I was responsible for "signalling in" the MTBs and
meeting the party when they came ashore. The signalling was to take the form of 3 "Ts" flashed every 2
minutes in Red from a point on the West shore of the
bay and also from a point just outside the bay to the
East.

On the journey up, Major CAMPBELL developed
dysentery badly, and, although he insisted on seeing
the job through, Lt-Col HASELDEN told me to
accompany him as 2nd-in-Command as far as the first
objective. My own plan was to station two of the RE
party at the Eastern signalling point, with a torch and

instructions as to how to signal in case I couldn't get back to them. I was then going back to the small house on the West side (which was to be Col HASELDEN's HQ) to report and to collect F/O SCOTT and his two Aldis lamps. I would substitute F/O SCOTT for the two REs and return myself to signal from the Western point. Signalling was not due to start until 0130 hours so there should have been plenty of time.

The rest of the Plan does not affect the remainder of the report.

Entrance

Owing to a slight miscalculation the party was late getting on to the EL ADEM road and it was dark soon after we had turned on to the main road towards TOBRUK. However, the entrance went smoothly and no check posts were encountered. Further delay was caused by the fact that, apparently considerable alterations (wire fences etc.) had been made where the track along the Southern bank of the harbour joined the main road. We were still some way off our debussing point when the bombing started.

After debussing, sorting stores, hiding German uniforms etc. the two parties set out.

Action

Immediately on leaving the trucks Major CAMPBELL's party had to negotiate a small minefield. This was done by an RE party with a detector, and caused considerable delay and necessitated the party walking in a long single file. In the middle of this operation a rifle was fired from the other side of the Wadi. This caused further delay. Eventually one section was sent forward (under Lt. ROBERTS) to investigate and I asked permission to reconnoitre the sandy beach. I walked right across the beach without encountering anything, and directed Lt ROBERTS to take his party up on the high ground to get round the back of whoever had fired the rifle. I then went back to Major CAMPBELL and guided one section across the beach, the rest following at intervals. Lt ROBERTS in the meanwhile engaged and put out of action a section of enemy who were manning a Spandau.

We had taken almost an hour to get across the Wadi. The same procedure of advance was adopted up the Wadi-side and on. I waited on top to guide Lt ROBERTS and the REs [Royal Engineers] who were labouring under heavy burdens of explosives etc. and it took some time to catch up with the rest, who I eventually found, had struck Eastwards away from the bay. Soon after that I met Lt DUFFY who said that all the positions near the Bay were empty and unused.

By this time the success signal from Lt-Col HASELDEN's party had been fired.

We proceeded to catch up Major CAMPBELL and soon afterwards came on a small wireless station which was put out of action with its personnel – mainly by Lt ROBERTS.

In climbing out of that Wadi I discovered it was already 0130 hrs. I urged Major CAMPBELL to fire the success signal, which was done. I then returned alone and as fast as I could towards the bay. This journey was made more difficult by the fact that I had to skirt a small enemy camp in a Wadi which we had missed on the way out. I found the Eastern Signalling point and was relieved to see that F/O SCOTT was signalling from the West side although he was far too high up. The REs had disappeared by this time, and, I presume that they returned to HQ on finding no guns to destroy. I had no watch and only an inadequate torch. I tried to time my signalling with F/O SCOTT's.

After a short while I saw two MTBs [Motor Torpedo Boats] come in. After that however no more appeared. My problem now was whether to stay signalling or to go to meet the landing troops and conduct them to HQ as I was supposed to be doing. I decided to try a compromise by wedging my torch in a rock and leaving it alight. I did this and started back but, before I had gone 200 yds I saw a light flashing out to sea and it appeared to be on an MTB proceeding *away* again. I rushed back to the torch and started to signal again. But nothing materialised. After another half hour I left signalling and started back towards the landing point. On the way back I found that my haversack and tommy gun had been taken from the Sangar where I had left them before climbing down to the rocks. I later ran into two enemy one of whom I hit with my revolver.

On reaching the landing point I found the two MTBs unloading. Lt MACDONALD appeared to be organising the landing, so I took one man with me with a tommy gun and returned at once to continue signalling. During all this time F/O SCOTT was still signalling from the West side.

By the time we got back to the Eastern signalling point the searchlights were sweeping the entrance to the harbour and our own shore. However I resumed signalling. Heavy fire was coming from the opposite shore of the harbour out to sea. Once the MTBs got caught in the searchlights and I could see their wake, and tracer bouncing off one of them. They were well to the East of us however, and it was obvious that there wasn't much chance of them getting in. One of the two MTBs slipped out past me during a slight lull, and appeared to get away safely. At "first light" I decided to abandon signalling and I returned to the landing point. By the time I got there dawn was breaking and I saw one MTB apparently aground. Sounds of rifle and LMG [Light Machine Gun] fire was coming from just over the West ridge of the Wadi, near where we had left the trucks. I hailed the MTB, but getting no answer, I walked around the bay and up the small Wadi to the house which was Lt-Col HASELDEN's HQ. Rifle fire was coming down the Wadi. I got to the house to find it deserted and I saw the heads of about a platoon of enemy lying covering the house from about 300 yds away. I walked back down the small wadi, and thinking I heard a shout aboard the MTB, I boarded her, but found no-one. I filled my water bottle and took what food I could find. Lt RUSSELL, Lt SILLITO, Pte HILLMAN and Pte WATLER then came aboard. Lt RUSSELL opened up with the twin Lewis guns forward on troops on top of the hill. I went to the engines to see if there was any hope of getting them started, but not even Pte WATLER – a mechanic – could help there. We then took all we could in the way of food and water and boarded one of the assault craft lying alongside. We paddled out into the bay but were forced to go ashore by being fired on from the rocks on the West side. We saw some of our own men dodging along the West side of the bay and there were large explosions coming from behind them. It was impossible to tell who they were, but I think they may have been the REs dealing with the guns on the point. We climbed through a minefield and into a Wadi. Here we were joined by Sgt EVANS. We made for the hills, having to hide frequently from low-flying aircraft. I looked back from the higher ground and saw what I now know to have been HMS ZULU with HMS SIKH in tow. The latter appeared to be burning and shells were bursting round. We were fired on heavily, going over a ridge, from the direction of BRIGHTON, but got safely into a large Wadi where we found about 15–20 others waiting. These included 2/Lt MACDONALD and Lt BARLOW, also those of the RNF who had been landed from the MTBs. We decided it was now useless to resist. No one knew what had become of Major CAMPBELL's party. It seemed clear that Col HASELDEN had been killed. We decided to take to the hills and make for Wadi SHAGRA North of BARDIA, where we had been told we would be picked up 5 days later.

Escape

We did not stop long in the big Wadi. Lts SILLITO and MACDONALD took their respective sections. I believe their intention was to make towards the coast further East and try to get taken off by the MTBs the same day. I have not heard of any of them since.

Lt BARLOW, Lt RUSSELL and myself went off up the Wadi with eight men. We found a small Wadi and lay up all that day among the bushes. At dusk we disposed of everything we did not require, divided what food we had into three and ourselves into three parties. We split up and made for the perimeter that night. Later in the night – after avoiding two enemy posts I joined up again with Lt BARLOW's party. Soon after we met, we bumped another enemy post and had to take hurriedly to the nearest Wadi. When we regathered Lt BARLOW was nowhere to be found, and I have not seen or heard of him since. After "bumping" several more posts we eventually got through the perimeter wire and lay up next day in a cave in a Wadi.

We had two nights of dodging camps etc. during part of which we walked on the road. We hid up every day in caves in the Wadis. On the fifth night, just as we were desperate for food and water we found the first Arab village where we were taken in, fed and given water. Pte HILLMAN acted as interpreter. The Arabs knew all about the TOBRUK raid. They also said they could not understand how the English managed to come all the way from KUFRA.

Going from village to village, we eventually reached the Wadi AM REISA. There was a large Carabinieri post at the shore end of this Wadi, the strength of which had recently been doubled, according to the Arabs. They also told us of boats cruising up and down at night – they said they thought they were British. One had landed a party one night and someone had shouted "Any British here?"

The Arabs then showed us to the Wadi KATTARA about 5 miles North of BARDIA. Here we found an Indian soldier of the 3/18th Garwhal Rifles who had escaped 3 times from TOBRUK and had been living there for 2 months.

We also found Pte WATLER. His story is as follows:

On leaving us on the night of the 14th, Lt RUS-SELL, Pte WATLER and one member of the SIG got through the perimeter and walked "all out" towards BARDIA along the road. They arrived at MERSA SHAGRA one day late. That night they ran into the enemy post in Wadi AM REISA and were fired on. In making their getaway Pte WATLER got left behind because of bad boots. Nothing further is known of the other two. The man with Lt RUSSELL spoke only German.

We lived in the Wadi KATTARA for four weeks being fed by the Arabs as best they could. We tried making fires by night to attract the attention of air-craft, but only got a stick of bombs extremely close. The only news or information we got was obtained from Italian, or German soldiers via the Arabs who sold eggs etc. on the road and engaged the soldiers in conversation. It was apparent that the enemy was very low in morale and very short of food. We had to take great care not to get caught because the Italians would undoubtedly have "wiped out" the village. As it was we saw no one during our four weeks there.

After three weeks Sgt EVANS unfortunately got dysentery and later we had to help him to the road by night and leave him to be picked up the next morning. The same happened a few days later to one of the Leslie twins and his brother went with him. The rains had come heavily and it was very cold and damp. I decided to move. The Indian stayed behind, and so the party consisted of Cpl WILSON, Pte WATLER, Pte HILLMAN and myself. I was lucky to have a German compass and a small German map, though the latter was not much use being 1:5,000,000. We had some tins of bully-beef, some goat meat and bread and ten water-bottles. We started on Oct 26th.

Apart from getting fired on on the second night our journey was uneventful. We did not see anyone from the day after we climbed through the frontier wire until we were picked up at HIMEIMAT on Friday Nov 18th with the exception of one convoy which looked very like an SAS patrol – near the SIWA–MERSA MATRUH track on Nov 5th. We walked south of the QATTARA depression for the last four days and thereby missed the "retreat".

In other words, the attack was a failure. The SAS, however, learned its lesson and were noticeably reluctant thereafter to undertake large-scale, spectacular operations. The regiment resumed its role as small-scale raiders of the Axis lines of communications, fuel dumps and airfields in North Africa.

DESERT PATROL

David Lloyd Owen

*Like Popski's Private Army and David Stirling's SAS,
the Long Range Desert Group (LRDG) owed its existence to the determination of one man.*

*Major Ralph Bagnold was a Signals officer who,
during the 1920s and 1930s undertook numerous journeys
through North Africa in Ford cars and trucks, and
became convinced of the need for a desert reconnaissance
force. GHQ Middle East begged to differ – until June
1940 when Italy declared war on Britain, and the self-
same GHQ Middle East realized that it had little idea of
Italian dispositions in North Africa. A month later the
Provisional War Establishment of the Long Range Desert Group was authorized, originally for eleven officers
and seventy-one men. Most of these were selected from a
New Zealand Division at a loose end in Egypt after their
ship had sunk. To transport the LRDG on its desert
endeavours, Bagnold – handily furnished with a chit
from General Wavell which stated: "I wish that any
request by Major Bagnold in person should be met instantly and without question" – scoured Egypt for thirty-
five Chevrolet 30-cwt trucks. The first LRDG missions
were purely reconnaissance, but Wavell quickly granted
the LRDG a "free hand to stir up trouble in any part of
Libya" (Bagnold). Success bred expansion, and patrols
from the Guards, the Yeomanry and Rhodesian forces
were added to the LRDG muster.*

*Captain David Lloyd Owen joined the Yeomanry
Patrol of the LRDG in mid-1941. In November Lloyd
Owen led the patrol for the first time as commander.*

I WAS NOT used to operating over the more cultivated soil of that part of Libya and a more than usually flat piece of going in that rough country enticed me with its promise of more speed. Quite unsuspecting, I told Springford to alter course and steer towards it. Coombs driving Alan Denniff was hot on my tail and one of the other trucks was level out to my right flank.

We covered the first hundred yards at a rollicking pace and suddenly I noticed the colour of the mud-pan getting a bit darker. Coombs was now only twenty yards behind us and the sight of us coming to a halt and Titch nearly being thrown over the handlebars made him laugh so much that he did not think of turning off to a flank. The third truck, about eighty yards away, suffered the same fate and within one hundred yards of each other there were three heavily laden trucks completely bogged.

Springford tried the first action of attempting to drive the vehicle out backwards. This merely served to dig our wheels in deeper. We then got out and dug a place behind the rear wheels in the hope that we could ride the truck up on the sand-channels – these were steel strips perforated with holes and about five feet long. Even these would not move us.

By now we were in the mud up to our axles and there were only two things to do. We first tried to bring one of the two remaining trucks up to tow us out. But that only bogged itself in the struggle and endeavour.

The situation was black. Four out of our five trucks were bogged down only fourteen miles to the west of Tmimi landing ground. German and Italian aircraft were flying above us all the time.

There was nothing for it but to unload each truck in turn and get it out as best we could. It was no mean task when each one was carrying a minimum of one and a half tons of stores. But we did it and after six of the more uncomfortable hours I have ever spent we eventually had the whole patrol on firm ground. It was now late and so we turned an ignominiously defeated tail towards the coast and hastened back into the desert.

We rejoined Frank Simms that evening and decided to

lay up for the first part of the following day and then move off again to the coast at about teatime. We had noticed that the majority of the enemy aircraft seemed to pack up for the night about then and movement would be safer.

For some strange reason more enemy aircraft flew over us that day than on any previous day. We felt that they must have been searching for us and only later did we discover that David Stirling's party with Jake Easonsmith had been attacked from the air on their way back to Siwa. Obviously the enemy had been alerted.

In the early evening Frank moved off to the north and I let him have twenty minutes start before following. I had decided to observe Jake's dictum and do the natural thing by moving blatantly along a track. Surely the average airman flying over us would never suspect us about a hundred miles behind his own front line?

It was getting cold and the sun had just gone down in a blaze of orange over to our left. The light was still good and we would probably have covered quite a reasonable distance before it was too dark to see any more. Frank and I had arranged to spend the night together and make an early start in the morning. But suddenly I heard Titch shout "Aircraft!" – it was the warning cry we most feared.

I looked round to see Titch grabbing the butt-handles of his Vickers gun and pointing it menacingly to our rear. Our five trucks were strung out in a long line on the track and just above the dust I saw a single-engined fighter come roaring over the last vehicle and down over the heads of us all.

It was an Italian. There was nothing for it but to wait and see what it would do. The suspense was painful as we watched it swing round us twice in a wide circle while the pilot was making up his mind whether or not to attack.

Jake's words came back to me. Be natural. Yes, that was the obvious thing to do until the pilot began to suspect us. So I shouted to everyone to hold their fire. He flew round once more in a rather wider circle and then came in straight at us just as though he was going to strafe us. Be natural! The words hummed through my brain.

All right, I would be; and I strode out a few paces from

my truck and waved in the most friendly way I could. Some of the others followed suit and we had the satisfaction of seeing the pilot wave back cheerily out of his cockpit and fly home in the dark to his dinner!

We all laughed a little nervously and felt sorry for that pilot for we hoped that he would get a frightful rocket later on if we were going to have the success we had planned.

It was getting dark and although we had not met Frank we decided to halt for the night. It was a cold and miserable night and there was some rain which added little to our comfort. I remember, too, that we had some difficulty in "shooting the stars", as clouds obscured those in which we were particularly interested. But it did not matter as we knew well enough where we were.

The next morning we started off very early as I wanted to try and find Frank. I did not know that he preferred a leisurely start and we had only gone about ten miles when I came across him and his patrol. They were just having breakfast and so we joined them over a cup of tea.

I discussed our plan for the day with Frank Simms and we agreed on a rendezvous where we would meet later on. There was no point in my hanging about in the open country where we were and so I decided to move on towards better cover in the north.

We thanked Frank and his men for their tea and, huddled in our greatcoats against the early chill of the morning, we drove off. The sky was overcast and there was still an atmosphere of grey and cheerless dawn. My morale was fairly low and I was longing for the sun to climb higher and warm my shivering body.

Springford was blowing on his hands to keep them warm, swearing all the while at his early rise from bed. "Cold this morning, Skipper, isn't it?"

"Yes, bloody awful," I replied rather shortly for I was in no mood for petty banter.

"I bet the Wops won't be up very early to-day. They like to wait about in bed until it's warmer. They know a thing or two, don't they?" he said with some feeling and a barely disguised meaning.

"Yes, but the early bird—" I began to say but suddenly

noticed that Springford was sitting up and taking a bit more interest.

"Titch," he shouted. "Do you see something moving to our left?"

Titch bestirred himself a little, grabbed the handles of his friend, the Vickers, and looked out towards the west.

"It's a truck," he cried.

"All right, we'll stop a moment and let's have a look at it through glasses," I said to Springford.

I took my glasses out of their case on the dashboard and had a look at the vehicle.

"It looks to me like a Ford lorry."

"Can't be," Titch replied.

"Damned well can be. They've captured lots of ours. Yes, I'm sure it is and I can see some men in the back. Let's get cracking and go and see who they are. Go on, Springford, drive on. We'll go in extended order and encircle them. Titch, don't shoot yet, we may get them by surprise."

"Let's scupper them, Skipper. We don't want any bloody prisoners," Titch replied.

"No, hold it for a moment," I shouted as we bumped across the desert.

We closed in on them. My truck was in the centre going straight for them and there were two others out on either flank. We were going as fast as we could and whoever owned the vehicle we were heading for must have been shaken by the sight of us charging at them.

"All right, Titch, give them a burst," I said. "That'll stop any funny business and we've got them cold now."

Titch's eyes suddenly brightened and a look of great determination came into his face as he made himself comfortable to fire across the few hundred yards that separated us from our quarry.

The machine-gun spat out one short burst which was quite enough to make the enemy capitulate. The vehicle jammed on its brakes and the occupants in the back stood up with their hands high above their heads. We closed in on them to find that there were three Italians and two native Libyan soldiers as our captives. They were in a very good new Ford 15-cwt truck and this was a useful capture. Otherwise they had very little with them.

The time was a quarter past seven in the morning and one of the Italians was in no mood for bravery. He spoke quite reasonable English and was prepared to air his knowledge of it. In fact, he was only too anxious to do almost anything to help us and told me that he had come from a small fort not far away and he indicated the direction to me.

I asked him where he was going and he explained that they were going on a few days leave to Derna and would return bringing with them the rations for their little outpost.

Some of the wags in my patrol told him they were sorry he wouldn't get his leave in Derna but that we would be delighted to take him back to Cairo. He thought that was a splendid idea and said that he had always wanted to see Cairo.

"You will, brother – if you're lucky!" snapped Titch.

"Thank you," said the terrified little man. "Thank you very much."

"OK. You be good then, and no monkey-tricks," Titch retaliated obviously in possessive mood.

"Tell me about your fort," I asked. "How many men are there?"

"Not many. 'Bout-a-twenty."

"What guns have they?"

"Some machine guns."

"Have they any sentries?"

"Oh, *si*! There is always a man on the roof."

"Let's go and beat them up, sir," Titch interrupted.

"Yes, let's," the others joined in.

"I think we will," I said. "Come on, little man, you come with me and show me the way."

"OK. Verra good, verra good," he muttered nervously.

So I told him to sit up on the back of my truck and he climbed rather apprehensively up beside Titch Cave, who made him feel the little rat he was.

We drove off in the general direction the Italian had indicated to me and found the going a bit rough. Our passanger knew a better way and showed me the route to avoid the worst of the country. We had gone a few miles when he suddenly pointed ahead of him and shouted, "There it is."

Not far off, as we came over a slight rise in the ground, I could see the little *Beau Geste* fort. It looked very serene and peaceful in the early morning and I decided to stop and have a look at it through my glasses. We were now about 600 yards off, and I could clearly see a man on the turreted roof of the building watching us through his glasses.

There was no point in dallying, especially as our Italian passenger said he thought the garrison would surrender if we looked really menacing. This was reassuring as I was not at all clear what would be the best tactics to employ when quite unarmoured 30-cwt vehicles were faced with attacking a fort. I felt boldness was probably the only advantage we had on our side and that we must exploit it to the full. Surprise had certainly gone – we could not look much like Italians at that short range.

I gave the order to advance and we careered forward in open formation. I felt very foolish for I had simply no idea what I would do if the opposition was determined. All went well until we were about 200 yards from the fort and then the defenders decided to open fire on us. This was awkward for I could not afford to endanger any of our trucks unnecessarily.

I pulled away a bit to the left and told everyone to dismount except for the drivers of the vehicles who would stay to guard the prisoners and give us covering fire. My Italian interpreter came, rather unwillingly, with me. We took some machine guns with us and advanced on foot towards some outhouses and stone sangars – an unaccustomed rôle for my patrol of Yeomanry from the 1st Cavalry Division.

We reached the cover of the buildings without casualties and there then began some intermittent and not very effective sniping between both the opposing sides. This went on for a while and did not seem to be getting us anywhere. There were only eight of us on foot and I did not see how we would succeed if we attempted to take the fort by storm. Anyway it was a stone edifice and the front door, which was in our view, looked a formidable structure. I did not think there would be much future in just charging at it.

We had reached a very awkward stalemate. It would be too ignominious just to get up and drive away. But I could not see how we could possibly win with our few men and very limited weapons: we certainly had nothing suitable for storming a fort.

Suddenly an idea came to me. It was only the remotest chance but it was just a hope that I might bluff the enemy into surrender. I called for my Italian friend, who lay cowering in the dust behind a wall and he came up to join me. I explained my plot to him. I wanted him to walk forward and shout to the commander of the garrison that I proposed to offer him an armistice so that he could come out and discuss terms of surrender. I explained that I had heavy reinforcements over the hill and that, if he did not give in, I would have to call them up.

My interpreter said that this was an excellent idea, but he did not like the thought of standing up and going forward. So I gave him a nip of whisky out of my flask, which was in my haversack slung over my shoulder. I had one, too, and we both felt better. I pushed him to his feet and with some courage he walked forward into the open. We had already ceased fire and the enemy held theirs as soon as they saw one of their own comrades advance towards them waving a grubby handkerchief.

The inevitable infuriating back-chat then went on at the tops of the voices of the negotiators. I could not find out what was going on and was getting impatient at the endless speeches my representative was making. I did not want to hang about here for ever, for it was more than likely that the fort had a wireless and was giving a running commentary to its superiors.

"Tell him to come out," I shouted. "Just tell him that. No more."

"OK. I tell him. I say he must come. He says he will not come. But I say he must come again," and off he went into another stream of shrill Italian. But at last I realized that he must have been imploring his superior officer to come out (if only to save his own skin) for the heavy door suddenly opened and the commander came forth to meet me!

I shouted to everyone to hold their fire and walked forward to meet my opponent. He came with a determined stride and as we shook hands, I was impressed that it was not the flaccid and flabby hand that I had expected. He was a stocky man with well-cut features and a pugnacious jaw. Dressed in the light blue-grey of the Italian Army he looked smart and soldier-like and he must have wondered what I was with no badges of rank on my shoulder and thick stubble on my chin.

I offered my adversary a cigarette and we stood together conversing through my interpreter. It was a fantastic situation. I explained about my reinforcements, which had many tanks with them and I told him that his days were numbered. I told him that we would treat him honourably and that they would thoroughly enjoy the delights of Cairo. I laid it on for all I was worth.

But the little man was made of sterner stuff than my interpreter had led me to believe and he was adamant in his determination to continue the fight. After about ten minutes of useless haggling I realized that I was beat, said I was very sorry that the inevitable would have to occur, as I had been so very keen to avoid further bloodshed, and shook hands once more with the enemy commander. He turned on his heel and walked back to the fort.

I went back to my position in the outhouses and said to Alan Denniff who was with me, "What on earth do we do now?"

"Can't think," he replied.

"I know, let's try firing a grenade from this damned thing," said Springford, who had grabbed the rifle with a discharger cup on its muzzle when he dismounted to join the battle, leaving Titch in charge of our truck and behind his beloved machine-gun.

"Do you know how to use it?" I asked.

"Not really, but I'll have a go."

We never used the weapon normally and I cannot think why we had it as it was only extra weight to carry. But we had tried everything else and there was no harm in having a bang with it. Rifles, pistols, machine-guns, Very lights – all had been tried so far and had made little impression on the enemy safely sheltered behind their stone walls.

After a few minutes, during which the grenade was primed and the rifle all set to fire, Springford said he was all ready and so I told him to fire. His preparations had been generally directed by Denniff and the men who were nearest to him. There was a reasonable chance that the average of their opinions would have hit on something approximating the correct range.

Springford fired and we watched the grenade leave the rifle and go hurtling up into the air. The direction at least was perfect.

All eyes now turned to the top of the tower and we only had to wait a few seconds before, to our utter consternation, we saw it bang with a splendid little explosion plumb on its target.

I remembered the essence of the principles of attack and knew that we must follow up this strike before the enemy had time to pick themselves up and to retaliate. The only thing to do now was to assault the place in the hope that we would frighten them into capitulation.

So we ran forward firing everything that we had got and shouting savage cries. This had the desired effect and, before we had blunted our noses in a futile assault on the stone building, we saw the main door swing open and watched the garrison pour out in their anxiety to surrender.

We stood a little foolishly and counted them as they ran out towards us. One, two, three . . . ten, eleven, twelve . . . and so on until there were seventeen. I have never seen a more morose, sullen and dispirited section of the human species than those seventeen miserable defenders of Mussolini's outpost of the Italian Empire at El Ezzeiat; for such was the name of the nearest place on the map to the fort.

The prisoners stood dejected in a heap outside their former home and we rushed in to see what there was to be had. There was not much. A certain amount of food and a few bottles of wine were collected and we found some documents. Otherwise there was little of any immediate value to ourselves. We destroyed three machine-guns, the rest of the stores and ammunition and generally left the place unfit for occupation without a major job of clearance.

I climbed up the stairs on to the roof and found the bodies of two men who had been manning the machine-gun when the chance grenade had put a speedy end to their existence on earth. I felt rather sorry for them as they had fought bravely and continued to remain at their post to the end in spite of the fact that they had been the only target we could see. Consequently each of us had done his best to dislodge them from their position and all our shots had been directed at them.

As I came down to have a final look round before leaving I saw a small door which was still shut. So I opened it carefully and burst in just in case there might still be somebody lying in wait. I found my wireless operator inside having a look at the set which was standing on a table.

"Does it work?" I asked.

"Yes, and it's still switched on. I expect they've been in touch with their base all the time, and I'll bet that was why they wouldn't surrender earlier."

"Well, we can't waste any more time here. Make a note of the frequency they're on and pinch anything else that's useful and then smash the thing to pieces," I said.

We had already been in the fort for forty-five minutes and it was now a quarter past nine. It was time to go, and so I gave the order to pack up and to set fire to anything that would burn. At any moment the enemy might send an aircraft over to investigate and we did not want to be caught driving away from El Ezzeiat.

The prisoners were bundled on to the back of our trucks and crowded into their own Ford lorry and we drove away as fast as we could possibly travel. There were more anxious eyes watching the skies than ever before and I think we all felt as guilty as small boys who had stolen the apples from the tree in the village policeman's garden.

We went back on our tracks for about thirty-five miles to where we knew of some good cover. I was only happy when all our vehicles were camouflaged into some large bushes in the bottom of a wadi and we had brushed away the tracks that we had made in the soft sand driving into it.

It was now about eleven o'clock in the morning and the first thing to do was to tell Guy Prendergast of what had occurred. I was rather pleased with my morning's work and enjoyed writing out a signal to tell him of our success.

"From Y2 Patrol. At 07.30 after capturing 3 Italians and Ford truck we ran into a small occupied fort at EL EZ-ZEIAT. After battle lasting one hour garrison of seventeen surrendered. Destroyed wireless set in communication with Mechili three MG's, quantity of stores and ammunition. Total 2 killed 20 captured and NO casualties to own side. Am now at . . . Await your instructions."

It took a bit of time to encipher the message but we got it through and were told to come back on the air again in an hour. Meanwhile I took stock of the situation. We had twenty prisoners and an extra vehicle. Luckily we had suffered no casualties ourselves worse than one bullet hole through the trouser leg of Private Devine, who had been left with his vehicle to guard the first bag of prisoners during the scrap. He was so incensed with this that when he saw us charge forward in the final assault he shouted to one of the prisoners, "Here, look after my horse," and he rushed forward himself to be in at the kill.

While waiting for the reply from Siwa I got to work on interrogating the prisoners through the interpreter. He was not quite so willing to help as he had been before as he was now under the watchful eye of his former commanding officer who was being a little truculent and defiant.

I discovered that there were two Italian Divisions in Derna and they told me that there were about 400 men in Mechili. This was all useful information. Otherwise they did not tell me much, except that they were suffering quite a lot of hardship from the cold as they had not been given any winter clothing. This was obvious as they were still shivering in their lightweight summer kit. They also told me that their rations were very inadequate and they were lucky to have anything at all sometimes.

I did not glean much else of value from them but they told me that they had knowledge of David Stirling's parachutists but never expected to see a motorized force appear in their peaceful little neighbourhood so far away from the front. It had been a nasty shock to them, they said.

We then had lunch and, in the inevitable manner that British soldiers have with their captives, the Italians were given everything they wanted. I suppose there was no good in being anything but pleasant to them for, although we gave no sign of the fact, we were in none too secure a position ourselves. There was no guarantee that the tables would not be turned and we might find ourselves waiting on our prisoners' mercy.

In the early afternoon a message came through and I sat down to decipher it in the confident anticipation that it would be a pleasant round-off to our successful little operation.

Not a bit of it! It was terse, to the point and written in a mood of ill-disguised irritation!

"Your orders were to operate offensively against transport in a certain area. Dispose of your prisoners and do what you were told."

This signal conveyed exactly the effect it was intended to have. I felt completely deflated and really very small. I had not looked on our action in the light in which I now saw it. My Commanding Officer was quite right. I had been told to go up to the Derna area and to disrupt the enemy's communications. My morning's work had done nothing towards that end!

Oh, dear! Something would have to be done, and done pretty quickly, to restore Guy's confidence in me. But it was not quite as easy as all that. "Dispose of your prisoners, and do what you were told." It was simple enough to do what I was told but the problem of the prisoners was a little more tricky.

There seemed to be three alternatives open to me. Either I could dispose of them in a literal sense, or I could leave them under guard and pick them up later or I could just leave them where they were. There were all sorts of problems. Disposal was not an attractive suggestion in any way. It violated the Red Cross Convention and the laws of war; it violated all my own moral principles and I could not

do it while there were other possible alternatives. To leave
them under guard would diminish my little force too much,
and to leave them without a guard gave them much too
reasonable a chance of having us followed up within a few
days.

I remember putting the problem to the men. There was a
definite school of thought which wanted blood. They saw
no other reasonable alternative. We could not afford to
guard them and we simply could not risk letting them go.
By now the prisoners knew far too much about our methods. But there were those among us who felt as I did. We
could not "bump them off" in cold blood and anyhow who
would do it?

We argued for an awful long time but there was no hurry
as I had decided that I would not move until dusk. There
were still two or three more hours of daylight and they were
very worrying ones.

In the end I had an idea. A compromise that would save
both our lives and our consciences and would enable us to
go on unhindered and do as we had been told. Whatever I
did we had to get rid of them. I had not enough food and
water to keep them for long and I could not possibly have
them hanging around our necks if we were to go and attack
transport.

There was only one answer. I reckoned that if I could
ensure that they did not reach any Italian garrison in less
than five days I would have a reasonable chance of getting
away with it.

I had not got enough food or water to stay out for longer
as we had already been away from Siwa for over two weeks
and it had always been intended that we were to return in
under three weeks.

I worked out that the prisoners must start from a point
eighty miles from any help and, therefore would have to
start thirty miles away further to the south from where we
then were. I would give them sufficient food and water to
spur them on to survival and, as Bill Kennedy Shaw said in
his book, "the general direction for a march on Rome".

I explained what I intended to do to Sergeant Carningham and, after we had given the prisoners a good hot meal,

he took two trucks with a few men as escort and set off into the desert. I knew they were very apprehensive as to their fate and I am quite sure they expected that they were off to die when I said good-bye to them.

Just before dusk Sergeant Carningham returned, told me that he had dumped the unfortunate devils in the desert and we had our evening meal. It was some months later that I heard that the prisoners had eventually reached their own lines safely for the German High Command were very incensed at what they considered savage treatment of prisoners at the hands of the piratical patrols of the LRDG. Little did they know how very lucky they were to be alive at all.

After we had supper we moved off in the dark towards the north and I planned to try and find some cover where we could lie up for the day and attack the main road the following night – 30th November. It was a cold and wet night and we had another miserable drive as it was difficult to see and even harder to navigate.

The only method we could use was for Alan Denniff to work out a compass bearing for the direction in which I wanted him to go. I would then drive for half an hour on a star which he had selected for me before halting to repeat the process. Meanwhile, Alan would take the speedometer reading of our peregrinations and, by a simple system of plotting distance and the deviations from his compass bearings, he would be able to tell reasonably well where we were.

I hoped to move to within about fifteen miles of Tmimi airfield in the dark and then go on at the first sign of light into some cover. But Tmimi had more than one airfield and when I moved on in the morning I came over a rise to find that we were practically on the edge of one of them. We had the unnerving experience of about six German planes roaring over our heads as they took off above us. This was too near as we wanted a secure hideout where we could sleep as we had only had one hour's rest during the night.

I moved off hastily to the Wadi Maallegh where the patrol had been before and where there was some good cover. We were glad to reach it and to get breakfast. We lay hidden all day, snatching what little sleep we could get; it was not very peaceful as there were aircraft over us frequently and we counted two hundred during the hours of daylight. One even flew almost at ground level down the wadi in which we were hiding and, of course, we suspected that they were all on the lookout for us.

During the day I went off with Titch Cave to go and see what we could observe of the main Tobruk-Derna road. We climbed to a high escarpment and there ten miles away we could see the road down below on the plain. There was little movement of traffic, but I was glad to have had an opportunity of seeing the country in the daytime.

After the night's rain we had been lucky to have fine weather until the evening when it began to pour down again. I never saw such rain, in the whole time I was in the desert, as came down that evening. We were soaked through and the wadi bed soon became a raging torrent of water. We even had to move some of the trucks higher up the banks to keep them out of it.

The lack of sleep and the damp were having an effect on me and I was feeling very low. I had contracted "that distressing and almost universal complaint" and was thoroughly uncomfortable. But there was no turning back now that we were poised all ready.

After dark that night I took twelve men in two of our trucks down towards the road. The wireless truck and two others I left in the Wadi Maallegh with their drivers. I felt it wiser to have only the minimum transport with us as I had decided to do the final attack on foot. The country was rough, rocky and with some deep wadis, and I could not be certain of a really speedy getaway if I took the trucks right down to the road.

When I was three miles from the main road we left the two trucks with their drivers and the remainder of us walked on in the dark to the road. We arrived there at nine o'clock and it was blowing a cold wind from the northeast as we settled down at ten-yard intervals on the edge of the road. We were lying on the slope of an embankment and it gave us some shelter from the wind.

After the rain the sky had cleared a bit and the stars were

twinkling in the arena of sky above us. Titch Cave was with me and we could just see the dark forms of the others lying on either side of us. It was silent except for the slight sound of the wind blowing across the desert.

Presently we saw some lights away to our left and realized that there were vehicles coming towards us. Soon we heard the noise of their engines and we got ready to act. I was lying in the middle of the men stretched over about a hundred yards of the roadside and my plan was to allow no one to fire until I gave the signal. Then, if I decided that the target was worthy of our efforts, I would blow a whistle at the critical moment and we would open up with every weapon we possessed.

The convoy of vehicles drew near. Only a hundred yards away . . . Their lights were on . . . I could count them . . . One, two, three, four. There may have been more . . . I was not sure . . . I was straining my eyes to see and count . . . No, I did not think there were any more than four, possibly five . . . That was not worth it . . . I hoped for at least ten or more . . . They drew level with me . . . My whistle still in my mouth with my frozen hand shaking slightly on my rifle . . . I did not give the signal . . . One, two, three, four, five, six lorries rumbled ponderously past us.

Six lorries. No, that was not worth the effort at that stage. And they had been empty – or so it seemed in the darkness – and there were only their drivers with them. Eventually the sound of their engines disappeared into the night and all was silent once more.

Titch spoke first. "They didn't know how near they were to their last moment. Lucky brutes."

"I'd like to meet them one day and tell them just how lucky they were."

"I wonder if they saw us. Their lights were bloody bright."

"I don't suppose they did and anyhow they wouldn't have been inclined to have done much about it even if they had. I think I won't go for anything less than ten unless it is petrol tankers."

"No," said Titch. "We haven't come all this bleeding way for nothing. We might just as well have a proper duffy

while we're here. Have some rum, sir? I've got a drop in a
bottle."

"Yes, I'd love some. I'm damned cold and I'm not feeling
frightfully good."

I took a swig from Titch's bottle and felt the warmth of it
course down inside me. It was good and I had another
mouthful. As I got up the others must have seen me for one
or two of them came over to talk to us.

We lay down again and waited. Nothing passed us until
three quarters of an hour later when two vehicles came from
the front and went on to Derna. Then there was complete
silence for two hours until at midnight one vehicle came
noisily along from the east. Some of us had fallen asleep.
Titch certainly had, and when someone went to wake him
they found that he was lying on his back on the embankment with a grenade in each hand – and he had removed the
safety pins from them, all ready to leap into instant action!

Once more we watched the approaching lorry and I had
no intention of firing at it because it was such a small target.
I was after bigger fish than this. But as it drew up alongside
me I suddenly saw that it was a large petrol tanker and I
blew my whistle and fired at point-blank range. It ran the
gauntlet down past four others each of whom fired at
equally short range.

To our utter consternation it drove serenely on, neither
speeding up nor slowing down. We all assumed that the
driver must have been deaf and the tanker armour-plated.
It had a trailer behind it and must have been capable of
carrying many hundreds of gallons of petrol. I simply do
not know what happened to that vehicle. It must have been
empty and must have had at least fifty bullet holes in it by
the time we had finished. But we could not claim a kill
which was disappointing after we had been on the road for
three hours.

Once more we waited. Twelve-thirty came and nothing
had gone by since the bullet-proof petrol tanker. I decided
that I could not hang about for too long. I had given our
position away and I had to have sufficient darkness to get
well clear of the area by sunrise. So I told the men that I
would attack the next thing that came along.

Just before one o'clock in the morning when our morale was at its lowest and we were all frozen stiff I saw some lights coming in from the direction of Tobruk. Maddening; I wanted to hit at stuff going the other way but it was too late to choose. The lorry came on slowly towards us and as it got to a point about fifteen yards away from me, Titch rolled a grenade out on to the road in front of it.

We all pulled our heads below the embankment and waited for the explosion. Once more we had incredible luck with a grenade and this one exploded right underneath a ten-ton lorry. At the same moment every possible weapon was brought to bear on it and the lorry stopped.

Titch – a little foolishly – scrambled up the embankment and hurled two more grenades into the back. At the same moment two men, whom we later discovered were officers, jumped out of the cab and were promptly shot dead. One more man somehow leapt out alive from the back of the lorry and he was despatched equally swiftly.

I managed then to stop the shooting and we all scrambled up on to the embankment to finish off the vehicle and count the dead. There were two officers and seven others left there that night. There was no future in hanging about and so we cut all the telephone cables and withdrew away from the road.

By then I was in a pretty poor state and very near collapse. I was in considerable pain and remember very little of our return journey except that, when we had nearly gone about half way to the two vehicles in which we had come forward from our hideout, an aeroplane came flying very low over where we were. Then I remember nothing else until we reached the two vehicles and heard from Alan Denniff, whom I had left in charge, that a motorcycle and a car had been to within fifty yards of where they were concealed.

This was disconcerting news and there was no time to be wasted. But for some odd reason one of our trucks would not start. The fitter was with the other three vehicles and there was nothing that we could do. I decided to abandon it and so we took off all the kit that was of any value to us, removed various essential parts of the mechanism and left it where it was.

We all piled on to the one remaining truck and I collapsed in the front seat. I can only remember Titch holding me in and, at one time, when I came round I heard him saying, "Look, they're still following." I looked round and saw vehicles with their lights some distance behind us.

Eventually we reached our first three vehicles and Titch lifted me up into the front seat of my own truck after I had fallen asleep on the ground while we spent five minutes getting everything sorted out and ready to move. We then drove away from the area as far as we could go in the remaining hours of darkness, followed for a while by the mysterious vehicles with lights on. But we gave them the slip and found some reasonable cover where we lay up in hiding for the whole of the 1st December.

Two days later – after another successful attack on enemy transport – Lloyd Owen's patrol reached the safety of the LRDG's base at Siwa.

As Julian Thompson notes in his study of British special forces during World War II, Behind Enemy Lines *(1998), the LRDG was the most "cost-effective" of them. At peak strength it numbered little more than 300 men, but still managed to carry out more than 200 operations. Nor were these limited to the Western Desert; the LRDG also saw service in in Greece, Yugoslavia and Italy. The LRDG was disbanded in 1945.*

HUNTED

John Verney

*Verney was an officer with L Squadron of the SBS.
During the 1943 Allied invasion of Sardinia, Verney's
detachment became trapped behind Italo-German lines.
The hunters became the hunted.*

NEAR THE TOP of the ridge we found a spring. Dawn was
nearly breaking as we halted to wait for it and slept for
a little. The daylight woke us. We were on a lonely range of
hills and felt much satisfaction contemplating the distance
we had come on the ground, though it was disappointingly
little – about five miles – on the map. As the hills seemed
deserted I decided to push on farther in the cool of the
morning. The sun always became unpleasantly hot after 10
a.m. and the hours between noon and 4 p.m. were almost
unbearable in anything except deep shade. After that the
heat relaxed rapidly till the sun set about 7.30 p.m. The
sensation of relief from the strain of the day was always
delicious in the remaining two hours of twilight before
darkness finally came.

Before leaving we shaved, for comfort but also for camouflage reasons. In our American cork helmets we could
hope to pass for German soldiers among Italians, but with
untidy beards the disguise would be less effective. We
managed to shave every third day during our march –
Amos's party of course could not. Razors had been a small
but particularly important item in the preparation of equipment for the expedition.

We had only covered a few hundred yards when we met a shepherd and his flock. We told him we were Germans. To our dismay he left his flock and walked with us. The same old homicidal doubts I hated so much ... We were debating in whispers what he could be up to when we came over a crest and saw the village of Sarule a quarter of a mile away. The shepherd stopped and pointing to it, told us to go there and people would give us cold milk and bread and cheese. We made a show of being delighted with the advice and started towards the village, looking back suspiciously to see if he was watching. But he had returned to his flock. We swerved away from the village and crawled into some low but adequately thick scrub, to spend the day.

The scrub gave very little shade and we spent a wretchedly uncomfortable day, dozing and sweating and wriggling ineffectually under the sparse foliage to escape the sun's rays. The date was now 12th July.

Amos and I, in planning this march, had originally decided to move "across country" the whole way – first eastwards as far as the coast and then south over the coastal hills, the summit of one of which, Mt. Alberu, was the RV. But now, seeing how slowly we covered map-distances over those rough hills, I thought we should never reach the RV in time. Personally, I preferred to take the risk of using roads at night, for the sake of the extra speed. Brown and Fry agreed with me. (Afterwards I learnt that all the other parties had come rapidly to the same decision after a short experience of marching across country in Sardinia.) So we decided to strike the road south of Sarule and follow it via Gavoi and Fonni over the Gennargentu range till it joined the main coast road, when we would consider the question again.

By the evening I felt alarmingly weak with hunger. The others admitted to feeling the same. We brewed tea on an inconspicuous fire and boiled up some dried mutton into a broth, but it was bulk we needed. Brown and Fry recalled every large meal they had ever eaten, describing vividly every dish – the savoury broth, the juicy steak, the fruit and pastry and cream. Then they amused themselves picturing the meals they would have when we got back, with the same mouth-watering emphasis on every detail, until I could have screamed with irritation.

I determined to obtain food from the village that night. Hunger and thirst warp your judgment and drive you to take chances which, reviewed afterwards on a full stomach from the security of an armchair by the fire, appear unjustifiable.

We approached the southern outskirts of the village after dark and found our road. Near it I saw a farmhouse, conveniently isolated. We walked up to the door of the kitchen which was open. Inside in the light sat two old ladies. I knocked and entered and asked to buy food. They were quite friendly and unsuspicious and seemed to accept the story that we were Germans whose truck had broken down on the road farther back and that we were now walking to Orani for help. They produced six eggs, a cheese and large flat biscuits in lieu of bread. We drank a lot of water, filled our bottles and loaded the food carefully in the packs. The question of payment raised a serious problem as I had only a 500-lire note, which of course they couldn't change. I gave it to them and said I would call back the next day in my truck with smaller money. We exchanged polite "*Buonanotte's*" and left. Not to have had some five and ten-lire notes was a bad oversight in the planning – it is just these little points which matter most and which get forgotten in the preliminary enthusiasm for the big Aim.

We filled ourselves up quickly on biscuits and cheese and then set off down the road. We met one or two peasants who answered our "*Buona sera*" without question, though generally if we saw them first and had time, we dodged off the road till they had passed. The road climbed steadily, winding round the contours and over bridges. As we walked through another village, about a hundred dogs began to bark in houses off the main street, but no one came out. We reached the outskirts of Gavoi at 2 a.m.

There beside the road stood a water-trough fed from a tap, and beside the trough two youths. They watched us in silence as we drank the water greedily and then they asked for cigarettes. Our cigarettes had English markings and we checked ourselves in time. No, we none of us smoked. And then, anticipating their questions, I asked how far it was to the nearest "other" Germans. I thought I was being rather subtle, appearing to assume that they knew we were Germans. "Do you speak German?" became my invariable technique on similar future occasions. The youths seemed friendly and gullible and told me of a German camp at Fonni. I was confident that they suspected nothing. They pressed us to come and drink a glass of wine before continuing our walk. Their house, they said, was only just round the corner. Brown and Fry urged me to leave at once, but I was seduced by the idea of wine. "I've got them taped," I assured them. "I'm sure they're genuine – there's no danger."

We followed the youths up a dark side street, and they stopped at a house. They knocked on the door. And then I realized just how badly I had miscalculated the simplicity of Sardinian peasants. Over the door hung a huge heraldic sign – the sort of sign which you see over the doors of police stations anywhere on the continent.

"It's late and I think we ought to be getting on, after all," I said hurriedly. I did not wish to behave too suspiciously, in case my worst fears were unfounded. We turned to go back but one of the youths clung to me, insisting that a glass of wine would take no time. The door was opened by a man in shirtsleeves and the other youth spoke to him in a low voice. I continued to regret politely that we must really be going and we walked away. I heard voices, excited voices, inside the police station behind me and then people running after us. Two *carabinieri* in uniform with rifles caught up with me. I changed my tactics. I became the haughty German officer. Did they speak German? No. Did I speak French? one of them asked. I did, and was able to tell him forcibly that I was in a hurry and what the devil was the fuss all about, anyway?

He seemed servile and apologetic. Would I wait just a minute longer till the "Brigadier" came? He was just coming now.

No, of course I wouldn't wait!

But then the "Brigadier" arrived, a fat elderly little man out of breath, accompanied by two or three of his soldiers.

Could he understand German?

He regretted he could not. Obviously he was confused and lacking in confidence. I spoke to him through the interpreter in French. My sudden command of that language surprised me. I had never spoken it so fluently before – perhaps I never will again.

I have forgotten what I said, except that my tone was very indignant and haughty, as was appropriate from a German officer affronted in such a manner by *carabinieri*. The "Brigadier" was pacificatory, apologetic, scared. He was sorry I had been delayed but how did a German officer happen to be walking over this mountain road at this hour?

I explained impatiently that I was walking for a bet. We Germans were great walkers. I had wagered my Colonel that I could walk in the night from Orani to Fonni. Now, unless I was quick, thanks to this interference, I should lose the bet. My Colonel was waiting for me at Fonni to attend an important conference. If I was late he would be angry.

The "Brigadier" wavered. I could see exactly the doubts and the fears revolving in his mind. He was, like all Italian soldiers, terrified of offending Germans, even such preposterously unlikely Germans. I felt I must clinch the matter quickly before I lost the advantage of surprise.

"Satisfied now?" I sneered. "Good night," I added fiercely, and walked off with Brown and Fry behind. A chorus of faint "good nights" followed us. We dared not obey the temptation to look behind us and we tried not to walk through that village faster than a mere bet should warrant. In such circumstances the mind shifts into the back, somewhere between the shoulder blades – and wishes it had eyes to see with. An unpleasant anticipatory sensation of vulnerability you have in your back, in such circumstances . . . But the shots we expected never came. Outside the village we left the road immediately, as a precaution. On the wild hillside we began to lose that constricted feeling in the windpipe and to breathe freely; our knees recovered their strength.

And I hope I had the good grace to say I was sorry.

I wished I knew just what those *carabinieri* had said to each other after we left. I believed they would telephone to the Germans at Fonni, discover the mistake and send after us. We kept across country for a time and then, striking the road, walked along it again listening carefully. About 4 a.m. we heard a horse coming towards us and hid in a convenient culvert. The horse clop-clopped by and we never saw the horseman, but I am sure now it was only a peasant riding off to his fields. Dawn was near and we climbed uphill to find a good bush. It was a bad area for bushes – more like English parkland with oak trees and bracken and we settled finally among some large rocks, with no prospects of shade except from their shadow.

A tense tiring day, though we boiled one egg each for breakfast and another for dinner and fed well off biscuit and cheese. There were flocks on the hillside round us all the time, scaring us with their bells and we had to keep watch in turns for fear of being caught asleep. The sun rose in the sky and the shadows of the rocks dwindled to nothing and we none of us obtained more than an aggregate of four hours' sleep during the day. My nervous system resisted the impulse to sleep. If I dozed from sheer tiredness, it was never for more than half an hour, when some subconscious alarm bell would ring – an echo of sheep bells inside my head and I would wake guiltily as might a sentry who nods at his post. I found it less wearing on the nerves to keep awake.

In the coolness of evening we read our maps and planned the night's march ahead. We had covered a gratifying distance on the map the previous night and we agreed to continue to walk on roads, in principle, except through villages which we would skirt, however tedious and slow the detour might be. Now, owing to the news of Germans in Fonni, it seemed better to cut straight across the hills to join the road again south-east of it, after which there were no villages marked on the map till after Gennargentu.

The valleys on that night all ran across the line of our march. Consequently, to avoid climbing up mountains and down again, I tried to work round their flank, without changing height more than necessary. In my anxiety to spare us the fatigue of climbing up and downhill too often, I strayed farther and farther off our course till we hit the road from Nuoro to Fonni. We followed it and arrived by dawn in a place like Windsor Great Park, within sight of Fonni. During the night we had found a potato field and from this day onwards we always boiled potatoes with the mutton – they gave us the much-needed bulk.

There was no ideal cover in the Great Park. We lay under a small oak tree and kept a careful watch. Shepherds and goatherds with their flocks and peasants on horseback passed nearby, but no one noticed us. We had brewed some tea at dawn on a discreet fire. The ashes smouldered on unseen by us, the dried leaves and grass caught alight and burst into a sizeable bush fire, which we heard before we saw it. We beat out the flames just in time, but the embers, in the tinder-dry undergrowth, were a menace for the rest of the day. We urinated on them in turns, to help keep them under control – it was impossible to extinguish them totally.

We hoped, when we set off, to reach the road south of Fonni within an hour or two, and to cover many miles along it that night. We should be crossing the Gennargentu range, and we could expect to find the road comparatively safe.

First we walked into a flock resting for the night, and the dogs went for us, with their infernal snarling barking. The shepherd called them off and he answered our grateful greeting, but it was the sort of thing which in our frayed nervous condition frightened us still, hours later. Next we met an old man who asked our business and who, when I told him we were Germans climbing Mt. Gennargentu for the exercise, strode away without a word. Then a small boy cutting a field of wheat with a sickle by moonlight. He stared hostilely and wouldn't speak. Another flock of shepherds with guns caused us to hide by a stream while they crossed it, and when we dared to start again, we met another peasant. He seemed friendly and insisted on showing us the best track on to the road which I told him we wanted to reach. On the way he led us to his family spending the night out in their fields, who begged us to stop with them. But we pressed on, keeping to the track he indicated till out of sight and then branching off it. Another flock suddenly, and dogs, and a shepherd who kindly put us back on the track to join the road. He also showed us a spring. We talked with him some time. He had fought with the English against "us" in the last war, he said. Now we were fighting together against the English. War was silly, wasn't it, and was hard on the poor soldiers who had to obey orders and didn't want to fight anyway? Like him in 1915, like ourselves now, out so late at night, carrying such heavy packs. A nice man.

He asked us how the battle was going in Sicily. This was our first definite news that it had begun and I questioned him about place names, but he knew very little. I assured him dramatically that we would kick the filthy English right off the island very soon. To my secret amusement he did not appear very convinced, though he made some polite and noncommittal reply. He was obviously pro-English and the temptation to confide in him was very great. But even if he was friendly, he would certainly talk about us to others. Mussolini had offered a reward for British parachutists, and I kept the impulse back.

It was 1 a.m. (15th July) when we finally struck the road. We were all of us footsore and stiff, and though we had been marching only three and a half hours more tired than we usually felt after a full night's march.

By 2 a.m. we reached the summit of the pass over Gennargentu and the road began its winding descent. In total distance and time we were well up to schedule, with every prospect of reaching the RV two or three days before the 24th July. So I decided to halt and give ourselves the chance of a thorough rest till the following night. We climbed off the road into adequate scrub, pulling our sleeping-bags over our heads and slept – the first real sleep since the night 6th/7th July on board the depot ship.

I was woken at 11 a.m. by the noise of goats grazing all round me – bells everywhere. The goatherd, wrapped in a black cloak, stood motionless against the skyline, staring apparently at us. An ominous sinister figure he made. Then the goats drifted on and their attendant spirit disappeared too, leaving me wondering whether he had really seen us – or if I had really seen him.

He and his goats passed by again in the evening. That sleep made a great difference to us all. Brown and Fry were both so tough and so cheery, they never looked as tired and stiff as I usually felt, and I had stopped early for my own sake rather than for theirs. However, they now confided that they, too, had been almost "done for" when I decided to halt and sleep. I knew they would have died rather than ask me to stop, such was our pride and our fear of letting each other down. Though I loved them for their trust and their loyal acceptance of my least reasonable prosposals (such as following the young men for a glass of wine), I found this sense of responsibility towards them a trying additional strain. At least it was pleasant now to feel that for once I had made a right decision.

We set off down the mountain again at a tremendous pace, bursting with energy and optimism and a determination to eat up the kilometre stones along that road. We counted ten of them in the first two hours. After that I plodded along in a sort of trance – the dumb misery of marching on a hard road; humming to the beat of my feet an inaudible chant indiscriminately composed from snatches of Beethoven, dance tunes or musical gibberish of my own improvization. The sheer boredom of marching always weighs on me more heavily than any pack.

We arrived outside Villanova about 3 a.m. and spent a laborious weary hour climbing round it. We branched off the road again as the first light of day appeared in the sky and found cover in a thick wood. We crawled into a large bush and fell asleep on ground comparatively soft with leaf-mould – not that the softness mattered much to us.

The shade was wonderful in that bush, owing to the trees around it. The sound of peasants with carts in the vicinity disturbed us all day, but we were well concealed – so well, that I watched a wild boar unaware of our presence pass the bush several times not six feet from my head.

I wondered, as we slipped back to the road after dark, what might be ahead of us in the night. I had grown to hate more than anything, more than the hunger or tiredness or boredom of long marching, the suspense which increased with every day of continued success and as the distance to the RV lessened. I hated more deeply with every day the sense of insecurity, the feeling that however safe we seemed to be one minute, some ghastly crisis might be impending in a space of seconds, that the bogey of sudden disaster lurked for us round the corner. At the start of each march I struggled to reconcile myself to bearing this cross and the cross each time seemed more and more unbearable. Now my spirit was, so to speak, still in the process of groaning, the nightly business of philosophic resignation was still in progress, when the bogey of sudden disaster stepped out.

The moon had only just risen and the light was obscure, when we saw a group of soldiers seated by the roadside ten yards ahead. Too late to avoid them, we walked boldly up to and past them. More and more Italian soldiers – for I saw to my relief they were Italian – obviously resting on a march, appeared beside the road. A company in numbers, with baggage carts still lumbering on to catch up the rest. We called "*Buona sera*" cheerfully and one or two replied. They were dozing and slow to suspect us. We were fifty yards beyond them when a voice shouted after us to halt. We marched on without looking back. Footsteps running on the road behind. I hesitated whether to run on or to stop and bluff. The latter seemed the best chance. Two soldiers caught us up. Who were we and so on? Germans from Fonni. But why were we walking on foot on this road? A training march, I explained. We Germans believed in keeping fit – we made a practice of marching long distances at night over mountains with heavy packs. I demonstrated my biceps and made other gestures indicating how tough and strong we were. They seemed impressed but not convinced.

"Well, we must get on . . . far to go . . . a hard life . . . Good night." And we sighed, as one soldier to another, as we turned away. A stream of straggling foot soldiers and a lorry containing more troops appeared coming towards us. I led off the road down a grassy hillside, dropping completely all pretence of self-assurance by running as fast as I could. At the best I hoped no one was watching us; at the worst, if they gave chase, the ground was in our favour. But I was afraid that if we kept on the road we should be

stopped again – perhaps by an officer, whom I could not
expect to bluff so easily.

No one came after us or fired. A bad beginning to the
night and one which made us keep off roads and move
cautiously along the shady side of river beds. But we ran
into nothing more alarming than a litter of wild boar in
some reeds. It was nice to frighten somebody else for a
change.

The railway line, two white ribbons threading through
the valley, accompanied us much of the way. We crept past
a small station, a pale ghostly building standing in its plot of
vegetables, where not even a dog barked. The station
marked the turning to Jerzu and as the time was by now
2 a.m., 17th July, we decided to use the road again.

We overtook an ox-drawn cart, a peasant lying asleep in
the back, while the ox pulled slowly uphill. The wheels
creaked noisily and we walked by without disturbing the
peasant and were soon out of sight ahead. The incident was
repeated, with very different consequences, two days later.

The road climbed a mountain and descended again till it
crossed a gorge and then zig-zagged up the other side to
Gairo Nuoro. We left the road and climbed down a precipitous goat track to the gorge, which I planned to follow
the next night past Jerzu, until eventually it joined the main
coast road. The gorge was a "deep romantic chasm" if ever
there was one, complete with "Alph", a sacred torrent
rushing down the bed between mighty rocks and boulders.
The moon was low to the west, casting one half of the gorge
into deep and chilly shadow. Here, surely, we could spend a
day unmolested and secure, and we began to search for a
suitable hide-up. First light was about to appear at any
minute.

We found an artificial channel, constructed of earth and
carrying water from the torrent along the hillside, presumably for irrigation purposes. My heart misgave me. We
followed it and came to two small terraces of beans. We
squatted despondently under the dividing bank among the
beanstalks. It was poor cover but dawn was breaking and
there appeared to be nowhere better. Those thrifty Sardinian peasants . . . I cursed their ingenuity and persistence

which could level up and cultivate even in such a place a small plot of earth.

"Mark my words," I said gloomily, "there is somewhere in these parts an aged crone whose only purpose in life is to totter out every day to this wretched crop of beans and to prune and count them with loving care."

I had hardly spoken when, glancing at the terrace above, I saw by the dim grey light of dawn an aged crone standing among the stalks. She had not seen us. She was dressed in black, a black shawl over her head and shoulders. With immensely loving care her bony fingers pruned the plants. Her lips moved inaudibly as though counting the pods. I watched her with horror.

I whispered to Brown and Fry to lie back and pretend to sleep. And I waited, holding my breath, while the crone moved slowly from stalk to stalk, working her way round every single one until she reached the end of that terrace. Then she staggered shakily down the bank on to our level. She began to work from stalk to stalk not ten yards away from us, and still she had not seen us.

I was lying back, too, with half-closed eyes, watching her. She was standing right over Brown and Fry when she caught sight of them and she stopped as if suddenly petrified. She stared and stared and her hand very slowly relaxed its clutch on the beans and travelled across to her mouth. I studied her old wrinkled face as I have never studied a face before. What was going on behind it? What would she do next? But the expression in those dark lacklustre eyes was insoluble.

Brown and Fry gave a wonderful performance. Lying there still harnessed in their packs and accoutrements, with their blond hair and pale, clear skins and charming youthfulness, they made a picture of tired, sleeping warriors, a picture which told its own story. Burne Jones would have revelled in the sight of them. I thought I could detect a trace of tenderness in the old witch's face, so far as mahogany is capable of becoming plastic to that extent.

Then out of the corner of her eye she saw me, but her scrutiny was abrupt. She turned and tiptoed away, like a mother leaving the room where her child is lying asleep. I could not see where she was and had to assume she had gone to betray us. I "woke" Brown and Fry and decided to make at once back up the gorge, so that if we were pursued we should at least have the advantage of a start uphill.

But as we left the terrace, there was the crone again working quietly on the terrace above. She stared at us as we passed and did not answer our greeting. Her expression was still inscrutable, but now I could interpret it. The blond sleeping-warrior act had got her maternal instinct. She had tiptoed away rather than disturb them. No doubt she had sons or grandsons of their age serving in the army overseas. The whole episode was very touching. All the same, we hastened back up the gorge, keeping among the boulders by the torrent.

We caught sight of a man walking along the irrigation channel in the same direction as ourselves. He was repairing the earth walls where our feet had crumpled them and there was no avoiding him. We looked round us for a place to hide – a desperate hunted feeling. Then we noticed a sort of crevice under the rock, behind which we had halted to be out of sight of the man. I stooped and looked in and saw that the crevice was the mouth of a narrow tunnel leading to a small cave. The tunnel was just wide enough for us to crawl through one at a time. The cave was ideal for our purpose, adequately lit by a window-like crack in the ceiling. A branch of the main stream, a trickle of clear water, flowed through it and there was just room on the pebbles either side of it for three men to lie down.

We felt almost perfectly safe; we had beautiful running water and the shade we lay in was unalterably cool all day. The pebbles made our sleep intermittent, but they were a price worth paying for the other joys. We washed and shaved before the light failed and our spirits were high when the time came to start.

We calculated to reach the main coast road that night and from then the RV would be in sight. The date was 17th July. We could hope to reach the RV by the 19th or 20th, which would leave four days in hand to rest or if necessary to search for the others or to descend to the pre-arranged point on the coast. Brown and Fry began to take our successful return for granted and to visualize in graphic terms the foodstuffs they hoped to find waiting at the base and all that they intended to eat thereafter in the submarine and on the Depot Ship and in the fleshpots of Algiers. I was pleased with their morale, though their optimism, which I knew was wildly premature, grated on my nerves. So many things could still go wrong between our present cave and the submarine. And my short experience of submarines had not filled me with confidence.

The gorge fell away more and more steeply and progress was painfully slow, scrambling down over rocks at the risk of damaging a limb. The packs had never seemed so uncomfortable and the belts bruised our hip bones raw with their weight of water-bottle, pistol, grenades, etc. I had slightly sprained both knees many nights before and had to bandage them for each night's march with the elastic bandages we wore on our ankles for the jump. The bandages now impeded me in the climbing and cut into the flesh behind the knees. It was a warm night and we sweated hard but were able to relieve our thirst from the stream as we went along.

After four hours' painful descent the gorge opened out into a wide fertile valley and the torrent lost itself over a broad sandy river bed. The valley, in the full moon, was a wonderful inspiring place; the mountains towered many thousand feet on either side, well wooded and terraced with vine and vegetables at their foot, gleaming with black rock towards their peak. We passed small white solitary cottages, and a tile-roofed chapel, but there was no sign of human life. For all its cultivation that valley was the stillest, most deserted spot I was ever in. Not even a dog's bark or a goat bell.

The sandy surface of the river bed gave a welcome relief to our limbs, jarred and stiff from the climbing. We covered the ground faster and at last, about 3.30 a.m., we saw the road ahead, where the valley finished.

We followed the road for a while, looking for signs of suitable cover, but the countryside was intensely cultivated with olives and vine. We were in a broad, apparently fertile valley, and at length there was nothing to do but branch off to the eastern range of mountains. The mountainside was also well cultivated. The chances of being detected there were too great and we eventually climbed the mountain to its summit, an exhausting business in our weak state. I loathe climbing mountains.

On top we found a few leafless bushes, but the surroundings were wild and the dawn had started. We flopped down and slept for an hour. Thereafter the noise of peasants on the move in our immediate neighbourhood prevented sleep. But in any case, we had reached that state of nervous exhaustion when the mind seems incapable of settling into unconsciousness.

The day was windless and the sun beat on us through the bushes until we almost cried. The hours dragged and time became an evil force smothering us. To help us defeat it we "brewed up" three times, using old tea leaves we had kept. The brew was black and stinking but the business of lighting a fire smokelessly and cooking tea and drinking it, sipping it slowly to spin out the minutes, took our minds off our misery.

I was worried by the question of water. Below in the valley I could see the river Pardu, but it was dry. We had seen no springs on the mountain and though the valley was green, I was afraid that all the surface water supplies might be dried up. This boded ill for the next five or six days. I had identified the peak of Mt. Alberu about twelve miles away and we could reach it possibly in the next night's march, certainly the night after. But our bottles held only enough water for three days on the scale of two pints per day. In this heat we sweated so much we could not manage on less if we were to remain strong enough to paddle or even swim out to the submarine. The idea of water and the possible shortage of it obsessed me more and more as the hours passed and I scanned the valley below in vain for signs of it.

Evening brought its delicious relief of coolness, but our thirsts remained and the strain of resisting the temptation to drink our bottles recklessly was agonizing.

We studied the ground and decided to descend to the valley and follow the river bed parallel to the road until we had passed Tertenia, the last village on our journey. "Silly to take any risks now, having come so far and with so many days in hand," we argued. Once past Tertenia we might rejoin the road for the last five miles until we reached the junction with the track which led off to Mt. Alberu. Once past Tertenia we would have some reason to consider our troubles over, except for the always doubtful question of finding the submarine. Brown and Fry were already disposed to consider themselves safe. What sort of rations would Bryan have for us at the base? Would there be lemon squash and tinned fruit? And so on, bless them. I cursed them at the time, silently.

Supposing we couldn't find Bryan or anyone else there . . . supposing we couldn't find the boats he had brought ashore . . . supposing . . . The alternatives of disaster were endless. And, anyway, we still had to march to the base successfully. So many things might happen.

I did not wish to dispirit the others. When I suggested that we should not congratulate ourselves too soon Brown exclaimed: "If I got caught now, I think I'd shoot myself." The juvenile Fry made a speculation about life as a prisoner of war and Brown, whose temper was usually placid, for once shut him up angrily.

The descent to the valley took an hour. I tried a short cut which failed and we had to force our way through clinging undergrowth over loose rocks in the dark, for the moon had not risen. We crossed the dry river bed and our thirst had become so intolerable I broke the resolution to avoid the road. I believed there might be water near it. We met a peasant and I asked him where I could find the nearest spring. He said there was *molto acqua* a mile farther along the road. We came to a house and asked again from a man and his wife, and they sent their children to guide us to the spring close by. We should never have found it otherwise, for the water was collected and carried in irrigation canals out to the fields where it disappeared.

We drank and drank, while the children stared in wonder. Then we soaked our heads and splashed the cold water down our backs and on our faces. And then we drank as much again. After filling the bottles we filled our cork helmets and carried them like basins in our hands when we continued the march. We returned to the river bed and the helmets slopped the water out as we stumbled along. When our thirst had fully returned we drank what water remained. It tasted of resin, which had been used in the manufacture of the helmets and smelt of our own hair and was altogether most unpleasant.

The moon had risen and the houses of Tertenia were easily distinguished. We skirted the village by a few hundred yards but, even so, a dog began to bark. We walked on to a field of tomatoes and ate some, unripe and sour. Then we joined the road again and with Tertenia behind us strode along it. The hour was about 2 a.m., 19th July. We had five miles to cover for the turning off to Mt. Alberu on our left.

There was still no sign of plentiful running water in the neighbourhood, which continued to worry me. I felt sure there was water, in springs and wells, but the difficulty was to find it without visiting houses. The take-off not being planned till 24th July, our water-bottles would not suffice, unless we found water on Alberu; otherwise we might have to walk back to the spring.

Ahead of us on the road we heard and then saw, as we caught up with it, an ox cart, like the one we had passed a few nights earlier. We could wait for it to draw ahead, but that would prevent us reaching the turn-off to Alberu before dawn. And I did not care to spend a day in the valley where the cover was insufficient, nor did I want to climb a mountain, unless it was Alberu. Alternatively we could leave the road and try to by-pass the cart. But the ground was rough and we might not be able to walk fast enough. Or we could simply walk on and overtake the cart. This was the lazy solution which appealed to me most and which I adopted. That is my only justification for what followed.

A man was sitting up, half-awake, on the tail board. And then I noticed several more men lying asleep behind him. I greeted the sitting man and asked if there was much water along the road. He said there was, in about a mile. We called "*Buona notte*" and in my confidence I slapped the bullock on the flank as I passed, causing him to swerve and no doubt stirring up the sleepers. However, we strode on and soon left the cart out of sight behind.

We always walked in single file. After ten minutes Brown said from the rear: "We are being followed."

"Are you quite sure?" I whispered, and kept walking.

"Three men, about a hundred yards behind."

"We'll walk faster. Don't look round yet, but when I say, glance back casually and see if they've dropped behind."

We lengthened and quickened our stride, but after some minutes Brown said the men were gaining on us.

"All right, we'll pretend to rest by the road. Make a business of off-loading the packs, as though it was a natural halt. We'll soon see what they want."

The three men came up to us and appeared friendly. Three ordinary peasants. Were they from the cart? In which case, where had it gone, because we could not hear its wheels, nor did it come in sight after five minutes.

I told the men we were Germans from Tertenia marching to Villapatzu: the old story. It came out quite slickly now. And the men seemed to accept it. But I wasn't happy about them, or about the story. I didn't know that there were any Germans in Tertenia. And it was suspicious that the men should have followed. And where was their cart? I tried hard to convince myself – and the others – that all was well. I refused to believe that anything could be wrong just when everything ought to have been nearly right. But I blamed my folly for having stuck to the road with more bitterness than I can describe.

I tried to chat naturally to the men about water. Could we get a drink anywhere? They led us to a spring, hidden in the bushes near the road, which we would certainly have missed. They seemed over-fond of us, unanxious to get on their way home and to leave us. I said we were tired and would sleep a while by the spring before continuing, and begged them, with how much politeness, not to bother to wait.

The mosquitoes round the spring were bad and the three men warned us not to stay or we might catch malaria. I countered that we had anti-mosquito cream. At last, to my relief, they showed signs of moving.

Then we heard the cart approaching. The men promptly pressed us to come back to the road and drink some wine. No, we didn't care for wine; we just wanted to stay and sleep. "Thanks very much all the same, please, please don't wait for us," and so on.

The men returned to the road to the cart. We looked about desperately for a good line of retreat, but the ground near the spring was boggy; we sank in to our knees and obviously we couldn't escape far without being heard or seen. But was this, after all, a trap? I could not, dared not, believe it was. There was still no apparent danger, nothing tangible to fear. Which was what made the incident so nightmarish.

The cart stopped and we could hear low voices of men talking. Unable to bear the suspense, I left the bushes and joined them. I said I had changed my mind and would like to buy their wine. They produced a small Italian army bottle of it, for which I gave them a 500-lire note. They laughed delightedly, all piled on the cart and drove on. I listened to their laughter growing fainter and fainter and felt better. I rejoined Brown and Fry and told them that they had only been simple peasants after all, who had just sold a penny-worth of wine for a pound and were chortling with joy at my expense. I believed the explanation because I wanted, desperately, to believe it. Then, allowing time for the cart to get well ahead, we started off down the road again.

I intended to leave the road and find cover as soon as I could, but the landscape on all sides was barren and open. There was no hope of reaching Alberu – all that mattered now was safety for the next day, if there was a next day. The premonition of calamity stifled me, try how I would to be optimistic. And when Brown whispered that we were still being followed I was not really surprised. I just felt rather sicker at heart than before.

There was only one man who might of course be a different one; it MIGHT be only a coincidence. We tried to out-walk him again and failed and stopped again by the roadside, this time pretending to urinate. The man caught up. I thought I recognized him, but I could not be sure. He did not speak but walked over to a shepherd who appeared with his flock suddenly nearby. They had been resting for the night by the road. I walked over, too, and asked him if we had already met at the spring. He denied it. The shepherd looked at me strangely, I thought. He was carrying a gun. Neither paid me any attention and went on talking together.

We waited and the man walked off, up the road ahead of us. The shepherd sat down with his flock. We followed the man until a bend placed him out of sight of us. Then we turned up the hill into some scrub, hoping that if he was hostile we might give him the slip. And at the same moment we heard the horses' hooves – how many horses we couldn't tell, but they were galloping down the hard road. And they grew louder and louder very quickly.

I saw now, only too clearly, what had happened. The peasants on the cart had sent back to Tertenia for help while they stuck to us.

We dropped our packs and crawled up the hill among the bushes. We might yet get away. I hoped the horsemen would ride on till they caught up the man. But the latter was running back down the road. As the *carabinieri* came round the bend we heard him shouting to them to stop – no doubt pointing in the direction we had taken. The shepherd appeared on the skyline above us, so it was useless to try and climb the hill undetected. We dived on top of each other into the thickest bush. There was still a chance the search would carry on up the hill, if they didn't find us at once.

We lay there while the *carabinieri* and peasants searched all round. They passed and repassed our bush without spotting us. I began to have hopes, however faint. I wondered whether we should have thrown grenades when the *carabinieri* were on the road instead of bolting and hiding. Now we were so cramped we could not even reach our revolvers without stirring the branches. A man was standing five yards away. We lay and prayed the search would move a little farther on, to give us time to relax our aching muscles. A twig moved, a leaf rustled; the man noticed. Before we knew it, we were the centre of an excited mob, shouting, firing their rifles in the air, pulling us by the limbs, seizing our arms and possessions, screaming orders at each other and at us – an experience

which might have seemed almost amusing if we had not felt
so bitterly humiliated.

> *Humiliated but not hurt. The Italians refused to pass
> Verney and his men over to the Wehrmacht who would, in
> line with Hitler's secret order for the extermination of
> Allied special forces, quite probably have killed them.*

22 SAS ESCAPE & EVASION EQUIPMENT

*Sabre squadron troopers always carry E & E equipment as
part of their belt order. There is no definitive layout, but the
belt order usually includes:*

1. *Belt, pouches and water bottles*
2. *SLR magazines*
3. *Rifle cleaning kit*
4. *Purse net*
5. *Fishing kit*
6. *Snares*
7. *Mess tin lid and rations*
8. *Torch and filters*
9. *Button-compass*
10. *Wire saw*
11. *Fire starting kit*
12. *Lock picks (note these are illegal in UK)*
13. *Clasp knife*
14. *Prismatic compass*
15. *Miniflares*
16. *Millbank bag for filtering water*
17. *Field dressing*
18. *Survival ration*
19. *Heliograph*
20. *Silk escape map*

*Other useful kit includes condoms (for collecting water, for use
as surgical gloves, for hiding things internally) and tampax
(for fire-lighting).*

Some of the kit will not be carried on the belt, but concealed in clothing, in case of capture. The wire saw is commonly fed into the waistband of trousers, and the fishing line into the seams of the tunic, for instance.

PANTELLERIA

John Cochrane

In early 1943, Major Geoffrey Appleyard of 2 SAS was personally requested by General Alexander to survey Pantelleria, an Italian-held island midway between Tunisia and Sicily. Appleyard reconnoitred Pantelleria twice; Lieutenant John Cochrane, a soldier with the Toronto Scottish serving with 2 SAS, accompanied one of Appleyard's "excursions".

O<small>UR PARTY CONSISTED</small> of Geoffrey, two sergeants, six men and myself. We left the submarine base, at Malta, in (if I remember correctly) His Majesty's submarine *Unshaken*, under the command of Lieutenant Jack Whitton, R.N.

After an uneventful trip we arrived off the coast of Mussolini's secret island fortress and for the next twenty-four hours Apple and Jack made a periscope reconnaissance of the fortifications in order to decide on the best place to make a landing.

At last after an intensive study of both air photographs and the beach defences, Geoff finally decided on a very high and particularly inaccessible cliff as the best landing place – naturally the success of the operation depended upon taking the enemy by surprise and off their guard – and the harder the climb the greater the surprise.

The raid had a twofold purpose – to spy out the best landing places for the Allied assault troops and secondly to try and find out the enemy's strength – the latter being very important as our own intelligence did not have much information on the subject.

In order to gain the necessary information, Geoff had been told to try and capture a sentry and bring him back with us in the hope that he would be able to supply us with the enemy's strength.

As in all his operations Geoffrey had to have the moon in his favour (that is, to land under the cover of darkness and work in the light of a rising moon). The whole plan was calculated to a split second – so many minutes to get ashore, so many minutes for the raid and so many minutes for the return to the submarine; all this was vitally important otherwise both the submarine and our party might have been discovered in an early dawn.

During exhaustive tests Apple had decided that RAF rescue dinghies were more suitable than canvas boats and these we blew up as the submarine surfaced half a mile off the coast and launched them over the side.

Leaving the submarine was a matter of minutes and I soon found myself following Geoff's dinghy ashore, each boat holding five men.

Our landing was uneventful, and after posting one sentry on the two dinghies Geoff started off in search of the way up that he had already seen from the submarine – no mean feat in the pitch blackness. We had one false start and then began the hardest climb any of us had ever experienced – we pulled ourselves up completely by instinct and every foothold was an insecure one, the rock being volcanic and very porous, crumbling away under our hands and feet.

By what seemed to be a miracle, Geoff finally got us safely to the top, covered in scratches, for we had decided to wear shorts so that in an emergency swimming would be easier.

We were nearly discovered as we reached the top of the cliff which was about a hundred feet high at this point. Geoff and the others were crawling away from the edge towards a path that they could dimly see and I was just pulling myself up over the edge when we heard men approaching. We all froze where we were and then to my horror I felt the edge of the cliff on which I was lying begin to crumble.

The sounds of marching feet and voices were coming much nearer and it became obvious that the Italian patrol was going to pass along the very path by the side of which Geoff was now lying, and there was I slipping slowly back over the edge and not daring to move a muscle for fear of dislodging some of the loose rocks.

Just as the patrol came level with Geoffrey, who was lying in the gorse not three feet from their feet, the worst happened. A large stone slipped out from beneath me and I waited tensely for the crash as it hit the rocks a hundred feet below me.

The crash came and Apple and the others prepared to let the patrol have it at short range. But the Italians, chattering to each other, apparently didn't hear a sound and passed by, little knowing how near to death they had been. We breathed again and prepared to start the work we had been sent to do.

Of course, the capturing of a prisoner in our case depended upon silencing him in the quickest way possible, and Apple had decided that the best plan was to crack our particular man on the head with a leaded hosepipe and then lower him down the cliff and away.

Because of the stiff climb we had encountered, Geoff changed the plan on the spur of the moment – it being impossible to lower or carry an insensible man down the route we had followed. He decided to jump on a sentry, half throttle him and when he had calmed him down, force him to make his own descent.

Apple therefore detailed me with two men to guard the route down and under no circumstances to give our position away unless directly attacked. He then crept away with the others to find a sentry.

Hardly had we settled ourselves into our position when the whole guard passed by on their relieving rounds – so close that we could have touched them had we stretched out our hands.

Geoff and his party also had to lie in the gorse further down the path as the guard passed them and then wait for things to settle down again.

Very close by they could hear an Italian sentry singing "O sole mio" and decided that he was their man. They crept silently up to him and then Geoff sprang for his throat. In the uncertain light he missed his hold and the sentry let out a scream of fear. Needless to say it was the only sound he made, because by this time four desperate men were sitting all over him and Geoff's fist was literally jammed down his throat – all to no avail, even though Geoff was whispering "*Amico! Amico!*" in his ear. The Italian reciprocated by getting his teeth well into Geoffrey's wrist.

The next sentry, about fifty yards away, heard the scream and came running through the gorse towards them. Herstall was nearest to this new danger and although armed only with a rubber truncheon gallantly rushed forward in an attempt to silence him. He was met by a burst of fire in the abdomen, and above the sound of firing I heard him call out to Geoff that he had been hit. That was the last anyone saw or heard of Herstall, because by now the whole guard was aroused and Apple and the other two survivors of his party were desperately fighting them on the cliff edge. Geoff accounted for at least three with his automatic and Sgt Leigh got one and possibly two.

By this time things had got so hot that just as my small party had decided to join in the fray Apple shouted, "Every man for himself," and as we turned to go back down the cliff I saw him, outlined against the gun flashes and tracer, dive over the edge along with Leigh and the other trooper.

I thought, as I scrambled madly down the cliff, that I'd seen the last of Apple, but when I reached the bottom he was already there with his two men. How they got down is a mystery because the piece of cliff where they went over was quite strange to them, they were being shot at the whole of the way down, and all the rock was loose and crumbling away. It had taken us nearly three-quarters of an hour to climb the cliff and they got down in about a minute and a half – Sgt Leigh put his knee out falling part of the way.

Somehow or other we all managed to find the boats and started to paddle like mad for the rendezvous with *Unshaken* which was lying submerged offshore.

By this time considerable activity had begun from the

shore – Very lights and machine guns were going off in all directions. Luckily they had no searchlights and we were soon out of Very light range.

We had arranged an emergency signal with Jack Whitton just in case of a hurried withdrawal – two grenades to be thrown into the sea, the explosions bringing Whitton to the surface in a hurry.

Geoff let the grenades off and *Unshaken* broke surface very close by. What a relief it was to see her! We clambered on board and down the conning tower in double quick time, while hefty sailors slit the rubber boats in little pieces and sank them.

Unshaken immediately submerged and set course for Malta. I'd like to say that the officers and crew couldn't have treated us with more consideration or kindness – they bound up our considerable cuts and bruises and insisted upon giving up their own comfortable bunks to those of us who had been more severely cut.

One last tribute I want to pay to our naval hosts. Jack's orders had been quite implicit: rather than endanger his submarine he was to abandon us to our fate. But luckily for us he had waited around, although we had been ashore longer than expected, and was prepared to cover our retreat with his 3-inch gun if necessary.

Pantelleria was captured shortly afterwards, an important stepping-stone to the Allied invasion of Italy itself.

OPERATION JUMBO

Ellery Anderson

*Following her defeat in 1945, Japan surrendered posses-
sion of the Korean peninsula to the Americans and
Russians. The Americans took the south of the country,
and established the Republic of Korea; the Russians took
the country north of the 38th Parallel and created the
communist Korean People's Republic. After a stream of
border incidents, the North invaded the South in June
1950. The UN condemned the communist aggression, and
dispatched a UN force under American leadership to
help the South Koreans. Among those serving with the
UN force was Ellery Anderson of the British Army. A
former Parachute Regiment and SAS officer, Anderson
convinced the Americans that a small special forces unit
could and should be dropped behind North Korean lines
to carry out sabotage. There were eight men in Anderson's composite UN unit: Anderson himself, plus three
Americans and four Koreans.*

O PERATION JUMBO WAS due to start at 9 o'clock on the
evening of March 17th, and by 7.30 all was ready and
we were on our way to the aerodrome. If ever I face
execution, the sensations and emotions of the death cell
will not be new. I do not know what thoughts were in the
minds of the others as we drove in the truck to the airfield,
but I have rarely felt so completely alone.

At last the time arrived, and we made the final adjust-
ments to our equipment, slinging the rucksacks containing

our change of clothing, explosives, food and radio across our chests, and buckling the parachutes to our backs. The straps of the parachutes held the rucksacks in position, and we waddled like a troop of ducks up the steps and into the plane.

I made my way towards the crew's cabin and sat down on one of the hard aluminium bucket seats, fastened my safety belt and tried to relax. The big door at the rear slammed, shutting out the last of the pale evening light. The engines revved up and died down, and then revved up again, the plane shuddered a little and began to move slowly towards its take-off position at the end of the runway. No one spoke and a pale yellow light from the roof of the plane shone down on the grim faces of the men lost in their thoughts.

For the first hour as we sat in the heated fuselage, some smoked in silence while others slept as best they could. As I sat smoking my pipe, a sudden overwhelming wave of confidence seemed to sweep through me. It was a momentary sensation but I saw clearly that we *were* going to succeed and that this tiny nucleus of a guerrilla army would grow and grow until it became an efficient, far-reaching and fast-striking force.

The navigator came aft from the cabin. "Crossing the bomb line any minute now, Captain," he yelled at me above the noise of the engines. The lights were dimmed and we sat in the eerie glow of a solitary screened bulb in the roof. The despatcher took off the jump door at the rear of the plane, and the cold night air rushed in, knife keen, alerting us all. Someone tapped my shoulder.

"Ten minutes."

I signalled to the others and we struggled awkwardly to our feet and clipped our static lines to the stay wire which ran the length of the roof of the plane. The despatcher came along the line carefully checking each hook to ensure that it was properly attached.

"Five minutes."

We stood up once again and shuffled along towards the open doorway. I was jumping first, followed by Bentham, Parker and the four Koreans, with Sergeant Monks bring-ing up the rear. The plane banked and turned, the note of its engines changing as it reduced speed, and through the open door I saw a clear dark sky lit by a galaxy of stars and, infinitely far below, an uneven carpet of tree-covered mountains.

I stood with my left foot well forward on the very edge of the plane and gripped each side of the door, looking straight ahead but every now and then casting a hurried glance to where, by my shoulder, were situated the two little lights, one red and one green. Although I waited tense and expectantly for the red light to flood the cabin, its very suddenness was startling when it did finally come on.

The thirty seconds between the red light, which was the order to stand by, and the green light, which was the order to jump, seemed endless. Once more I looked out ahead of me into the dark night sky as the lights changed and for a moment I caught the green eerie glow before the despatcher slapped my shoulder. There was a rush of air, a jerk as the canopy developed, and then utter stillness and quiet as I floated down.

Soon I could see the details of the drop zone; terraced paddy fields like a cul de sac surrounded on three sides by steep mountain ranges. Feet and knees together I hit the ground and rolled over. The breath was knocked out of my body and, instead of the soft landing I had expected, the ground was frozen hard and the sharp rice stubble scratched my face and hands as I struggled out of my parachute. Suddenly I realized one factor which I had not taken into consideration during planning. While it was spring in Pusan, here, two hundred miles north, winter still held firm. High above, the drone of the plane grew fainter and fainter as it continued on its way north to drop eight decoy parachutes some fifty miles away in the hope that, if they were found, they would add a certain amount of confusion and possibly mislead the enemy.

By the time the sound of the plane had faded into the silence of the night, the rest of the party had gathered around me and we rested momentarily while we regained our breath. We now faced our first change of plan.

It is inevitable that, however carefully one may plan down to the last final detail, and however successful rehearsals may be, an operation of this kind rarely goes as expected, and I had now to decide what was to be done with our parachutes. Obviously, they could not be buried in this frozen ground as we had originally intended. Therefore, we had to take this added burden with us into the hills and there find some spot to hide them. And so, with our rucksacks on our backs and our 'chutes piled on top, we moved grotesquely towards the dark outline of the mountains in front of us.

We had covered approximately a quarter of a mile when we heard the distant drone of the returning plane. We stopped, and as it passed over the area I took a chance and flashed the two letters "O.K." towards it. The pilot must have been looking out for us as we had arranged and he briefly snapped his navigation lights on and off.

Slowly we moved across the broken surface until we reached the thin scrub that nuzzled the lower slopes of the mountains. Once through this sparse bush we began the steady ascent through trees that stood like impersonal figures reluctant to let us pass. After what appeared an interminable time but must have been only a few minutes, we seemed to be in a suitable place in which to bury our parachutes. We stopped and each man moved off a little way until he found a convenient spot.

After another half-hour's climb, we reached the crest of the hill. There was no point in going on any further, as in another few hours it would be dawn. I searched for a convenient place in which to lie up, and eventually found a small rocky gully, overgrown with thick bush. We huddled together and, despite the bitter cold, were soon asleep.

At about four o'clock it began to rain, a hard, driving rain, and, listening to the steady drip, drip and the groaning of the branches above, it was comforting to know that any search party would find it difficult and even impossible to find us in such a storm.

All that day we lay in the gully, wet, cold and tired, but cheerful. If we had been dropped in the right place, we should be about twenty miles from our objective and all we had to do was follow the line of hills towards the east. In the afternoon the weather cleared a little and from somewhere in the valley below the shrill voices of children floated up towards us. Later the silence was shattered by the sharp crack of a rifle, followed by a flight of frightened magpies wheeling in the sky. We froze into immobility, hardly daring to breathe, but no other shots followed and we were left to speculate as to what was going on around us.

By six o'clock it was almost dark and we ate a hasty meal of raisins and chocolate before dragging ourselves stiffly from our hideout. The sky was overcast. A thick blanket of low black cloud covered the moon as we stumbled silently along, and even with the help of a compass, I found it difficult to keep direction on the narrow slippery path that twisted along the crest. As we became accustomed to the darkness, our pace increased. By four o'clock in the morning, we had covered approximately eighteen or twenty miles.

Our objective was to close the Kyongwon railway line, south of Wonsan, between Osan-ni and Huch'ang-ni. This could not be achieved satisfactorily by blowing up the line anywhere along its length. A detachment of Royal Marine Commandos had already tried this, and within 48 hours the line had been repaired. Nor was it any use to derail a train, for gangs of labourers would soon be recruited locally to clear it. Therefore, it had been decided that the only satisfactory way to block the line was to derail a train inside a tunnel.

We were tired and cold when once more we sought shelter and sleep in the thick undergrowth beside the path. At dawn we were awake again and, shivering with cold, made a scant silent breakfast of chocolate and biscuits. It was another cold bleak day and before long the first flakes of snow began to fall.

Leaving the main party, I set out with one of the Koreans, whom we called John, to reconnoitre our position and, if possible, locate the railway line which was our target. If we had been dropped in the right place, and my calculations were correct, it should lie some five miles to the east of our present position.

After three miles the ridge began to swing sharply to the

south and at this point we climbed a small outcrop of rock. Below us lay a narrow valley with a steep mountain range beyond it. In the valley stretched the railway line, like an evil black snake, its head hidden in the darkness of a tunnel which cut through the mountainside. I sent John back to bring up the others and settled down among the rocks with my binoculars to study the layout of the land and the approach to the tunnel. It was no more than a mile away below me.

John returned with the others and soon they had settled down in the lee of the rock, each man silent as he searched the area through his binoculars to familiarize himself with it. The tunnel seemed to be unguarded and no sign of life appeared in the now whitening valley below. This did not surprise me as there must have been hundreds of tunnels along this stretch of line alone, and to guard them all would have required a division. Fifty yards from the mouth of the tunnel a rice-straw shelter had been built which might possibly have been used as a temporary guard-post, but we saw no movement. More probably, this shelter was used from time to time by parties of gangers maintaining the line.

Once more I went over the details of the plan which we had rehearsed again and again during the final phase of our training. As soon as it was dark we would move down the side of the mountain to the valley, follow the track to the mouth of the tunnel, and Parker, John and his friend Luke would take up a position from where they could cover that entrance and the approaches to it. The rest of us would move a hundred yards into the tunnel and there Sergeant Monks and I would begin to set the charges while Bentham and the two other Koreans, whom we called Matthew and Mark, went on a further hundred and fifty yards to cover us from the other end. The charges had been prepared and it should take us no more than two minutes to get in position, six to lay the charges, two minutes to get away – ten minutes altogether. After that we would make our way up the steep wooded mountainside that flanked the track to the east until we reached the ridge which lay two miles beyond. From there we would have two nights in which to cover the 25 miles to the point on the coast where the United States Navy would pick us up.

The only people we had seen since landing were two solitary women making their way along the railway track probably to pick up cinders and coal dropped from the passing trains. It seemed that the intelligence reports were right and that this particular stretch of the line, although in constant use, was unguarded.

It was still snowing at half-past nine as we began to descend the steep slippery mountainside, stumbling and sliding and falling among rocks and trees. The night was black as we crouched together beside the embankment which lay invisible ahead of us. We moved cautiously in single file until I could feel rather than see the embankment rising in front of me. We turned left and moved carefully towards where the mouth of the tunnel must lie.

The ground began to rise gradually and I sensed that the tunnel lay just in front. I led the way up on to the track and moved slowly forward until my hands came into contact with the cold, damp, slimy archway of the tunnel. Now we moved quickly; Parker and his party crouching down beside the track covered the line to the south, while the rest of us entered the tunnel. The fresh night air gave way to the bitter, acrid smell of smoke. Once we stopped to listen yet no sound reached us but the steady dripping of the moisture from the vaulted roof above.

We moved down the tracks from sleeper to sleeper and when I had counted about a hundred and fifty we stopped. Monks and I dropped our rucksacks beside the track, and Bentham, with Matthew and Mark, moved on to take up their positions. Monks and I lay down beside the line, and as I scraped away the loose stones from under the track midway between two sleepers, he unpacked the demolition kit. He handed me one end of a fuse, which I quickly tied round my wrist, and then made his way five yards up the line. While I was putting the pressure switch under the track and wedging it tight, I could hear the faint scraping of stones and knew that Monks was fixing the charge under one of the rails. Then he was back beside me, whispering that all was set.

He handed me another length of fuse, which I joined to the first, while he set a similar charge on the other rail five yards nearer the entrance. Soon he was back once more and holding a shaded torch for me as I carefully connected the fuse to the pressure switch, which was now held tight under the rail with small stones. We now went over the whole system to recheck it, and satisfied at last, Monks made his way to Parker at the tunnel mouth while I collected Bentham and his party before joining him. The whole operation had taken us a much shorter time than I had anticipated and it had been surprisingly easy – almost too easy.

Our withdrawal lacked the cautious restraint of our approach. We slipped and stumbled as we scrambled upwards among the tree-covered slippery side of the mountain. All about us was darkness and, hemmed in by the silent trees, we dared not stop. We scrambled up and up oblivious of the noise we made and our cuts and bruises, until finally I judged that we must have put sufficient distance between us and the tunnel to rest.

After the noise of our withdrawal, an oppressive silence once more enfolded us, broken only by the sad sighing of the wind. Although exhausted, there was no thought of sleep as we waited.

We must have been sitting there for about an hour before I was aware that some other sound had joined the sighing of the wind. Faintly at first, it was there and then it was gone, but finally it came to stay; the sound of a train approaching from the south.

On and on it came, slowly and relentlessly, louder and louder, until the sound suddenly decreased and we knew that the engine must have entered the tunnel. The very mountains seemed to hold their breath with us. Still we waited and still nothing happened. I had a sickening feeling that something must have gone wrong and that the train would run straight through the tunnel.

Then came one explosion immediately followed by a second, welling up from the valley and echoing from mountain to mountain like a great exultant shout. In an instant we were all on our feet, jumping up and down in excitement, all sense of caution forgotten. It was hard to resist the temptation to run back down the hill and look at the damage, but we turned our backs on the tunnel and set off once more into the night.

When we had reached the highest part of the range, we turned south and continued for another hour before finally seeking the shelter of a wet, inhospitable gully. My first duty now was to let Base HQ know that we had accomplished what we set out to do. And so, before we finally settled down to rest, we set up our radio and while the generator whined, I crouched under the cover of my poncho and sent the code word that announced our success.

For five minutes nothing was heard but the whining of the generator and the tapping of the key, punctuated by pauses as I switched over and waited to receive an acknowledgement. At last it came and with it a request to stand by to receive an urgent message later. We packed up the generator and, taking it in turns to keep a listening watch, switched the set on to receive for five minutes every half-hour. The rest of us huddled together trying to sleep as best we could under a blanket of teeming rain.

Monks took the first watch and before I fell asleep I wondered what this urgent message could possibly be. Of one thing I felt certain. It would not be good news, and added to this, I was beginning to feel the first symptoms of malaria.

"They're on the air, sir!" It was Parker shaking me. I scrambled to the set and put on the headphones, took out my notebook and pencil and waited. Parker started to operate the generator while I listened to the call sign coming faintly through. I switched over and acknowledged it, and then back to receive. The high-pitched morse was being transmitted with slow deliberation and I wrote down the letters untidily on the moist pad resting on my knee. As the message took shape my heart sank. NEGATIVE PHILADELPHIA REPEAT NEGATIVE PHILADELPHIA STOP WHOLESALE REPEAT WHOLESALE STOP CONFIRM GOOD LUCK STOP.

With a heavy heart I sent the reply: CONFIRM WHOLESALE OUT. I repeated it twice and then switched off the set. Parker looked at me enquiringly. "The Navy can't make it," I said, "and we'll have to walk." Parker shrugged his shoulders and smiled faintly. At that moment he was too tired to care and so was I.

The essence of this brief and cryptic message was that we had to change our plans drastically. It was no longer a case of a two-day march to the coast, there to be picked up by the Navy at a pre- arranged point. Now we were committed to the first of our alternative escape routes. This entailed an overland journey of about 120 miles to a point near the coast south-south-east of our present position. If and when we arrived there, we were to come on the air again and confirm our position so that helicopters operating from the ships of the East-coast Fleet could fly in and evacuate us.

It was a depressing thought and the journey would take us a week or more to complete, but at least it was better than the third alternative, which would have been to make our way directly south and attempt to cross the enemy lines. In this event, we stood an even chance of being shot by either the Chinese or the Americans.

We packed up the radio, cleaned our weapons and checked our equipment and then gathered round to study the map once more and the route we were to take. The main problem was to obtain food. Although I knew before we started that we might have to prolong our stay behind the lines for more than our scheduled six days, we could only carry the minimum amount of food, priority being given to the explosives, ammunition and the radio. If anything had to be left out, it had to be food. At the time I felt that it was a justifiable risk and that if we had to adopt an alternative escape route we must take our chance and live on meagre rations or, if necessary, off the land.

The second problem was that of the enemy's Security Forces. As soon as the wreck of the train had been reported, the Northern Korea Security Forces would go into action and it seemed obvious that if they believed, as they assuredly must, that this act of sabotage had been carried out by members of United Nations Forces, then they would do everything in their power to intercept us in our escape. As they had not enough troops to surround the area completely and cover every inch of the ground, they would have to set up checkpoints on our most likely line of withdrawal. Thus I felt sure that they would establish such a system between the tunnel and the most direct route to the coast; and, secondly, they would not only alert their reserve forces at the front to watch out for us, but would probably establish a security net across the route running directly from the tunnel to the front line, in the hope that we would stumble into it. In planning the alternative routes, we had anticipated such a reaction by the enemy and therefore had chosen a route which lay midway between these two security screens.

As soon as it was dusk and the dark banks of cloud rolled across the sky, we once again shouldered our rucksacks and set off towards the south-east. There was no need to hurry now; caution and patience must be our watchwords. We had hardly covered a mile or so before I heard a shout and a groan behind me and then a crashing of bushes. I spun round just in time to see Parker fall heavily and lie groaning a few yards down the slope at the side of the path. While John and I went to help him the others sat dejectedly in the rain. Parker lay propped against a tree, groaning and cursing softly. At first he could not stand and I thought he must have broken his ankle but after a few minutes' rest he was able to get to his feet and, without the weight of his pack, and with the help of a stick he could hobble slowly and painfully along. His ankle had been badly sprained but a tight bandage eased the pain and gave him a little support. Between us we carried his equipment and despite his pain he did his best not to slow us up.

That night we covered a bare ten miles. During the following day as we lay up Parker kept applying cold compresses to his now badly swollen ankle, and by evening it seemed to be a little better. It was still causing him a great deal of pain but never once did I hear him complain. Once he even suggested that he should be left behind as he felt that he was endangering the safety of the whole party.

At the end of three nights' travel Parker's ankle seemed to be much better and we were now increasing our distance to between twelve and fifteen miles each night. By the fifth night we had put sixty miles between us and the tunnel.

Two mornings later, when I estimated there to be only thirty miles between us and the area of our expected pickup, I was awakened by the crack of a rifle shot, followed quickly by two more.

· We rolled clear of our equipment, grabbed our weapons and, huddling against the protective tree trunks, formed a defensive circle. We waited tensely for the high staccato shots of the encircling enemy, the explosion of grenades and the clatter of automatic weapons. Nothing broke the heavy silence.

"Parker, you take charge here; Monks and I are going to have a look. If we're not back within an hour you know what to do, don't you?"

"Yes, sir, but I hope to God you are!"

Monks and I slid down the side of the hill in the direction from which the shots had come. Suddenly we came to a slight clearing from the edge of which we could look down into the valley. There, 500 yards below, lay a group of mud huts, and under the shelter of the overhanging thatch squatted a number of North Korean soldiers.

"How many do you think, Monks?"

"Maybe forty or fifty," he answered. "Wonder what they're up to?"

"They don't look as if they are particularly interested in us, thank God – anyway not yet," I replied. "They wouldn't be sitting there chattering and laughing like that if they thought we were sitting up in these hills behind them, but I hope nobody has seen us and reports it later. We'd better go back and join the others now, and as soon as it's dark we'll get on our way again."

Back among the others I explained what we had seen. There could be no sleeping that day, no unnecessary movement, and talking was to be the absolute minimum.

At last dusk came and we prepared to move. We were nearly out of food and the first effects of hunger were becoming apparent. We were physically and mentally exhausted; scratches and cuts had turned septic, and our clothes were torn, wet and filthy.

Two nights later hunger had become so acute that I reluctantly decided to risk stealing some rice. In the morning, I took Matthew with me in search of an isolated house which might afford us some food. About three miles further on from our resting-place, on the other side of the valley below, we saw a clearing across a stream. In a corner of this clearing stood a dilapidated mud house, its straw-thatched roof badly in need of repair. A wisp of smoke hung in the air above it and suspended under the over-hanging roof above the doorway were a number of earthenware pots. On the broken planks of the raised porch stood large jars. We knew Korean peasants kept much of their food in such jars and at night they slept soundly. Even if someone approached their houses and their mangy, starving mongrels yelped a warning, they would take no action. Ostrich-like, they lay in pretended sleep in order to avoid unnecessary trouble. It seemed an ideal place from which to steal some rice.

"Do you think you will find this place tonight?" I asked Matthew.

He looked at the house in silence, then stared about him. "Yes, I find it, OK," he replied in his peculiar mixture of stilted English and American idiom.

That evening we started a little earlier than usual, hoping to reach the point on the track from which we could see the house before darkness fell. When we arrived at the place, we stopped, and before Matthew and his friend Mark started off, I told John to explain to them exactly what they were to do so that there could be no misunderstanding. They were each to take enough food to last us for four days.

I estimated that they would need a maximum of an hour and a half to make the trip and return. If they were not back within two hours we would have to move on. If they were surprised or ran into any trouble they must fire their carbines to warn us and then make their way as best they could to our rendezvous at the pick-up point, but in no circumstances were they to follow the route which we had planned to take and, above all, they were to make sure they were not followed. I reminded them once again that if they did not return within the allotted time, we would have to move on without them. No one can keep from talking for ever and other men's lives would be at stake. They both knew and appreciated this and understood the risk they were taking.

When John had finished speaking, they nodded, turned and silently slipped away into the night. I glanced at my watch from time to time and the minutes ticked slowly by – a quarter of an hour, half an hour, an hour, they should be there by now, and it was a comforting thought that we had heard no sudden sound of shots or the dull explosion of a grenade. An hour and a quarter, an hour and a half, and we began to get ready to move. Then suddenly the two hours were up and still no sign of Matthew and Mark. It was time to go but somehow I could not force myself to leave them. We waited impatiently, straining our ears, but no sound broke the silence. Another quarter of an hour went by and still they had not returned. We had heard no shots and so presumably they were at least still alive unless, of course, they had been ambushed and quietly captured. Perhaps they had lost their way and were searching desperately to find us, stumbling blindly among the trees and under-growth.

They were twenty minutes overdue and when I gave the order to move, it was a depressed party that slowly put on their rucksacks and moved on. All the time I hoped against hope that I should hear their hurrying footsteps on the narrow path behind us and welcome back those two solemn, loyal and brave men. But when they had crept away from us earlier that evening, they had moved into darkness and oblivion for ever. God knows what their fate may have been, but I hope that somehow they managed to survive and are now living once again the life of peace they so richly deserve.

When we stopped that night, we ate the last of our rations and I began to feel the first positive effects of the fever which had been coming on for the last few days. My head ached abominably, I shivered with alternate flashes of heat and cold, and waves of nausea swept over me. I had been swallowing aspirins in prodigious quantities but they had no effect. I had thought at first it must be malaria and hoped that soon it would run its course, for at the moment I had more important things to worry about.

We set up our radio again and for twenty minutes I sent out our call sign pausing every now and then for acknowledgement which never came. We checked the set and it appeared to be working all right. The outgoing signal was strong but something had either gone wrong with our receiver or else our signals were not reaching Base.

When we tried to call Base next morning, the result was no better. Finally I sent a coded message "blind" without hope of acknowledgement: ESTIMATE E.T.A. WHOLESALE FORTY EIGHT REPEAT FORTY EIGHT HOURS and followed it with the time of transmission.

When we carried out the daylight reconnaissance of our position the following morning, Monks suddenly exclaimed: "Look, sir! Isn't that our pick-up point over there?" I looked in the direction in which he was pointing. "There, that long low hill – over to our left, the one where the trees seem to have been cut down along the ridge."

I looked at it through my binoculars. It certainly looked like the place and according to my reckoning it should be somewhere in the vicinity. Even if it was not the right place it could not be very far away. It would certainly serve as a good point from which we could be evacuated by helicopter, and it seemed to be only two or three miles from where we now stood.

A wonderful feeling of elation swept over us both and even the stern hard eyes of Monks twinkled with excitement. He smiled, I think for the first time since I had known him: "Well, that sure is a gladsome sight, ain't it?"

We almost ran back to tell the others and then I felt desperately sick. The fever which I now had was obviously not malaria and I was becoming worried, for I knew I should have to have all my wits about me for the finale. By the evening I felt a little better and had none of the pains of hunger which the others were obviously feeling. When we set off again, I found that Monks was walking almost at my shoulder and Parker had taken his place at the rear. I remember very little about the next twelve hours except that it was Monks who helped me along all the time and I borrowed from his seemingly inexhaustible supply of strength and courage.

Sometime that night we stumbled out of the trees into the clearing on the mountain. We moved back into the shelter of the wood and I could go no further. I lay down and as in a dream saw figures bending over me and gently wrapping ponchos around me.

Monks and Bentham set up the radio and again unsuccessfully tried to contact Base. I remember saying, "Oh, throw the thing away – give it up, it's no use." They both turned to me and smiled and went on trying. Presently I heard the generator die down and Monks came over. "No soap, I'm afraid, sir, but I sent it blind again and told them we were ready."

When I woke next morning, the fever seemed to have abated a little and the first thing I saw was Monks at the radio. Around me the others lay curled up as snugly as dogs before an open fire. I got up and staggered over to Monks. He had his headset on but had discarded his key and was talking into the rubber mouthpiece of the handset. "Do you receive me? Do you receive me? Over. Over." He flicked the switch across to receive and the whine of the generator died down. A look of concentration spread across his face and he pressed the headphones close against his ears the better to hear the faint murmur of the reply.

Eventually he switched off the set and stood up. "Well, I think we got through, sir."

He said that he had had no success in calling the Base but that after sending his message blind again he had tried the emergency frequency on which the First US Marine Division holding the sector of the line closest to us had been asked to keep a listening watch. He had passed his message and it had been acknowledged but when he tried to contact them again, he could get no reply.

Now there was nothing but the inevitable waiting. We had no food and only a little water left, but now we had hope. Morale had risen and the men were more cheerful and confident than they had been since the sound of the explosion that had wrecked the train. They were talking excitedly, already tasting their first moments of freedom.

It must have been about two o'clock in the afternoon when the silence about us was shattered by the screech of a jet as it flew above our heads. No one had seen it coming, no one had heard its approach. We jumped to our feet and ran to the edge of the clearing in time to see the plane climb, and bank steeply. "It's one of ours!" and then followed hectic activity as we laid out our phosphorescent recognition panels and made ready the last of our plastic explosive to burn as flares. When we looked up again there was no sign of a plane and I wondered whether it would come back or if there ever *had* been a plane, so silent was the world again. But soon it was over us once more, this time much higher, but I was certain the pilot must see our recognition signals and pick us out as we waved frantically to him. He banked and came in once more screeching so low above our heads that we instinctively ducked, and as he climbed this time he gave two half rolls as he headed eastward.

I think it was John who first saw them: two tiny specks in the sky to the east and above them circled the fighters. As we watched them growing nearer and nearer two other planes flew over us, and as the distant specks took shape, we heard the distinctive throb of the helicopters' rotors. Then, like a huge roaring dragonfly, the first hovered above us. Monks and I pushed John and Luke forward and as the hoists was lowered we secured it under John's arms and he was slowly winched up into the hovering plane. Down came the hoist again and up went Luke, and for a third time the hoist came down. "All right, Monks, that's your lot – up you go." He slipped the harness over his head and under his arms and, without looking back, disappeared into the fuselage of the helicopter. With an angry roar it gathered speed and climbed high into the sky.

Almost immediately the second helicopter was coming in for Parker, Bentham and myself. I ached in every joint and my head throbbed like a gigantic pulse, but in my fevered mind one last act of defiance obsessed me, one last gesture I must make before leaving. I staggered back to where our discarded equipment lay in confusion. I took up the carbines one by one and smashed them against a tree and finally shattered our radio with shots from my automatic. It seemed strange that the only time any of us had fired a single shot throughout the entire operation was to destroy

the one thing that had saved our lives, but somehow it
seemed more fitting than for it to be captured as loot.

Other parachute operations followed, but with the in-
volvement of the Chinese in the Korean War from
November 1950, "behind-lines jobs" were judged politi-
cally inappropriate.

UNDERWATER TAXI

Terence Robertson

The conspicuous development of airborne special forces during the Second World War has tended to obscure the fact that commando units between 1939 and 1945 were often transported to their destinations by more gravity-accepting means. (Ironically, this was particularly the case with the nascent Special Air Service in North Africa, which was many times driven over the sands to its destinations by the Long Range Desert Group.) Where secrecy was paramount and the geography appropriate, wartime special forces were invariably inserted by submarine. Of the Royal Navy's underwater taxis, HMS Seraph was perhaps the most famous. Dubbed the "Secret Mission Submarine" by the wartime press, her other clandestine duties included the landing of the American General Mark Clark in North Africa before the invasion of Tunisia.

CAPTAIN BARNEY FAWKES, commanding officer of the 8th Submarine Flotilla at Gibraltar, glanced again at the message on his desk. It was a signal, signed "Jellicoe", from Combined Operations Headquarters asking that Captain A.R. McClair of the Special Boat Section be granted an interview and given help within reason.

Since the landings in North Africa, Fawkes had been plagued by Combined Operations with its offshoots, and by cloak-and-dagger set-ups like SOE, the Special Operations Executive; then had come the OSS – Office of Strategic

Services, an American organization; more recently he had met the Special Services of the French Army, under Colonel Rivet. They all wanted him to provide submarines for their nefarious activities. Curiously, one organization never told the other what it was doing.

He reflected bitterly on a recent case in which the OSS had wanted a submarine to take a party to Rome, where they had business with the Vatican. The SOE had wanted a submarine at the same time to take a party to Rome, where they wished to blow up a bridge. Both parties refused to travel in the same submarine! Fawkes had appealed to the Commander-in-Chief, who had been advised by an army liaison officer to release the submarines.

The result: the SOE had landed first, blown up the bridge and retired; two days later the OSS had landed at the same spot, reached the sabotaged bridge and as the detour would delay them twenty-four hours and upset their schedule they had abandoned their mission and returned to the submarine. Meanwhile, one of the submarines had been badly depth-charged and would be out of commission for at least four months. No wonder Fawkes looked at this latest request with angry suspicion.

Captain McClair was shown into his office, a young, carefree officer with just the faintest hint of the swashbuckler about him. Fawkes groaned inwardly.

"Well, what is it you want?"

"A submarine, please, sir," replied the young man confidently.

Fawkes blanched. "Would you care to give me the reason?"

"Well, sir, I'm not sure that I should. Job's frightfully hush-hush, you know."

Fawkes hoped he looked suitably impressed. "Really, now. You know I meet a lot of you fellows from time to time and I always insist on knowing the reason before I hand over a submarine. They're rather expensive toys to be chucked around casually."

"Well, I've been told to take a party to Italy, sir. You see, we are in contact with the partisan forces behind the German lines there and they want certain equipment. They have tremendous military value, these chaps, with masses of guerrilla activities which cause Jerry no end of trouble, you know. Now they must have some radios, machine-guns, pistols and ammunition, sir. So we want to dump it somewhere along a convenient bit of coast and tell them where to pick it up."

"I see," replied Fawkes wearily. "Are you sure you can't get it to them any other way?"

"No, sir. Air would bungle the thing somehow – you know how they work, don't you, sir." The young officer said this with the air of a superior conspirator.

"Oh, yes, of course, you're so right," said Fawkes, not really knowing why the Air Force should not drop this sort of stuff. He seemed to have heard that they were doing it pretty well in France and the Low Countries.

"In any event, they've said they can't spare the aircraft, sir," went on McClair. Fawkes sat back. This was the real reason, he thought. So, as a last resort, Jellicoe was trying for a submarine.

"All right, McClair, I'll place the matter before the Commander-in-Chief. If he says you can have a submarine then you may look over the side of this ship and take your pick."

Captain McClair rose to his feet, saluted and left the room. Fawkes drafted a signal to Sir Andrew Cunningham suitably worded to give the impression that there were no submarines available. But the C-in-C thought the request was reasonable and told Fawkes to place one at McClair's disposal.

When he received this reply Fawkes paced the quarterdeck for a while and then reached a decision. *Seraph* had returned with bad luck from her last patrol. She would take McClair and his party to Italy. This was the sort of thing she did better than most, and at least she could be relied upon to bring the Army back safely.

Lieutenant Bill Jewell, the captain of the *Seraph*, was proud of his ship and those who manned her. They were veterans of eight patrols into enemy waters, and *Seraph* was as efficient as any submarine in the Service. Brass shone, metal valve handles gleamed, the diesel pistons sparkled from hours of patient polishing and thin layers of clean engine oil over all the bright work gave evidence of regular attention. Throughout the passageway through the bulkheads which separated the compartments there was an air of orderliness with movables stowed neatly into place so that nothing was in the way. Living in *Seraph* was a tight affair, but it was as clean, tidy and spacious as a meticulous First Lieutenant, David Scott, could make it.

His fastidiousness was not without reason: *Seraph* had passed from childhood quickly, and now was growing older more rapidly than was normal under the conditions of war. She had begun to feel the need of affectionate hands to massage life into her tiring mechanism and overworked engines – the latter could wish for none more clever than those of her new engineer, Stevenson. For it was on her efficient working that the safety of her crew depended. Whether on secret mission or operational patrol their only link with Algiers and home was *Seraph*. Faulty mechanism, tired engines or sluggish steering gear could mean disaster. If only for that reason there were no drones aboard her.

This knowledge gave Jewell a quiet confidence when he was called into Fawkes's office on August 26th, 1943, to be introduced to McClair and briefed on his coming voyage.

"Now, Bill," said the Captain, "you are going back to the Tyrrhenian, but don't think it's going to be another patrol like the last one. Remember I told you I might have something more up *Seraph*'s street when you came back last time? Well, this is it. McClair and his party want to take some secret equipment to the Italian mainland.

"They would like to be taken inshore a little to the right of Genoa, where they will select a likely place for paddling the stuff ashore, burying it and coming back with you. Actually I've compromised a bit with McClair. When the operation is completed, you will patrol between Corsica and the mainland. I think that might prove more profitable than down the Sardinia end. McClair's party will have to stay aboard for the rest of the trip and come back here with you."

Jewell glanced at McClair with some satisfaction. At least

the man was only a junior officer; he had no intention of sacrificing his bunk for an Army captain.

"When will the stores come aboard, sir?" he asked.

"Tomorrow, then you sail on the following day – the 27th. I'll give you your sailing orders tomorrow evening."

With a slight nod, Fawkes indicated he was busy and the two officers left, McClair promising to return the next day to help in loading the equipment. With him would be his party – Captain A. Croft of the Inshore Special Service Unit, and Sergeant J. Thompson of the Special Boat Section, Combined Operations.

Next day the three soldiers reported aboard, a steady stream of crates and sacks following, to be stowed away below. Apart from the Commandos, only Jewell knew that the stores consisted of two-way radio transmitters and receivers, Stens, machine-guns, pistols, signal lamps, ammunition, grenades and containers of special explosives for sabotage. He shuddered slightly when McClair pointed to one case vanishing down the fore hatch and muttered:

"That's a good one for 'em. Full of knives sharper than razors and as light as stilettos."

Seraph sailed into the Mediterranean on August 27th with a fair wind and sea causing her lean shape to plunge forward in a sliding roll. Her bows were under water, riding through it, and the foaming waves swished down her sides to lose themselves in the thin wake churned from her propellers. There was an air of renewed energy and keen anticipation among the crew, who looked forward to this adventure of gun-running behind enemy lines.

The passage into the Tyrrhenian Sea was undisturbed, although two aircraft sightings through the periscope sent *Seraph* into the depths, where there was no risk of an inquisitive pilot sighting her grey-black shape outlined beneath the blue surface of the sea. On the 31st the Italian mainland came over the horizon.

McClair joined Jewell on the bridge that evening after dark and said softly: "I'd like to have a look at some of the bays around here. How about starting by the Portofino promontory?"

Jewell nodded. They decided to consult the navigator

and his charts, but when Lieutenant Davis met them in the control-room he introduced a sour note.

"Well, sir, I suppose you know an enemy minefield has been reported right along this coast." Jewell didn't.

McClair whitened. "Can't be helped," he said. "We promised these Italians we would 'cache' thec stuff somewhere in there." He stabbed a finger at the coastline on the chart.

Jewell shrugged. "OK, if that's where you want to go, that's where we'll take you."

Davis warned him they were nearing the suspected minefield and he automatically remembered the rules by which the submarine war was played – the most important being to dive deep under a minefield and stay deep until you were certain the roof was clear. *Seraph* dived to 200 feet. The asdic operator switched on the mine-detector unit, which beamed above, below and ahead to give warning of the many-horned iron spheres which had claimed so many of her sister submarines.

At two knots, she crept ahead. Inside, the crew's mood changed as the word passed from one compartment to another that they were entering a minefield.

Jewell pulled a magazine from behind an instrument panel and sat down to read; Lieutenant Edsell bent intently over the chart table; David Scott stood by the fore and after hydroplane operators ready to act instantly should the detector react to a mine. In the for'ard torpedo room there was silence. These men could not but sense that if the bows were blown in they had very little hope of survival. Of the soldiers Sergeant Thompson seemed the most at ease. Always cleaning knives, guns or leather belts, he had become a favourite among the crew who had made him an honorary member of the mess deck.

Edsell broke the silence. "We've been going an hour now, sir. Bottom's beginning to slope a little from the fifty-fathom mark."

"Right. Let's go up to a hundred and fifty feet, Number One."

The heavy muggy air, coupled with the tension, produced a sweatiness which grew worse as time forced itself round the clock until another hour had passed.

"Cross the thirty-fathom mark now, sir, and bottom slopes a little quicker from here on," reminded Edsell.

Jewell looked up from his magazine. "How much longer before we clear this minefield?"

"About another forty minutes, sir."

"Take her up to a hundred feet, Number One."

A slight bump thudded through the submarine. Eyes swung round, stomachs knotted. Nothing happened. Whatever it had been, *Seraph* had shaken herself clear.

Now there were more glances at the clock. The word had spread that Lieutenant Edsell had estimated forty minutes before they were clear. Not long now.

Suddenly, Edsell unbent and announced cheerfully, "We're clear, sir, and I think we ought to go up. Frankly," he grinned in mock astonishment, "I'm surprised we haven't touched bottom. Only a couple of miles off the coast now, or should be."

Soft chatter broke out and a few experimental bangs were heard as men tested their nerves. When they found the noise no longer startled them, they began chuckling with relief.

Jewell could see nothing threatening through the periscope, the asdic operator found no evidence of shipping in the neighbourhood, so *Seraph* surfaced, drained the water from her back and settled down on even keel. The watch and the soldiers climbed to the bridge to see how accurate Edsell's navigation had been. Too good, thought Jewell, as he altered course away from the coastline little more than half a mile away.

For the next hour *Seraph* prowled the tiny bays and coves searching for one which suited McClair's perfectionist mind. This was a tiny cove marked on the chart as Casa Dell-Oro. When he had finished sweeping the hilly background to the beach with his binoculars, McClair at last announced the journey's end. Here they would bury the treasure store of arms as ordered in Operation Burrow.

Seraph withdrew to seaward while the boats were brought out on deck, but the exercise was soon interrupted when a lookout sighted several darkened shapes approaching from the south. Back down the fore hatch went the boats and quickly she vanished from sight. It was a convoy of two small merchant ships escorted by two destroyers. *Seraph* was ideally placed for an attack but, to his chagrin, Jewell had to let the enemy pass unmolested. An attack at that stage might only compromise the purpose of their visit to this coast – the arms cache.

When the convoy had passed into the night, she surfaced again and moved towards the shore, coming to stop inside the cove about 300 yards from the beach. The Commandos had brought two boats – a folbot and a self-inflating rubber dinghy similar to those used by the RAF. It promised to be a difficult operation, as *Seraph* was rolling heavily in a ground swell.

The folbot was launched first and immediately capsized in the swell, as had been feared, and all efforts were now concentrated on the rubber dinghy. It could be inflated by hand pump or by releasing a bottle of carbon dioxide attached to its side. As the latter might be needed urgently in an emergency ashore, the hand pump was used on the fore deck. Once launched it rode the swell comfortably and was quickly loaded with the precious stores for the guer- rillas. An astonishing weight in guns, ammunition and radio sets rode safely in the dinghy. When it appeared likely to fold up and sink, the three soldiers jumped in, waved and paddled away towards the beach. *Seraph* went astern out of the cove, turned to seaward and submerged out of sight in case there should be alert guards in the neighbourhood.

The Commandos found the beach; what there was of it offered little assistance in getting ashore. More rocks than sand, and the heavy surf made the safety of boat and stores uncertain. Before reaching the surf, McClair leaped out and waded ashore to reconnoitre the beach and cliffs.

Twenty-five yards inland he found a thick barbed-wire barrier running along the coast and a few yards the other side a guard hut showing a light. He hurried back to the beach in a crouching run, signalled the boat and waded out to steady it as the surf took hold and threatened to toss the valuable cargo overboard.

A few minutes later it was beached and the stores were

being stacked behind some rocks. The light still shone from the guard hut only 50 yards away. It was a still night with little wind, and every sound carried. Dressed in overalls and rubber-soled slippers the Commandos merely scuffled as they placed each crate carefully on the ground. A rattling stone, an uncontrolled cough or sneeze, a stumble against a rock or bush, and the guards would come running to investigate.

Working silently with hand signs to do their talking, the soldiers had the boat emptied in a few minutes and crawled back to the barbed-wire entanglement. Sergeant Thompson drew a pair of wire-cutters from his pocket and, while the two officers held each strand of wire to avoid flip-backs, he clipped a gap 4 feet high and 3 across.

They had worked together as a team doing this sort of thing many times before and it was accomplished deftly and without noise. First through was Croft, who ran up to the hut, listened, and ran down to the left. About 20 yards from the hut he found a bush growing by itself among the rocks and easily recognizable to the partisans who would come one night armed with spades to dig up the stores.

Then he returned to the gap in the wire, reported by signs to McClair and took Thompson back to the beach to help carry the crates up to the bush. For the next hour the three damp but sweating soldiers dug into the ground, cursing to themselves when they struck slate and rock. By the time the hole was deep enough to satisfy their exacting standards, it was past 1 a.m.

McClair beckoned to his companions, who continued with the burial while he moved up to the guard hut to listen by the lighted window for a moment before disappearing into the rocks behind. Ten minutes later he emerged from the shadows to confirm by signs that there were no other guards and assisted in replacing the earth over the stones. Not a pebble rolled away to arouse suspicion in the hut; not a branch of the bush was touched, not a twig broken underfoot to crack a warning of intruders.

Once they had returned through the gap in the barbed

wire, there was another important chore – each strand of cut wire had to be rejoined and made to look as undisturbed as possible. The joins would have to be good enough to remain unnoticed for at least forty-eight hours. Once again training made it comparatively simple for these three young intruders, who were soon back on the rocky beach carefully obliterating their footsteps by brushing a dead branch over the sand behind them.

They had some trouble in persuading the rubber dinghy to stay right side up in the surf but, after several anxious moments, the three were settled in, over the surf and out into the calm swell. By the time they passed through the entrance of the cove and looked back, the light in the guard hut had vanished behind a hill.

Seraph was on the surface waiting for their return. Breathing heavily, the trio were dragged inboard and taken below for a rub down and glasses of brandy. David Scott deflated the rubber dinghy and manhandled it down through the conning-tower hatch. Half-way down it jammed and in trying to free it the toggle of the carbon dioxide bottle caught on a jagged piece of metal. The stopper came out with a faint hiss. In seconds Scott was gassed, his struggles to come up for air growing feebler until he subsided into unconsciousness. Jewell wrote in his report of proceedings:

"We heard a faint commotion going on in the tower hatch and looked down to see the First Lieutenant temporarily asphyxiated by the accidental release of the dinghy's self-inflation device. We pulled him up to the bridge, had the offending boat removed and stowed away and then turned to see what could be done about Lieutenant Scott. Fresh air was his cure and after a minute or two, his eyes blinked open and he climbed slowly to his feet completely unaware of what had happened."

After this incident, *Seraph* turned seawards and dived towards the minefield – she would have to pass through it again to clear the coastline into open sea. Once again the crew and their passengers would have to suffer the agonizing suspense of three hours' waiting while *Seraph* nosed her way clear of danger. She had been lucky the first time but there was a limit to luck. Before dawn, however, they were safely into the Tyrrhenian Sea to begin seeking out the enemy.

With dawn approaching rapidly, *Seraph* was preparing for the morning dive. Supper had been served and the dishes cleared; smokers had thrown away their last cigarette stubs and the bridge personnel had taken their last gulps of fresh air for the next twelve hours. From the west appeared the dark shapes of ships. Startled, *Seraph* dived and looked at them from the hidden vantage-point of periscope depth. It was an E-boat obviously on an anti-submarine sweep. Hoping she had not been seen, *Seraph* crept past her, glancing back every few seconds to satisfy herself she was not being followed. At 10 a.m. a second E-boat, accompanied by a schooner, joined the first. There was considerable flashing of signal lights and the first hunter departed with the schooner, leaving the second to continue the search. This was sufficient activity to arouse speculation as to whether the Commandos had left some trace ashore of their operations. Then the E-boat began dropping depth charges in a line, luckily away from *Seraph*.

By midday, the enemy was obviously bored with duties or had completed the pattern of firing, for he picked up speed and headed for the Portofino point.

At 6 p.m. yet another E-boat appeared, intent on maintaining the hunt and, reluctantly, *Seraph* moved away from the hunting-ground to less crowded waters where she could surface and dispatch her report to Algiers.

Transmitting began at 10.30 p.m. but the long message, including the Commando report for Combined Operations headquarters and the exact location of the burial ground, took until five in the morning

Now that they were safe, the three soldiers chattered away in high delight at the experience. They had been shaken and not a little scared, like all the others, but they had a story to take back to Combined Operations headquarters which few Army men could equal.

SUBMARINE LANDINGS:
TACTICS AND TECHNIQUES

TRANSFERRING AT SEA

From a surface ship, the transfer procedure is quite simple. The landing craft are inflated and sent over the side. A scrambling net is let down, and the operational team instal themselves in the inflatables, stow their equipment and set off on their long journey to the beach.

And it will be a long journey. To maintain security, the mother ship will never come above the horizon as seen from the shore – maybe a distance of more than 20 miles.

Outboard engines are notoriously noisy. There are electric versions which are almost silent, but they have a very limited range. To get around this problem the landing craft may be towed in close to shore by a purpose built tug – low to the water and fitted with a heavily-silenced inboard engine. The landing craft then make their way the last two or three miles to the beach under their own steam – or rather, by the muscle power of the Special Forces team who are paddling.

Transferring from a submarine to the landing craft is either a lot easier, or a lot more difficult, depending on which one of the three methods is chosen. If the submarine can come to the surface, the inflatables can be dropped over the side, the landing party boards, and away they go. In one interesting variation to this method the boats are placed on the deck of the submarine and the crew get aboard then the submarine submerges gently beneath them.

Submarine Landing

Alternatively, the submarine commander comes up to just below the surface, exposing only the very tip of the conning tower and presenting a very small picture, even to enemy radar. The landing party exits and either swims to the landing point, on a compass bearing, or inflates the boats in the water and paddles in.

The most secure technique of all requires the landing party to exit the submarine underwater, usually with the boat completely stationary and sitting on the bottom. Team members wearing SCUBA (Self Contained Underwater Breathing Apparatus) then emerge from a hatch connected to an airlock and swim under water to the landing place.

6 Points For Leaving a Surfaced Submarine

1 *Crew members and troops should be fully briefed on the debarkation plan.*
2 *Inspect all your kit before the debarkation.*
3 *Wait for the crew to man their debarkation stations first before going to yours.*
4 *Swimmers debark in pairs from the conning tower of the submarine, which will surface with its decks awash.*
5 *Form up in the control room with all your kit. If there is space the first pair can be in the conning tower ready for the submarine to surface.*
6 *If possible, rehearse the whole debarkation procedure before you do it in a tactical situation.*

Special Forces personnel who undertake missions like this have to be highly trained and very, very fit. If it's necessary to use this "locking out" technique with technicians or mission specialists of any kind, then the lead pair will exit with inflatable boats and set them up on the surface. The rest of the team can then make "free ascents" using the submarine's ordinary escape hatch, join up with the divers, and make their way to the beach in the normal way.

UNDERWATER INFILTRATION

As radar and anti-aircraft weapons become increasingly effective, underwater infiltration has become an increasingly important method if infiltrating Special Forces troops. The key to any successful infiltration may be summed up as Short, Simple and Secure. Underwater operations using SCUBA equipment provide an extremely secure method of infiltrating short distances by water.

SHALLOW DEPTH

Try to make your approach at the shallowest possible depth

so that your air supplies last longer, and you and your
equipment do not suffer the problems associated with sustained diving at great depths. There is another reason,
swimmer detection systems find it harder to detect people
at shallow depths.

SECURITY

Part of the team should land ahead of the main body to check
that the beach is clear. Surfacing and removing their masks
outside the surf zone the security team goes ashore and signals
"Clear" to the rest of the troops when it has examined the
beach area.

COMBAT LOADS

Combat loads must be light and small and should include only
equipment, weapons and ammunition needed for the mission.
You must have a proper equipment unloading plan and pre-
ferably have it rehearsed before landing.

Precautions at Sea

1 Is the area used frequently by passing enemy patrol
   boats?
2 Fishing boats can cause embarrassing confrontations and
   must be avoided.
3 Rocks and any other hazards that are likely to make
   navigation difficult have to be noted and passed on.
4 Sometimes underwater obstacles will be in the way, so a
   route through to the shoreline has to be checked.
5 A close check on weather conditions is important and prior
   to the raiding force landing a met report should be sent
   back.
6 You need a secure landing point that will enable the
   raiding force to disembark safely and without making
   any noise.
7 The reconnaissance team will have been given a time and a
   date for bringing in the raiding troops and by this time
   all their work must be complete. They should know the
   lie of the land like the back of their hands and in particular
   which routes afford the best cover. Having checked the

state of the sea and sent their met report back they will then stand by at the landing area to receive the raiding troops.

SWIMMER DELIVERY VEHICLE

The furthest reasonable distance the swimming team should have to cover is 1,500 metres. If the submarine cannot approach this close to the target area then swimmer delivery vehicles should be used to reduce fatigue.

ON THE WAY IN

In anything but a flat calm it will be impossible to see the shore for most of the journey in, except when you get up onto the crest of a wave. Even then you probably won't have time to get a fix on your objective. You have to navigate by compass and that's satisfactory as long as you know where you are.

Unfortunately, the seas and oceans never stand still. Except for a very short period at high and low tides (called "slack water"), they are constantly in motion – and not just straight in to the beach and out again either. On top of that there are coastal currents with which to contend, and though they may run in the same direction all the time they certainly don't always run at the same speed.

These factors are much worse in some parts of the world than in others. The Mediterranean, for example, has no tides to speak of, while the Bay of Fundy and the Bristol Channel have up to 15 metres between low and high water. And around the Channel Islands there are four tides a day instead of two!

It's impossible to compensate for all this, and the commander of the mother ship will have calculated the transfer point to take account of all the known factors. Even so, the landing party will have to work hard to keep on course and will be grateful for all the help they can get.

CHOOSING A LANDING PLACE

The ideal site for a seaborne landing has very similar features of a good airborne drop zone; it's easy to identify from a distance; is free of obstacles; has good and secure access and evacuation routes for both the transportation group and the reception committee and is largely free from enemy activity. The main differences lie in the sea and under it.

Any reasonably competent observer can evaluate an inland drop zone just by looking around carefully. To do the same for a seaborne landing requires a certain amount of training in the science of hydrography. Tides and currents are more difficult to deal with than underwater obstacles – at least these don't move around all the time!

Navigation at sea or even on inland waterways is much more difficult than on land, chiefly because it's difficult to know exactly where you are at all times. Modern small radar equipment can solve this problem but leaves you exposed if the enemy detects the radar emissions.

A better solution is offered by satellite navigation (satnav) hardware, which will tell you where you are to within 100 metres anywhere on the earth's surface. Because it's completely passive (it transmits nothing itself but only receives) you don't risk giving away your position when you use it.

FIND THE BEACH

If there's no reception committee on the beach, the landing party will navigate for themselves, using the compass, sun or star sights and shoreline observation and will be rather lucky to hit the beach at precisely the right place except under the easiest possible conditions.

If there is a beach party it can help with visible light, well shielded and only allowed to shine out to sea; infra red beacons, which the boat party can pick up using special goggles; underwater sound; and radio.

The surf zone doesn't stretch very far out from the shore. When the landing party are close to its outer limit they stop and maintain position. Scout swimmers get into the water, approach the beach and check it out. When they are sure there's no enemy activity they signal the rest of the party to come in.

There are no exceptions to this procedure. Even though there may be a reception committee waiting with established peri- meter security and reconnaissance patrols, the landing party still performs its own reconnaissance.

THE RAID GOES ASHORE

The transit to the area may take some time and distance will depend entirely on fuel consumption. The troops must also be prepared for a wet and bumpy ride and must wear adequate clothing.

At a certain distance from the objective the boats slow their engines to cut down on noise. At this point their greatest ally will be wind and the crash of the sea, which will disguise any noise they make. From there they move slowly up to a rendezvous point, within a visible distance of their landing site. It is important to note that good radar can pick up and identify small boats and you should remember this when planning the route.

Once at this RV point the troops wait for a pre-arranged signal from the reconnaissance team ashore to notify them that all is clear to move in. It may be that something has occurred ashore and therefore no signal will be given, in which case the boats will return.

Having received the signal, the boats move in with engines cut and the troops paddling. This depends on the weather conditions, but it is essential that from here on as little sound as possible is made. One man in each boat has a gun trained on the shore as a precaution. Once in, everyone disembarks as quickly and quietly as possible and moves to a given area to await the next stage. Meanwhile the boats wait in the most concealed area, along with a guard force, their bows pointing back out to sea.

The raiding force commander and his team leaders are then given a final brief by the recce team commander. This gives everyone an opportunity to confirm any last minute details and to make any changes. Once everyone is satisfied, the team leaders carry out a briefing for their teams and then at a given time, they move off.

It may be necessary at this stage for teams to split and approach the target from different angles. In this case each team is led by one member of the recce force, who takes them up to a starting line. Quite often the recce team acts as a fire support group giving whatever help they can when required.

From The Mammoth Book of the Secrets of the SAS and Elite Forces, *ed. Jon E. Lewis, Robinson, 2002.*

EAGLE CLAW

Ian Westwell

After the overthrow of the Shah in 1979, a tide of anti-Americanism lapped over Iran; the USA had been the prime backer of the Shah and his hated secret police, the Savak. On 4 November of that year, 400 students occupied the US embassy in Tehran and took 56 US citizens hostage. The response of the Jimmy Carter administration was prompt: an Iran working group was formed on 4 November, and two days later planning for the rescue of the hostages began. The unit tasked with the mission was Charles Beckwith's Delta Force.

SHORTLY BEFORE 1800 hours on 24 April 1980, a lone MC-130E Hercules special operations transport thundered down the sun-baked runway at Masirah, an island off the coast of Oman, and rose gracefully into the darkening sky. Aboard, huddled shoulder to shoulder in the aircraft's cavernous cargo hold, their weapons secured to webbing above their heads, were members of the US Special Forces' Delta Force and their pugnacious commander, Colonel Charles Beckwith. After months of delay, uncertainty and detailed planning, Operation Eagle Claw, the daring bid to rescue 56 US nationals held in the Iranian capital of Tehran was finally under way.

Delta Force, a branch of the Special Forces formed in 1978, had been intensively trained for just such a mission. The men were ruthlessly professional and highly motivated, yet they faced enormous, almost insurmountable, logistical and planning problems. The teams, operating under the strictest security precautions to preserve the element of surprise, would have to penetrate deep into Iran, enter the capital in some strength yet remain undetected, rescue the hostages, who were dispersed in several different groups, and then carry out a withdrawal in the face of any number of possible Iranian military responses. Everyone recognized that transport, both in the air and on the ground, was the vital key. Unfortunately, Delta Force lacked its own transport capability, and outsiders, drawn from other units of the armed services, would have to be used.

Early plans involving insertions by parachute or by trucks driven to Tehran from Turkey were studied in detail and then rejected. Beckwith saw that long-range, heavy-lift helicopters would have to be used to fly the rescuers into Iran and to carry the hostages out. Carrier-based RH-53D Sea Stallions operated by the Marines fitted the bill, but despite their endurance, they could not reach Tehran in one hop – a refuelling stop somewhere in the desert south of the capital would have to be organized. Beckwith duly formulated a highly complex plan and, although he still had some nagging doubts about the ability of certain elements to perform their respective jobs, he remained confident that his plan would succeed.

Eagle Claw called for the various assault teams to fly at low level from Masirah to Desert One, an isolated spot in the Dasht-e-Karir some 300 miles south-east of Tehran, in three MC-130E transports. Three KC-130 tankers carrying fuel for the helicopters would also fly to Desert One. Once on the ground, a 12-man Road Watch Team would secure the landing strip, while Delta Force unloaded the rescue equipment. Some 30 minutes later, eight Sea Stallions, launched from the USS *Nimitz* stationed in the Gulf of Oman, would rendezvous at Desert One. After refuelling, the helicopters would take the 118-man rescue team towards a hide site nearer Tehran. After leaving Beckwith and his men, the RH-53s were then to proceed to a second hide site some 15 miles to the north and remain in hiding until called in to evacuate the hostages.

Delta Force would be met by two Department of Defense agents who would take the men to a wadi five miles from the landing zone, where they would spend the daylight hours in hiding. After sunset the agents would return with two vehicles: one to drive 12 men into Tehran to pick up the six transports to carry Delta into the capital; the other for Beckwith to undertake a final, on-the-spot reconnaissance of the route to the objective.

With the transport ready, Delta Force would begin the drive to Tehran at around 2030 hours on the second day. Beckwith had divided his command into three teams for the actual rescue mission – each had a specific objective. Red and Blue Elements, each 40 men strong, would provide the cutting edge. Red was to secure the western end of the embassy compound, take out any guards stationed in the motor pool or power plant, and free any hostages held in the staff college or commissary. Blue was to seize the southern sector of the compound and then rescue the prisoners held in the deputy chief of mission's residence, the ambassador's house and the chancellery. Outside the embassy, White Element's 13 men were to stop any Iranians from interfering with the operation and to cover the withdrawal.

The two assaults would go in simultaneously, after a massive explosion had blown a hole in the compound's outer wall. Meanwhile, a 13-man Special Forces team would storm the Foreign Ministry, where three hostages were being held separately from the main group. The various rescue attempts were expected to take place between 2300 and 2400 hours.

With the hostages freed, the Sea Stallions would be called in from their stand-by position somewhere to the north of Tehran, and, depending on the situation, would either land in the compound or in an adjacent sports stadium. Four AC-130E gunships would be available to deal with any Iranian response: one flying over Tehran to prevent Iranian troops from reaching the embassy, one over the nearest military airfield to discourage any airborne pursuit, and two in reserve to deal with any contingency.

Once aloft, the Sea Stallions were to fly with all speed to the airfield at Manzarieh, some 35 miles to the south of the capital. By this stage, the base would have been secured by a company of US Rangers flown in by C-130 Hercules transports, and three C-141 Starlifters would be on hand to fly out both the rescuers and the hostages. As there would be no chance of saving the Sea Stallions, they were to be destroyed and left behind.

In its final form, the plan was worryingly complex, and required several distinct forces to work in perfect unison. However, Beckwith had one over-riding concern: the helicopters. Their pilots would have to fly blind into Tehran at ground level to beat the radar defences, and any substantial losses would effectively end the mission. Although the planners had argued long and hard on the number of Sea Stallions required, all recognized that there had to be a minimum of six able to fly on to Tehran from Desert One; this number would guarantee sufficient capacity for all the hostages to be flown out.

Despite Beckwith's misgivings, the plan was given the presidential seal of approval, and Delta Force left its base at Fort Bragg in North Carolina, arriving at Masirah on 24 April. After last-minute checks over their equipment, the various assault teams, dressed in nondescript jeans, dust-covered brown boots and black combat jackets, boarded their MC-130Es at 1630 hours. One and a half hours later, the first transport, containing Beckwith, Blue Element, the Road Watch Team and Colonel James Kyle (the air force officer in charge of operations at Desert One), was airborne, quickly followed by the other two transports and the three tankers.

Flying on a northern course, the lead Hercules crossed into Iran near the town of Chah Bahar and dropped to 400ft for the low-level flight to Desert One. The Hercules was more than halfway to the preliminary objective when Kyle tapped Beckwith on the shoulder and said, "The helicopters are launched. All eight got off." Everything was going to plan, and at 2200 hours the first Hercules arrived over Desert One, flew a single circuit of the landing zone (LZ) and made a safe, if somewhat bumpy, landing.

With clockwork precision, the Road Watch Team left the cargo hold and raced off to secure the LZ's perimeter. All was quiet. Suddenly, headlights cut through the night sky, illuminating the transport. Beckwith shouted out, "Stop that vehicle," and opened fire. The vehicle, a Mercedes bus, screamed to a halt, and members of Blue Element surrounded it. At gunpoint, the 45 passengers were searched and placed under guard. No one had escaped; the mission remained uncompromised. However, over to the west of the LZ, a more serious incident was about to unfold. A second vehicle, a fuel tanker, hove into view. As the tanker, headlights ablaze, continued towards Desert One, it was taken out by a round fired from an M72 grenade launcher. Immediately, the night sky erupted with a vivid flash as its cargo of fuel exploded, illuminating the whole area. Worse, its driver escaped the inferno and made an unopposed getaway in a second vehicle. Although aware of this potentially disastrous turn of events, Beckwith ordered the mission to continue.

It was time for the other five Hercules to arrive. A few moments after the first troop-carrier had powered into the orange-black sky, on its return journey to Masirah, the second Hercules, with Red Element on board, made a perfect landing. After the aircraft was unloaded, its pilot taxied to a remote corner of the strip to make room for the remaining planes which arrived over the next few minutes. Once they were on the ground, the Hercules that had brought in Red Element took off for the return journey to Masirah. Everyone settled down to wait for the arrival of the eight Sea Stallions, scheduled to make the rendezvous in the next 30 minutes.

The helicopters were the key to the next phase of the mission and, at Desert One, Beckwith paced the desert like a caged tiger waiting for their arrival. Though he did not know it, the Sea Stallions had left the *Nimitz* dead on time, at 1930 hours. However, they were soon in trouble. At about 2145, No. 6 helicopter was forced to make a landing due to irreparable mechanical problems. Its crew was picked up, but now only seven choppers could make it to Desert One. The margin for error allowed by the planners was already being eroded.

The remaining Sea Stallions were also having problems

after running into two totally unexpected and vicious sandstorms. The one flown by the force commander, Major
Seiffert, and No. 2 chopper made forced landings to ride
out the worst of the storms. Luckily, after over 20 minutes
on the ground, the storms passed and both crews resumed
their journeys to Desert One. However, No. 5 Sea Stallion
suffered a major mechanical failure and, unable to carry on
with the mission, was forced to return to the *Nimitz*. There
was no longer any margin for error.

The first helicopter to reach Desert One, No. 3, arrived
50 minutes late, guided in by the burning fuel tanker; the
remaining five straggled in over the next 30 minutes.
Despite the delay, there was still a chance that Delta could
reach the hide site before first light. However, Beckwith
was informed that No. 2 helicopter was all but inoperable,
and that left only five choppers serviceable. After a quick
discussion with Kyle, who contacted senior military offi-
cials monitoring the operation in Egypt, it was decided that
the raid was no longer feasible. Beckwith ordered his men to
load their equipment on the Sea Stallions. The daring
attempt to free the embassy hostages had been forced to
abort because of the systems failure of a complicated piece
of machinery. Courage alone could count for little in this
situation.

However, before Delta could depart, No. 4 helicopter
needed refuelling. Only one tanker had any spare fuel, and
to make way for the helicopter, No. 3 Sea Stallion had to be
moved. Overloaded, the chopper shuddered into the air,
attempted to bank, failed, and crashed into the fuel tanker.
The effect was instantaneous and wholly catastrophic: the
two machines errupted in flames, covering the area with
red-hot debris. Five crewmen in the Hercules died instantly, as did three Marines in the chopper; the Delta
men in the tanker were lucky to escape with their lives.
Beckwith had no choice but to get his men onto the
remaining transports and evacuate Desert One. After nearly
five hours on Iranian soil, Delta Force returned to Masirah.

The mission was an undoubted failure – the hostages
would not, in the event, be released until January 1981 – but
Delta Force could not be held responsible. The blame lay

with the combination of unfortunate mechanical problems and the onset of freak sandstorms. Without these disastrous setbacks, the US hostage crisis might have ended in April, and the men of Delta Force would certainly have been acclaimed as heroes. Operation Eagle Claw taught the US Special Forces a number of grim lessons that would not quickly be forgotten.

After the failure of the rescue mission, the United States and Iran cautiously entered negotiations over the hostages. Following a complicated deal involving the unfreezing of Iranian assets in the USA, the embassy hostages left Iran at 12.33 p.m. on 20 January 1981. By then, tarnished by the debacle in the desert, Carter had been electorally ejected from office, and it was Ronald Reagan who welcomed the hostages home.

DELTA FORCE

Delta was the brainchild of Colonel Charles Beckwith, and eventually came into being on 19 November 1977. Its official name is Special Forces Operational Detachment Delta, presumably after the other Operational Detachments ("A", "B", and "C" Teams) into which the Special Forces are divided. The prime role of Delta is to deal with terrorist incidents affecting the USA and its interests, as a result of studies conducted after the Olympic Games massacre in Munich in August 1972 and the Mogadishu rescue of October 1977. The inspiration for Colonel Beckwith's force was the British 22nd Special Air Service Regiment with which he served in 1962–3, being one of the few US Special Forces' exchangees to gain selection. He developed a great love for the regiment and, on his return to the US Army, tried for a number of years to persuade it to form a unit with the same organization, purpose and functions as the British regiment.

Once his dream had been made reality, Colonel Beckwith proceeded to organize Delta into squadrons (initially there was only "A" Squadron, but this was split in 1979 to form "B"

Squadron as well) which are subdivided into troops of 16 men.
The basic group, or "chalk", is the 4-man patrol, but the
troops can operate in groups of 2, 4, 8 or 16 men. Selection and
training in Colonel Beckwith's time closely followed the SAS
pattern, and had a strong element of weeding out "cowboys"
and an accent on intelligence and self-reliance. Very high
standards of marksmanship are required: snipers must score
100 per cent hits at 600 m (650 yd) and 90 per cent at 1000 m
(1100 yd). Special Forces personnel volunteering for Delta
are often surprised at the degree of competence demanded by
SAS criteria.

Little more is known about Delta, as befits a "child" of the
SAS, and Colonel Beckwith has now retired from the US
Army.

From The World's Elite Forces by Bruce Quarrie,
Octopus Books Ltd, 1985.

JUNGLE FIGHTERS

Jonathan Reed

In the early 1960s, the former British colony of Malaya sought the formation of a new political power in South-East Asia, which was to comprise Malaya itself, plus Singapore, and the Bornean states of Sabah, Sarawak and Brunei. While Britain supported the incorporation of her Bornean territories, the plan was vehemently opposed by President Ahmed Sukarno of neighbouring Indonesia who had his own designs for the island of Borneo. In April 1963 Sukarno began to infiltrate insurgents from Kalimintan (the Indonesian southern part of Borneo) into the British parts of the island; in response, the British organized a force of Malaysian, Commonwealth and British troops, including 22 SAS.

"I REGARD 70 troopers of the SAS as being as valuable to me as 700 infantry in the role of hearts and minds, border surveillance, early warning, stay behind, and eyes and ears with a sting!" So wrote Major General Walter Walker, Commander British Forces, Borneo, in January 1964.

In the early hours of 28 April 1965 a four-man team of soldiers from the 22nd Special Air Service Regiment (22 SAS) waited patiently, SLRs at the ready, by the side of a river located some 9,000yd inside Indonesian territory. The team, led by Captain Robin Letts, had been ordered to reconnoitre the area around Berjonkong and Achan, where the Indonesians were known to have forward bases. During his recce, Letts discovered a waterway used by the enemy to ferry men and supplies to the border, and decided to set up an ambush. Positioning his men inside the loop of the river, with one man to his right, one to his left, and the other covering the left flank, Letts awaited the arrival of Indonesian boats.

He did not have to wait long. At 0815, two-and-a-half hours after the team had taken up their positions, a boat appeared, followed by a second and then a third. Each boat contained three soldiers, two paddling and the other, holding a rifle, standing astern acting as sentry. As the first boat reached the man to Letts' right, the second Letts himself, and the third the man to Letts' left, the SAS team opened fire. It was all over within four minutes. Four Indonesian bodies lay floating in the water; two more lay dead in their boats, while two others lay prostrate on the river bank; the ninth enemy soldier had fled in panic into the adjacent swamp. The ambush had succeeded. Letts' team collected their bergens and "scooted" back towards the safety of Malaysian territory, happy in the knowledge that they had made the enemy feel insecure even on his own home ground.

That the SAS had been given such a mission was no real surprise, since by that time 22 SAS had spent over two years on the jungle frontier which divided Indonesian Borneo (Kalimantan) from Malaysian Borneo. Indeed, almost as soon as the SAS arrived in Borneo, in January 1963, it had been deployed along the border to act as a defensive intelligence network. At the time, the British commander in Borneo, Major General Walter Walker, faced the twin threat of an internal uprising from the Clandestine Communist Organisation (CCO), a subversive movement based mainly on Chinese settlers in Sarawak, and of external invasion from Kalimantan. Apart from a small number of local forces, Walker had only five battalions of men available to meet these threats, an insufficient force to maintain internal security over the 80,000 square miles of territory on his side of the border, and at the same time to guard against possible attack from the other side. In the event, Walker decided to hold back the bulk of his men as a reaction force, ready to respond to troubles from within or incursions from without. At the same time he decided to deploy the available SAS squadron (about 70 men) along the border to warn of any Indonesian incursions.

The SAS had been allotted a most difficult task. One squadron, totalling not even 100 men, was being asked to keep watch along a jungle frontier almost 1,000 miles long, a frontier so wild and rugged that in some places it had not even been mapped. But then the SAS had extraordinary qualities. More so than any other regiment, the SAS possessed the ability to operate in inhospitable terrain for long periods of time, living off the land without regular re-supply; moreover, having taken part in the counter-insurgency campaign of the Malayan Emergency (1948–60), many SAS troopers spoke or understood Malay, the *lingua franca* of the frontier tribes. These attributes proved to be invaluable, because in practice the only effective means of controlling the border was to enlist the support of the border tribes, the native people who lived in settlements located on hillsides or in river valleys.

Fortunately for the SAS, many of these tribes were well disposed towards the British. Nevertheless, the tribesmen's loyalty could not be taken for granted, particularly as the favourite sport of some of them was headhunting. In an effort to win them over, SAS personnel operating in small teams of three to four men went into the settlements and stayed there for weeks or even months, helping with the planting, harvesting and weeding of crops, giving medical assistance and at all times respecting the customs and traditions of the natives. In return, the natives provided the SAS teams with news of any useful findings, such as spoors or bootmarks left in the jungle by the Indonesians.

Such information was relayed back to squadron headquarters on high-frequency radios and was supplemented by other information – about border-crossing points, jungle tracks, potential sites for ambushes and helicopter landings, and so on – gathered by the SAS teams on the patrols they carried out in their respective areas. So successful were these activities that by the time the Indonesians began their cross-border incursions, in April 1963, the SAS had already won over many of the tribes and had provided the security forces with "eyes and ears" along the frontier.

In the months that followed, the SAS continued their frontier duties, winning "hearts and minds", collecting intelligence and detecting and tracking enemy incursions, as well as helping to train a force of native irregulars called the Border Scouts. Inevitably, though, as the Indonesians stepped up their guerrilla incursions, the regiment's role was modified. By early 1964 SAS personnel were not only detecting incursions but were also helping infantrymen to intercept the infiltrators; the infantry, deployed from forward bases or dropped into the jungle by helicopter, were guided into ambush positions by SAS teams. Later that year SAS teams led ambush parties or "killer groups" over the border into Kalimantan, to hit the enemy before he could penetrate Malaysian territory.

These offensive forays, ultra-secret operations codenamed "Claret", called for the utmost skill and care. Any trace of British presence on Indonesian soil could have caused severe embarrassment to the British government. After all, Britain was not at war with Indonesia and wanted to avoid any accusation that she was escalating the conflict (it was for this reason, and also because of the risk of killing friendly tribesmen, that air strikes into Kalimantan were ruled out). Claret missions were, therefore, subject to definite limitations. They were to be undertaken only by experienced jungle troops and were to be guided by the SAS and the Border Scouts, who were to reconnoitre the target areas beforehand. They were also limited in terms of depth of penetration – initially to 3,000yd.

By the end of 1964, Claret operations had proved to be politically acceptable and militarily feasible. Consequently, when Walker learnt of a divisional strength build-up of high-quality Indonesian troops opposite the First Division (the western part of Sarawak) in December 1964, he sanctioned Claret missions to a depth of 10,000yd. The Indonesians seemed to be planning a major offensive against the First Division, and Walker believed that by threatening their forward bases and lines of communication he would force them to concentrate on defensive rather than offensive plans. In effect, Walker saw Claret operations as a means of denying the Indonesians the military initiative.

At first, during December 1964 and the early months of 1965, Claret teams were ordered to concentrate primarily on reconnaissance, a natural prerequisite to strikes in that the Kalimantan side of the border with the First Division had not previously been investigated to any great extent. Accordingly, SAS teams went over the border to identify Indonesian bases, infiltration routes (actual and potential) and lines of communication, by land and water.

Perhaps typical of such operations was a four-man patrol that set out early in January 1965 to recce the area south of Gunong Brunei, where the Koemba river ran close to the border. This patrol, led by Trooper Bennett, had to negotiate steep hills, thick jungle, rocky streams and a 300yd wide swamp before reaching the river. All the same their endeavours were worth while. They brought back valuable information about the area and also managed to earmark ambush positions – particularly promising in the latter respect was a high rock from which movements along the river, and along an established track linking Seluas and Siding, could be watched.

If Letts' team had carried out a recce that ended up as an engagement, it was not long before such engagements became standard practice. By early May 1965, Major General George Lea, who had succeeded Major General Walker two months previously, had decided that Claret operations should begin in earnest. One of the objectives chosen was a major supply route, the Koemba river near Poeri. A four-man team of SAS troopers led by Don Large was ordered to investigate river traffic near Poeri and to engage a suitable target.

Large's team had taken on a well-nigh impossible mission. Six previous attempts had been made to reach this sector of the Koemba river – and each had been foiled by

heavy going across swamps. The general feeling in headquarters was that this new attempt would also fail, but
Large himself remained optimistic, even though soon after
setting out from a landing position, on 10 May 1965, the
patrol ran into difficulties. On their second day in the jungle
the team heard enemy soldiers ahead; they had to take a
detour through thick undergrowth, and to do so without
making a noise or leaving tracks was an endeavour that
tested their jungle skills to the limit.

Worse was to follow. After crossing undetected over a
main jungle track on the third day, and another main track
(possibly used by the Indonesians for cutting off Claret
teams) on the fourth day, the team made for a loop in the
river, where Large believed they would find the tail of a
spur leading to the river bank. To their chagrin all they
found was more swamp – and each probe they made
seemed to lead them into deeper swamp. After spending
the night on a mud island, the team pressed on westwards,
hoping to find higher ground. As they inched their way
forward they heard the sound of boat engines – heavy
diesels – but saw no sign at all of the spur. Failure began to
seem inevitable, but Large refused to admit defeat. Taking
breakfast on dry land, the team talked over their predicament and decided to persevere – to go back into the swamp
and to head downstream with a view to finding a causeway
to the river.

Progress was painfully slow, though they were at least
encouraged by the sound of diesel engines, which indicated that they must be close to the river. And then, to
their surprise and amazement, they found high land
rising to 30ft. It was the spur! They emerged from the
swamp and began to negotiate the spur, soon entering a
narrow belt of jungle. After crossing the jungle, they
came to a rubber plantation. Skirting round this they
saw before them the Koemba river, fast-flowing and some
40yd wide.

Having at last found his objective, Large wasted no time
and proceeded to establish an observation post. He dis-
counted the area to his right because there was little cover
near the bank, and also rejected the area to his left, which,

although well covered, was the first place the enemy would expect them to go. He settled for the area to his front, a 10ft-high river bank with a ditch on the near side. This position had its disadvantages, the greatest of which was that the team would have to pull back across open ground on their way out. But it afforded a good view of the river, a ditch in which to rest, and reasonable cover (in the form of scrub and a tree) for both bank and ditch. It was also the sort of place the enemy would least expect an ambush site, or so Large hoped.

During the afternoon Large observed movements on the river and planned his ambush. He came to the conclusion that the best means of fulfilling his strategic objective – to make the enemy feel that their major supply lines were threatened – would be to destroy a boat carrying war cargo. As regards tactics, he decided that his best bet would be to wait until a boat had negotiated the river bend and then open fire from astern; this would offer a good chance of causing serious damage and would limit the crew's opportunity to return fire. His plan of action was for his team members – Walsh, Millikin and Scholey – to move forward to firing positions, 3yd apart; he himself would move in behind them to direct the firing, to watch out for other boats and to keep an eye on the rear.

Having established their positions and plan of action for the ambush, Large and his team settled down to an unpalatable meal of uncooked meat-blocks – they were unable to use their solid-fuel stoves or light a fire for fear of giving themselves away – and then managed to catch some sleep. They were to spend the next day fulfilling the first part of their orders – to establish the pattern of river traffic. It soon became apparent that headquarters was fully justified in its assumptions about the importance of the river. Among the vessels the team saw go past were a military supply launch and a luxury motor cruiser. The latter was a tempting target, but it appeared to be the flagship of some VIP. Large was mindful of the political consequences that might result from the destruction of such a vessel and so let it alone. He also let pass a 40ft launch that carried soldiers, confident that a more suitable target would appear the next day – something it would be well worth while waiting for.

The next morning, having radioed for permission "to engage opportunity target". Large and his colleagues waited eagerly. He allowed free passage to a two-man canoe and to a 30ft launch in the hope that a bigger prize might present itself. Five hours later none had done so, and as the sun became obscured behind thick cloud and rain began to pour down. Large's team-mates began to curse their leader's decision to let so many boats past on the previous day. But just then, with visibility fading, another launch appeared. It was a big one too, about 40ft long and 8ft wide; there were two sentries astern, it appeared to be carrying cargo, and soldiers were resting beneath its large canopy. As the launch passed by, 45yd distant, Large beckoned his men to their firing positions. Within half a minute they unleashed 60 rounds against their target, killing the two sentries and holing the boat. The stricken vessel listed in the water. As smoke belched from it, soldiers emerged from beneath the tarpaulin and jumped overboard as fast as they could. It was their only option, for, seconds later, the whole vessel was engulfed by flames.

Mission accomplished, the SAS men collected their effects together and took off along the spur as quickly as possible. However, there was a shock in store for them as Large found his path blocked, at head level, by a deadly snake – a king cobra – but fortunately the snake decided not to attack, and the team made rapid progress. By evening they had crossed the cut-off path. On the following day, having signalled for a helicopter on the SARBE (search and rescue beacon), they were winched out of the jungle and flown back to base. Large's sortie had accomplished a great deal. The team may only have destroyed one launch, but the psychological effect was devastating. The Indonesians now felt that their main supply routes were insecure and were compelled to re-deploy troops to guard them.

Other cross-border raids took place during the succeeding months, forcing the enemy further onto the defensive. In these subsequent raids, the role of the SAS was to act as guides, rather than sole participants, but that hardly mattered. The SAS men had done their bit. They had pioneered a tactic that was to force the Indonesians to abandon their forward bases and, in truth, to deny them any real chance of success.

INTERROGATION

Bruce Marshall

*The Special Operations Executive (SOE) was formed in
1940 from an amalgamation of various British secret
service departments, and charged with the co-ordination
of "all action, by way of sabotage and subversion, against
the enemy overseas". As an unconventional warfare unit,
the SOE had few, if any peers, in the Second World
War; in one four-week period of 1943 alone, the SOE
and its network of French agents carried out 3,000 acts of
sabotage on the French railways. It was SOE agents who
assassinated Reinhard Heydrich, Reichsprotektor of Bo-
hemia and Moravia, in 1942, SOE agents who blew up
the German atomic research facility at Vermork in Norway in 1943, and it was the SOE who trained the Karen
tribesmen who killed 17,000 Japanese soldiers in the last
weeks of the war.*

*Frederick Yeo-Thomas was typical of the indepen-
dent-minded men (and women) who joined the "Old
Firm", as SOE was known to its operatives. Thirty-
eight years old when the Second World War broke out,
Yeo-Thomas was refused service with RAF aircrew
because of his age, but was taken on as an AC2 interpreter because of his fluent French, courtesy of his many
years living in Paris. Eventually, Yeo-Thomas found his
way to SOE HQ at Baker Street in London, where he
organized the supply of equipment to the French Resistance. However, this was far too desk-bound a job for
Yeo-Thomas, who pestered his superiors to allow him to
parachute into France to co-ordinate the Resistance
groups. They did, and Yeo-Thomas became a founding*

father of the French secret army in the south known as the Maquis. Inevitably, Yeo-Thomas's activities in France came to the notice of the Germans, who ordered the Gestapo to capture "Shelley" (the code-name by which Yeo-Thomas was known to the Germans and French; his more famous alias was "White Rabbit"). In February 1944, only four months before D-Day, Yeo-Thomas parachuted into France for the last time. Landing about 250 miles from Paris, and spraining his ankle in the process, he quickly made his way to the capital to meet his Resistance contacts. In the event of capture, he had a cover story to hand, in which he was Dodkin, an RAF pilot who had been shot down and forced to bale out.

B ECAUSE OF REPEATED hold-ups by German police in the Métro, Yeo-Thomas had to do a great deal of walking: seven or eight contacts a day in widely separated parts of Paris laid a considerable strain on his as yet imperfectly healed left ankle. He had to take the usual precautions against being followed and to make sure that his contacts were not being trailed when he met them. For the Gestapo was more than ever alert.

In view of the constant danger, Tommy kept changing residences. One of his hideouts was at No. 11 Rue Claude Chahu, in the flat of a fearless Danish woman in the French Resistance, Suni Sandöe. He was staying there on March 21st, 1944, when he had an appointment with Antonin, a new *agent de liaison* lent to him by Pichard, the Chief Air Operations Officer of the French Resistance. The appointment had been fixed for eleven o'clock at the Passy Métro station, situated, unlike most others, on a bridge above ground; Antonin was to walk down the steps on the left and Tommy was to come up them on the right; they were to cross in front of the newspaper kiosk next to the ticket office and to feign surprise when they met.

At eleven o'clock precisely Yeo-Thomas passed the kiosk, but Antonin was not there. Ordinarily Yeo-Thomas would not have broken his security rule of never waiting for an unpunctual contact, but the appointment was very important. He therefore went down the steps on the other side of the station and came up again, using the same steps as before. Having ascended the first flight and still seeing no sign of Antonin coming towards him he hesitated as to whether to pay a surprise visit to his father, whose flat was only a hundred yards distant. Deciding to put duty before pleasure, he continued up the steps, meeting a crowd of people coming down from the train which had just arrived and feeling fairly safe in the other crowd which was climbing the steps towards the station. As he drew level with the last flight leading up to the ticket office five men in civilian clothes pounced on him, handcuffed him and began scientifically to search his pockets. Just then Antonin, escorted by another two Gestapo men in civilian clothes, passed by on the other side of the steps, looked at Tommy and was led away.

"*Wir haben Shelley*," Tommy's captors shouted with glee. "We've got Shelley."

As soon as Yeo-Thomas had been handcuffed two of the Gestapo men set about pushing back the excited crowd: they forbade access to the station and threatened to shoot anybody attempting to approach their prisoner. Then Tommy was quickly hustled up the steps, through the crowd and propelled into a Citröen with a uniformed driver which had been waiting at the corner of the Boulevard Delessert. He was made to sit in the back with two policemen on either side of him. As soon as the car started these two men began to take it in turn to punch him in the face. "Shelley," they cried, "*Wir haben Shelley. Englischer Offizier. Terrorist. Schweinhund.*"

This horrible little litany of imprecation continued until they reached the Gestapo Headquarters in the Rue des Saussaies, and so did the cruel blows. Tommy said that he was surprised to find himself "thinking in a completely impersonal manner just as though it were another person being beaten up and it was a very extraordinary feeling". It must have been. What was even more extraordinary was that during this painful passage to prison he was able to think out what he was going to say when he was interrogated.

It was clear that the Dodkin story would no longer serve in its entirety: the fact that the Gestapo men had greeted him as Shelley seemed to indicate that Antonin had talked. (He learned later that the *agent de liaison* had been arrested while carrying in his pocket contrary to all regulations, a piece of paper marked: SHELLEY PASSY II.) The Gestapo knew and had long known that Shelley was a British officer, but they did *not* know the name of the British officer. If they discovered his real identity and failed by normal methods to make him speak they would certainly arrest his father and torture the old man in his presence. Dodkin he would have to be, but not a baled-out Dodkin. All this he thought out while his face was being battered in the car.

When they reached their destination he was yanked violently out of the car and, with a pistol pointed at his back, was propelled into the lift. His abrupt arrival in an office on the third floor astonished the three men sitting there. "*Wir haben Shelley*," the leading policeman shouted as Tommy was pushed into the room. At this the three men rose from their chairs and began to punch him and kick him. Then they locked the door, stripped him naked and made him stand on a telephone directory. Enraged by the discovery of his tear-gas pen and revolver in a special holster strapped to his thigh, they started in on him again. They tore from his neck the small brown canvas sachet which a Russian countess had given him as a charm at the beginning of the war, and laid it on a desk beside the other objects which they had removed from his pockets: among these were his forged identity papers, the keys of four of his Paris apartments, and two monocles which he had worn to disguise himself. The discovery of the last particularly infuriated his tormentors, for they flung them on the floor and trampled on them. The spectacle was so ridiculous that Tommy laughed aloud in spite of his pain; this earned him another beating-up.

"I don't know how long this went on," Yeo-Thomas said. "To me it seemed hours, but in all probability it was only an hour and a half." Although so dazed that the room was swimming before his eyes, he was still able to think fairly clearly. Two desires were in his mind: to avoid betraying his friends and to escape from his agony. He could do both if only he could get at the signet ring containing the poison tablet which the thugs had omitted to remove from his left hand. Sooner or later, he felt, they would be bound to unhandcuff him and then he could slide open the top of the ring, swallow the tablet and put himself beyond treachery and pain.

He was still standing on the telephone directory when a tall, broad-shouldered man with cold steel-grey eyes and a cruel mouth entered the room. Tommy's tormentors stood sharply to attention, extended their arms in the Nazi salute and said *"Heil Hitler!"*

"Heil Hitler!" said the newcomer, returning the salute and stopping in front of Yeo-Thomas, who even on his perch was a head shorter. Looking down at the prisoner, the tall man spat in his face and gave him a crashing slap on the cheek which sent him careering against the wall. Unable to use his hands, Tommy collapsed on the floor, where the tall man kicked him every time he tried to get up. *"Schwein-hund, salaud, terroriste,"* the brute cried in bilingual rage, as he bent down, pulled Yeo-Thomas to his feet and flung him into a chair.

Very deliberately, the new thug drew up another chair and sat down in front of Tommy, staring at him with his expressionless, icy eyes. Tommy describes the man's eyes as being like "twin daggers, trying to pierce his brain". Knowing that the man's purpose was to make him lower his own eyes, Yeo-Thomas looked him full in the face. Once again the heavy fist crashed on to his lips and nose.

At a word of command from the new thug two of the other men pounced on Yeo-Thomas and dragged him out of the chair and began to unfasten his handcuffs. The moment he had been waiting for seemed to have arrived. But just as his handcuffs were removed the big man noticed the ring. *"Dummkopf,"* he roared at the assistants, himself grabbed Tommy's hand, removed the ring and slipped it into his pocket. Yeo-Thomas was ordered to put on his clothes again.

As he dressed he made quick calculations: he had been arrested at five minutes past eleven; it must now be about three o'clock. Maud, an agent with whom he had had an appointment at one o'clock, would now be aware that something was wrong. When also he failed to turn up for his emergency rendezvous at six o'clock she would know for certain that he had been arrested. Within twelve hours all his letter-boxes would have been closed down, his meeting-places changed and his contacts warned not to keep their appointments. In the meantime, to protect his network, he must, as was the rule for captured agents, hold out for at least forty-eight hours.

As soon as he was dressed the big man made a sign to his companions and sat down behind a desk. Tommy was dragged from the chair into which he had deliberately slumped, propelled to the desk and dumped down again in the chair which had been brought up behind him. On the desk were laid out the objects which had been removed from his pockets and from his person: from them his gold fountain pen, his wristwatch and banknotes of higher denomination were already missing; but his pistol was still there, with the barrel pointing towards him and nearer to him than to his inquisitor. Intending to shoot the big man and then himself, he lifted his manacled hands and laid them on the edge of the desk. Nobody seemed to notice this gesture.

"*Vous avez joué et vous avez perdu*," the big man began. "You've had your flutter and you've lost. But nothing will happen to you if you're reasonable and listen to sense. But if you don't . . ."

Tommy did not answer; it was always a few seconds gained.

"Well, are you going to talk?"

Once again he did not answer.

The big man sprang up and crashed his fist on to Tommy's mouth. "I'll make you speak all right." With the help of his two assistants, he started hitting the prisoner again. They did not desist until Yeo-Thomas crumpled up under their onslaught. The big man went back behind his desk and rang a bell.

Pretending not to have completely recovered conscious-ness, Tommy leaned forward in his chair and slowly slid his hand across the desk towards the pistol; but the big man saw the gesture, laughed, picked up the pistol and put it in a drawer.

"So you thought you'd use it, *cochon?*" was all that he said.

A young, fair, good-looking German with blue eyes and a pink complexion answered the bell. The big man, ordering him to go out and bring back a typewriter, called him "Ernst", and the young man called the big man "Rudi". Tommy made a mental note of the names. When Ernst had fetched a typewriter he sat down at a corner of the desk, inserted a form, a carbon and a blank sheet into the machine and waited in silence.

"Name?" Rudi rapped at Yeo-Thomas.

"Shelley." That at least it was no good denying.

"Fool. Your real name."

"Kenneth Dodkin." This answer seemed to be accepted, for Rudi went on to ask:

"Your serial number?"

"47,685."

"Rank?"

"Squadron Leader."

"Branch of the Service?"

"Royal Air Force."

"Address?"

"I do not require to reply to that question."

"You will reply all the same."

"I shall not."

Rudi got up, walked around the desk, and using both his hands, began to slap Tommy's face from one side to the other, cutting the already bruised cheeks with his heavy signet ring. Yeo-Thomas swayed in his chair; the two assistants propped him up so that Rudi could go on hitting him.

At last Rudi stopped and sat down behind the desk again.

"Listen," he said, suddenly changing to a friendly tone. "It's no good being obstinate. Now I'm going to ask you a few questions; all you've got to do is to answer and it'll be all finished with. I say, what about a cigarette?" He took a cigarette from a gold case, stuck it between Tommy's bruised lips, lit it with a gold lighter. "That's better, isn't it?" he said as he watched Yeo-Thomas take a couple of puffs. "You see, we're not such brutes after all. If you're reasonable you've got nothing to fear. And when you've answered we'll give you some food and something nice to drink."

Tommy did not reply, nor did he make any sign; he went on puffing at his cigarette. Ernst sat expectantly at his typewriter.

"I may as well tell you that it's no use telling us any lies," Rudi went on. "Your *agent de liaison* has made a clean breast of everything. We know all you've been doing here since the beginning of the year. We know that you know all about the arms dumps. You've only got to tell us where they are and we'll leave you alone."

Behind his sore face Yeo-Thomas almost smiled. Rudi had been too clever; if Rudi had been as well informed as he pretended to be he would have known that his prisoner had not been in France at the beginning of the year; and Antonin, who had been working for Tommy only for a week, could not have given him much information. Rudi was bluffing; to gain time Yeo-Thomas decided to bluff too.

"Then he's talked?" he asked.

"Naturally."

Tommy pretended to be shocked and distressed.

"Did he tell you I had an appointment for this afternoon?"

"We know everything, I tell you."

"In that case it won't do much good my talking, will it?"

This unexpected piece of logic made Rudi's face harder again.

"This is no time for joking," he said. "We know that you have an appointment this afternoon. All I want to know is with whom and where."

"What time is it now?" Tommy asked.

"Half-past four."

"In that case it's too late because my appointment is for a quarter to five."

"Where?"

"At the Porte Maillot."

"With whom?"

"With a woman who's bringing me a message."

Rudi picked up the telephone and ordered a car to stand by immediately. One of the guards was sent to fetch another two thugs in civilian clothes, to whom instructions were given by Rudi in German too rapid for Yeo-Thomas to understand. "*Heil Hitler!*" said the thugs and ran from the room; removing Tommy's revolver from the drawer and pocketing it, Rudi prepared to follow them.

"What's this woman like?" Rudi asked.

Yeo-Thomas gave him a fantastic description of an imaginary woman who, he said, would be carrying a bouquet of flowers in one hand and a newspaper in the other.

"If you're lying you'll pay for it," Rudi shouted as he rushed after the other two men.

Yeo-Thomas knew only too well that he would soon pay dearly for having sent Rudi on a wild-goose chase; but he had gained time and so far he had not talked. His two guards watched him stolidly out of their square, unimaginative, unpitying faces. Ernst moved from his typewriter to Rudi's chair and began examining the property which had been removed from Tommy's person.

Through the slits which were all he now had for eyes Tommy tried to examine his possessions too. There was only one, he thought, which was really dangerous: the bunch of keys, of which one belonged to a flat in the Rue de la Tourelle. Of his use of this flat only two people knew. One was in prison, but the other was the agent called Maud. When he failed to turn up for his six o'clock appointment, she would give the place a wide berth. He must therefore avoid answering any questions about the keys until after six o'clock, when, if the persistence of his tormentors became too painful, he would tell them which was the key of the flat in the Rue de la Tourelle. The Germans would then rush round to the flat and, when they found nobody there, bait a trap which would immobilize a couple of their men for a few days. He was still thinking all this out when Rudi burst into the room livid with rage.

As Rudi had promised, Yeo-Thomas paid for having

lied: he was knocked down on the floor, picked up and knocked down again. Eventually he was picked up for the last time and thrown back on to his chair; Rudi resumed his seat at the desk.

"You've made me lose my time, *salaud*."

"I told you you'd be late," Tommy said. "She can't have waited. It's not my fault."

Rudi glared at him. "Where are the arms dumps you know of?"

"I know of none."

"Are you going to talk: yes, or no?"

"I don't know anything, I tell you."

"We'll see if you know nothing." Rudi signed to the two guards who grabbed Tommy's arms and jerked him to his feet. Taking from a drawer a long chain and an ox-gut whip with a flexible steel rod inside it, Rudi swished the latter threateningly in the air. Tommy was propelled out of the room, up steps and along a narrow passage lined on one side with small circular windows which looked like portholes; he guessed that he was being taken to a torture chamber.

He had a rough journey: every time he stumbled from weakness he was jerked up by the handcuffs, which bit deeply into his flesh. At the end of the passage a door opened and he was flung on to the tiled floor of a bathroom, through the open window of which blew in a freezing draught. He was dragged to his feet and two men pulled off his trousers and underpants; his hands were unmanacled while his jacket and shirt were torn off and then handcuffed again behind his back. While Rudi bent and twisted the chain tightly round his ankles Ernst opened the cold-water tap and filled the bath.

"Where are the arms dumps?" Rudi asked.

"I don't know."

The ox-gut whip came slashing down on Tommy's chest, searing it and raising a weal; Yeo-Thomas gritted his teeth.

"So you're going to be pig-headed, are you?"

Aching in every joint, Tommy remained silent. He was forced to sit on the edge of the bath. Rudi bent down again, caught hold of the chain around his ankle and gave it a twist and a tug, drawing him into the bath. One of the men scooped water up in the palm of his hand and splashed him with it.

"Where are the arms dumps?" Rudi asked again.

"I don't know."

Rudi crashed his big fist into Tommy's jaw and, as he staggered, pushed him headlong into the bath, so that his face was under the water while his legs stuck up in the air. With his hands manacled behind his back, Yeo-Thomas was helpless. Panicking, he tried to kick, but his legs were caught and held in a powerful grip. His eyes were open and he could see faces distorted by the water wavering above him. His mouth came open and he swallowed water. His lungs felt as though they were bursting. He made another attempt to kick himself out of the bath but the vice-like grip still held him. He tried to lift himself up with his hand-cuffed arms and failed. Swallowing more water, he became limp: the strength went out of him and he began to lose consciousness; he was drowning and he knew it.

He came to feeling an agonizing pain in his chest. Water was gushing out of his mouth and there was a big wavering black shadow in front of his eyes. The shadow slowly dissolved into lighter filmy circles which shimmered like hot air on a summer's day. As the circles became faces Tommy realized that he was lying on the tiled floor of the bathroom and looking up into Rudi's sadistic eyes. He could breathe only in gasps and his heart, in his own phrase, was "thumping like bellows in a forge". He had been pulled out of the water just as he had been about to drown and given artificial respiration.

He was lifted to his feet.

"Where are the arms dumps?"

"I . . . don't . . . know."

Thrown brutally back into the bath, his head hit the edge. Once more the water engulfed him. Once more he tried in vain to kick and to push himself up with his handcuffed arms. Once more he swallowed water. Once more he felt himself drowning. His mouth opened and the water poured in. There were rushing noises in his ears. As before he was hauled from the bath just as he was about to drown and was artificially revived.

"Where are the arms dumps?"

"I . . . don't . . . know."

He was thrown back into the bath several times. Kicking and swallowing water, oblivion succeeding consciousness and consciousness oblivion, he lost count of his torments and soon was unable to trace their sequence. As soon as he saw the distorted faces of Rudi and Ernst he lost sight of them again. He no longer had the strength or the desire to kick. He was brought round for the last time by a kick from a heavy boot and knew from the agony that he was still alive. He was lying on the bathroom floor, with walls, bath and faces swirling around his head. Abominably sick and with his stomach as large as a barrel, water came gushing out of his mouth on to his chest. Numb with cold, he was dragged to his feet, on which he could no longer stand as the chain had stopped the circulation. As he tottered he was struck heavily over the head with a rubber cosh and again collapsed.

When he had recovered from the sickening effects of this blow he was hustled, still dripping with water, back to Rudi's office. The chain was removed from his feet and he was pushed into a chair while his underpants and trousers were slipped on. His handcuffs were loosened, but fastened again as soon as he had been thrust into his shirt and jacket. Once again Rudi sat at his desk facing him.

"Where are the arms dumps?"

"I don't know."

"Haven't you had enough, *ordure*? Well, we'll see."

At a sign from Rudi the two guards produced rubber coshes with which they began to beat him. He was beaten on the head, arms, legs, and body. He did not cry out. Still less did he speak.

"Where are the arms dumps?"

"I don't know."

Each time that he said this the beating up started all over again. He saw flashes before his eyes; the furniture and Rudi's face began to float in the circles. In the end he lost consciousness.

When he came to, lying on the floor, he pretended that he was still unconscious by keeping his eyes closed; this was not difficult because his eyelids were now so swollen that he could scarcely see out of them. He felt sore and bruised all over. He said that he did not know that it was possible to have so many pains in so many places at the same time.

When his tormentors saw that he had recovered consciousness he was picked up and dumped in his chair again. The handcuffs were cutting into his wrists and making them ache. He was beginning to feel hungry too, having had only a cup of coffee for breakfast and nothing since.

Rudi faced him with a malevolent grin, holding up the bunch of keys.

"What keys are these?"

"They are keys." The question which he had feared had come. The keys had been found in his possession and he could not disown them. However, the lights in the room were already on and through the window he could see that it was dark outside: it must therefore be after six o'clock. Maud would know by now that he had been arrested and would take care not to go near the flat in the Rue de la Tourelle. But in order to protect the owners of the flats to which the other three keys belonged he must not yield even harmless information easily.

"For what doors?"

"For no doors. The keys are cover. A man looks suspicious if he doesn't carry keys, so to be in the swim I had some made."

"I warn you once again not to take me for a fool. I want to know what doors they open."

"I tell you they open none."

"Where did you sleep last night?"

"I don't remember."

"In that case I shall force you to remember."

Rudi rose from his seat and, with the key ring hooked round one of his fingers, approached Yeo-Thomas; using the keys as a flail, he lashed his face with them until the blood began to flow.

"Now are you going to tell me, *salaud*?"

With his face pouring with blood, his eyes streaming and his nose feeling as though it were on fire, it was not difficult for Tommy to let his head fall on his chest as though he were in such agony he could not speak. He allowed Rudi to go on scourging his face with the keys for a little longer and then he deliberately flopped.

"There's only one that works," he said at length. "It's the big one."

"Where does it work?"

"33 Rue de la Tourelle, Porte de St. Coud."

"Couldn't you have said so earlier, *ordure*? Making me waste my time like this. If you've been lying again you'll pay for it."

After giving some instructions over the telephone, Rudi took the keys and walked out of the room. Yeo-Thomas was picked up and dragged from the room and across the landing. A padlocked door on the same floor was opened and he was thrown into a cell about three feet wide, five feet long and ten feet high; on one side was an opening about a foot square with an iron bar across it. Jerked to his feet, he was flung on to a chair, over the back of which his hand-cuffed hands were slipped. One of the guards gave him a parting blow on the jaw; then they both left, slamming and padlocking the door behind them. Not a ray of light came from the aperture which he had seen when the door had been open; he was in complete darkness.

For the first time since his arrest he was alone. He was all aches and pains. His head was buzzing and his nose felt as big as a pumpkin. His jaw hurt terribly and all his teeth were loose. His mouth was full of the salt taste of blood, his eyes burned and the handcuffs were cutting into his wrists. Worn out, he sagged on his chair and the handcuffs bit more deeply into his flesh. Tommy tried to sleep, but every time his head fell forward his handcuffs jabbed him back to agonizing wakefulness.

When at length he was taken back to the interrogation room Ernst was still sitting at the desk, and Rudi was standing menacingly beside him.

Rudi glared at Yeo-Thomas.

"You've made me lose my time again. You haven't been in that flat for months."

A soldier came in and laid on the desk a tray on which were food and a bottle of wine. Rudi and Ernst sat down and began to eat and drink. They did not speak as they ate, although they kept glancing at their prisoner from time to time. At last they finished eating and ordered the guards to take him back to the tiny cell on the other side of the landing. There he was thrust on to the chair as before, with his hands slipped over the back, and left in pitch blackness.

Unable to sleep with his arms fastened behind the chair, he attempted to free them. But each movement he made was agony, and when he attempted to rise to his feet his legs and his shoulders were so stiff that all that happened was that the chair slid back until it reached the wall. Finally he fell forward, the chair tipped, his forehead struck the wall in front of him and his arms were free. With difficulty setting the chair upright again, he sat on it and, although more comfortable, found that he had less room than before as his handcuffed arms now intervened between his body and the back of the chair. He then shuffled the chair into a corner of the cell and leaned his head against the wall. With pain racking him from head to foot and wanting desperately to blow his nose, he eventually dozed.

He was awakened by the noise of the bar outside being lifted and of the padlock being opened, and by a shout of "*Raus!*" Luckily the guards did not notice that he had freed his arms from the back of the chair. Yanked out of the cell, he was pushed back into the now familiar room where two new interrogators awaited him. Smaller than Rudi and Ernst, the new inquisitors were clean-shaven and bull-necked and had glistening, beady eyes. Both began firing questions at him at once, starting not where Rudi and Ernst had left off but, in the evident desire of trapping him in a contradiction, where they had begun. Tired and sleepy, it was fortunate that Yeo-Thomas knew his story by heart.

As previously the interrogation was punctuated with punches, slaps and insults. He was knocked off his chair and kicked as he lay helpless on the floor. After about an hour he was taken back to the bathroom, undressed and the all-but-drowning process began again. He had now, how-ever, elaborated a new technique: as soon as his head went under water he kicked vigorously and then, just as he felt himself about to lose consciousness, let himself go limp. As before he swallowed a lot of water and underwent what he euphemistically terms discomfort, but the icy cold dispelled his torpor and he was brave enough to derive consolation from the thought that he was still gaining time. He was alternately half-drowned and artificially revived for about another hour until he deliberately collapsed and took his own time to recover. Dragged back to the interrogation room, he was forced to sit and watch his tormentors eat their breakfast of hot coffee and croissants. Then he was beaten up again until he was almost insensible.

Nearly past caring what happened to him, he was left to recover from the blows. But he was not left alone for long. Rudi and Ernst soon turned up again and started in as soon as they arrived:

"Where are the arms dumps?"

"I don't know."

Although the keys weren't mentioned again, Rudi made his prisoner pay for having sent him on two useless errands and prevented him from exploiting his capture; his questions were accompanied by mighty beatings-up, and another visit was paid to the bathroom, where the half-drowning treatment was again vainly employed.

In the afternoon a new master and a new technique were tried. Yeo-Thomas was driven to No. 84 Avenue Foch, where an armed escort awaited him. He was led into a small office, where a small, studious-looking man, whose spectacles increased his appearance of benignity, sat at a typewriter; beside him stood a giant of about six-foot-five dressed in SS uniform with skull and crossbones on the collar. The giant, lifting Tommy almost with one hand, placed him on a chair in front of his new inquisitor, who for quite five minutes examined him with dispassionate, silent curiosity. Then, when he had filled his typewriter with foolscap and carbon, he leaned back in his swivel chair and joined his hands professionally on his chin.

"I am not like the others," he said, speaking in the customary correct Gestapo French. "I shall not hurt you. If you are sensible we shall be good friends. Come now, you will do yourself no good by obstinacy. You've had your flutter and you've lost. Now all you've got to do is to answer my questions."

Yeo-Thomas did not answer; although the repetition of the flutter phrase amused him he was very much on his guard.

"Your name?"

"Kenneth Dodkin."

"Your number?"

"47,865."

"Your rank?"

"Squadron Leader."

"Your Branch of the Service?"

"Royal Air Force."

"Your address?"

"I do not require to answer that question."

"Where are the arms dumps?"

"I don't know."

Unlike Rudi and Ernst and their second strings, the little man did not threaten: he just typed down Tommy's answers.

"You know Cadillac?" ("Cadillac" was one of the code names of a very important agent named Bingen.)

"Cadillac? I know nobody of that name. It's the trade name of an American car, isn't it?"

An ominous look came into the little man's eyes.

"It would be as well if you were to refrain from playing the fool. I happen to know that you know Cadillac."

"You are making a mistake."

The little man shook his head sorrowfully.

"My friend, you are going to force me to resort to methods I don't like very much."

Yeo-Thomas did not answer; he found this detached manner of examination much more disturbing than Rudi's brutal onslaughts

"Where is Cadillac?"

"I tell you I don't know Cadillac."

"What a very great pity. You are forcing my hand, you know."

"I can't very well tell you that I know Cadillac when I don't know him."

"And Pic? Do you know him?" (Pic was one of the code names of Pichard, the Chief Air Operations Officer of the Resistance.)

"Yes, I know Pic." This time Tommy could not lie, knowing that Antonin, who had been Pichard's *agent de liaison*, had almost certainly admitted the connection between his normal master and himself.

"What does he look like?"

Almost as much to test his inquisitor's knowledge as to protect his friend, Yeo-Thomas gave of Pichard a description which was the contrary of reality: omitting to mention that Pichard had a mutilated hand, he made him short and plump instead of tall and thin and when asked the colour of the Air Operation Officer's hair, stated that he could not say because Pichard, who in fact, was always bareheaded, never took off his hat. To his surprise his bluff succeeded.

"It's just as well you've told us the truth," the little man said. "You see, we arrested Pichard yesterday."

Realizing that his interrogator had lied and did not know as much as he pretended, Tommy tried to stall for time by answering dilatorily the next very insidious questions and by feigning surprise at their nature. But suddenly the little man asked him once again:

"Where is Cadillac?"

"I don't know Cadillac."

"You're lying and I know it. You know Cadillac very well. What's more you knew him in London. He's a Jew."

"You know more than I do."

"Dear me! I can see that my method doesn't suit you at all. Well, I have a friend who is not quite so gentle." The little man picked up the telephone and spoke in German.

Presently a strongly-built, bullet-headed man with small, piercing, piglike eyes came in and, without a word, crashed his heavy fist into Tommy's face. The small inquisitor looked on with an expression of regret and commiseration.

Led out of the office by the giant, Yeo-Thomas was handed over to two guards who escorted him to a small room on the fourth floor, where they were immediately joined by the bullet-headed man. The links on his handcuffs were attached to a hook on the end of a long double chain which hung from a pulley on the ceiling; the other end was pulled and, as his heels left the ground, the steel of the handcuffs was forced deeply into his wrists. Agony shot through his shoulders, a red film obscured his eyes and, unable to restrain himself, he groaned. As he fainted he heard the bullet-headed man laugh. In intermittent spells of consciousness he suffered pain worse than any he had so far endured. Not until it was dark did they loosen him, and at once he crumpled up on the floor.

When he came to he felt that he had reached breaking-point. He was afraid that if they tortured him again he would speak and tell them all about the arms dumps and the whole Resistance Movement.

But there was to be no more torture for him that night: flat out after more than twenty-four hours' almost continuous interrogation and chastisement, he was half-carried to a small cell at the top of the building, from which he was almost at once removed to another room in which sat the giant and a mean-looking NCO. There he had to spend the night chained by his arms and legs to a settee. Hungry and thirsty, he was refused food, but was eventually given a mug of water. The only time he managed to sleep was during the short period when his guards were snoring; otherwise as soon as he dozed off he was shaken awake by the mean-looking NCO who roared at him: "*Nicht schlaffen.*"

When dawn came the giant went out and brought back bread and sausage and a steaming jug of hot coffee for himself and his companion. The sight and the smell of the warm food made Tommy feel hungry and cold and he asked hopefully for a drink: he was given another mug of water.

As the morning grew lighter he knew that the moment was fast approaching when he would again writhe under the torments of his captors. He was at the end of his tether: he felt that if they did anything too painful to him this time he was bound to break down and speak. He wished for death because it was only in death that he could be sure of not speaking. Terror tore through him when his chains were undone and he was pulled to his feet. But his resolution returned as he thought of his friends who trusted in him.

In another office on the fourth floor, with the giant seated

behind him, he faced a new, sinister and menacing interrogator:

"Are you still going to be pigheaded? Or are you going to
talk?"

"I have nothing to say."

"I can see quite clearly that you are a liar. But we have
methods of making even liars talk, methods you don't know
yet."

Yeo-Thomas made a quick calculation: already he had
held out for almost forty-six hours; in another two hours he
would have accomplished the statutory forty-eight, and
then, perhaps, he could afford to let slip a few unimportant
details. In the meantime he must still strive to gain time.

"You know Cadillac, I think. His real name is Bingen. He
is a Jew."

This unexpected knowledge relieved Tommy. In view of
his role in the Resistance, he could not deny knowing
Bingen; if he had denied knowing him under his code name
of Cadillac it had been in order to avoid being forced to
admit that, while he was ignorant of his whereabouts, he
could get into touch with him when he wanted.

"I didn't know he was called Cadillac," he said.

The German seemed surprised.

"Do you mean to tell me that you didn't know that
Cadillac and Bingen were one and the same person?"

"No. You see, everybody has several names and one can't
be expected to know them all."

"But you know where he is."

"No."

"Yes, you know quite well and what's more you're going
to tell us."

"How can you expect me to tell you where he is when I
don't know myself?"

But the new inquisitor seemed to know all the tricks of
the trade.

"In that case you must have a permanent rendezvous
with him. Where is that rendezvous?"

"I have no permanent rendezvous with him. In any case
he must know by now that I have been arrested." In spite of
his pain, hunger and weariness he still had the energy to lie

fluently: "You see, I had an appointment with him yester-day. As I didn't turn up he will know what has happened. So even if I wanted to I couldn't find him."

"Ha, ha! So you had an appointment with him yesterday? And you won't tell us, *Schweinhund*? That's another thing you've still got to pay for." The interrogator suddenly abandoned his threats and spoke in honeyed tones. "Listen. I am certain that you know where to find him. If you will tell us we'll be kind to you. I think perhaps we could release you. We'll organize an escape. You see how simple it is? Nobody will ever know that you have talked."

Battered, caked with blood, trembling in every limb, Yeo-Thomas looked the German full in the face out of his puffed eyelids.

"I can't tell you where to find Bingen," he said. "And even if I could I wouldn't."

His defiance made the inquisitor splutter with rage.

"You're the friend of a dirty Jew," he shouted. "I'm beginning to think that you must be a Jew yourself."

"I am not a Jew and I don't know if Bingen is one and in any case it's none of my business."

The inquisitor again became persistent and threatening: "Where are the arms dumps?"

Seated within three feet of a window, Tommy gathered all his strength for a desperate leap across an intervening table: provided that he got through the window quickly enough there was every chance, as the office was on the fourth floor, that he would kill himself or at least hurt himself so badly that he would not recover.

"Where are the arms dumps? You have suffered, I know, but I promise you that you shall suffer much more if you do not answer my question."

He sprang and, taking his captors by surprise, jumped clean over the table. His head hit the glass pane and smashed it and his shoulders passed through. But the giant was too quick for him: seizing Tommy by the ankles, he pulled him back into the room and sat him back on his chair, to which he was now securely fastened by chains hurriedly brought by a soldier.

"So you are frightened, are you?" the interrogator said

with a leer. "Well, now's the time to speak. If you don't it'll be very unpleasant for you indeed."

Tommy did not answer: he knew that if he spoke it would be to beg for mercy.

"Well, we shall see," the interrogator said as he rose.

Accompanied by his inquisitor and an escort, Yeo-Thomas was driven back to the Rue des Saussaies, where another glaring and cursing interrogator awaited him in a different room with a long table in it.

"Now you'll speak," the thug roared at him. "You're afraid. It's now or never."

Desperately terrified, Tommy remained silent. Five new thugs came in. Thrown on to the table, chains were fastened round his legs and attached to the desk in such a manner that his feet were spread out. Two men held down his arms; with rubber coshes the other three rained thudding blows on his face, legs and body. The thugs slammed away till he fainted.

When he came to he found himself lying on a couch with broken springs in an empty, bare room. Through the only window, barred and high up, he could see that it was already dark outside; it had been morning when they had started beating him up. His suffering soon sent him back into semi-consciousness in which his sore body seemed to float away from him like a balloon.

He began to lose track of the sequence of events. He remembers being questioned, but recollects the questions only hazily:

"What is your name?"

"Kenneth Dodkin."

"Your serial number?"

"47,685."

"Where are the arms dumps?"

"I don't know."

"Where have you been living for the past few weeks?"

This last was the dangerous question and he knew it, but his interrogators knew it too, and they came back to it again and again. One inquisitor, a fair, good-looking man of twenty-six or twenty-seven called Mizzlewitz, was, however, more subtle and less brutal than his colleagues:

"I know where you live. It's no use your trying to gain time."

"If you know where I live why do you ask me?"

"Because we have several of your addresses and we want to arrest everybody whom we suspect of helping people like you."

"When you talk like that it's quite clear to me you don't know where I live."

"I'll prove it to you that I do. You live at 11 Rue Claude Chahu."

"What makes you think that?"

"I don't think; I know. And what's more I know that you weren't the only person to use this address."

Flabbergasted, Tommy did not reply.

"If you tell me the names of the persons who sheltered you I promise you that no harm will come to them."

Still Tommy did not answer.

"Not that it matters really. Our men are there already and they'll soon find out from the concierge," said Mizzlewitz.

Tommy knew that whether the Gestapo men were or were not at 11 Rue Claude Chahu they could soon force the concierge to tell them that a stranger answering to his description had stayed from time to time in Suni Sandöe's flat on the ground floor. Whatever he did or did not say Suni Sandöe was now blown. If she had already been arrested she would be beaten up until she admitted that she knew him and they would ultimately be confronted; there was, however, every chance that she had gone into hiding. The only thing that he could now do to help her was to represent her as ignorant of the nature of his activities. This he did, and Mizzlewitz said that he could now go back to the Rue des Saussaies, from which, in his fuddled state, he did not recollect having been removed.

Rudi slapped him on the face when he got back and had him flung once more into the tiny cell opposite his office. Still handcuffed and sore, Tommy sat on the chair and waited until he was taken to be interrogated by a sallow-faced, dark-haired, black-jowled man with bad teeth, who asked him in a rough voice questions about sabotage. Yeo-Thomas sagged on his seat and ignored his questions. He was then conducted again to the bathroom and, as far as he can remember, half-drowned and artificially revived six times.

He did not know whether it was night or day when he was taken to his next interrogation, which was conducted on entirely different lines, by a man of about fifty and by a slim young man with horn-rimmed glasses.

"They've been rather unkind to you, I see," the young man said "It's unfortunate, but that's war for you. I expect you're rather hungry."

Almost immediately a soldier carried in a tray on which was a jug of hot soup, a cup and a plate of sausage sandwiches.

"It's not much, but at four o'clock in the morning Maxim's is shut," the young man said. He came round, undid Tommy's handcuffs and fastened his sore, stiff arms in front of his body, and with the handcuffs looser than before. "I'm afraid I'll have to put them back again afterwards. And you mustn't say I've done this, because I'm not supposed to be humane."

Warmed by the food, Tommy felt his strength returning. Knowing that his clemency was part of a technique, he waited warily for the first question.

He was shown a photograph of an agent known as Clo, who had been Air Operations Officer for the Bordeaux area and whom he knew to be dead.

"Do you know who this is?"

"I think so."

"I think that you know very well indeed who it is, but unfortunately he is dead."

Tommy pretended to be surprised.

"I didn't know that: poor chap."

Many more questions followed, but they were kindly and not too persistently put, and showed a vast superficial knowledge of Resistance plans and as vast an ignorance of the details. Yeo-Thomas was, therefore, able to appear co-operative by restricting the truth of his replies to what his interrogators already knew and giving them false information about what they obviously didn't. He was shown a faulty chart of General de Gaulle's Free French Secret

Service, purporting to give the names of all the component officers and their duties; pretending to be impressed by its accuracy, he increased the war establishment by giving the names of non-existent officers to whom he ascribed almost fantastic duties; this information was gravely inscribed on the chart and he was given two more cigarettes as a reward.

At noon he was collected by two guards from Rudi's section, and, on his way downstairs, was horrified to meet Suni Sandöe, also under the escort of guards. Surprisingly he was allowed to say a few words to her and tried to convey to her that she must pretend to have been ignorant of his activities and deny having seen any arms in her flat. He learned later that, having neglected to go into hiding, she had been arrested in her flat in the Rue Claude Chahu.

Later that day, which he was astonished to discover was only Friday, he was again interrogated by Rudi, who seemed very pleased with himself and was unexpectedly benign. When this interview ended at dusk, he was made to enter a large room in which, seated on chairs evenly spaced but staggered so that no two were side by side, were assembled Commandant Palaud, second-in-command of the Paris area, Doyen of the Free French Secret Service, Anne-Marie, Yvonne and Georges of Pichard's secretariat and circuit, Chaland, saboteur and executioner of traitors, and others. Palaud's face was puffed and swollen, his clothes were torn and his hands smeared with blood. Anne-Marie's hair was dripping with water and lay in wet strands down her pale face; and most of the others looked tired and worn. Yeo-Thomas now understood the reason for Rudi's good humour: the catch was certainly a good one.

About two hours later, when it was dark, there were shouts of "*Raus! Los! Schnell!*" Accompanied by guards armed with sub-machine guns, the prisoners were marched downstairs into a hallway, where Rudi and Ernst checked their names off on a list. "Dodkin" seemed to be the first name on this list, for it was Tommy who was made to lead the way into the prison van waiting outside; inside the van he was propelled along a narrow passage lined with steel doors and locked into a dark cell with only a vent to give him air. Other doors slammed and they were off, bound for the notorious prison of Fresnes.

After more brutality at Fresnes, Yeo-Thomas was sent to Buchenwald concentration camp to be executed. At the last moment, he escaped and made his way to the Allied lines.

INTERROGATION: A SURVIVAL GUIDE

To the army on the move, taking prisoners is more than a waste of time, it's a waste of precious manpower to guard them and rations to feed them. It's often only some respect for the laws of warfare and the fear that they would be treated the same way themselves that keep them from shooting everybody.

To the intelligence specialist, though, the prisoner is not a waste of time. He's precious. He may be pure gold. The information about troop strengths and positions that he has in his head – perhaps not even realising that he has it – could be the difference between a battle lost and a battle won.

The US Army knows this, and spends a lot of time training its men how to combat enemy interrogation techniques. Field Manual FM 21–76 is the source for this section on how to get through a hostile interrogation while giving away as little information as possible.

The Laws of War

The news of your capture is supposed, under the Geneva Convention to be passed to a body called the Protection Power, often the Red Cross/Red Crescent, so that they can pass it on to your own government. That's the only reason for giving away even such simple information as your name, rank, number and date of birth.

If you're captured by a terrorist group, they probably won't do this – even some governments don't which is why so many US prisoners of the Viet Cong and Pathet Lao are still recorded as MIA (Missing in Action) following the war in South-East Asia.

The Geneva Convention

The Geneva Convention is an international agreement first formulated in 1864 to establish a code of practice for the treatment of wartime sick, wounded and prisoners of war. These are the major elements of the Geneva Convention as it affects prisoners of war.

1 Interrogation. A PoW is required to provide only his name, rank, service number and date of birth. The use of physical or mental coercion to obtain information from PoWs is prohibited.

2 Movement. PoWs must be moved under humane conditions.

3 Environment. The internment environment must not be unhealthy or dangerous.

4 Food. Food must be of sufficient quality and quantity to maintain good health.

5 Clothing. Suitable clothing must be provided.

6 Health, Hygiene and Wellbeing. The detaining power must ensure that adequate hygienic facilities are provided. The PoW is entitled to treatment by medical personnel from their own country, where available. The seriously wounded or sick are entitled to special treatment and may be transferred to a neutral nation.

7 Protected Personnel. Captured medical personnel and chaplains are treated as protected personnel and are to be free to circulate among the PoWs tending to their spiritual welfare and health.

8 Religion, Recreation, Education and Exercise. Each PoW has the right to practise his religion, and to engage in physical exercise, education and recreation.

9 Work. All enlisted personnel below NCO rank are subject to work details, but these shall not be dangerous or unhealthy. NCOs may be called up to work in a supervisory capacity; officers may work voluntarily. The Geneva Convention prohibits the use of PoWs for mine clearance

and lays down working conditions, pay, fitness for work and the treatment of PoWs working for private individuals.

10 **Outside Contacts.** PoWs have the right to write to their families on capture. The convention outlines postal privileges and rights pertaining to the receipt of packages.

11 **Complaints.** PoWs have the right to complain to the military authorities of the detaining powers, and to representatives of the neutral protecting powers recognized by both sides.

12 **Representatives.** The senior PoW will be the prisoners' representative. In a camp where there are no officers or NCOs the representative will be chosen by secret ballot.

13 **Legal Proceedings.** PoWs prosecuted and convicted for offences committed before capture retain the protection afforded by the convention. They may not be tried for any action which becomes illegal after the act is committed. The captors may not use force to gain a confession.

14 **Punishment.** Cruel and unusual punishments, torture, collective punishments or unfair punishments by a biased court are prohibited.

15 **Escape.** Attempted escapes, or non-violent offences committed only to aid escape and not involving theft for personal gain, the wearing of civilian clothes or the use of false papers are subject only to laid-down disciplinary action.

Your Conduct

You don't have to tell them what branch of the service you're from, though they may be able to guess that themselves from your uniform and equipment. Some personnel traditionally get a hard time, notably members of Special Forces units and fliers.

Try not to get noticed and singled out for interrogation. Don't exhibit bravado or humility. Just fade into the background.

There's no point in not being respectful and polite – in fact, to behave in any other way is extremely stupid. It will only earn you harsher treatment and probably get you beaten up and deprived of food.

At the same time, don't give the interrogator the idea that

you might be willing to co-operate. All you'll succeed in doing is to prolong the interrogation.

There's a world of difference between acting ignorant and acting dumb. The interrogator may say something like "We know there's a build up of troops at such-and-such a location. Does it contain armour?" If your answer were "I don't know, Sir, I've never been in that location," it sounds a lot more convincing than "Piss off". But beware of seeming to be trying to be helpful.

Watch out for apparently innocent enemy personnel such as doctors, nurses, orderlies and cleaners. Never talk in front of them; they could well be intelligence agents, operating under-cover – perhaps not even revealing themselves to other enemy agents on the spot.

The enemy interrogator will be very keen to turn you into a collaborator too. The two main methods are threats – of physical torture or death, to you or to another member of your squad, or promises – of better treatment, medical attention for someone badly wounded and not treated properly or almost anything else that seems attractive. After all, they can promise you anything – you're not going to get it anyway.

The Interrogator's Skill

The interrogator prepares himself before interrogating his prisoner. He adopts a three-phase approach:

1 **Research:** *He gathers all the information he can about all his prisoners.*
2 **Selection:** *He chooses which prisoners to interrogate and determines the information he wants.*
3 **Extraction:** *He puts into operation his varied mix of extraction techniques.*

1 Intelligence

The interrogator studies any information he may have ac-quired from initial searches, overheard conversations and background material gleaned by intelligence workers operating in the captive's own country.

2 Weak or strong?
He also builds up a picture of the PoW's make-up; is he weak or strong? Can he take punishment? What gets to him? Is he cold or emotional? How has he adjusted to PoW life?

3 Softening up
You'll be softened up, either by rough treatment, starvation, thirst, sensory deprivation, sleeplessness or solitary confinement. The interrogator will set up the place where he'll ask his questions so that it's intimidating and unfriendly.

4 Disgrace
He will try to destroy your confidence by disgracing you in the eyes of your fellow prisoners or your family or comrades at home or will simply try to make you feel ashamed of yourself.

5 Lesser of two evils
The captor will give you a choice between two evils, one of which is less damaging than the other. He knows that you will choose the least damaging and that is the one he can use for his own purposes.

6 The File
Your interrogator may start by asking you a harmless question about yourself. If you give a false answer he checks his intelligence file on you and gives you the right one. You begin to think this guy knows everything. "What's the use of holding out?" Don't give in. He is telling you the little he does know; if he knew everything he wouldn't have to question you further.

7 Hidden eyes and ears
You may have looked and found nothing, but the enemy has probably bugged the camp, so watch what you say, everywhere.

8 The silent treatment
You may be put into solitary confinement or held in a room with an interrogator who says nothing. Don't be afraid of silence; come to terms with it.

9 Repetition and monotony
Your interrogator may ask you the same question in the same tone over and over again. Let him, if you get riled he'll win; if you maintain control the psychological victory will be yours.

10 What's the use?
"Why hold out?" "Why suffer?" "You are at our mercy." "We'll get the information out of you anyhow." "Make it easier on yourself." These are all statements that you must learn to resist.

THE DOUBLE GAME

As well as trying to convince you that other prisoners have been cooperating he will try to get information from you about them which in turn will allow him to put subtle pressures on anyone you talk about. Don't give out any information about any of your comrades. Don't admit to being in the same unit with them.

BE ON GUARD

Watch out for false questionnaires "for the Red Cross", for instance. The aid organizations need to know nothing more than your name, rank, number and date of birth. Any information you provide on a form like this is only for the enemy intelligence officer's use.

Never make any statement of any kind. Not in writing, nor spoken where it might be recorded.

Don't try to impress the interrogator by boasting about things that you and your unit have done whether they're true or not. He's not going to let you go because you make yourself out to be some sort of superman!

At the same time, don't try to deceive him by volunteering false information, no matter how subtly you think you do it. He knows the wide intelligence picture and will ask you the same questions over and over again, perhaps with days in between. He'll record everything you say, and look for differences in your answers.

Don't look into the interrogator's eyes. You may give away information without meaning to. Pick out a spot between his eyes or in the centre of his forehead and concentrate on that.

Once he has you talking, it won't take a skilled interrogator long to get the truth out of you. Don't put yourself into a position where you find that you're having a conversation with him. Let him do all the talking, and limit your answers to "No" and "I don't know anything about that".

Never drop your guard. You can be taken off for further interrogation at any time, at any hour of the day or night.

Try to win a victory every time you're interrogated, no matter how small. Having worked out how, pass it on to your fellows, so that they are morally stronger.

The longer the interrogation goes on, the safer you are. More prisoners will be arriving and needing your interrogator's time and your information will become more and more out of date.

What will prolong the nightmare is your partial co-operation. One snippet of useful information will convince your interrogator that he may be onto a good thing, and he'll carry on until he gets the lot, no matter what it takes.

FORCING CO-OPERATION
These are some techniques that PoWs have been subjected to in recent times.

1 Torture
Technique: extreme dislocation of body parts e.g. arms, legs, back etc. by twisting or pulling; beating, slapping, gouging, kicking; inserting foreign objects such as bamboo slivers under the fingernails; electric shocks.
Effect: crippling; partial or total temporary or permanent loss of use of limbs and senses; loss of normal mental functioning; extreme pain; lowering or breaking of ability to resist captor's demands. TORTURE IS THE MAJOR MEANS OF FORCING COMPLIANCE.

2 Threats
Technique: threats of solitary confinement, non-repatriation, death or beatings to oneself or other PoWs; threats regarding future treatment; threats against family.
Effect: unreasonable anxiety; loss of hope and confidence; despair.

3 "Now and then" treatment
Technique: occasional favours such as release of food packages and better living conditions; promise of big rewards for helping captors.
Effect: tempts the PoW to go along with captors; presents the captors in a favourable light; makes resistance to questioning seem a bad idea.

4 Isolation or solitary confinement
Technique: total or partial isolation by rank, race, degree of compliance etc. or total solitary confinement.
Effect: keeps PoW away from anyone who can give any kind of support, moral, physical, psychological.

5 Hints that captors are in full control of everything in camp
Technique: use of information from other sources to make PoW believe the captors know more than they really do.
Effect: makes PoWs suspicious of each other and makes resistance seem futile.

6 Show of power over life and death
Technique: use of executions or torture; introduction and withdrawal of better conditions and medical care; complete control over physical aspects of camp.
Effect: breeds extreme caution and the belief that the captor is boss.

7 Deliberately caused physical deterioration
Technique: extremely long interrogation sessions; long periods in leg irons and stocks; bad food.
Effect: drastic lowering of resistance to interrogation.

8 Enforcement of minor rules and commands
Technique: overly strict demands for compliance with instructions and expected courtesies; forcing PoW to write or verbally repeat nonsensical words or phrases.
Effect: causes automatic obedience to commands.

9 Lowering of self-respect of PoW
Technique: lack of privacy; ridicule and insults; prevention of

washing; keeping living conditions filthy, insanitary, full of vermin etc.
Effect: humbles PoW and makes giving in an attractive prospect.

10 Control over physical senses
Technique: placing in isolation with no stimuli or giving extreme stimuli such as no light or sound or too much light or sound; dripping water on forehead.
Effect: makes PoW think that captors have total physical control; causes extreme discomfort and distress.

From The Mammoth Book of the Secrets of the SAS and Elite Forces, *ed. Jon E. Lewis, Robinson, 2002.*

OPERATION LEOPARD

Bruce Quarrie

Since the inception of the French Foreign Legion in 1831, more than 34,000 legionnaires have died in combat. "The Army of Strangers" has long been France's fire brigade, rushed to the front line of every war in which she has had an interest, from Algeria in 1831 to Iraq in 2003. If anything, the fire-brigade nature of the Legion has increased post-1945, as the Legion increased its mobility with the formation of parachute units, eventually designated the 1st and 2nd Foreign Parachute Regiments (Regiment Etranger Parachutiste). The Foreign Legion paras fought valiantly – if in vain – at Dien Bien Phu in Indo-China, bloodily and effectively in Algeria, but in 1961 1REP was disbanded after mutinying against de Gaulle's granting of independence to Algeria. A cloud of suspicion clung to 2REP, which it studiously countered by developing itself into a hyper-trustworthy and hyper-effective air commando. Over the past forty years, the 2nd REP has found many chances to demonstrate both its effectiveness and its loyalty, but nowhere more so than Zaire in 1978.

THERE WERE ABOUT 2,300 Belgian, French, Italian, Portuguese and other white technicians and their families living in the New Town of Kolwezi in May 1978. During the previous year, an attempt to invade Shaba Province from camps in Angola had been made by the Katangese rebels of the Congolese National Liberation

Front – FNLC – who were armed and trained by Cuban instructors. It had been repelled by General Mobutu's Zaïrean army, stiffened by Moroccan and French advisers. Now the FNLC were back, and this time they drove the small garrison out of the town without difficulty.

They seemed to have no strategic plan for advancing further towards the provincial capital, Lubumbashi, and they made no very serious attempts to fortify the town against counter-attack. Their precise strength is unknown, but there were between 1,500 and 4,000 men armed with modern Soviet and Belgian small arms, machine-guns, mortars and rocket launchers, and supported by a few captured Zaïrean Army AML armoured cars. The FNLC seemed content to settle down to a leisurely, medieval sack of the town. They smashed in the doors of shops and houses, helping themselves to what they wanted. At first under some kind of discipline, they later degenerated into drunken savages. The European quarter was searched repeatedly, though in a random fashion. The first unfortunates to fall prey to the FNLC's impromptu "courts" and firing parties were those whom they decided were "Moroccan and French mercenaries": anyone who had an Arab appearance, or a French passport. Later, the violence became an end in itself. Men, women and children, black and white alike, were tortured, raped, murdered and mutilated. The stench of death and the sound of swarming flies haunted the wrecked, empty streets. For days on end, terrified families hid in their barricaded bungalows, helpless to intervene as their neighbours suffered.

The situation in Kolwezi was known: a radio operator at the Gécamines offices had stayed on the air long enough to inform his head office at Kinshasa, the national capital. The Zaïrean Army was obviously incapable of mounting a serious operation. The Belgian government – the logical choice for a rescue mission, since they had intervened before in their former colony to rescue hostages, and since the largest group of whites at Kolwezi were Belgians – was indecisive. It was willing to supply transport, and an escort to bring out refugees – but not to fight. At last, after four days, an appeal from President Mobutu reached Paris, through the offices of the French ambassador and military advisors in Kinshasa. The appeal was accepted, and, early on the morning of 17 May, a warning order reached Lieutenant Colonel Erulin of the 2^e REP at Calvi. His regiment was placed on six hours' notice of immediate movement.

The paras would carry minimal kit on the drop: two water canteens, two ration packs, a poncho, a sweater, and ammunition. Even this last was in short supply. Most of the legionnaires would jump over an unprepared and "hot" drop zone armed with – incredibly – just 40 rounds each for their FSA-49/56 self-loading rifles, or about 200 rounds for the MAT-49 sub-machine-gun, plus perhaps four hand grenades. Their mission briefing told them little more than that they were to get on the ground, deal with any opposition as best they could, rescue civilians wherever they found them, and hold on till further orders. They could expect no re-supply for three days. Fanshawe's platoon was less than amused to be told that there would be no medical back-up in the first wave: each man was on his own, with the contents of his small personal first aid pouch.

The emplaning process the following morning nearly drove Fanshawe crazy with frustration. Zaïrean and French jumpmasters got in each other's way; awkwardly loaded, red-eyed paras shuffled aboard the strange aircraft with no idea of the correct loading procedure; and "sticks" (sections of paras) became muddled. At last, at about 11.30 on 19 May, the five aircraft lumbered into the sky. They carried, crowded in their bellies in intense discomfort, Lieutenant Colonel Erulin and just 405 of his 1st, 2nd and 3rd Companies, and a reduced HQ. After four hours of hot, miserable flight, Sergent-Chef Fanshawe was shouting and shoving his muddled sticks of paras into some sort of order as they shuffled towards the door. The green light came on and, to a welcome of machine-gun fire, the 2^e REP tumbled awkwardly into thin air in the regiment's first full combat drop since Dien Bien Phu. It was just a day and a half since the unit had received its movement order thousands of miles away in Corsica.

"DZ Alpha" was an expanse of scrub, huge termite hills

and patches of tall grass at the eastern end of the Old Town. The 1st Company was tasked with moving south to the Jean XXIII School; the 2nd with marching west through the town towards the hospital (where it was thought civilians might be held hostage) and the Gécamines compound (from whose motor pool the paras hoped to acquire transport). The 3rd Company was to take the Impala Hotel and Post Office, and set up a blocking position on the bridge leading across the railway towards the New Town.

Not surprisingly, the drop was badly scattered: ten paras were so thoroughly lost that they did not rejoin their comrades until the next day. Sergent-Chef Fanshawe hit the ground a kilometre off course, only 100 m (110 yd) from his objective – the railway overpass. Quickly releasing his harness, he dashed for the bridge. He could see many parachutes hung up in the tall bush, but, thanks to the 90 sq m (108 sq yd) area of the big American canopies, there turned out to be surprisingly few injuries – even Misse and his AA-52, who hit the ground particularly hard, was only shaken. Even more surprising was the lack of organized opposition. Apart from those first bursts of firing, the drop zone was almost eerily quiet.

It was later discovered that the FNLC had indeed got wind of the forthcoming rescue, and many of them had fled for the Angolan border. Plenty remained, however, scattered all over the Old and New Towns in hidden positions, waiting to fight it out. The companies assembled as fast as possible, heading off towards their objectives without waiting for stragglers, as they were terribly aware of the need for speed if a massacre of hostages was to be prevented.

Just south of the railway overpass to the New Town, Fanshawe managed to assemble all but six of his 2nd Platoon, and established a blocking position. He was agonizingly short of support weapons, and faced the possibility of a major attack with only two light machine-guns, nine rifle grenades, and one LRAC anti-tank launcher with just two rounds. He had not been in position long when three captured AML armoured cars charged out of the New Town on to the approach to the overpass. At the last minute, the leading AML was knocked out cleanly, only

50 m (55 yd) from the 2nd Platoon positions, with one of the precious rockets. After firing several rounds of 90 mm and 60 mm shells from their cannon, the other two armoured cars retreated in a hail of small-arms fire. The bridge was not attacked again before nightfall, but heavy firing could be heard all around.

The 1st and 2nd Companies were advancing through a maze of alleys, shanties and patches of scrub in a hectic, confused running fight. They came under constant harassing fire, and dealt with each position as they met it, fast and hard; but they could build up no picture of the overall situation against such a dispersed enemy. As they pushed on they saw dreadful sights in the streets and the wrecked buildings. The "Tigers" had been as brutal in their treatment of the native inhabitants as of the whites. The first of the Europeans were now showing themselves, often running dazedly into the middle of firefights in their confused delight at seeing white soldiers. Erulin's HQ team tried to keep a tally of them by radio, and assembled several hundred of them in the Jean XXIII School when it was secured that evening.

Shortly before nightfall, the transport aircraft reappeared overhead with the second wave of the 2^e REP. Erulin "waved them off" to Lubumbashi, however, with orders to return at first light. His three companies had secured all the main objectives for the day, and he did not want disoriented troopers falling all over the drop zone in the dark, and shooting at each other in their confusion.

The temperature fell quickly. Huddled in their ponchos in hastily dug rifle pits, the paras sat out the night of 19/20 May – their third without sleep – wherever darkness found them. Swallowing dexedrine tablets from their first aid pouches, they tried to keep alert. There was heavy gunfire all over Kolwezi throughout the night, as prowling units of the FNLC ran into Legion positions without warning. At about 22.00 one group made another attempt on Fanshawe's bridge-block, led – rather strangely – by an FNLC Major in a Volkswagen "Beetle"! After a brisk exchange of automatic and rifle fire, and some rocket-propelled grenades from the FNLC, the attack was beaten off. (The VW was shot to pieces by the two AA-52s, enabling Fanshawe to examine the Major's papers.) Later, Fanshawe heard that a larger enemy unit and an AML armoured car had been prowling his area, but they did not attack.

At first light on the 20th the second wave dropped: the mortars, reconnaissance platoon and remaining HQ element on "DZ Alpha", and the 4th Company on "DZ Bravo", east of the New Town. In not much more than an hour they had combed right through the New Town, silencing all resistance and releasing the European inhabitants from their long ordeal. Meanwhile, the 1st Company finally cleaned up the southern area of the Old Town, and the 2nd mopped up the western area. The reconnaissance platoon moved north, clearing Camp Forrest and the old Gendarmerie barracks, and part of the 3rd Company pushed south into the labyrinth of the Manika housing estate. The HQ was established at the Impala Hotel. From here, Erulin was able to begin organizing the evacuation of the Europeans from the airstrip some way outside the town, where Belgian troops and various medical teams had now landed.

Some of the clashes on the 20th had been heavy. Sergent-Chef Daniel of the 4th Company was killed during the clearing of the Metal-Shaba estate that afternoon, and other paras were wounded. The 4th was quickly supported by the 2nd, the mortars and the reconnaissance platoon, and some eighty rebels were killed. Here, as all over Kolwezi, large numbers of weapons and explosives were found, including two recoilless rifles, heavy bazooka-type cannon. Many legionnaires, short of ammunition for their FSA-49/56 rifles, helped themselves to FN/FALs, Russian AK-47 assault rifles, and American M-16 Armalites from the rebel booty.

The night of the 20th was disturbed only by sporadic sniping, and some paras at last managed to have a few hours' sleep. Ambush positions secured all routes into the cleared area, and the men lying awake on guard had plenty to think about. Hideous sights encountered in the New Town had filled them all with a grim rage. In a single charnel-house room in block P2, no less than thirty-eight men, women and children had been found heaped in a pile. Nevertheless, a large number of Europeans had been saved, some after miraculous escapes. The Pansalfin family had emerged from a tiny hiding place in the cavity between their house's double walls. One woman had been found in the hospital, with her limbs riddled with bullets, having lain for nearly twelve hours, holding her dead baby, under the bodies of her neighbours.

The operation was by no means over. For another week, using requisitioned civilian lorries, and their own jeeps and trucks which arrived after driving from Lubumbashi on the 21st, the 2^e REP spread out on wide-ranging patrols, covering more than a 300 km (190 mile) radius. On the 21st there was fighting during the clearing of Kapata to the south-west, and casualties were taken during a fierce clash near Luilu, where several searches were carried out during the period 24–28 May. On that day most of the regiment finally pulled out and drove to Lubumbashi, some of them having received no rations since the first drop.

By 4 June the 2^e REP was back in Corsica. They had saved more than 2,000 lives, killed more than 250 rebels, and captured 163; and accounted for two armoured cars, four recoilless cannon, 15 mortars, 21 rocket launchers, 10 machine-guns, 38 sub-machine guns, and 216 rifles. They had lost 5 legionnaires, and 25 had been wounded.

THE FRENCH FOREIGN LEGION: CODE OF HONOUR

Laid down in the early 1900s, the Code of Honour remains the guide for all those who volunteer for the French Foreign Legion.

Code of Honour

1 Legionnaire: you are a volunteer serving France faithfully and with honour.

2 Every Legionnaire is your brother-at-arms, irrespective of his nationality, race or creed. You will demonstrate this

by an unwavering and straightforward solidarity which must always bind together members of the same family.

3 Respectful of the Legion's traditions, honouring your superiors, discipline and comradeship are your strength, courage and loyalty your virtues.

4 Proud of your status as a legionnaire, you will display this pride, by your turnout, always impeccable, your behaviour, ever worthy, though modest, your living-quarters, always tidy.

5 An elite soldier, you will train vigorously, you will maintain your weapons as if they were your most precious possession, you will keep your body in the peak of condition, always fit.

6 A mission once given to you becomes sacred to you, you will accomplish it to the end and at all costs.

7 In combat, you will act without relish of your tasks, or hatred; you will respect the vanquished enemy and will never abandon neither your wounded nor your dead, nor will you under any circumstances surrender your arms.

All who apply to join the French Foreign Legion are interviewed, but only 20 per cent are accepted into the "The Process", namely IQ, physical and character tests at the Legion headquarters at Aubagne. Successful candidates are then offered a five-year unconditional contract, but in fact selection is not yet finished: prospective Legionaries have to pass the four-month preliminary training course at Castelnaudary, before being assigned to a regiment. Top recruits may volunteer for the elite airborne 2 REP, based in Corsica, whose 1,300 officers and men wear the coveted grenade-and-dragon badge.

RECON

Frank Camper

The first Long-Range Reconnaissance Patrols (LRRPs) were formed in the mid-1960s, as a reactive necessity to the US Army's lack of units capable of reconnaissance behind North Vietnamese lines. Initially granted only "provisional" status and formed by individual brigades, the "Lurps" were redesigned as Rangers in 1969, and made separate companies of the 75th Infantry Regiment. The LRRP usually operated in four-to-eight man patrols, with most personnel graduates of the MAC/V RECONDO (Reconnaissance Commando) School at Nha Trang. During the Vietnam War, the LRRP conducted some 23,000 long-range patrols which, aside from reconnaissance, performed hunter-killer tasks; according to one estimate, LRRPs accounted for 10,000 NVA and Vietcong killed in action.

Below, Frank Camper recounts his first LRRP mission, operating out of a US firebase close to the Cambodian border in February 1967.

T HE DAWN ARRIVED cold and foggy. Mott gave the signal and we came to our feet and entered the ghostly forest, the mist smothering our footfalls.

For an hour there was no noise to disturb the unreal quality of the morning as we trod softly through the dew-soaked bushes. My trouser legs and boots became as chilly and damp as if we'd forded a stream.

You move with care and caution when your life depends

on it. We lifted our feet high as we walked, setting them down slowly, toeing twigs and roots out of the way, pausing every few meters to kneel and listen.

When blue sky finally shone through the treetops, and we stopped to rest, we found a trail and made radio contact with the firebase. I had counted a thousand meters we'd traveled, a third of the way to our objective.

No small infantry patrols had been sent into this area, for fear of losing them. Three companies operating out of the firebase were working east from us, in hopes they might drive the NVA this way, west toward Cambodia.

I covered tailgun, Steffens watched the flanks, and Payne and Mott held the center. Mott had a long conversation with the firebase over the radio, his map before him, weapon and hat laid aside.

Mott marked the location of the trail on the map, while the rest of us guarded both approaches. "We'll go north as long as this trail holds out," he said. "You take point."

I resolved to shoot first and ask questions later, switching to full automatic and proceeding up the path. This was baiting the tiger and we all knew it. One of the laws of jungle warfare is that if you want enemy contact, get on a trail.

I began to sweat from nervous tension, finding myself frequently holding my breath rather than risk the noise of inhaling or exhaling.

The team followed me, imitating my every move, watching my reactions, stepping where I stepped. The suspense was numbing.

In many places the overhead was so dense the sunlight couldn't penetrate. The trail was dim, beset by shadows, the rightful province of the ambusher.

The trail had a destination. I spied the first bunker far enough in advance so that I could blend down into the shrubbery gracefully. The team behind me went to earth so quickly it seemed a breeze had blown and, like smoke, they had disappeared.

Something was wrong. We were too close to the bunkers not to be dead already if the NVA were alert. I took a good look around. The bunkers seemed to be deserted. Soil had sunk between the logs and the firing ports were covered with withered camouflage.

I signaled for the team to stay down, and I checked out the nearest hole by creeping over to it. I was right. These were all old fortifications. I gave an all-clear whistle, and the team came out.

"Looks like a company or more dug in here," Mott said, surveying the positions. He took out his notebook and began to make a diagram of the bunkers.

We began to recover from the exertion of the day, muscles unknotting, fatigues drying out, stomachs growling for food. I pulled a chicken-and-rice from my rucksack, boiling a canteen cup of water to reconstitute it, and sat back to wait.

I hadn't eaten all day, and I was starving. The ration slowly absorbed the water, swelling the packet. I had twenty minutes to wait for the dehydrated ration to reconstitute, but it seemed like an hour to my empty stomach.

To top off a hard day, a plague of sweat bees descended on us. They buzzed and lit everywhere, coming right back after being swatted off, trying to crawl into the corners of my eyes and into my mouth. I draped a handkerchief over my face.

I made a mistake then. My attention wandered for just an instant. I heard a slight sound near where I sat, and looked swiftly around to see what it was.

I found myself looking straight into the eyes of an NVA. He had come out of nowhere! I was sitting nearly out of his line of vision as he glanced in my direction. He acted as if he had not seen me. I was too stunned to move. He continued to look around, seemingly oblivious to my presence.

Then he casually turned to my left and walked out of sight. I couldn't function. Had he seen me? We had looked each other in the eye! I snap-rolled into a depression in the earth against some roots, flicking the safety off my CAR. I detected no sound. He had to be still out there. Probably just a short distance away, crouched in the underbrush.

I looked back and saw Payne as he repacked the radio equipment. I waved at him. He didn't look up. I motioned frantically, Payne totally not noticing me for what seemed to be one eternity.

When Payne finally saw me, he reacted by tapping Mott and going down into the thicket. We waited. Disaster on the first day? Maybe not. My heart knocked against my ribs so loudly I wasn't sure I could hear anything else.

Payne inched up to me. I indicated. *One dink, moving that way*, in a sign language. Payne pointed to himself, and to the right flank, then to me and to the left, motioning we should go out and get our visitor.

We tried the impromptu pincers movement, but only found each other and the trail on which the man had made his escape. "This is how he got up on me without making any noise," I whispered to Payne. The trail was well used and wide.

We crawled back to the old bunkers to wait and listen.

I reached over and pulled my ration package to me, still hungry despite the circumstances. I found I was shaking so badly trying to eat, I was spilling half the rice off my spoon. When we had finished trying to eat, Mott told us to prepare to move, pointing to the trail.

The trail passed on through the bunkers and went for higher ground. I walked forward a few meters and found another trail branching off ours.

"We'll go north as long as the trails do," Mott said. "I believe they'll take us right to the Red Warrior LZ. And start looking for a good place to spend the night. I want to find a good one before it gets too late."

I agreed. This place was too damn active for us to be stumbling around in the dark. I searched carefully as we advanced, turning down any place that didn't afford maximum protection. It was easy to stay on our compass course. All I had to do was move from one trail to another. We were in a network.

It was hours before I came across some good high ground, and I led us up into it. It was so steep it was hard for us to climb. That was fine. Anyone trying to do it at night would make a hell of a lot of noise.

I pulled up from tree to tree, resting in place occasionally. I reached the top dripping with sweat and bleeding from thorn pricks and grass slices, but I didn't just barge in. I hugged the hillside below the crest, listening, calculating how fast I could jump backward and get away if the hill was already claimed for the night.

I peeked over a fallen log and scanned the hilltop. Safe so far. Loping in a crouch, I covered the distance across the small knoll and took cover behind a tree, looking down the opposite slope.

It wasn't as steep on the far side, being part of a ridge. I waved the team up, and we secured the hill for the night, spreading out. I chose the lower part of the slope, the team assuming its usual defensive position: team leader and RTO in the center, point and tailgun at the far ends.

A stick thrown by Mott hit me in the back while I waited. I turned and felt my heart sink as he gave me the *Be quiet* sign. Payne had his M-16 ready, his attention on something near us.

I picked up my weapon, moving nothing but my arm, believing we were about to be attacked. Mott and Payne sneaked into the foliage, moving with absolute silence. Then I heard it for myself.

A short distance away people were walking by, the scuffing of sandals on packed dirt very clear, voices in Vietnamese conversing without fear of detection.

They walked away. I had edged downward until I was absolutely flat against the ground. I realized we'd camped right beside another trail. Mott looked up at me, the whites of his eyes showing all around his pupils.

We dared not try to leave the hill – they would catch us for sure – but if we stayed here, all it would take was for one of them to get lucky and step off the trail, and zap, instant catastrophe.

When it became fully dark, we pulled in together. Payne made the last radio report of the day by only keying the handset and saying nothing aloud. We just couldn't afford it. We didn't unpack anything, lying with our rucksacks beside us.

Later, lights began to flash in the sky toward the firebase we had left. No one was asleep, so we raised our heads, hearing the sound of gunfire drift in on the wind. They were getting hit again.

The firebase responded with its artillery, firing out rounds in all directions and ranges. Flares went up, and tracers arced over the jungle, red for ours, green for theirs. A burning parachute flare fell into the treetops near us and took away our night, until it sputtered out.

Several stray artillery shells sailed in and hit our ridge-line, sounding much louder at night, the blasts echoing into the valley. Even a marker-round canister or two came whistling down and smashed into the trees; all too near for us.

And we soon had company again. A North Vietnamese squad rushed by us on the hidden trail, equipment bumping, heading for the action.

The night and the battle progressed. More NVA went past us, all involved in their own problems, none even guessing we were in pissing distance.

Then a roar greater than the fight below us vibrated through the valley. I glanced up and saw what appeared to be a million red tracers plunging out of the night sky.

Puff! The old C-47 cargo plane with the electric Gatling guns! Puff belched another terrific volley, an unbelievable column of pure bullets that soaked the forest below like a deadly rain.

That was the end to the fighting. No army could stand up to Puff. The dragonship's engines droned lazily over-head, occasionally spraying around the firebase with a breath more deadly than anything imagined in King Arthur's day.

Then it started coming our way! We had no arrangement for radioing anybody to get Puff away from us, the mini-guns drowned out everything, and I expected the fire to nail us to the hill. I had heard of men being killed accidentally by Puff, hundreds of meters from the "beaten zone."

All things considered, it was a long night. The NVA retreated on our trail until dawn, trickling by, disorganized, carrying their wounded and dragging heavy loads.

As soon as it was light enough to see, we were ready to leave. Payne made the radio report, having to repeat himself to be understood, he spoke so low into the mike.

We needed speed, and got off the ridge the fast way, via

last night's highway. It was a fresh trail, leading into the hills.

Once we were on low ground and headed for the old Red Warrior LZ, we ducked off the trail and took to the woods again. Evidence of enemy movement was everywhere we looked.

The layer of leaves on the ground had been trodden down in many places by men walking in single file. The dampness of the morning dew betrayed them. The untouched leaves glistened damply. The disturbed leaves were dull. It was easy to see the winding routes Vietnamese patrols had taken only hours before.

We covered the distance to the LZ before noon and without incident, being very careful. I had point again, and saw the first of the NVA fortifications that circled the old LZ.

We stealthily slipped into the old bunker line, the clearing visible ahead of us. The team lay back as I advanced to scout the LZ. I parted the high grass and peered into a vast open field. In the center, like a target, was the landing zone itself, the scars of the battle only now being reclaimed by nature. The pitifully shallow fighting holes had begun to vanish under patches of grass and shrubs.

The line of fire from the NVA position to the LZ was absolutely clear. No wonder they got their butts kicked, I thought dismally. It was so easy to imagine the horror out there, exposed from all sides, the helicopters being shot down, no place to run.

It took time, but we walked completely around the LZ, charting the positions and marveling at them. It was very slow work, checking for booby traps, pacing off yardage, guarding and watching.

Every bunker was firmly roofed over, the mortar pits looked like wells, and trenches connected all the heavy weapons positions. Anti-aircraft guns had been set in between the recoilless rifle and mortar emplacements, so a chopper flying across the LZ would be like a clay pigeon launched before a crowd of skeet shooters.

It was nearly dark when we had finished the reconnaissance job and had eaten. We sent a long radio report back, describing the patrol up to this point. But as Payne signed us off and packed his mike and antenna, Steffens reached down to his feet and pulled up a strand of buried wire.

"Commo wire!" he exclaimed in a loud whisper. It was gray Chinese issue, not the black U.S. Army wire. "Follow it," Mott ordered.

Steffens ripped the line out of the earth until he came to a tree. It joined a terminal there, spliced into another line. Steffens held up the fistful of wire.

The splice was insulated by paper, and the paper was still fresh. We looked it over closely. They had recently wired this place, expecting to use it again. That answered all our questions for this mission.

Mott pointed to the slight rise toward the west. "Let's get into those thickets," he said, "and take cover for the night. Steve, lead out."

Steffens led us to an entanglement of dried bamboo and vines, and we crawled in like rabbits into a warren. After dark, we moved a hundred meters away on our hands and knees before we slept, to confuse any NVA that might have spotted us earlier.

The stars came out brilliantly and we rested, secure in the dense underbrush, wondering what the NVA were doing tonight. My apprehension was subdued, but it did not go away. We had enjoyed incredible luck so far. It could not continue.

We stayed late in our haven, eating our LRRP rations and making coffee, organizing our gear and watching the LZ through a hole in the foliage. The sun was high by the time Mott announced our next move.

"We're taking a straight 270 degrees west," he told me, "right to the border. We have enough rations to stay out two more days."

I was given the point again, and I kept a steady pace, pausing only long enough to examine a bit of evidence here or there that the enemy had also been this way.

It was as hot as two hells by noon. The forest had become lush jungle, enmeshed in swampy lowland and thick, green mossbeds along the streams. We ran out of energy pushing through the mass of it, sweat pouring off us, a direct sun cooking us unmercifully.

We found a slight clearing and fell into it, throwing our gear down and gasping for breath. Payne wiped the sweat from his neck with his flop hat. "Where the fuck are we?" he asked, his voice weak from the exertion.

Mott slipped his map from his thigh pocket. "About right here, I think," he said, indicating a place on the border. So this was Cambodia. It didn't look a bit different from Vietnam.

"We need to get an exact fix on where we are." Payne insisted. Steve looked around. All we could see was swamp and rain forest infested with vines. "Can't tell anything from here," he stated.

"I'll climb that tree," Payne volunteered, gazing at a tall stand of trees about a hundred meters away. Steve picked up his rifle. "I'll pull security for you," he said. Payne stripped off his shirt and boots, and slung a pair of binoculars over his neck.

He came back down skinned up a bit, but loaded with information. "I'd put us right on the border," he said as he dressed. "I could orient my map and get those mountains and these streams lined up just right."

Mott considered that briefly, then stood and pulled on his rucksack. "Okay. We're on our way home now. Camper, take the point. Back azimuth 90 degrees, let's go."

I aimed my compass, the arrow pointing our way back. We slopped through the swamp, trying to keep on the more solid ground as the humidity made the air itself dense and oppressive. Sweat ran in my eyes, and my uniform was chafing and binding, as wet after ten minutes' walking as if I'd dived into the stream.

As I walked through the grass and water, watching where I put my feet, I saw the footprint. It was a tire-tread sandal print, freshly made in the sandy soil alongside the water.

I felt a shock race straight up my spinal cord. They were here, close. Mott looked at the print. "Turn around, go the other way!" he whispered.

I hurried past the team and retraced our steps. The guy

who had made that print was only a few minutes ahead of us. I damned the circumstances that had put us here.

I was cautious, measuring my progress in minutes of life and not meters of ground. Mott whistled. I looked around and he motioned for me to hurry, by pumping his fist up and down like a drill instructor ordering double-time.

I signaled an unmistakable refusal. Mott waved me aside and took point himself. I let him go by and fell in behind. He began to move fast, without caring how much noise he made.

We got out of the swamp and climbed a bombed-out hillside, finding ourselves in a morass of dying elephant grass. Mott hadn't slowed down at all. I wondered if he was giving any thought to where he was taking us.

A semi-path through the grass attracted Mott. It had been pushed down before. We tromped on through the grass, chasing Mott, getting more lost by the meter.

Suddenly Mott seemed to fall in a most awkward way, his hat and rifle flying. I thought he'd tripped over a vine. I stopped, and sidestepped off the trail, squatting down, expecting Mott to get back to his feet.

Mott was scrambling to free his rifle from the vines. "Sarge," I whispered, "what's wrong?" Mott looked back at me, his face a mask of terror. Something was very wrong. "Dinks?" I asked. Mott could see something I couldn't.

"Shoot!" I said.

He did nothing. "Goddammit, if you're not going to fire, I am!" I threatened, unsure of the situation. I lifted my weapon and was flipping it off safe when a shot exploded from in front of me, blowing the grass back in my face. My ears rang.

I pulled the trigger instinctively, but my CAR fired just once. I almost had heart failure. I glanced down and saw the selector was only on semi.

I didn't take the time to flip it to full auto. I blasted out the whole magazine in a sweeping fan, my trigger finger moving like lightning.

The shit hit the fan for real then. A deafening cascade of small-arms fire erupted from in front of us. I saw Mott twitching, and thought he was being shot. Bullets hit all around him. I changed magazines, though I wouldn't realize I had done so until I found the empty mag in my shirt later.

Leaves flew off their branches around us and dirt hit my face as near misses bracketed me. I cringed, waiting for the impact of the rounds in my body.

I changed to automatic, somehow making my hand obey, as a Vietnamese jumped up surprisingly close, his AK-47 smoking from muzzle to magazine well, trying to see if he had hit Mott.

I was already pressing the trigger again as he exposed himself, and it was only by chance he was in my line of fire. He never saw me. I swung a burst across his chest and he disappeared, arms flung wide, his weapon spinning through the air.

Unhurt, Mott launched himself off the ground and passed me screaming, *"Go! Go! Go!"* I needed no urging. I was right behind Mott, running as I'd never run before.

It sounded like a firing range behind us. What had Mott done, stumbled into a platoon? I raced through the woods, dodging trees, breaking down vines, losing sight of Mott. My hat was knocked off. Where were Payne and Steffens? The NVA were shooting at me with every jump.

I ran into the clearing we'd passed earlier. It was six inches deep in napalm ashes, and I saw Mott ahead of me, leaving a wake of dust behind him like a whirlwind.

I caught up with him when he tried to leap through a forked tree stump and became stuck. I grabbed him by the seat of the pants and lifted as I passed, literally flipping him over the fork; he regained his feet and outran me.

The swamp was straight ahead, and I caught sight of Payne and Steffens waiting there for us. Mott and I dived into the swamp, totally out of breath. The gunfire had ceased.

Mott grabbed for the radio handset from Payne, getting me caught in the middle and tangled in the cord. I accidentally burned myself on my weapon, the short barrel and flash suppressor as hot as a furnace. "I got one, I got one . . ." I heard myself saying.

"My map, I think I lost it," Mott croaked. In my own

semi-stupor of exhaustion I heard that statement. A map was gold to the NVA, especially one of ours marked with patrol routes and coordinate codes.

Steffens watched the grass. "We gotta get the hell out of here, I think they're coming after us!" he warned. Mott radioed battalion again. "Three-Three, I am changing to another location, wait out," he said, and began to slog out of the damp. "Let's go," Mott said nervously.

We trotted to higher ground, so tense an insect couldn't have moved without catching our eye. We found a break in the trees and laid out an aircraft marker panel; Payne hastily set up the radio and Steffens and I staked out the security.

Steffens cursed; his weapon was malfunctioning. He discovered it wouldn't change to automatic and had to be pried off safe with his knife. Payne swapped weapons with Steve while Mott called in our position.

We could see two helicopters in the air about five klicks away, and I hoped the firebase would relay our situation to them. But the minutes ticked past and the choppers flew on. "FAC's coming," Mott said excitedly, "get that panel out where he can see it!"

Talk about service. The small green spotter plane was on our radio frequency before Payne could move the panel. Mott keyed the handset and FAC rode the beam in. Payne stood and held the orange panel up like a big bedsheet — what a target.

"He's got us!" Mott said. Payne gratefully dropped the panel. "He says there's a bomb crater six hundred meters west of here, and to get to it!" Mott said.

The two helicopters had caught FAC's call and banked back toward us. Help at last! We ran to the crater, the drumming of the rotor blades getting closer.

I was the first man on the top. It must have been a hell of a bomb that had cleared this hill; it was as bare as a baby's butt. Only one tree was left standing, and it had no bark or limbs.

I saw the crater, the only cover anywhere, and made for it as fast as my rapidly expiring legs would take me. Two helicopters were approaching us in the sky from the east. We'd have transport in a matter of minutes.

But surprise! The NVA had beaten us to the hill. I saw one hiding in a bush, looking the other way. His khaki uniform gave him away.

"Steve, there's one!" I yelled to Steffens, who was close behind me, firing a full magazine at the bush. The man wasn't there anymore when I hit empty. Steffens saw another dink at the far end of the hilltop and blasted him at fifty meters, from the hip.

I saw the man scream and go down. I reached the bomb crater, and the team piled in on me. The NVA ambush was sprung, and its fire was unleashed on us, kicking dirt up all around our hole.

It was a small crater, and the whole team with rucksacks crowded it badly. The first helicopter came in low, trying to find a place to pick us up. Ground fire drove it away.

We threw red smoke toward the trees and Mott called the spotter plane for support. The second Huey was a gunship. He radioed Mott, asking for an azimuth to the enemy from the smoke. Mott quickly supplied that information.

The gunnie made a firing pass, quad M-60s stuttering, hot brass cartridge cases pelting us. The trees in the fire swayed in the onslaught, grass and brush disintegrating in billows of dust.

I crammed another magazine in my weapon and hammered it out in one pull of the trigger, putting out suppressive fire to our left flank. Steve emptied magazines off to the right, and Mott and Payne peppered the front.

"Get down! Rockets!" Mott shouted in the din, and we pressed into the soft earth of the bomb crater. The Huey barreled in like a fighter plane, rocket pods flaring, streaks of fire roaring over our hole, and the tree line exploded into a deafening storm of roots and flying splinters.

"He's coming back!" Mott said, his voice sounding distant to my numb eardrums. The chopper cleared out his rocket racks, dumping everything. The projectiles went by just a few meters over our heads, but one caught our lone tree.

It was a white-phosphorus missile. It hit the very tip of the only standing obstruction on the hilltop and went off, showering us with a thousand arcing bits of incandescent particles. If there had been somewhere to go, we'd have unassed that crater then.

Incoming fire halted completely after the last rocket run. The gunship chose a new direction to rip up the trees from, and blazed down, machine guns running wild. We added as much of our fire at the tree line as we could, our hole filling with expended cartridge cases.

The smoke from the burning trees covered the hill thickly. We lost our visibility and had to stop shooting as Mott announced, "Slick coming in, cease fire!"

The rotor wash from the Huey blew the smoke down and outward as it hovered in carefully. I stepped on Payne's shoulder as I jumped out of the hole, and Mott scrambled out and outran me again as we dashed for the helicopter.

Mott had so much speed built up, he ran all the way around the ship and came in through the opposite door. Payne made it out of the hole and ran at the helicopter, but something was wrong with his balance. I didn't realize it then, but all during the firefight my CAR-15 muzzle had been inches from his ear, and the firing had temporarily upset his equilibrium. Payne slammed into the door gunner's machine-gun mount, and had to be pulled bodily into the helicopter.

I was third, as I had slowed down to cover Payne, raking the trees with one of my last magazines, and as I ran for the doorway, firing at the enemy with just one hand holding my CAR-15, my last two or three rounds punctured the tail boom of our own helicopter.

Now we were all in but Steve. He had remained in the crater and continued to fire, dutifully covering his team, performing his tailgun job to the last. He rose and made the dash, the strain showing on his face. His Starlight scope fell from under his rucksack flap.

He knew it fell. He stopped, his eyes still on us, and turned, going back after the instrument.

The rotors were spinning at takeoff speed, and our skids were off the ground. Payne was lying nearly unconscious on the deck, and the smoke was still obscuring the trees.

Steffens got to us just as the pilot propelled us upward. Mott and I desperately grappled at Steve's pack straps, hoisting him in, his feet dangling out during the fast, high climb.

I took one breath and collapsed against the bulkhead, watching the burning hill get smaller in the distance. My Lord, we were out of it.

SPECIAL FORCES ARMOURY: EXPLOSIVES

Blowing things up has long been a primary tool of the warrior. First there was the mysterious Greek Fire. Later there was gunpowder. Later still there was Alfred Nobel, who just before the start of the twentieth century discovered and marketed commercial high explosives. (His dismay at the use of his products in war impelled him to create the prizes given in his name.) And later still the variety of explosive pyrotechnics has grown to the point where they are viewed by professionals not as blunt instruments but as precision tools.

Consider if you will that skilled use of conventional explosives (in shaping initial shock waves) is the key to producing a nuclear detonation. A very different kind of shaped charge, using a differently formulated explosive, will "carefully" drop a single obsolete building without harming the structures on either side, while precision-guided munitions, armed with another explosive formulation and dropped by a stealth bomber, will find their way unerringly into an enemy's headquarters.

Special Forces soldiers are skilled with a variety of explosives (though they normally carry only a couple of types at any one time).

Explosives can be generally classed into two types – "slow" (or "push") and "fast" (or "burning"). TNT (Trinitrotoluene) is a "slow" explosive.* That is, its primary destruction mechanism is the shock wave or "front" of explosive gases created during detonation. TNT destroys or disassembles targets by structurally blowing them over or apart.

---

* TNT is also the measure of all other explosive pyrotechnics. Thus nuclear weapons are measured in kilo- and megatons of TNT.

This is in contrast to "fast" explosives like C4 (Composite Explosive Four — better known as "plastique"), which detonate very quickly and can actually burn (i.e. break the molecular bonds) through structural materials like steel. C4 tends to be more useful to SF soldiers than TNT, since it is quite safe to handle; has a higher explosive yield per measure; and, because of its "plastic" character, it can be cut and shaped into more efficient charges. At normal temperatures (50° F/ 10° C to 120° F/49° C) C4 has the same consistency of molding clay or frozen ice cream. Usually issued in one-pound blocks, you can cut and shape it and even burn the stuff without causing a high-order detonation. (In a high-order detonation, the entire charge goes off all at once, as opposed to a low-order or "string" series of explosions.) This kind of explosive requires an electrical detonator, blasting cap, or other precision igniter (a burning fuse will not usually cause a detonation in fast explosives).

By way of example, a two-lane steel-girder bridge that might require a TNT charge of up to 300 lb/136 kg to "push" it over can be dropped by "burning" the steel structural beams with less than 100 lb/45 kg of C4. When you are asking a twelve-man Special Forces ODA team to carry on their backs for most of a week the explosive "payload" to destroy a target, it is easy to see which they prefer to use, the target allowing.

Of course, it is important to pay attention to that last point. Every target is unique, requiring a tailored approach to take it down. Special Forces weapons (18B) and engineering (18C) sergeants are skilled in assessing the quantities and types of explosives needed to "drop" a particular target. In making that assessment, these men use many of the same techniques that Air Force planners have developed to plan air strikes with precision weapons. They use builder's blueprints, satellite reconnaissance photos, and any other available information. Nobody wants to have to hit a target twice. This is especially true of SF soldiers, for whom a failed raid or strike means a target sure to be better protected the next time around.

One final consideration: while precision air strikes sometimes fail to be "precise" (as in the time a B-2 strike hit the Chinese Embassy in Belgrade), SF teams can destroy their targets with absolute certainty. There are just some targets that are better destroyed by men on the ground than satellite-guided bombs. For one thing, they can eyeball a building to make sure the target is not a foreign embassy or babyfood factory.

Not all explosive jobs are as heavyweight as dropping a bridge or building. There are other times, for example, when you're only called upon to create an opening or breach in a wall. For this kind of job, very small explosive charges can be used with greater safety and reliability than mechanical cutters or battering rams. In fact, such breaches can frequently be cut with Detonation Cord (called "Det Cord" in the field). Det Cord is a synthetic rope impregnated with explosive and has a burning speed measured in thousands of feet per second and a temperature high enough to burn through thin metal. Det Cord can cut breaches and burn thin metal, and it is frequently used as a flying fuse (i.e. an old-fashioned burning fuse such as you've seen in movies and cartoons) for larger explosive charges. A deployed ODA even on a "noncombat" mission will usually carry a supply of explosives and detonation gear, just in case a real-world contingency develops in their neighborhood.

Special Forces soldiers are not only skilled with conventional explosives, they are equally skilled in improvising where the situation calls for it. That is to say, they can take commonly available materials and turn them into a useful explosive charge. For example, fertilizers and diesel fuel are quite effective if mixed and placed properly (this mixture was used against the World Trade Center in New York and Federal Building in Oklahoma City). And many other explosive concoctions are possible in the field.

From Special Forces, *Tom Clancy, The Berkley Publishing Group, 2001. Copyright (C) 2001 Rubicon, Inc.*

THE ABDUCTION

W. Stanley Moss

Parachuted into Crete in 1942, SOE operatives Major Patrick Leigh Fermor and Major Stanley "Billy" Moss organized partisan resistance to the 22,000 Germans garrisoning the island. On 26 April 1944, Fermor and Moss pulled off their most daring escapade: the kidnap of Major General Karl Kreipe, the commander of German forces in Crete.

I T WAS EIGHT o'clock when we reached the T-junction. We had met a few pedestrians on the way, none of whom seemed perturbed at seeing our German uniforms, and we had exchanged greetings with them with appropriately Teutonic gruffness. When we reached the road we went straight to our respective posts and took cover. It was now just a question of lying low until we saw the warning torch-flash from Mitso, the buzzer-man. We were distressed to notice that the incline in the road was much steeper than we had been led to believe, for this meant that if the chauffeur used the footbrake instead of the handbrake when we stopped him there would be a chance of the car's running over the edge of the embankment as soon as he had been disposed of. However, it was too late at this stage to make any changes in our plan, so we just waited and hoped for the best.

There were five false alarms during the first hour of our watch. Two *Volkswagen*, two lorries, and one motor-cycle combination trundled past at various times, and in each of them, seated primly upright like tailors' dummies, the steel-helmeted figures of German soldiers were silhouetted against the night sky. It was a strange feeling to be crouching so close to them – almost within arm's reach of them – while they drove past with no idea that nine pairs of eyes were so fixedly watching them. It felt rather like going on patrol in action, when you find yourself very close to the enemy trenches, and can hear the sentries talking or quietly whistling, and can see them lighting cigarettes in their cupped hands.

It was already one hour past the General's routine time for making his return journey when we began to wonder if he could possibly have gone home in one of the vehicles which had already passed by. It was cold, and the canvas of our German garb did not serve to keep out the wind.

I remember Paddy's asking me the time. I looked at my watch and saw that the hands were pointing close to half-past nine. And at that moment Mitso's torch blinked.

"Here we go."

We scrambled out of the ditch on to the road. Paddy switched on his red lamp and I held up a traffic signal, and together we stood in the centre of the junction.

In a moment – far sooner than we had expected – the powerful headlamps of the General's car swept round the bend and we found ourselves floodlit. The chauffeur, on approaching the corner, slowed down.

Paddy shouted, "Halt!"

The car stopped. We walked forward rather slowly, and as we passed the beams of the headlamps we drew our ready-cocked pistols from behind our backs and let fall the life-preservers from our wrists.

As we came level with the doors of the car Paddy asked, "*Ist dies das General's Wagen?*"

There came a muffled "*Ja, ja*" from inside.

Then everything happened very quickly. There was a rush from all sides. We tore open our respective doors, and our torches illuminated the interior of the car – the bewildered face of the General, the chauffeur's terrified eyes, the rear seats empty. With his right hand the chauffeur was reaching for his automatic, so I hit him across the head with my cosh. He fell forward, and George, who had come up behind me, heaved him out of the driving-seat and dumped him on the road. I jumped in behind the steering-wheel, and at the same moment saw Paddy and Manoli dragging the General out of the opposite door. The old man was struggling with fury, lashing out with his arms and legs. He obviously thought that he was going to be killed, and started shouting every curse under the sun at the top of his voice.

The engine of the car was still ticking over, the hand-brake was on, everything was perfect. To one side, in a pool of torchlight in the centre of the road, Paddy and Manoli were trying to quieten the General, who was still cursing and struggling. On the other side George and Andoni were trying to pull the chauffeur to his feet, but the man's head was pouring with blood, and I think he must have been unconscious, because every time they lifted him up he simply collapsed to the ground again.

This was the critical moment, for if any other traffic had come along the road we should have been caught sadly unawares. But now Paddy, Manoli, Nikko, and Stratis were carrying the General towards the car and bundling him into the back seat. After him clambered George, Manoli, and Stratis – one of the three holding a knife to the General's throat to stop him shouting, the other two with their Marlin guns poking out of either window. It must have been quite a squash.

Paddy jumped into the front seat beside me.

The General kept imploring, "Where is my hat? Where is my hat?"

The hat, of course, was on Paddy's head.

We were now ready to move. Suddenly everyone started kissing and congratulating everybody else; and Micky, having first embraced Paddy and me, started screaming at the General with all the pent-up hatred he held for the Germans. We had to push him away and tell him to shut up. Andoni, Grigori, Nikko, and Wallace Beery were standing at the roadside, propping up the chauffeur between them, and now they waved us good-bye and turned away and started off on their long trek to the rendezvous on Mount Ida.

We started.

The car was a beauty, a brand-new Opel, and we were delighted to see that the petrol gauge showed the tanks to be full.

We had been travelling for less than a minute when we saw a succession of lights coming along the road towards us; and a moment later we found ourselves driving past a motor convoy, and thanked our stars that it had not come this way a couple of minutes sooner. Most of the lorries were troop transports, all filled with soldiery, and this sight had the immediate effect of quietening George, Manoli, and Stratis, who had hitherto been shouting at one another and taking no notice of our attempts to keep them quiet.

When the convoy had passed Paddy told the General that the two of us were British officers and that we would treat him as an honourable prisoner of war. He seemed mightily relieved to hear this and immediately started to ask a series of questions, often not even waiting for a reply. But for some reason his chief concern still appeared to be the whereabouts of his hat – first it was the hat, then his medal. Paddy told him that he would soon be given it back, and to this the General said, "*Danke, danke.*"

It was not long before we saw a red lamp flashing in the road before us, and we realized that we were approaching the first of the traffic-control posts through which we should have to pass. We were, of course, prepared for this eventuality, and our plan had contained alternative actions which we had hoped would suit any situation, because we knew that our route led us through the centre of Heraklion, and that in the course of our journey we should probably have to pass through about twenty control posts.

Until now everything had happened so quickly that we had felt no emotion other than elation at the primary success of our venture; but as we drew nearer and nearer to the swinging red lamp we experienced our first tense moment.

A German sentry was standing in the middle of the road. As we approached him, slowing down the while, he moved to one side, presumably thinking that we were going to stop. However, as soon as we drew level with him – still going very slowly, so as to give him an opportunity of seeing the General's pennants on the wings of the car – I began to accelerate again, and on we went. For several seconds after we had passed the sentry we were all apprehension, fully expecting to hear a rifle-shot in our wake; but a moment later we had rounded a bend in the road and knew that the danger was temporarily past. Our chief concern now was whether or not the guard at the post behind us would telephone ahead to the next one, and it was with our fingers crossed that we approached the red lamp of the second control post a few minutes later. But we need not have had any fears, for the sentry behaved in exactly the same manner as the first had done, and we drove on feeling rather pleased with ourselves.

In point of fact, during the course of our evening's drive we passed twenty-two control posts. In most cases the above-mentioned formula sufficed to get us through, but on five occasions we came to road blocks – raisable one-bar barriers – which brought us to a standstill. Each time, however, the General's pennants did the trick like magic, and the sentries would either give a smart salute or present arms as the gate was lifted and we passed through. Only once did we find ourselves in what might have developed into a nasty situation – but of that I shall write in a moment.

Paddy, sitting on my right and smoking a cigarette, looked quite imposing in the General's hat. The General asked him how long he would have to remain in his present undignified position, and in reply Paddy told him that if he were willing to give his parole that he would neither shout nor try to escape we should treat him, not as a prisoner, but, until we left the island, as one of ourselves. The General gave his parole immediately. We were rather surprised at this, because it seemed to us that anyone in his position might still entertain reasonable hopes of escape – a shout for help at any of the control posts might have saved him.

According to our plan, I should soon be having to spend twenty-four hours alone with Manoli and the General, so I thought it best to find out if we had any languages in common (for hitherto we had been speaking a sort of anglicized German). Paddy asked him if he spoke any English.

"*Nein*," said the General.

"Russian?" I asked. "Or Greek?"

"*Nein*."

In unison: "*Parlez-vous français?*"

"*Un petit peu.*"

To which we could not resist the Cowardesque reply, "I never think that's quite enough."

But it was in French that we spoke, and continued to do so. The quality is scarcely commendable.

Presently we found ourselves approaching the Villa Ariadne. The sentries, having recognized the car from a distance, were already opening the heavily barbed gates in anticipation of our driving inside. I hooted the horn and did not slow down. We drove swiftly past them, and it was with considerable delight that we watched them treating us to hurried salutes.

We were now approaching Heraklion, and coming towards us we saw a large number of lorries. We remembered that Micky had told us that there was to be a garrison cinema show in the town that evening, so we presumed that these lorries were transporting the audience back to various billets. We did not pass a single vehicle which was travelling in the same direction as ourselves.

Soon we had to slow down to about 25 k.p.h., because the road was chock-full of German soldiers. They were quick to respond to the hooting of our horn, however, and when they saw whose car it was they dispersed to the sides of the road and acknowledged us in passing. It was truly unfortunate that we should have arrived in the town at this moment; but once again luck was with us, and, apart from a near-miss on a cyclist, who swerved out of our way only just in time, we drove down the main street without let or hindrance. By the time we reached the market square in the centre of the town we had already left the cinema crowd behind us, and we found the large, open space, which by daylight is usually so crowded, now almost completely deserted. At this point we had to take a sharp turning to the left, for our route led us westward through the old West Gate to the Tetimo road.

The West Gate is a relic of the old days when Heraklion was completely surrounded by a massive wall, and even to-day it remains a formidable structure. The gate itself, at the best of times not very wide, had been further narrowed by concrete anti-tank blocks; and a German guard was on duty there for twenty-four hours a day.

I remember saying "Woops" as I saw the sentry signalling us to stop. I had proposed to slow down, as on the previous occasions, and then to accelerate upon drawing level with the sentry; but this time this was impossible, for the man did not move an inch, and in the light of the headlamps we saw several more Germans standing behind him. I was obliged to take the car forward at a snail's pace. We had previously decided that in the event of our being asked any questions our reply would be simply, "*General's Wagen*," coupled with our hopes for the best. If any further conversation were called for Paddy was to do the talking.

George, Manoli, and Stratis held their weapons at the ready and kept as low as they could in the back seat. The General was on the floor beneath them. Paddy and I cocked our pistols and held them on our laps.

The sentry approached Paddy's side of the car.

Before he had come too near Paddy called out that this was the General's car – which, after all, was true enough – and without awaiting the sentry's next word I accelerated and we drove on, calling out "*Gute Nacht!*" as we went. Everyone saluted.

We drove fast along the next stretch of road.

The General, coming to the surface, said he felt sorry for all the sentries at the control posts, because they would surely get into terrible trouble on the morrow.

The road was clear of traffic, and it was not long before we had put several kilometres between ourselves and Heraklion. Soon we had passed the last of the control posts, and the road began to rise from the plain and wind gradually uphill. Up and up we went. We had seen the massive mountain forms in front of us as a target, but now we were among them; and high above, like a white baby curled upon a translucent canopy, we saw the crescent of the moon.

Suddenly we felt quite distant from everything that had just happened – a terrific elation – and we told one another that three-quarters of the job was now over, and started discussing what sort of celebration we would have when we got back to Cairo. We sang "The Party's Over"; and then I lit a cigarette, which I thought was the best I had ever smoked in my life.

At a quarter-past eleven we arrived at the point on the road where Manoli, Stratis, the General, and I were to leave the car. We had been driving for an hour and three-quarters, and during the latter part of the journey the road had spiralled up and up, so that we were now at a considerable altitude, and we felt that until dawn at least we were out of harm's way.

As Paddy and I got out of the car the General called to us, begging us not to leave him alone with the Cretans – so dramatically, in fact, that I'm sure he imagined he would have his throat slit the moment our backs were turned. Paddy assured him that he was not going to be left alone, that I was going to accompany him; and on hearing this the General gave a great sigh of relief. We told him to come out of the car, and he hastily obeyed. Paddy gave him a smart salute, saying that he would meet him, together with the rest of us, on the morrow at Anoyia; and then he clambered into the driving-seat with George next to him.

Paddy had not driven a car for over five years, and it was with fits of suppressed laughter that we watched him trying to put the hand-brake into gear and pressing the horn instead of the starter. After several starts and stalls, off he went, and we watched the car going on up the road, swerving from side to side and grinding along in bottom gear, until the tail-lamp disappeared round a bend. With only two kilometres to go, I hoped he would complete the journey all right.

We set off with the General in a southerly direction. There was no path or track, and we were obliged to scramble up and down cliffs, across streams, and through heavy undergrowth. This was very hard going for the General, and although he was quite co-operative and did not try to hinder us in any way, it was inevitable that we travelled very slowly. Stratis, contrary to his assurances, had little idea of the route which we were trying to follow, and consequently our progress was more or less guided by our reading of the stars. The General said that his leg had been badly hurt when he had been dragged out of his car, and indeed he walked with a pronounced limp. I considered it unnecessary to continue walking behind him with my revolver at his back, so I searched him for concealed arms – he had none – and then walked with him, helping him over obstacles and, with Manoli's assistance, carrying him across streams. We were foolish enough not to drink from these streams, for it was not long before we came to a dry expanse of country, and it was three o'clock in the morning before we reached a spring.

The spring was almost dry, and in order to get any water out of it we had to tie some string round the lid of an emergency-ration tin, which we let down some twenty feet and dragged in the mud until it was full. It took us a long time to quench our thirsts, for we were only able to bring up about a quarter of an inch of water each time. The General said that he was very hungry, for he had eaten nothing since luncheon, so I gave him a few raisins which were mixed up with the dust in my pockets, and for these he was more than thankful.

We moved on again. The General became talkative and started discussing General Brauer's* reactions to hearing of this "Hussar Act," as he called it. He supposed that Paddy and I must be very happy and pleased with ourselves, but added that the job was not yet over. And then he asked me if we were Regular soldiers. When I replied that we were not he seemed greatly upset, for he had just realized, it appeared, that his career had ceased to exist. He was the thirteenth child, he said, of a family of fifteen; and his father, a poor man, was a pastor, so it was really he himself who was the family's breadwinner. A major general's pay,

---

* General Brauer was Commander of the Fortress of Crete, as opposed to Kriepe, who was the Divisional Commander. Both Brauer and Kreipe's predecessor, General Muller, were sentenced to death at a War-crimes trial in Athens in December 1945.

he explained, was pretty good in the German Army, and, what was more, he had been expecting his promotion to the rank of lieutenant general to come through at any moment. (He was, in fact, already wearing the insignia of a lieutenant general, but I think this was due rather to his local appointment than to eager anticipation.)

JUST CAUSE

David Eshel

*Panama is a tiny country of enormous strategic impor-
tance; it lies along both sides of the Panama Canal, the
short-cut between the Atlantic and Pacific oceans. Free
passage through the Canal is vital to the economic and
military interests of numerous nations, but none more so
than Panama's mighty neighbour to the north, the USA.
Long-time good neighbours, relations between Panama
and the US corroded in the 1980s, when Panama's
military leader, General Noriega, was indicted in US
courts on counts of drug-trafficking. In December 1989,
Noriega declared a state of war, and a US Marine
officer in Panama City was killed. In response, the
US President, George Bush, ordered an invasion of
Panama by US forces.*

*The invasion plan, code-named "Just Cause", called
for twenty-seven objectives in Panama and alongside the
Canal to be taken in twenty-four hours – that is, by
midnight 21 December 1989. Committed to Just Cause
were some 23,000 US troops, spearheaded by detachments of the Navy SEALs and 1st Ranger Battalion.*

F IRST INTO ACTION were a team of US SEALs, who set
off from an American naval base on Panama shortly
before midnight on 19 December to neutralize a Panamanian patrol boat, *President Porras*, which the planners
thought might interfere with the American operations.
Clad in tight-fitting black spandex diving suits, the naval

Commandos boarded two fast raiding craft and silently slipped out to sea. Having crossed the channel leading to the Panamanian docks, the boats sailed along the shore lined with mangrove trees. Reaching their destination some 50 metres from the objective, which was fully lit, the divers took a compass bearing and then slipped silently into the water, navigating by compass board and depth-gauge which were fitted in front of their equipment, visible in the dark with the aid of special glow lamps. Each swimmer carried explosive charges in waterproof packs. After a short underwater swim, the SEALs reached the *President Porras* undetected; one team fitted their demolition charges on the propeller shaft, while the others attached their charges under the boat. Suddenly, the boat's engines started and the divers swam off to seek cover. The boat's crew had woken up by now and started to toss hand-grenades into the water, but the swimmers were already too far away to suffer any casualties. As they waited, four loud explosions shattered the still night. Shots began to come from some nearby vessels, but they were wildly inaccurate, and the divers were already well on their way back.

Just after midnight on 20 December, the first US paratroops started to drop on to Torrijos International Airport. Seven hundred men of the 1st US Ranger Battalion made their combat drop from a low 500 feet into the darkness from several C-130 Hercules transports which had flown straight over from the USA. Their mission was to secure the airfield for a bigger drop to follow.

Lieutenant James Johnson, son of the commander of the 82nd Airborne Division, was among the first men out of his C-141 Starlifter. The young officer carried a heavy load, including his personal weapon, Claymore mine and radio – the whole totalling 35 kilograms. It was 0212 as he stepped out of the door into the tropical night. Below he could see coloured tracer bullets whizzing in all directions, but he had no time for aesthetic appreciation, since he realized that he was heading for a sharp drop on some thick overgrowth. His parachute caught on a large tree but when he untangled his harness he fell quite smoothly to the ground.

Many of his team were not so fortunate: some of them

dropped in a nearby marsh and had to be drawn out very carefully, as their heavy load could have dragged them under. Others dropped heavily and sprained ankles or broke legs. The supply drop which followed was a catastrophe. Some Sheridan tanks of 73rd Armoured Battalion were dropped on the airfield, but, of the first eight, one became mired in the swamp and another smashed into the ground as its parachutes did not open. Another important piece of equipment, a fire control truck, landed upside down. Assembling the troops and supplies took much longer than had been expected, and the officers had great difficulty in getting their men together, as some of them had to hack their way through head-high elephant grass using their combat knives.

By 0430, however, Lieutenant Johnson was able to radio his commander that he had most of his men assembled. At this time they were supposed to be boarding the Black Hawk helicopters, but these did not arrive until three hours later. Johnson and his men boarded quickly, but by then the sun was up, which obviously would make things more difficult.

The plan was for the Black Hawks to fly in formations of six aircraft, each carrying sixty paratroopers. The flight would be guided in by scout helicopters and AH-64 Apaches, whose first mission this would be. After a landing zone had been secured, some AH-1 Cobra gunships would hover nearby to cover and support if needed.

The first task for the 82nd Ready Brigade was the capture of Panama Viejo, which overlooked the bay at the eastern end of Panama City. US intelligence had gained information that 250 of Noriega's most loyal troops, the notorious UESAT, were stationed there. Johnson's platoon was assigned to capture three observation posts near the fort. As they touched down on the adjacent beach, the men were covered by a hail of automatic fire from a barracks located on some nearby high ground. While Johnson and his men started to move out, another wave of helicopters came in to land, but the paratroopers jumped out into deep mud which had been stirred up by the previous landings. Some of them sank up to their armpits and had to be pulled up by their landing gear, hooked to choppers hovering overhead. Others formed a human chain to pull each other out, while all the time bullets whizzed over their heads. They were free from the quagmire within minutes, but valuable time had been lost.

Now the supporting Cobras went into action, attacking the barracks and a nearby anti-aircraft gun, which was knocked out before it had even opened fire. Johnson and his men then stormed the barracks, where resistance stopped as soon as the Americans set foot in the compound.

Things did not go so easily, however, in the city: Panamanian Defence Force (PDF) troops ran through the streets, firing automatic weapons and lobbing grenades through the windows of houses, and, as they wore jeans, it was impossible to distinguish them from the ordinary Panamanian citizens, making it very difficult to fight them. Also hiding in the crowds which thronged the streets were men of Noriega's so-called "Dignity Battalions" or Dinbats, actually no better than street gangs out for personal gain but dangerous for all that: they were known to have brutally murdered some opponents of Noriega in earlier times.

As the fighting escalated, the Hotel Marriott in downtown Panama City became the focus of attention. Some American civilians who had been staying there were rounded up by masked men of Noriega's forces, were brutally abused and in fear of their lives. An airline pilot managed to get away in the confusion and phoned the White House in Washington for help. The message got through to General Stiner at For Bragg, who in turn radioed Lieutenant Colonel Harry Axson, commanding the paratroop battalion which was just entering the city from the direction of Fort Viejo. The colonel immediately ordered one of his companies to the hotel – but they had to get there first.

Advancing through heavy fire, hugging the sides of the buildings, the troopers ran from cover to cover, dodging the bullets which pinged around them. Just as the first men reached the doorway of the hotel, a large truck rounded the corner of the street at high speed, brakes squealing, and from it some UESAT men wearing protective vests blazed away with machine-guns. The truck zigzagged between the American paratroopers, who frantically raced for cover, but not before two of them had been wounded. Some paratroopers returned the fire and even managed to set light to the truck's cabin, but the shooting continued. Then one paratrooper, Specialist James Smith, went and stood directly in the path of the truck; aiming his grenade-launcher, he let go and scored a direct hit; the truck shuddered to a halt and, reloading quickly, he followed it up with another shot which sent the truck swerving into a building. Their way clear, the company raced into the Hotel Marriott and rescued the frightened civilians.

Another task force, which had set out at daybreak to capture a hill fortress on top of Tinajitas hill, was undergoing a terrible ordeal. Intelligence elements had estimated that a battalion of Noriega's best PDF forces were defending the fort. The landing zone designated for the US task force was on a low ridge about one kilometre south-west of the fort; as the Black Hawks came in to land soon after eight in the morning, they drew fire from the defence forces above them, and mortar fire fell near the landing zone, hitting two of the choppers. The paratroopers assembled, however, and set out to climb to the summit. It turned out to be an arduous climb: drenched in sweat in the hot tropical sun, the men soon became exhausted as they climbed through the elephant grass which reached high above their heads. It was only 700 metres to the top, but, at a crawling pace, in those conditions and under constant fire, it seemed a lot further. The PDF mortar men, from their position on top of the hill, had time to correct their range, and coolly pick off the advancing Americans, 22 of whom were wounded and two killed during the climb and the assault which followed. By that afternoon, however, the fort had been captured and the PDF fled to a nearby village.

Several kilometres from Tinajitas stood Fort Cimmaron where Noriega's most loyal units were stationed. US intelligence officers had feared that the nearby electricity plant which controlled the power for the entire city might be destroyed and a *coup de main* strike was planned to secure the fort as quickly as possible. The force assigned to capture the fort was supported by two Sheridan tanks and gun-mounted Humvees, but they had set off late, having had to wait until the vehicles could be manhandled from the marshlands where they had been dropped earlier. When the motor column came near the fort and the men were preparing to strike, it emerged that most of the PDF battalion guarding it had melted away during the night. The few men who had stayed behind fought back, but were quickly subdued by superior firepower.

As special Commando forces secured all the strategic sites along the canal zone, there still remained one more very important objective, in fact the main point of the exercise: the capture of the dictator himself. General Noriega had been in the officers' mess at the airfield when the first Ranger battalion dropped shortly after midnight, but as they began to assemble on the ground he jumped into his limousine and headed for the city, dodging the roadblocks which were just being set up along the route. Throughout the day US agents had been searching for him all over the city; finally they came to believe that he had taken refuge in his headquarters, the Comandancia, and this was to become the scene of the last violent battle.

The Comandancia was a complex of several concrete buildings, sited in the southern part of the city not far from the seashore; it was well defended, with thick walls, capable of withstanding a powerful attack. In order to assault such a target General Stiner had assigned a lot of firepower to reduce the expected strong resistance. Two AC-130 Spectre gunships were detailed to support Apache gunships and several Sheridan tanks. Since its impressive performance in Vietnam the Spectre had been modified to carry, apart from many rapid-firing automatic cannon, a powerful 105mm howitzer which could accurately hurl forty-pound projectiles. The Apaches could launch Hellfire anti-tank missiles, able to penetrate even the thickest walls.

This was all very well in theory, but as the convoy of vehicles, including the Sheridan tanks, approached the buildings, it came under heavy RPG fire which knocked out two APCs, one of which exploded, killing two and wounding eighteen of its passengers. The burning vehicles blocked the street, but the two Sheridans manoeuvred round them and fired point-blank at the compound, while the wounded men were dragged out of the blazing hulks.

Now it was time for the infantry, who dashed forward. The tanks stepped up their fire and from above the Spectre and Apaches destroyed the upper floor. Within minutes the whole compound was ablaze but snipers still continued to fire from the ruins. General Stiner therefore detached a Ranger company to reduce the target and they, together with the paratroopers, overcame any remaining resistance.

Noriega, however, if he had been in the Comandancia, was not to be found. It was to be another two weeks before he gave himself up; he had been hiding in a private apartment.

Operation Just Cause was the largest US intervention since the Second World War involving airborne troops. Twenty-three US soldiers had died and more than 300 were wounded, while the civilian toll, never finally established, was probably several hundred. Many of the US special forces who were engaged in Panama would use the skills they had learned there two years later – and halfway round the world – in Operation Desert Storm.

US ARMY SPECIAL FORCES

[The Special Forces Creed]

I am an American Special Forces soldier. A professional! I will do all that my nation requires of me.

I am a volunteer, knowing well the hazards of my profession.

I serve with the memory of those who have gone before me: Rogers' Rangers, Francis Marion, Mosby's Rangers, the first Special Service Forces and Ranger Battalions of World War II, The Airborne Ranger Companies of Korea. I pledge to uphold the honor and integrity of all I am – in all I do.

I am a professional soldier. I will teach and fight wherever my nation requires. I will strive always, to excel in every art and artifice of war.

I know that I will be called upon to perform tasks in isolation, far from familiar faces and voices, with the help and guidance of my God.

I will keep my mind and body clean, alert and strong, for this is my debt to those who depend upon me.

I will not fail those with whom I serve. I will not bring shame upon myself or the forces.

I will maintain myself, my arms, and my equipment in an immaculate state as befits a Special Forces soldier.

I will never surrender though I be the last. If I am taken, I pray that I may have the strength to spit upon my enemy.

My goal is to succeed in any mission – and live to succeed again.

I am a member of my nation's chosen soldiery. God grant that I may not be found wanting, that I will not fail this sacred trust.

DANGEROUS ENCOUNTER

Derrick Harrison

Captain Harrison was dropped into occupied France as part of 1 SAS's Operation Kipling, which was to provide cover for the Allied airborne landings scheduled for the Orleans Gap in August 1944. In the event, the Orleans landing were cancelled, and the 107 men and forty-six jeeps of C Squadron turned their hands to daring patrols and attacks in the Auxerre region. One such patrol led Harrison into a dangerous encounter.

WE MOVED OFF, my own jeep in the lead. As we rolled down the narrow track towards the road I found myself wondering where all these rumours started. Admittedly our French friends were prone to exaggerate, but I could not understand Roger dashing off like this on the strength of a rumour. Still . . .

We were about to turn into the road when I caught sight of a curl of thick smoke above the trees over to the right. I stopped the jeeps and Stewart came running forward. I pointed. "See that? What do you make of it?"

"Looks as though it's over towards Les Ormes – something big on fire. What are we going to do?"

"Carry on and keep our eyes open. It may be further than we think."

At top speed we raced away along the bumpy, dusty road towards the ever-growing column of smoke. Breasting the top of the hill outside Les Ormes I signalled the jeep behind to stop. Together we screamed to a halt. Ahead of us the road forked.

From the left came the crackle of firing. A number of buildings were ablaze. The crossroads on which we had halted was not more than a hundred yards from the village, but all the noise seemed to be coming from the far end. While I debated what to do a woman on a bicycle came pedalling for dear life down the left-hand fork towards us. Head down, she came quickly on with her grey hair blowing in the wind. Tears streamed down her lined face. With surprising agility she leapt from her bike.

"Quick, messieurs," she called out, "save yourselves . . . the Boches . . . there." She pointed to the burning buildings. "Now I go to bring the maquis back."

"Just a moment." She hesitated as she made to remount her bicycle. "Quickly, how many Boches are there?"

She shrugged her shoulders. "Two hundred . . . three hundred," she hazarded. "Who knows? A lot. Yes, a lot. Too many for you, monsieur. Now I must go."

"Wait a minute. We'll go. With our jeeps it will be quicker." I had made a quick decision. "Leave it to us."

Astonishment showed in her face. "Thank you, monsieur. Thank you, thank you." She climbed back on to her bike and cycled slowly back into the burning village. The rest of the patrol gathered round.

"Well," I asked, "what do you think? Go for the maquis or attack the village ourselves?" It was a hard decision. In my own mind I had made it already, but I wanted the reactions of the others.

We were five in all. Fauchois was the first to speak. "I say attack." Fauchois had been sent to us from the French SAS He carried false papers showing him to be a Canadian to ensure that, should he be captured, his family would not suffer. He was keen, dependable, and ever anxious to get at the "*sales Boches*".

I turned to ask Curly Hall.

"If we go to Aillant for the maquis I think it will be too late when we get them here."

"Brearton?"

Brearton was Stewart's driver, and like Stewart, an extank man. His reply was short and to the point. "Let's have a crack at them."

"And you, Stewart?"

"I feel like Hall. We haven't time to go for the maquis."

"Good. That's just what I feel. But we can't make an open attack. I suggest we take this right-hand fork into the part of the village that is quiet. Once in, we can drive through the village at speed with our guns going. We'll have the element of surprise and should be able to shoot our way out of anything we meet. The odds are something like fifty to one, but I hope they'll get such a shock that we'll pull it off."

Union Jacks fluttering in the wind, we tore down the road, round the bend and into the village. Even as we came into the square I saw him. He was dressed in SS uniform, walking towards us, pistol in hand. He looked up in surprise – and died.

I took in the scene in an instant. The church in the middle of the square . . . a large truck . . . two German staff cars . . . the crowd of SS men in front of the church.

The staff cars and the truck burst into flames as, standing in my seat, I raked the square with fire from my twin machine-guns. The crowd of SS men stampeded for cover. Many of them died in those first few seconds in front of the church, lit by the flickering flames of the burning vehicles.

Even as I fired I shouted to Hall to reverse. The jeep jerked to a halt about thirty yards from the church. The Germans who had escaped the first fury of our assault were now returning our fire. I turned to see why Hall had not got the jeep moving back. He lay slumped over the wheel. The tell-tale gouts of blood told their own story. Curly Hall was dead.

Still firing, I pressed the starter with my foot. The engine was still, hit by the burst of fire that had got Hall. Then my guns jammed. No time to try and put them right. I dashed round to use the rear gun. It fired one burst, and stopped.

There was now only the single gun by the driver's seat. I got round to it, managed to fire a couple of short bursts before that, too, jammed. A dud jeep and three jammed guns. Hell, what a mess!

I had forgotten all about the second jeep. Now I could hear its guns hammering away over my shoulder. It was drawn up against the wall of the road leading into the square. There were Germans at the upper windows of the building immediately overlooking us. Stewart's Colt cracked again and again as they tried to fire down on us.

All this I took in in a flash. My own plight was too desperate, standing as I was in the middle of the crossroads. I reached over and snatched up my carbine. Thank heavens it was semi-automatic. I fired off the fifteen rounds in the magazine . . . changed the magazine. Blast this broken finger. The damned splint gets in the way. Another magazine.

I fired wherever I saw movement. A German made a dash for safety. I fired from the hip and he pitched forward on to his face. Now I grabbed Hall, lifting him from the jeep. A sniper stepped from a doorway on my right. I took a quick pot-shot and dropped him. Aim was instinctive.

I managed to get Hall to the centre of the crossroads. The Germans redoubled their fire. I started shooting again. I could see tracer streaming towards me. I weaved backwards and forwards like a boxer as if to dodge the flying bullets. There came a shout behind me.

"Look out. The orchard on your left."

There was a low stone wall to the left. I ran to it. On the other side was the orchard. Germans were advancing through it at the double. I fired as fast as I could pull the trigger. They disappeared.

Back to the jeep. Fauchois had run forward and was trying to drag Hall back to the second jeep. "Get back, you fool. Get back," I yelled. The Germans were concentrating their fire on him now. No sense in having another man killed.

Standing by the disabled jeep I kept up a rapid rate of fire. How many magazines left? I didn't know. Suddenly I remembered it was my wedding anniversary. With complete inconsequence I found myself thinking: Lord, my wife will be furious if I get myself killed, today of all days.

My right hand jerked and went numb. I looked down. It

was smothered in blood. With my fingertips I fished out another magazine from the pocket of my smock and after much fumbling managed to clip it into the carbine.

With both hands partly out of commission now, my aim was getting erratic. The Germans, who had seen me jump when hit, increased their fire. The sound of firing from the second jeep had stopped. I dared not look round. Keep on firing, keep on firing . . . the words went round and round in my head.

A German stepped from behind one of the trees to take a more careful aim. I raised my carbine, now slippery with blood, and squeezed the trigger. Nothing happened. I lowered the carbine. My hand jerked again as the marksman's bullet snicked across my knuckles.

I looked down. Two rounds were jammed in the breech. No time to put it right now. I grabbed for my Colt. The holster was empty. I swore. The damn' thing must have jerked loose in the fight. Nothing for it but to get that jammed magazine out. Resting one foot on the jeep I wrestled with it as best I could with my gammy hands. The Germans were still firing, but there was nothing I could do about it until I got that carbine firing again.

The new magazine was in. Miraculously I was still alive. I raised the carbine. From behind came a shout. "Dash for it!"

I heard the wild revving of an engine. The second jeep had been turned round. Stewart, Brearton and Fauchois were already in it. They shouted again. Firing as I ran, I dashed crabwise towards them. The jeep moved forward even as I leapt for it. Fauchois seized the rear guns and poured a last, long burst into the square. In a cloud of dust we disappeared down the road.

Straight into the nearest woods we drove, down a narrow, almost non-existent ride at breakneck speed. Swinging violently round a bend I was nearly flung from my seat. To save myself I grabbed at the guns. A final burst rent the air, narrowly missing the engine.

Back in camp I broke the news that Hall was dead. It was hard news to tell. He had been with me ever since I joined SAS, always bright, cheery and philosophical. I also knew that, had I not stood up in my seat to fire that first burst, I would have taken the shots that killed him.

At nightfall Stewart Richardson took a patrol back into Les Ormes. The Germans had left. The news he brought back gave us some consolation. No one knew just why the SS men had swooped on the village. Some said they were the advanced guard of a German convoy and they were protecting its passage through the area; others, that it was a reprisal raid for our presence in the area.

However that may be, they had, apart from burning houses, seized twenty men for execution. It was that execution which we had so unexpectedly interrupted outside the church. The first two of the doomed men had been shot as we arrived. The other eighteen escaped in the confusion. Besides the truck and two staff cars destroyed by our fire, the Germans had lost about sixty men dead and wounded. The rest had withdrawn as soon as we broke off the fight.

Derrick Harrison won the Military Cross for his part in the action at Les Ormes.

OPERATION BARRAS:
22 SAS SIERRA LEONE, 2000

A hostage situation in Sierra Leone was successfully resolved on the morning of 10 September 2000 as a force of 150 British paratroopers, led and directed by SAS soldiers, assaulted the West Side Boys' camp where eleven British and one Sierra Leonean hostages were being held. On 25 August 2000, the eleven soldiers from the Royal Irish Regiment along with their military liaison from Sierra Leone, were taken hostage by a "renegade militia", known as the West Side Boys, who are said to be perpetually drunk and drugged. The soldiers were in Sierra Leone as part of a 200-strong force training the government army in the country. British forces in the country launched an immediate search operation, but helicopter over-flights proved useless, and failed to locate the missing patrol. At this time, reports surfaced that a twelve-man Special Air

Service (SAS) team was sent to the country to attempt a rescue. That same day, 27 August, the West Side Boys demanded the release of their leader, General Papa, from prison, along with food and medicine, in exchange for the British troops. Two days later, on 29 August, one of the captured soldiers was allowed to meet with a hostage negotiating team, and assured them that the soldiers were being treated well, and that no one was injured. Around this time, the British government admitted that the captured patrol might have been deep inside rebel territory, rather than on the main highway. The situation improved on Wednesday, 30 August, when five of the eleven British soldiers were released, in exchange for a satellite phone and medical supplies. The other soldiers would not be released until the other demands were met. As negotiations continued, 5 September saw the arrival of over 100 elite British paratroopers from the 1st Battalion Parachute Regiment in Senegal in preparation for a possible military resolution to the crisis. The SAS had been on the ground for several days before the eventual assault, conducting reconnaissance among the swamps of Occra hills where the hostages were held. Supposedly, the hostages were lined up in front of firing squads for mock executions. The SAS had learned with the help of eavesdropping devices that the West Side Boys were discussing moving the hostages to higher hills. When the order for the rescue operation was given, the SAS operators moved to their final vantage point to guide in the paras. As dawn broke on Sunday, 11 September the order to move was issued. At 06.16 three Chinook helicopters and two Westland Lynx gunships took off from Freetown airport. Flying at 200 miles per hour, they headed towards Rokel creek, the site of the rebel camp. At 06.30, the assault began as the lead Lynx helicopter began strafing the banks of the river. One Chinook landed near the huts, as soldiers disembarked from it and immediately shot the guards. This task most certainly fell to the SAS soldiers due to their expertise in hostage rescue. A firefight ensued, as the West End Boys opened up on the rescue force with a heavy machine gun, killing one paratrooper. A second force of SAS and paras, moving in through a valley from the south, soon overwhelmed them, as more of the rescue team took casualties. The hostages were hustled into the helicopter and, 20 minutes

after the start of the operation, were safely airborne. The
hostages were removed to a waiting ship off the coast of
Freetown, the Sir Percival. During this time two other Chi-
nooks landed at a secondary camp south of the first position,
and the paras, with the second Lynx gunship providing cover,
engaged in a vicious firefight with the West Siders. Fighting on
this side of the creek took up to an hour and a half, the British
forces using mortars. The last of the rescue force were airlifted
around 16.00, after a mopping-up operation, which saw the
capture of the West Side Boys' leader, Foday Kallay. The
British forces suffered one death, one serious injury, and eleven
"light injuries". The West Side Boys lost twenty-five fighters,
along with eighteen captured.

From Elite Forces, *Richard M. Bennett, Virgin Books,*
2003. Copyright (C) 2003, Richard M. Bennett.

The SAS trooper killed in the action was Brad Tinnion.
He was awarded a posthumous Mention in Dispatches.

FIGHTING FIRE WITH FIRE

Eric Bailey

The first Allied special forces, 22 SAS and US Delta Force troops, arrived in Afghanistan within 72 hours of the 9/11 terrorist attack on the USA. These crack troops, reinforced by contingents of Navy SEALs, USMC "recons", Green Berets, the Rangers and Royal Marines SBS, were deployed in identifying Taliban and Al Qaeda targets for strike aircraft. The Taliban, with their strange penchant for women's make-up, were soon in disarray, but their militant guests, Al Qaeda, were made of stiffer stuff, and fanatically resisted every attack by allied units. Moreover, the Al Qaeda leader, Osama bin Laden fled to the White Mountains in south-eastern Afghanistan, where he holed up in the vast Tora Bora cave complex alongside 1,000 of his best warriors. Bin Laden's stronghold was subjected to repeated poundings by cluster bombs and "daisy cutters", dropped by the USAAF, and attacks by local Afghan militias in the pay of the US. Even so, parts of the stronghold proved impervious to such conventional assaults – at which US Central Command in Florida decided to send in the special forces. In the last week of November, the Colonel and Regimental Sergeant Major of 22 SAS led a raid on one section of the Tora Bora complex, which ended in an epic battle, with the RSM wounded and fighting hand to hand with his K-bar knife. Three days later, the Regiment took another turn at assaulting bin Laden's lair.

T HEY HAD TABBED for three hours to get to the cut-off.
Hard going, over scree and boulders, 12,000ft up in
the White Mountains of Afghanistan, where your body
screamed for a good lungful but didn't get it. But there
was no snow, and no bergens to carry: just the light kit of
belt rations, survival gear and tiny stoves – vital for making
a brew. To the eight men who crested the dark ridge –
carefully, in order not to be skylined by any fighters below –
it seemed as if there might be plenty of time for making
brews on this operation. A few even felt pangs of disappointment that it might well be the other lads – three hours
back around the mountain – who would be the ones to
smoke bin Laden out of his cave.

The men, led by a lean, rangy sergeant we shall call
Degsy, were from a 40-strong group of SAS – believed to be
A or G Squadron – who had been moving from cave to cave
in the Tora Bora complex. And they knew they were close
to looking Al Qaeda, and bin Laden, in the eye.

Three days earlier, there had been an epic confrontation
in which four soldiers, including the Regimental Sergeant
Major, had been wounded. It was desperate fighting, much
of it hand to hand with knives. One trooper had lost a leg –
but Al Qaeda had lost what became known as The Battle of
the Caves, along with scores of men. Then there had been
some humint – human intelligence – that more Al Qaeda
were massed in a second cave complex, and the company
had been detailed to mount an attack. The plan involved a
frontal assault by 30 troopers to drive the enemy further
into the caves. Any who got out would flee over the top of
the mountain or round the sides – so Degsy's group were
detailed to take up a position on the south side and wait to
cut off any stragglers.

From a distance, the eight might have passed for local
tribesmen. Their combat uniforms were hidden under heavy
local robes and some wore the traditional pie crust hat. All
had beards. Although the eight men were travelling light,
they were loaded up with firepower. They had two "gimpys" – the 7.62mm General Purpose Machine Gun no
longer issued in the Army but a favourite with the SAS
for its utter reliability and crude efficiency. The two machine

gunners were carrying 2,500 belt rounds of armour-piercing ammo. The remaining six each had an M203 – a standard M16 rifle fitted with a 40mm grenade launcher under the barrel. Each had eight magazines with 30 rounds of mixed tracer and armour-piercing rounds in each – as well as eight "bombs" for the grenade-launchers and a further 800 belt rounds for the gimpys. They were not aiming to run out.

The main attack was due to begin at 1730 hours, just as dusk was falling. By then, Degsy's group had reached their position – and were amazed at what they saw. The moon was waning, but it was cold and clear and they could make out dark sockets of caves and tunnels on the south side of the mountain. Were these linked to the caves where the main attack was about to take place? Degsy ordered one of the lads to get on the net to the main group – but there was no radio signal and they could not get through. There was nothing for it but to sit and wait.

The mountainside came down into a small gorge, so Degsy chose a spot on the other side directly opposite the tunnel entrances and about 150 metres away – a good range for the M203 bombs. All of the lads found their own cover, spreading out so as not to present a concentrated target but keeping within shouting distance. They set up the gimpys on their tripods so that they could lay down enfilading fire, making a killing zone around the cave entrances. There was the metallic clack of guns being readied. They tried the net again but there was nothing. After that there was to be no gobbing off without a good reason. Then they lay down in silence, focused hard on the caves opposite, and waited for the enemy.

When the main force launched their attack on the complex on the north side of the mountain, something odd happened. There was some resistance but nothing like the firestorm which had erupted from Al Qaeda fighters during other assaults. Nothing had been heard from the cut-off group, which was odd but not too worrying. The main group applied themselves to mopping up what resistance there was, and cleaning out the many entrances. It took some hours but, as each cave came up empty, the troopers couldn't help wondering: where had the enemy gone?

Degsy's group were about to find out. They had been in their positions for around three hours, keeping warm as best they could and scanning the entrance to the caves across the gorge with their night-sight goggles. When the first shadow moved, the news was whispered along the line: they were coming out. But there was silence as more shadows joined the first, then more, then more. The Al Qaeda fighters did not look as if they were expecting trouble: clearly they had come through a prepared labyrinth of tunnels from the north side of the mountain, and they appeared to be strolling out into the night air. Contact!

Degsy watched with growing concern as the few became a score, and still more were emerging. His lads were clearly going to be hopelessly outnumbered – and, if the enemy were allowed to spread out, they would easily outflank them. There was a hurried fudhl and Degsy considered pulling back, an option none of them fancied. They had plenty of ammo and, for now, a decent position. But eight men against, perhaps, hundreds? "Oh f*** it," snorted Degsy. "We're going to sort this out." The gimpys opened up first: an awesome cannonade laid down at 750 rounds a minute with enough velocity to cut a tree in half.

Normal practice is to conserve rounds – the Regiment does not blast away like Rambo – but, just then, a lot of lead was needed. The gimpy rounds, rattling through the guns on belts, smashed and scattered the group across the gorge, and the muffled plop of M203 rounds began. The tracers zipped across the gorge, but these were single shots carefully aimed.

Some Al Qaeda had been hit but others had taken cover and began to fire back, letting rip with their AK-47s and the occasional whump of a rocket-propelled grenade not well enough aimed. All the SAS had infrared sights on their M203s – but the terrorists had some, too, so, for a few hellish minutes, the firing was incessant.

Their fire became more sporadic but it was evident there were a lot of the enemy: still they were pouring out of the tunnel and running for cover. The SAS tactics were to stop them breaking out into wider positions and forming up into groups: formidable objectives for such a tiny force. The only way to do it was to keep the outer edges of the group pinned down with accurate fire.

Degsy ordered the imposition of weapons discipline: each man was numbered, and they were nominated in twos to watch for movement and fire next. He would shout "1 and 4" and those two men stayed on their night-sights until they had fired. In the meantime, the six others could rest their eyes, distribute ammo and reload. The gimpys fell silent for long periods, letting off short bursts only when a live target was spotted.

As night became the early hours, the constantly shifting shadows across the gorge indicated that the terrorists were still trying to fan out. But, whenever they grouped up, the next SAS man to fire would slip his hand forward to the M203 grenade launcher trigger. There would be a characteristic pop and the bomb would go screaming in. The radio was tried again but was still U/S.

From across the gorge there was the groaning of martyrs in the making, and constant jabber as they tried to decide what to do next. From Degsy's lads there was silence, and the cold determination to hold their position, freezing fingers held lightly on triggers, eyes filled only with the ghostly red world of the night-sight, ears with the whizz and clatter of AK-47 rounds pinging off the rocks they crouched behind.

Hours later, as the first sun cast long shadows across the gorge, scores of Al Qaeda terrorists lay dead. All of the M203 bombs, and virtually all of the gimpy ammunition, had gone. Degsy's men had only a few mags of M203 rounds left. The mouth of the cave was dark, and it was uncertain exactly how many Al Qaeda were still in there – but it was a lot. That was the moment when reinforcements from the main SAS group arrived, having secured the cave complex on the north side of the mountain, and tabbed round to see what had happened at the cut-off. They brought ammunition – but still the SAS squadron was hopelessly outnumbered. As the day wore on, the fight continued: the terrorists by now making desperate attempts to escape and being cut down with withering and accurate fire. But, as dusk loomed again, ammunition was running short. There was only one option: airstrike.

Moving the radio back along the line enabled the group to get in touch with the Head Shed, who could authorise an American bombing run – but it would have to be a "daisy-cutter", and that meant someone on the ground highlighting the target with a laser designator, and staying there while the bomb was guided in. One of Degsy's men volunteered.

The laser designator is like a large TV remote control with a wand which has to be pointed precisely at the target – but to find a good position the operator would have to expose himself to enemy fire. Covering fire would be laid down and the laser locked on to the mouth of the cave as the silent, menacing vapour trails of a B-52 appeared overhead. Once the bomb aimer in the aircraft had picked up the fix, the SAS could withdraw but there would be perilously little time before the fearsome "daisy-cutter" – a weapon designed to devastate large areas – would impact. And it was no good standing up and running back – the terrorists were still there in numbers and might have construed it as a retreat: it was vital they stayed pinned down.

The "daisy-cutter" is an awesome bomb: vacuum-packed with petroleum jelly, it bursts open 50ft above ground, splattering its incendiary load, instantaneously igniting it in a seismic explosion. But it's not the vaporising fuel which does the damage, it's the immense shockwave it forces downwards, burrowing into every crevice and hiding place.

To avoid danger, troops should be at least 1,000 metres from the edge of a "daisy-cutter" blast. But the SAS – and particularly the soldier with the laser guidance system – were well inside that when the world exploded. Some had ear defenders, others covered their ears with their hands, all had lain down in whatever cover they could find. There was a blinding light and the terrible sound of suction, a rush of air and then silence. The aim had been deadly accurate.

Whoever had been inside the cave was not there any more. Thousands of rounds had been expended; scores of Al Qaeda were dead, with no casualties to the SAS.

It was about 24 hours since Degsy's group had dug in, not expecting a contact; the action that had followed, to become known as the Siege of the White Mountains, is likely to earn Degsy and the soldier who operated the laser designator VCs.

Desperate fatigue and powerful hunger ensued. They folded out the legs on their hexy stoves and lit the white blocks of solid fuel: enough heat for a brew. Some dug rations out of their belt packs. They didn't speak much. Then they tabbed off the mountain and found a heli. Job done.

In the four-hour battle, 27 enemy were killed, 30 wounded and 30 captured. Yet, despite such efforts by the SAS, bin Laden escaped the allied attacks on Tora Bora to slip over the snow-covered mountains into Pakistan.

GULF WAR II: SHOOT & SCOOT

In an unfortunate echo of the ill-lucked Bravo Two Zero mission during the first Gulf War, the rematch against Saddam Hussein also saw an SAS team stranded deep behind enemy lines, and having to draw deep on their personal wells of courage and training to exit Iraq alive.

On 26 March 2004, D-Day +6 of Gulf War II, sixteen men from 22 SAS's Air Troop climbed aboard an American C-130 aircraft, to be parachuted into the desert south-west of Mosul. Their task was to reconnoitre the Republican Guard's defences around the city. According to intelligence supplied by the US Special Forces Command, the drop zone was free of Iraqi troops.

The intelligence was erroneous. On landing, the SAS patrol called in an RAF Chinook, which landed four "pinkies", the specially adapted 110 Land Rovers used by the Regiment on desert missions. The pinkies carried both front-and-rear mounted General Purpose Machine Guns with the roll bar mounted with either Mk19 automatic grenade launcher or a Milan anti-tank rocket.

Within only a matter of hours of driving north towards Mosul, the SAS patrol was intercepted by a forty-strong Iraqi force, and four troopers were caught away from their vehicle. Two of the troopers scrambled over to the rest of the patrol, but the other two had to "leg it" into the desert. Affectionately nicknamed Big (in ironic honour of his small stature) and Monty (in acknowledgement of his resemblance to Britain's victor at El Alamein), the two SAS soldiers began a desperate fighting retreat towards the remote desert of west Iraq, where enemy troops were likely to be fewer in number.

Meanwhile, their comrades had "floored" their pinkies to an emergency RZ and had been extracted by helicopter. The captured pinky of Big and Monty was displayed to the world by a jubilant Iraqi Ministry of Information.

Hiding in the desert posed desperate problems for Big and Monty, for it was flat with next-to-no cover. They dared only move in the twilight and the dark. Several times enemy soldiers got on their trail, and Big and Monty had to employ a traditional SAS technique known as "shoot and scoot" – heavy fire followed by a quick departure. They lived off emergency rations of water and food.

By the third night, Big and Monty, in an epic trek, had travelled 60 miles in less than 72 hours, and judged themselves to be far away enough from Iraqi troops to use their SARBE emergency rescue beacon, which sent out an electronic positioning signal to Coalition command centre. Later, as they lay up in the darkness, Big and Monty heard the most welcome sound of all – the deep whumpf-whumpf of an RAF Special Forces flight Chinook coming to the rescue.

APPENDIX I
THE REVOLT IN THE DESERT – SPECIAL FORCE OPERATIONS, ARABIA, 1917

Colonel T.E. Lawrence

When, in 1941, David Stirling conjured the notion of a small mobile force fighting a guerrilla war in the beneficent vastness of the desert he was, to a degree, reinventing the wheel. Colonel Thomas Edward Lawrence of the British Army had been struck by the same idea twenty-three years previously whilst serving as an intelligence officer attached to Arab forces in revolt against Germany's First World War ally, Turkey. Under Lawrence's leadership, Arab fighters fought a tenacious campaign against the Turks' main line of communication in Syria, the Hejaz railway. More even than this, Lawrence's Arab irregulars were able to capture, in July 1917, the important Red Sea port of Aqaba. These were not mere pin-pricks; by tying down thousands of Turkish (and even some German) troops, Lawrence had a profound effect on the Middle Eastern theatre of war.

In other words, T.E. Lawrence achieved what would become the holy grail of special forces operations: for a small outlay, there is a war-winning result.

W E STARTED AN hour before noon on June 19, 1917.
Nasir led us, riding his Ghazala – a camel vaulted and
huge-ribbed as an antique ship; towering a good foot above
the next of our animals, and yet perfectly proportioned,
with a stride like an ostrich's – a lyrical beast, noblest and
best bred of the Howeitat camels, a female of nine remembered dams. Auda was beside him, and I skirmished about
their gravities on Naama, "the hen-ostrich", a racing camel
and my last purchase. Behind me rode my Ageyl, with
Mohammed, the clumsy. Mohammed was now compa-
nioned by Ahmed, another peasant, who had been for six
years living among the Howeitat by force of his thews and
wits – a knowing eager ruffian.

Our present party totalled more than five hundred
strong; and the sight of this jolly mob of hardy, confident
northerners chasing gazelle wildly over the face of the
desert, took from us momentarily all sorry apprehension
as to the issue of our enterprise. We felt it was a rice-night,
and the chiefs of the Abu Tayi came to sup with us.
Afterwards, with the embers of our coffee fire pleasantly
red between us against the cool of this upland north-
country, we sat about on the carpets chatting discursively
of this remote thing and that.

Nasir rolled over on his back, with my glasses, and began
to study the stars, counting aloud first one group and then
another; crying out with surprise at discovering little lights
not noticed by his unaided eye. Auda set us on to talk of
telescopes – of the great ones – and of how man in three
hundred years had so far advanced from his first essay that
now he built glasses as long as a tent, through which he
counted thousands of unknown stars, "And the stars – what
are they?" We slipped into talk of suns beyond suns, sizes
and distance beyond wit. "What will now happen with this
knowledge?" asked Mohammed. "We shall set to, and
many learned and some clever men together will make
glasses as more powerful than ours, as ours than Galileo's;
and yet more hundreds of astronomers will distinguish and
reckon yet more thousands of now unseen stars, mapping
them, and giving each one its name. When we see them all,
there will be no night in heaven."

"Why are the Westerners always wanting all?" provokingly said Auda. "Behind our few stars we can see God, who is not behind your millions." "We want the world's end, Auda." "But that is God's," complained Zaal, half angry. Mohammed would not have his subject turned. "Are there men on these greater worlds?" he asked. "God knows." "And has each the Prophet and heaven and hell?" Auda broke in on him. "Lads, we know our districts, our camels, our women. The excess and the glory are to God. If the end of wisdom is to add star to star our foolishness is pleasing." And then he spoke of money, and distracted their minds till they all buzzed at once. Afterwards he whispered to me that I must get him a worthy gift from Feisal when he won Akaba.

We marched at dawn, and presently Auda told me he was riding ahead to Bair, and would I come? We went fast, and in two hours came upon the place suddenly, under a knoll. Auda had hurried on to visit the tomb of his son Annad, who had been waylaid by five of his Motalga cousins in revenge for Abtan, their champion, slain by Annad in single combat. Auda told me how Annad had ridden at them, one against five, and had died as he should; but it left only little Mohammed between him and childlessness. He had brought me along to hear him greatly lament his dead.

However, as we rode down towards the graves, we were astonished to see smoke wreathing from the ground about the wells. We changed direction sharply, and warily approached the ruins. It seemed there was no one there; but the thick dungcake round the well-brink was charred, and the well itself shattered at the top. The ground was torn and blackened as if by an explosion; and when we looked down the shaft we saw its steyning stripped and split, and many blocks thrown down the bore half choking it and the water in the bottom. I sniffed the air and thought the smell was dynamite.

Auda ran to the next well, in the bed of the valley below the graves; and that, too, was ragged about the head and choked with fallen stones. "This," said he, "is Jazi work." We walked across the valley to the third – the Beni Sakhr – well. It was only a crater of chalk. Zaal arrived, grave at sight of the disaster. We explored the ruined khan, in which were night-old traces of perhaps a hundred horse. There was a fourth well, north of the ruins in the open flat, and to it we went hopelessly, wondering what would become of us if Bair were all destroyed. To our joy it was uninjured.

This was a Jazi well, and its immunity gave strong colour to Auda's theory. We were disconcerted to find the Turks so ready, and began to fear that perhaps they had also raided El Jefer, east of Maan, the wells at which we planned to concentrate before we attacked. Their blocking would be a real embarrassment. Meanwhile, thanks to the fourth well, our situation, though uncomfortable, was not dangerous. Yet its water facilities were altogether insufficient for five hundred camels; so it became imperative to open the least damaged of the other wells – that in the ruins, about whose lip the turf smouldered. Auda and I went off with Nasir to look again at it.

An Ageyli brought us an empty case of Nobel's gelignite, evidently the explosive which the Turks had used. From scars in the ground it was clear that several charges had been fired simultaneously round the well-head, and in the shaft. Staring down it till our eyes were adjusted to its dark, we suddenly saw many niches cut in the shaft less than twenty feet below. Some were still tamped, and had wires hanging down.

Evidently there was a second series of charges, either inefficiently wired, or with a very long time-fuse. Hurriedly we unrolled our bucket-ropes, twined them together, and hung them freely down the middle of the well from a stout cross-pole, the sides being so tottery that the scrape of a rope might have dislodged their blocks. I then found that charges were small, not above three pounds each, and had been wired in series with field telephone cable. But something had gone wrong. Either the Turks had scamped their job or their scouts had seen us coming before they had had time to re-connect.

So we soon had two fit wells, and a clear profit of thirty pounds of enemy gelignite. We determined to stay a week in this fortunate Bair. A third object – to discover the condition of the Jefer wells – was now added to our needs for food, and for news of the state of mind of the tribes between Maan and Akaba. We sent a man to Jefer. We prepared a little caravan of pack-camels with Howeitat brands and sent them across the line to Tafileh with three or four obscure clansmen – people who would never be suspected of association with us. They would buy all the flour they could and bring it back to us in five or six days' time.

As for the tribes about the Akaba road, we wanted their active help against the Turks to carry out the provisional plan we had made at Wejh. Our idea was to advance suddenly from El Jefer, to cross the railway-line and to crown the great pass – Nagb el Shtar – down which the road dipped from the Maan plateau to the red Guweira plain. To hold this pass we should have to capture Aba el Lissan, the large spring at its head, about sixteen miles from Maan; but the garrison was small, and we hoped to overrun it with a rush. We would then be astride the road, whose posts at the end of the week should fall from hunger; though probably before that the hill tribes, hearing of our successful beginning, would join us to wipe them out.

The crux of our plan was the attack on Aba el Lissan, lest the force in Maan have time to sally out, relieve it, and drive us off the head of Shtar. If, as at present, they were only a battalion, they would hardly dare move; and should they let it fall while waiting for reinforcements to arrive, Akaba would surrender to us, and we should be based on the sea and have the advantageous gorge of Itm between us and the enemy. So our insurance for success was to keep Maan careless and weak, not suspecting our malevolent presence in the neighbourhood.

It was never easy for us to keep our movements secret, as we lived by preaching to the local people, and the unconvinced would tell the Turks. Our long march into Wadi Sirhan was known to the enemy, and the most civilian owl could not fail to see that the only fit objective was Akaba. The demolition of Bair (and Jefer, too, for we had it confirmed that the seven wells of Jefer were destroyed) showed that the Turks were to that extent on the alert.

It might be that Jefer really was denied to us; but we were not without hope that there too we should find the technical work of demolition ill-done by these pitiful Turks. Dhaif-Allah, a leading man of the Jazi Howeitat, one who came down to Wejh and swore allegiance, had been present in Jefer when the King's Well was fired by dynamite placed about its lip; and sent us secret word from Maan that he had heard the upper stones clap together and key over the mouth of the well. His conviction was that the shaft was intact, and the clearing of it a few hours' work. We hoped so; and rode away from Bair all in order, on the twenty-eighth of June, to find out.

Quickly we crossed the weird plain of Jefer. Next day by noon we were at the wells. They seemed most thoroughly destroyed; and the fear grew that we might find in them the first check to our scheme of operations, a scheme so much too elaborate that a check might be far reaching.

However, we went to the well – Auda's family property – of which Dhaif-Allah had told us the tale, and began to sound about it. The ground rang hollow under our mallet, and we called for volunteers able to dig and build. Some of the Ageyl came forward, led by the Mirzugi, a capable camel boy of Nasir's. They started with the few tools we had. The rest of us formed a ring round the well-depression and watched them work, singing to them and promising rewards of gold when they had found the water.

It was a hot task in the full glare of the summer sun; for the Jefer plain was of hard mud, flat as the hand, blinding white with salt, and twenty miles across; but time pressed, because if we failed we might have to ride fifty miles in the night to the next well. So we pushed the work by relays at speed through the midday heat, turning into labourers all our amenable fellows. It made easy digging, for the explosion which shifted the stones had loosened the soil.

As they dug and threw out the earth, the core of the well rose up like a tower of rough stones in the centre of the pit. Very carefully we began to take away the ruined head of the pile: difficult work, for the stones had become interlocked in their fall; but this was the better sign, and our spirits rose. Before sunset the workers shouted that there was no more packing soil, that the interstices between the blocks were clear, and that they heard the mud fragments which slipped through splashing many feet below.

Half an hour later came a rush and rumble of stones in the mouth, followed by a heavy splash and yells. We hurried down, and by the Mirzugi's torch saw the well yawning open, no longer a tube, but a deep bottle-shouldered pit, twenty feet across at the bottom, which was black with water and white in the middle with spray where the Ageyli who had been clearing when the key slipped, was striking out lustily in the effort not to drown. Everybody laughed down the well at him, till at last Abdulla lowered him a noose of rope, and we drew him up, very wet and angry, but in no way damaged by his fall.

We rewarded the diggers, and feasted them on a weak camel, which had failed in the march to-day; and then all night we watered, while a squad of Ageyl, with a long chorus, steyned up to ground-level an eight-foot throat of mud and stones. At dawn the earth was stamped in round this, and the well stood complete, as fit in appearance as ever. Only the water was not very much. We worked it the twenty-four hours without rest, and ran it to a cream; and still some of our camels were not satisfied.

From Jefer we took action. Riders went forward into the Dhumaniyeh tents to lead their promised attack against Fuweilah, the blockhouse which covered the head of the pass of Aba el Lissan. Our attack was planned for two days before the weekly caravan which, from Maan, replenished the client garrisons. Starvation would make reduction of these distant places easier, by impressing on them how hopelessly they were cut off from their friends.

We sat in Jefer meanwhile, waiting to hear the fortune of the attack. On its success or failure would depend the direction of our next march. The halt was not unpleasant, for our position had its comic side. We were within sight of Maan, during those minutes of the day in which the mirage did not make eyes and glasses useless; and yet we strolled about admiring our new well-lip in complete security, because the Turkish garrison believed water impossible here or at Bair, and were hugging the pleasant idea that we were now desperately engaged with their cavalry in Sirhan.

I hid under some bushes near the well for hours, against the heat, very lazy, pretending to be asleep, the wide silk sleeve of my pillow-arm drawn over my face as veil against the flies. Auda sat up and talked like a river, telling his best stories in great form. At last I reproved him with a smile, for talking too much and doing too little. He sucked his lips with pleasure of the work to come.

In the following dawn a tired horseman rode into our camp with news that the Dhumaniyeh had fired on the Fuweilah post the afternoon before, as soon as our men had reached them. The surprise had not been quite complete; the Turks manned their dry stone breastworks and drove them off. The crestfallen Arabs drew back into cover, and the enemy, believing it only an ordinary tribal affray had made a mounted sortie upon the nearest encampment.

One old man, six women and seven children were its only occupants. In their anger at finding nothing actively hostile or able-bodied, the troopers smashed up the camp and cut the throats of its helpless ones. The Dhumaniyeh on the hill-tops heard and saw nothing till it was too late; but then, in their fury, they dashed down across the return road of the murderers and cut them off almost to the last man. To complete their vengeance they assaulted the now weakly-garrisoned fort, carried it in the first fierceness of their rush, and took no prisoners.

We were ready saddled; and within ten minutes had loaded and marched for Ghadir el Haj, the first railway station south of Maan, on our direct road for Aba el Lissan. Simultaneously, we detached a small party to cross the railway just above Maan and create a diversion on that side. Especially they were to threaten the great herds of sick camels, casualties of the Palestine front, which the Turks pastured in the Shobek plains till once more fit for service.

We calculated that the news of their Fuweilah disaster would not have reached Maan till the morning, and that they could not drive in these camels (supposing our northern party missed them) and fit out a relief expedition, before nightfall; and if we were then attacking the line at Ghadir el Haj, they would probably divert the relief thither, and so let us move on Akaba unmolested.

With this hope we rode steadily through the flowing mirage till afternoon, when we descended on the line; and, having delivered a long stretch of it from guards and patrols, began on the many bridges of the captured section. The little garrison of Ghadir el Haj sallied out with the valour of ignorance against us, but the heat-haze blinded them, and we drove them off with loss.

They were on the telegraph, and would notify Maan, which beside, could not fail to hear the repeated thuds of our explosive. It was our aim to bring the enemy down upon us in the night; or rather down here, where they would find no people but many broken bridges, for we worked fast and did great damage. The drainage holes in the spandrils held from three to five pounds of gelatine each. We, firing our mines by short fuses, brought down the arch, shattered the pier, and stripped the side walls, in no more than six minutes' work. So we ruined ten bridges and many rails, and finished our explosive.

After dusk, when our departure could not be seen, we rode five miles westward of the line, to cover. There we made fires and baked bread. Our meal, however, was not cooked before three horsemen cantered up to report that a long column of new troops – infantry and guns – had just appeared at Aba el Lissan from Maan. The Dhumaniyeh, disorganized with victory, had had to abandon their ground without fighting. They were at Batra waiting for us. We had lost Aba el Lissan, the blockhouse, the pass, the command of the Akaba road: without a shot being fired.

We learned afterwards that this unwelcome and unwonted vigour on the part of the Turks was accident. A relief battalion had reached Maan that very day. The news of an Arab demonstration against Fuweilah arrived simultaneously; and the battalion, which happened to be formed up ready with its transport in the station yard, to march to barracks, was hurriedly strengthened by a section of pack artillery and some mounted men, and moved straight out as a punitive column to rescue the supposedly besieged post.

They had left Maan in mid-morning and marched gently along the motor road, the men sweating in the heat of this south country after their native Caucasian snows, and drinking thirstily of every spring. From Aba el Lissan they climbed uphill towards the old blockhouse, which was deserted except for the silent vultures flying above its walls in slow uneasy rings. The battalion commander feared lest the sight be too much for his young troops, and led them back to the roadside spring of Aba el Lissan, in its serpentine narrow valley, where they camped all night in peace about the water.

Such news shook us into quick life. We threw our baggage across our camels on the instant and set out over the rolling downs of this end of the tableland of Syria. Our hot bread was in our hands, and, as we ate, there mingled with it the taste of the dust of our large force crossing the valley bottoms, and some taint of the strange keen smell of the wormwood which overgrew the slopes. In the breathless air of these evenings in the hills, after the long days of summer, everything struck very acutely on the senses; and when marching in a great column, as we were, the front camels kicked up the aromatic dust-laden branches of the shrubs, whose scent-particles rose into the air and hung in a long mist, making fragrant the road of those behind.

The slopes were clean with the sharpness of wormwood, and the hollows oppressive with the richness of their stronger, more luxuriant growths. Our night-passage might have been through a planted garden, and these varieties part of the unseen beauty of successive banks of flowers. The noises too were very clear. Auda broke out singing, away in front, and the men joined in from time to time, with the greatness, the catch at heart, of an army moving into battle.

We rode all night, and when dawn came were dismounting on the crest of the hills between Batra and Aba el Lissan, with a wonderful view westwards over the green and gold Guweira plain, and beyond it to the ruddy mountains hiding Akaba and the sea. Gasim abu Dumeik, head of the Dhumaniyeh, was waiting anxiously for us, surrounded by his hard-bitten tribesmen, their grey strained faces flecked with the blood of the fighting yesterday. There was a deep greeting for Auda and Nasir. We made hurried plans, and scattered to the work, knowing we could not go forward to Akaba with this battalion in possession of the pass. Unless we dislodged it, our two months' hazard and effort would fail before yielding even first fruits.

Fortunately the poor handling of the enemy gave us an unearned advantage. They slept on, in the valley, while we crowned the hills in wide circle about them unobserved. We began to snipe them steadily in their positions under the slopes and rock-faces by the water, hoping to provoke them out and up the hill in a charge against us. Meanwhile, Zaal rode away with our horsemen and cut the Maan telegraph and telephone in the plain.

This went on all day. It was terribly hot – hotter than ever before I had felt it in Arabia – and the anxiety and constant moving made it hard for us. Some even of the tough tribesmen broke down under the cruelty of the sun, and crawled or had to be thrown under rocks to recover in their shade. We ran up and down to supply our lack of numbers by mobility, ever looking over the long ranges of hill for a new spot from which to counter this or that Turkish effort. The hill-sides were steep, and exhausted our breath, and the grasses twined like little hands about our ankles as we ran, and plucked us back. The sharp reefs of limestone which cropped out over the ridges tore our feet, and long before evening the more energetic men were leaving a rusty print upon the ground with every stride.

Our rifles grew so hot with sun and shooting that they seared our hands; and we had to be grudging of our rounds, considering every shot, and spending great pains to make it sure. The rocks on which we flung ourselves for aim were burning, so that they scorched our breasts and arms, from which later the skin drew off in ragged sheets. The present smart made us thirst. Yet even water was rare with us; we could not afford men to fetch enough from Batra, and if all could not drink, it was better that none should.

We consoled ourselves with knowledge that the enemy's enclosed valley would be hotter than our open hills; also that they were Turks, men of white meat, little apt for warm weather. So we clung to them, and did not let them move or mass or sortie out against us cheaply. They could do nothing valid in return. We were no targets for their rifles, since we moved with speed, eccentrically. Also we were able to laugh at the little mountain guns which they fired up at us. The shells passed over our heads, to burst behind us in the air; and yet, of course, for all that they could see from their hollow place, fairly amongst us above the hostile summits of the hill.

Just after noon I had a heat-stroke, or so pretended, for I was dead weary of it all, and cared no longer how it went. So I crept into a hollow where there was a trickle of thick water in a muddy cup of the hills, to suck some moisture off its dirt through the filter of my sleeve. Nasir joined me, panting like a winded animal, with his cracked and bleeding lips shrunk apart in his distress; and old Auda appeared, striding powerfully, his eyes bloodshot and staring, his knotty face working with excitement.

He grinned with malice when he saw us lying there, spread out to find coolness under the bank, and croaked at me harshly, "Well, how is it with the Howeitat? All talk and no work?" "By God, indeed," spat I back again, for I was angry with every one and with myself, "they shoot a lot and hit a little." Auda almost pale with rage, and trembling, tore his headcloth off and threw it on the ground beside me. Then he ran back up the hill like a madman, shouting to the men in his dreadful strained and rustling voice.

They came together to him, and after a moment scattered away down hill. I feared things were going wrong, and struggled to where he stood alone on the hill-top, glaring at the enemy; but all he would say to me was, "Get your camel if you want to see the old man's work." Nasir called for his camel and we mounted.

The Arabs passed before us into a little sunken place, which rose to a low crest; and we knew that the hill beyond went down in a facile slope to the main valley of Aba el Lissan, somewhat below the spring. All our four hundred camel men were here tightly collected, just out of sight of the enemy. We rode to their head, and asked the Shimt what it was and where the horsemen had gone.

He pointed over the ridge to the next valley above us, and said, "With Auda there"; and as he spoke yells and shots poured up in a sudden torrent from beyond the crest. We kicked our camels furiously to the edge, to see our fifty horsemen coming down the last slope into the main valley like a run-away, at full gallop, shooting from the saddle. As we watched, two or three went down, but the rest thundered forward at marvellous speed, and the Turkish infantry, huddled together under the cliff ready to cut their desperate way out towards Maan in the first dusk, began to sway in and out, and finally broke before the rush, adding their flight to Auda's charge.

Nasir screamed at me, "Come on," with his bloody mouth; and we plunged our camels madly over the hill, and down towards the head of the fleeing enemy. The slope was not too steep for a camel-gallop, but steep enough to make their pace terrific, and their course uncontrollable; yet the Arabs were able to extend to right and left and to shoot into the Turkish brown. The Turks had been too bound up in the terror of Auda's furious charge against their rear to notice us as we came over the eastward slope: so we also took them by surprise and in the flank; and a charge of ridden camels going nearly thirty miles an hour was irresistible.

The Howeitat were very fierce, for the slaughter of their women on the day before had been a new and horrible side of warfare suddenly revealed to them. So there were only a hundred and sixty prisoners, many of them wounded; and three hundred dead and dying were scattered over the open valleys.

A few of the enemy got away, the gunners on their teams, and some mounted men and officers with their Jazi guides. Mohammed el Dheilan chased them for three miles into Mreigha, hurling insults as he rode, that they might know him and keep out of his way. The feud of Auda and his cousins had never applied to Mohammed, the political-minded, who showed friendship to all men of his tribe when he was alone to do so. Among the fugitives was Dhaif-Allah, who had done us the good turn about the King's Well at Jefer.

Auda came swinging up on foot, his eyes glazed over with the rapture of battle, and the words bubbling with incoherent speed from his mouth. "Work, work, where are words, work, bullets, Abu Tayi" . . . and he held up his shattered field-glasses, his pierced pistol-holster, and his leather sword-scabbard cut to ribbons. He had been the target of a volley which had killed his mare under him, but the six bullets through his clothes had left him scathless.

He told me later, in strict confidence, that thirteen years before he had bought an amulet Koran for one hundred and twenty pounds and had not since been wounded. Indeed, Death had avoided his face, and gone scurvily about killing brothers, sons and followers. The book was a Glasgow reproduction, costing eighteenpence; but Auda's deadliness did not let people laugh at his superstition.

He was wildly pleased with the fight, most of all because he had confounded me and shown what his tribe could do. Mohammed was wroth with us for a pair of fools, calling me worse than Auda, since I had insulted him by words like flung stones to provoke the folly which had nearly killed us all; though it had killed only two of us, one Rueili and one Sherari.

It was, of course, a pity to lose any one of our men, but time was of importance to us, and so imperative was the need of dominating Maan, to shock the little Turkish garrisons between us and the sea into surrender, that I would have willingly lost much more than two. On occasions like this Death justified himself and was cheap.

Meanwhile our Arabs had plundered the Turks, their baggage train, and their camp; and soon after moonrise, Auda came to us and said that we must move. It angered Nasir and myself. To-night there was a dewy west wind blowing, and at Aba el Lissan's four thousand feet, after the heat and burning passion of the day, its damp chill struck very sharply on our wounds and bruises. The spring itself was a thread of silvery water in a runnel of pebbles across delightful turf, green and soft, on which we lay, wrapped in our cloaks, wondering if something to eat were worth preparing: for we were subject at the moment to the physical shame of success, a reaction of victory, when it became clear that nothing was worth doing, and that nothing worthy had been done.

Auda insisted. Partly it was superstition – he feared the

newly dead around us; partly lest the Turks return in force; partly lest other clans of the Howeitat take us, lying there broken and asleep. Some were his blood enemies; others might say they came to help our battle, and in the darkness thought we were Turks and fired blindly. So we roused ourselves, and jogged the sorry prisoners into line.

Most had to walk. Some twenty camels were dead or dying from wounds which they had got in the charge, and others were over weak to take a double burden. The rest were loaded with an Arab and a Turk; but some of the Turkish wounded were too hurt to hold themselves on pillion. In the end we had to leave about twenty on the thick grass beside the rivulet, where at least they would not die of thirst, though there was little hope of life or rescue for them.

Nasir set himself to beg blankets for these abandoned men, who were half-naked; and while the Arabs packed, I went off down the valley where the fight had been, to see if the dead had any clothing they could spare. But the Beduin had been beforehand with me, and had stripped them to the skin. Such was their point of honour.

To an Arab an essential part of the triumph of victory was to wear the clothes of an enemy; and next day we saw our force transformed (as to the upper half) into a Turkish force, each man in a soldier's tunic, for this was a battalion straight from home, very well found and dressed in new uniforms.

In the end our little army was ready, and wound slowly up the height and beyond into a hollow sheltered from the wind; and there, while the tired men slept, we dictated letters to the Sheikhs of the coastal Howeitat, telling them of the victory, that they might invest their nearest Turks, and hold them till we came. We had been kind to one of the captured officers, a policeman despised by his regular colleagues, and him we persuaded to be our Turkish scribe to the commandants of Guweira, Kethera and Hadra, the three posts between us and Akaba, telling them that if our blood was not hot we took prisoners, and that prompt surrender would ensure their good treatment and safe delivery to Egypt.

This lasted till dawn, and then Auda marshalled us for the road, and led us up the last mile of soft heath-clad valley between the rounded hills. It was intimate and home-like till the last green bank; when suddenly we realized it was the last, and beyond lay nothing but clear air. The lovely change this time checked me with amazement; and afterwards, however often we came, there was always a catch of eagerness in the mind, a pricking forward of the camel and straightening up to see again over the crest into openness.

Shtar hill-side swooped away below us for hundreds and hundreds of feet, in curves like bastions, against which summer morning clouds were breaking; and from its foot opened the new earth of the Guweira plain. Aba el Lissan's rounded limestone breasts were covered with soil and heath, green, well watered. Guweira was a map of pink sand, brushed over with streaks of watercourses, in a mantle of scrub; and, out of this, and bounding this, towered islands and cliffs of glowing sandstone, wind-scarped and rain-furrowed, tinted celestially by the early sun.

After days of travel on the plateau in prison valleys, to meet this brink of freedom was a rewarding vision, like a window in the wall of life. We walked down the whole zigzag pass of Shtar, to feel its excellence, for on our camels we rocked too much with sleep to dare see anything. At the bottom the animals found a matted thorn which gave their jaws pleasure; we in front made a halt, rolled on to sand soft as a couch, and incontinently slept.

Auda came. We pleaded that it was for mercy upon our broken prisoners. He replied that they alone would die of exhaustion if we rode, but if we dallied, both parties might die: for truly there was now little water and no food. However, we could not help it, and stopped that night short of Guweira, after only fifteen miles. At Guweira lay Sheikh ibn Jad, balancing his policy to come down with the stronger; and to-day we were the stronger, and the old fox was ours. He met us with honeyed speeches. The hundred and twenty Turks of the garrison were his prisoners; we agreed with him to carry them at his leisure and their ease to Akaba.

To-day was the fourth of July. Time pressed us, for we

were hungry, and Akaba was still far ahead behind two defences. The nearer post, Kethira, stubbornly refused parley with our flags. Their cliff commanded the valley – a strong place which it might be costly to take. We assigned the honour, in irony, to ibn Jad and his unwearied men, advising him to try it after dark. He shrank, made difficulties, pleaded the full moon; but we cut hardly into this excuse, promising that to-night for awhile there should be no moon. By my diary there was an eclipse. Duly it came, and the Arabs forced the post without loss, while the superstitious soldiers were firing rifles and clanging copper pots to rescue their threatened satellite.

Reassured we set out across the strand-like plain. Niazi Bey, the Turkish battalion commander, was Nasir's guest, to spare him the humiliation of Beduin contempt. Now he sidled up by me, and, his swollen eyelids and long nose betraying the moroseness of the man, began to complain that an Arab had insulted him with a gross Turkish word. I apologized, pointing out that it must have been learnt from the mouth of one of his Turkish fellow-governors. The Arab was repaying Caesar.

Caesar, not satisfied, pulled from his pocket a wizened hunch of bread to ask if it was fit breakfast for a Turkish officer. My heavenly twins, foraging in Guweira, had bought, found, or stolen a Turkish soldier's ration loaf; and we had quartered it. I said it was not breakfast, but lunch and dinner, and perhaps to-morrow's meals as well. I, a staff officer of the British Army (not less well fed than the Turkish) had eaten mine with the relish of victory. It was defeat, not bread, which stuck in his gullet, and I begged him not to blame me for the issue of a battle imposed on both our honours.

The narrows of Wadi Itm increased in intricate ruggedness as we penetrated deeper. Below Kethira we found Turkish post after Turkish post, empty. Their men had been drawn in to Khadra, the entrenched position (at the mouth of Itm), which covered Akaba so well against a landing from the sea. Unfortunately for them the enemy had never imagined attack from the interior, and of all their great works not one trench or post faced inland. Our advance from so new a direction threw them into panic.

In the afternoon we were in contact with this main position, and heard from the local Arabs that the subsidiary posts about Akaba had been called in or reduced, so that only a last three hundred men barred us from the sea. We dismounted for a council, to hear that the enemy were resisting firmly, in bomb-proof trenches with a new artesian well. Only it was rumoured that they had little food.

No more had we. It was a deadlock. Our council swayed this way and that. Arguments bickered between the prudent and the bold. Tempers were short and bodies restless in the incandescent gorge whose granite peaks radiated the sun in a myriad shimmering points of light, and into the depths of whose tortuous bed no wind could come to relieve the slow saturation of the air with heat.

Our numbers had swollen double. So thickly did the men crowd in the narrow space, and press about us, that we broke up our council twice or thrice, partly because it was not good they should overhear us wrangling, partly because in the sweltering confinement our unwashed smells offended us. Through our heads the heavy pulses throbbed like clocks.

We sent the Turks summonses, first by white flag, and then by Turkish prisoners, but they shot at both. This inflamed our Beduin, and while we were yet deliberating a sudden wave of them burst up on to the rocks and sent a hail of bullets spattering against the enemy. Nasir ran out barefoot, to stop them, but after ten steps on the burning ground screeched for sandals; while I crouched in my atom of shadow, too wearied of these men (whose minds all wore my livery) to care who regulated their febrile impulses.

We had a third try to communicate with the Turks, by means of a little conscript, who said that he understood how to do it. We walked down close to the trenches with him, and sent in for an officer to speak with us. After some hesitation this was achieved, and we explained the situation on the road behind us; our growing forces; and our short control over their tempers. The upshot was that they promised to surrender at daylight. So we had another sleep (an event rare enough to chronicle) in spite of our thirst.

Next day at dawn fighting broke out on all sides, for hundreds more hill-men, again doubling our number, had come in the night; and, not knowing the arrangement, began shooting at the Turks, who defended themselves. Nasir went out, with ibn Dgheithir and his Ageyl marching in fours, down the open bed of the valley. Our men ceased fire. The Turks then stopped, for their rank and file had no more fight in them and no more food, and thought we were well supplied. So the surrender went off quietly after all.

As the Arabs rushed in to plunder I noticed an engineer in grey uniform, with red beard and puzzled blue eyes; and spoke to him in German. He was the well-borer, and knew no Turkish. Recent doings had amazed him, and he begged me to explain what we meant. I said that we were a rebellion of the Arabs against the Turks. This, it took him time to appreciate. He wanted to know who was our leader. I said the Sherif of Mecca. He supposed he would be sent to Mecca. I said rather to Egypt. He inquired the price of sugar, and when I replied, "cheap and plentiful", he was glad.

The loss of his belongings he took philosophically, but was sorry for the well, which a little work would have finished as his monument. He showed me where it was, with the pump only half-built. By pulling on the sludge bucket we drew enough delicious clear water to quench our thirsts. Then we raced through a driving sandstorm down to Akaba, four miles further, and splashed into the sea on July the sixth, just two months after our setting out from Wejh.

Vessels steamed up the Gulf of Akaba. Feisal landed, and with him Jaafar, his staff, and Joyce, the fairy godmother. There came the armoured cars, Goslett, Egyptian labourers and thousands of troops. To repair the six weeks' peace, Falkenhayn had been down to advise the Turks, and his fine intelligence made them worthier our opposition. Maan was a special command, under Behjet, the old G.O.C. Sinai. He had six thousand infantry, a regiment of cavalry and mounted infantry, and had entrenched Maan till it was impregnable according to the standard of manœuvre war. A flight of aeroplanes operated daily thence. Great supply dumps had been collected.

By now the Turkish preparations were complete; they began to move, disclosing that their objective was Guweira, the best road for Akaba. Two thousand infantry pushed out to Aba el Lissan, and fortified it. Cavalry kept the outskirts, to contain a possible Arab counter-stroke from the Wadi Musa side.

This nervousness was our cue. We would play with them and provoke them to go for us in Wadi Musa, where the natural obstacles were so tremendous that the human defending factor might behave as badly as it liked, and yet hold the place against attack.

To bait the hook, the men of neighbouring Delagha were set busy. The Turks, full of spirit, put in a counter-stroke, and suffered sharply. We rubbed in to the peasantry of Wadi Musa the rich booty now enjoyed by their rivals of Delagha. Maulud, the old war-horse, went up with his mule-mounted regiment, and quartered himself among the famous ruins of Petra. The encouraged Liathena, under their one-eyed sheikh, Khalil, began to foray out across the plateau, and to snap up by twos and threes Turkish riding or transport animals, together with the rifles of their occasional guards. This went on for weeks, while the irritated Turks grew hotter and hotter.

We could also prick the Turks into discomfort by asking General Salmond for his promised long-distance air raid on Maan. As it was difficult, Salmond had chosen Stent, with other tried pilots of Rabegh or Wejh, and told them to do their best. They had experience of forced landing on desert surfaces, and could pick out an unknown destination across unmapped hills; Stent spoke Arabic perfectly. The flight had to be air-contained, but its commander was full of resource and display, like other bundles of nerves, who, to punish themselves, did outrageous things. On this occasion he ordered low flying, to make sure the aim; and profited by reaching Maan, and dropping thirty-two bombs in and about the unprepared station. Two bombs into the barracks killed thirty-five men and wounded fifty. Eight struck the engine-shed, heavily damaging the plant and stock. A bomb in the General's kitchen finished his cook and his breakfast. Four fell on the aerodrome. Despite the shrapnel our pilots and engines returned safely to their temporary landing ground at Kuntilla above Akaba.

That afternoon they patched the machines, and after dark slept under their wings. In the following dawn they were off once more, three of them this time, to Aba el Lissan, where the sight of the great camp had made Stent's mouth water. They bombed the horse lines and stampeded the animals, visited the tents and scattered the Turks. As on the day before, they flew low and were much hit, but not fatally. Long before noon they were back in Kuntilla.

Stent looked over the remaining petrol and bombs, and decided they were enough for one more effort. So he gave directions to everyone to look for the battery which had troubled them in the morning. They started in the midday heat. Their loads were so heavy they could get no height, and therefore came blundering over the crest behind Aba el Lissan, and down the valley at about three hundred feet. The Turks, always somnolent at noon, were taken completely by surprise. Thirty bombs were dropped: one silenced the battery, the others killed dozens of men and animals. Then the lightened machines soared up and home to El Arish. The Arabs rejoiced; the Turks were seriously alarmed. Behjet Pasha set his men to digging shelters, and when his aeroplanes had been repaired, he disposed them innocuously about the plateau for camp defence.

By air we had perturbed the Turks; by irritative raids we were luring them towards a wrong objective. Our third resource to ruin their offensive was to hinder the railway, whose need would make them split up the striking force on defensive duties. Accordingly we arranged many demolitions for mid-September.

I decided also to revive the old idea of mining a train. Something more vigorous and certain than automatic mines was indicated, and I had imagined a direct firing, by electricity, of a charge under the locomotive. The British sappers encouraged me to try, especially General Wright, the chief engineer in Egypt, whose experience took a sporting interest in my irregularities. He sent me the recommended tools: an exploder and some insulated cable. With them I went on board H.M.S. *Humber*, our new guardship, and introduced myself to Captain Snagge, in command.

Snagge was fortunate in his ship, which had been built for Brazil, and was much more comfortably furnished than British monitors; and we were doubly fortunate in him and in this, for he was the spirit of hospitality. His inquiring nature took interest in the shore, and saw the comic side even of our petty disasters. To tell him the story of a failure was to laugh at it, and always for a good story he gave me a hot bath, and tea with civilized trappings, free from every suspicion of blown sand. His kindness and help served us in lieu of visits to Egypt for repairs, and enabled us to hammer on against the Turks through month after month of feckless disappointment.

The exploder was in a formidable locked white box, very heavy. We split it open, found a ratchet handle, and pushed it down without harming the ship. The wire was heavy rubber-insulated cable. We cut it in half, fastened the ends to screw terminals on the box, and transmitted shocks to one another convincingly. It worked.

I fetched detonators. We stuffed the free ends of the cable into one and pumped the handle; nothing followed. We tried again and again ineffectually, grieving over it. At last Snagge rang his bell for the gunner warrant officer who knew all about circuits. He suggested special electric detonators. The ship carried six, and gave me three of them. We joined one up with our box, and when the handle was crashed down it popped off beautifully. So I felt that I knew all about it and turned to arrange the details of the raid.

Of targets, the most promising and easiest-reached seemed Mudowwara, a water station eighty miles south of Maan. A smashed train there would embarrass the enemy. For men, I would have the tried Howeitat; and, at the same time, the expedition would test the three Haurani peasants whom I had added to my personal followers. In view of the new importance of the Hauran, there was need for us to learn its dialect, the construction and jealousies of its clan framework, and its names and roads.

These three fellows, Rahail, Assaf and Hemeid, would teach me their home affairs imperceptibly, as we rode on business, chatting.

To make sure of the arrested train required guns and machine-guns. For the first, why not trench-mortars? for the second, Lewis guns? Accordingly, Egypt chose two forceful sergeant-instructors from the Army School at Zeitun, to teach squads of Arabs in Akaba how to use such things. Snagge gave them quarters in his ship, since we had, as yet, no convenient English camp ashore.

Their names may have been Yells and Brooke, but became Lewis and Stokes after their jealously loved tools. Lewis was an Australian, long, thin and sinuous, his supple body lounging in unmilitary curves. His hard face, arched eyebrows, and predatory nose set off the peculiarly Australian air of reckless willingness and capacity to do something very soon. Stokes was a stocky English yeoman, workman-like and silent; always watching for an order to obey.

Lewis, full of suggestion, emerged bursting with delight at what had been well done whenever a thing happened. Stokes never offered opinion until after action, when he would stir his cap reflectively, and painstakingly recount the mistakes he must next time avoid. Both were admirable men. In a month, without common language or interpreter, they got on terms with their classes and taught them their weapons with reasonable precision. More was not required, for an empirical habit appeared to agree with the spirit of our haphazard raids better than complete scientific knowledge.

As we worked at the organization of the raid, our appetites rose. Mudowwara station sounded vulnerable. Three hundred men might rush it suddenly. That would be an achievement, for its deep well was the only one in the dry sector below Maan. Without its water, the train service across the gap would become uneconomic in load.

Lewis, the Australian, at such an ambitious moment, said that he and Stokes would like to be of my party. A new, attractive idea. With them we should feel sure of our technical detachments, whilst attacking a garrisoned place.

Also, the sergeants wanted to go very much, and their good work deserved reward. They were warned that their experiences might not at the moment seem altogether joyful. There were no rules; and there could be no mitigation of the marching, feeding, and fighting, inland. If they went they would lose their British Army comfort and privilege, to share and share with the Arabs (except in booty!) and suffer exactly their hap in food and discipline. If anything went wrong with me, they, not speaking Arabic, would be in a tender position.

Lewis replied that he was looking for just this strangeness of life. Stokes supposed that if we did it, he could. So they were lent two of my best camels (their saddle-bags tight with bully-beef and biscuits) and on the seventh of September 1917, we went together up Wadi Itm, to collect our Howeitat from Auda in Guweira.

For the sergeants' sake, to harden them gently, things were made better than my word. We marched very easily for to-day, while we were our own masters. Neither had been on a camel before, and there was risk that the fearful heat of the naked granite walls of Itm might knock them out before the trip had properly begun. September was a bad month. A few days before, in the shade of the palm gardens of Akaba beach, the thermometer had shown a hundred and twenty degrees. So we halted for midday under a cliff, and in the evening rode only ten miles to camp for the night.

Next day, in the early heat, we were near Guweira, comfortably crossing the sanded plain of restful pink with its grey-green undergrowth, when there came a droning through the air. Quickly we drove the camels off the open road into the bush-speckled ground, where their irregular colouring would not be marked by the enemy airmen; for the loads of blasting gelatine, my favourite and most powerful explosive, and the many ammonal-filled shells of the Stokes gun would be ill neighbours in a bombing raid. We waited there, soberly, in the saddle, while our camels grazed the little which was worth eating in the scrub, until the aeroplane had circled twice about the rock of Guweira in front of us, and planted three loud bombs.

The aeroplane was the quaint regulator of public business in the Guweira camp. The Arabs, up as ever before dawn, waited for it: Mastur set a slave on the crag's peak to sound the first warning. When its constant hour drew near the Arabs would saunter, chatting in parade of carelessness, towards the rock. Arrived beneath it, each man climbed to the ledge he favoured. After Mastur would climb the bevy of his slaves, with his coffee on the brazier, and his carpet. In a shaded nook he and Auda would sit and talk till the little shiver of excitement tightened up and down the crowded ledges when first was heard the song of the engine over the pass of Shtar.

Every one pressed back against the wall and waited stilly while the enemy circled vainly above the strange spectacle of this crimson rock banded with thousands of gaily-dressed Arabs, nesting like ibises in every cranny of its face. The aeroplane dropped three bombs, or four bombs, or five bombs, according to the day of the week. Their bursts of dense smoke sat on the sage-green plain compactly like cream-puffs; writhing for minutes in the windless air before they slowly spread and faded. Though we knew there was no menace in it, yet we could not but catch our breath when the sharp-growing cry of the falling bombs came through the loud engine overhead.

Gladly we left the noise and heart-burning of Guweira. So soon as we had lost our escort of flies we halted; indeed there was no need of haste, and the two unfortunate fellows with me were tasting of such heat as they had never known, for the stifling air was like a metal mask over our faces. It was admirable to see them struggle not to speak of it, that they might keep the spirit of the Akaba undertaking to endure as firmly as the Arabs; but by this silence the sergeants went far past their bond. It was ignorance of Arabic which made them so superfluously brave, for the Arabs themselves were loud against the tyrannous sun and the breathlessness; but the test-effort was wholesome; and, for effect, I played about, seeming to enjoy myself.

In the late afternoon we marched farther and stopped for the night under a thick screen of tamarisk trees. The camp was very beautiful, for behind us rose a cliff, perhaps four hundred feet in height, a deep red in the level sunset. Under

our feet was spread a floor of buff-coloured mud, as hard
and muffled as wood-paving, flat like a lake for half a mile
each way; and on a low ridge to one side of it stood the grove
of tamarisk stems of brown wood, edged with a sparse and
dusty fringe of green, which had been faded by drought and
sunshine till it was nearly of the silvered grey below the
olive leaves about Les Baux, when a wind from the river-
mouth rustled up the valley-grass and made the trees turn
pale.

We were riding for Rumm, the northern water of the
Beni Atiyeh: a place which stirred my thought, as even the
unsentimental Howeitat had told me it was lovely. The
morrow would be new with our entry to it; but very early,
while the stars were yet shining, I was roused by Aid, the
humble Harithi Sherif accompanying us. He crept to me,
and said in a chilled voice, "Lord, I am gone blind." I made
him lie down, and felt that he shivered as if cold; but all he
could tell me was that in the night, waking up, there had
been no sight, only pain in his eyes. The sun-blink had
burned them out.

Day was still young as we rode between two great pikes of
sandstone to the foot of a long, soft slope poured down from
the domed hills in front of us. It was tamarisk covered: the
beginning of the Valley of Rumm, they said. We looked up
on the left to a long wall of rock, sheering in like a thousand-
foot wave towards the middle of the valley; whose other arc,
to the right, was an opposing line of steep, red broken hills.
We rode up the slope, crashing our way through the brittle
undergrowth.

As we went, the brushwood grouped itself into thickets
whose massed leaves took on a stronger tint of green, the
purer for their contrasted setting in plots of open sand of a
cheerful delicate pink. The ascent became gentle, till the
valley was a confined tilted plain. The hills on the right
grew taller and sharper, a fair counterpart of the other side
which straightened itself to one massive rampart of redness.
They drew together until only two miles divided them; and
then, towering gradually till their parallel parapets must
have been a thousand feet above us, ran forward in an
avenue for miles.

They were not unbroken walls of rock, but were built sectionally, in crags like gigantic buildings, along the two sides of their street. Deep alleys, fifty feet across, divided the crags, whose planes were smoothed by the weather into huge apses and bays, and enriched with surface fretting and fracture, like design. Caverns high up on the precipice were round like windows; others near the foot gaped like doors. Dark stains ran down the shadowed front for hundreds of feet, like accidents of use. The cliffs were striated vertically, in their granular rock; whose main order stood on two hundred feet of broken stone deeper in colour and harder in texture. This plinth did not, like the sandstone, hang in folds like cloth; but chipped itself into loose courses of scree, horizontal as the footings of a wall.

The crags were capped in nests of domes, less hotly red than the body of the hill; rather grey and shallow. They gave the finishing semblance of Byzantine architecture to this irresistible place, this processional way greater than imagination. The Arab armies would have been lost in the length and breadth of it, and within the walls a squadron of aeroplanes could have wheeled in formation. Our little caravan grew self-conscious, and fell dead quiet, afraid and ashamed to flaunt its smallness in the presence of the stupendous hills.

For hours the perspectives grew greater and more magnificent in ordered design, till a gap in the cliff-face opened on our right to a new wonder. The gap, perhaps three hundred yards across, was a crevice in such a wall; and led to an amphitheatre, oval in shape, shallow in front, and long-lobed right and left. The walls were precipices, like all the walls of Rumm; but appeared greater, for the pit lay in the very heart of a ruling hill, and its smallness made the besetting heights seem overpowering.

The sun had sunk behind the western wall, leaving the pit in shadow; but its dying glare flooded with startling red the wings each side of the entry, and the fiery bulk of the farther wall across the great valley. The pit-floor was of damp sand, darkly wooded with shrubs, while about the feet of all the cliffs lay boulders greater than houses, sometimes, indeed, like fortresses which had crashed down from the sheer heights above. In front of us a path, pale with use, zig-zagged up the cliff-plinth to the point from which the main face rose, and there it turned precariously southward along a shallow ledge outlined by occasional leafy trees. From between these trees, in hidden crannies of the rock, issued strange cries; the echoes, turned into music, of the voices of the Arabs watering camels at the springs which there flowed out three hundred feet above ground.

Mohammed turned into the amphitheatre's left-hand lobe. At its far end Arab ingenuity had cleared a space under an overhanging rock: there we unloaded and settled down. The dark came upon us quickly in this high prisoned place; and we felt the water-laden air cold against our sunburnt skin. The Howeitat who had looked after the loads of explosive collected their camel drove, and led them with echo-testing shouts up the hill path to water against their early return to Guweira. We lit fires and cooked rice to add to the sergeants' bully-beef, while my coffee men prepared for the visitors who would come to us.

The Arabs in the tents outside the hollow of the springs had seen us enter, and were not slow to learn our news. In an hour we had the head men of the Darausha, Zelebani, Zuweida and Togatga clans about us; and there mounted great talk, none too happy. Aid, the Sherif, was too cast down in heart by his blindness to lift the burden of entertainment from my shoulders; and a work of such special requirements was not to be well done by me alone.

At dawn on the sixteenth of September 1917 we rode out from Rumm. Aid, the blind Sherif, insisted on coming, despite his lost sight, saying he could ride, if he could not shoot, and that if God prospered us he would take leave from Feisal in the flush of the success, and go home, not too sorry, to the blank life which would be left. Zaal led his twenty-five Nowasera, a clan of Auda's Arabs who called themselves my men, and were famous the desert over for their saddle-camels. My hard riding tempted them to my company.

Old Motlog el Awar, owner of el Jedha, the finest she-camel in North Arabia, rode her in our van. We looked at her with proud or greedy eyes, according to our relationship with him. My Ghazala was taller and more grand, with a faster trot, but too old to be galloped. However she was the only other animal in the party, or, indeed, in this desert, to be matched with the Jedha, and my honour was increased by her dignity.

The rest of our party strayed like a broken necklace. No one group would ride or speak with another, and I passed back and forth all day like a shuttle, talking first to one lowering sheikh, and then to another, striving to draw them together, so that before a cry to action came there might be solidarity. As yet they agreed only in not hearing any word from Zaal as to the order of our march; though he was admitted the most intelligent warrior, and the most experienced. For my private part he was the only one to be trusted farther than eyesight. Of the others, it seemed to me that neither their words not their counsels, perhaps not their rifles, were sure.

We put our mid-day halt in a fertile place, where the late spring rain, falling on a sandy talus, had brought up a thick tufting of silvery grass which our camels loved. The weather was mild, perfect as an August in England, and we lingered in great content, recovered at last from the bickering appetites of the days before the start, and from that slight rending of nerve inevitable when leaving even a temporary settlement. Man, in our circumstances, took root so soon.

Late in the day we rode again, winding downhill in a narrow valley between moderate sandstone walls, till before sunset we were out on another flat of laid yellow mud, like that which had been so wonderful a prelude to Rumm's glory. By its edge we camped. My care had borne fruit, for we settled in only three parties, by bright fires of crackling, flaring tamarisk. At one supped my men; at the second Zaal; at the third the other Howeitat; and late at night, when all the chiefs had been well adjusted with gazelle meat and hot bread, it became possible to bring them to my neutral fire, and discuss sensibly our course for the morrow.

It seemed that about sunset we should water at Mudowwara well, two or three miles this side of the station, in a covered valley. Then, in the early night, we might go forward to examine the station and see if, in our weakness, we might yet attempt some stroke against it. I held strongly to this (against the common taste) for it was by so much the most critical point of the line. The Arabs could not see it, since their minds did not hold a picture of the long, linked Turkish front with its necessitous demands. However, we had reached internal harmony, and scattered confidently to sleep.

In the morning we delayed to eat again, having only six hours of march before us; and then pushed across the mud-flat to a plain of firm limestone rag, carpeted with brown, weather-blunted flint. This was succeeded by low hills, with occasional soft beds of sand, under the steeper slopes where eddying winds had dropped their dust. Through these we rode up shallow valleys to a crest; and then by like valleys down the far side, whence we issued abruptly, from dark, tossed stone-heaps into the sun-steeped wideness of a plain. Across it an occasional low dune stretched a drifting line.

We had made our noon halt at the first entering of the broken country; and, rightly, in the late afternoon came to the well. It was an open pool, a few yards square, in a hollow valley of large stone-slabs and flint and sand. The stagnant water looked uninviting. Over its face lay a thick mantle of green slime, from which swelled curious bladder-islands of floating fatty pink. The Arabs explained that the Turks had thrown dead camels into the pool to make the water foul; but that time had passed and the effect was grown faint. It would have been fainter had the criterion of their effort been my taste.

Yet it was all the drink we should get up here unless we took Mudowwara, so we set to and filled our waterskins. One of the Howeitat, while helping in this, slipped off the wet edge into the water. Its green carpet closed oilily over his head and hid him for an instant; then he came up, gasping vigorously, and scrambled out amid our laughter, leaving behind him a black hole in the scum from which a stench of old meat rose like a visible pillar, and hung about us and him and the valley, disconcertingly.

At dusk, Zaal and I, with the sergeants and others, crept forward quietly. In half an hour we were at the last crest, in a place where the Turks had dug trenches, and stoned up an elaborate outpost of engrailed sangars, which on this black new-moon night of our raid were empty. In front and below lay the station, its doors and windows sharply marked by the yellow cooking fires and lights of the garrison. It seemed close under our observation, but the Stokes gun would carry only three hundred yards. Accordingly we went nearer, hearing the enemy noises, and attentively afraid lest their barking dogs uncover us. Sergeant Stokes made casts out to left and right, in search of gun positions, but found nothing that was satisfactory.

Meanwhile, Zaal and I crawled across the last flat, till we could count the unlighted tents and hear the men talking. One came out a few steps in our direction, then hesitated. He struck a match to light a cigarette, and the bold light flooded his face, so that we saw him plainly, a young, hollow-faced, sickly officer. He squatted, busy for a moment, and returned to his men, who hushed as he passed.

We moved back to our hill and consulted in whispers. The station was very long, of stone buildings, so solid that they might be proof against our time-fused shell. The garrison seemed about two hundred. We were one hundred and sixteen rifles and not a happy family. Surprise was the only benefit we could be sure of.

So, in the end, I voted that we leave it, unalarmed, for a future occasion, which might be soon. But, actually, one accident after another saved Mudowwara; and it was not until August 1918 that Buxton's Camel Corps at last measured to it the fate so long overdue.

Quietly we regained our camels and slept. Next morning we returned on our tracks to let a fold of the plain hide us from the railway, and then marched south across the sandy flat, seeing tracks of gazelle, oryx and ostrich, with, in one spot, stale padmarks of leopard. We were making for the low hills bounding the far side, intending to blow up a train; for Zaal said that where these touched the railway was such a curve as we needed for minelaying, and that the spurs commanding it would give us ambush and a field of fire for our machine-guns.

So we turned east in the southern ridges till within half a mile of the line. There the party halted in a thirty-foot valley, while a few of us walked down to the line, which bent a little eastward to avoid the point of higher ground under our feet. The point ended in a flat table fifty feet above the track, facing north across the valley.

The metals crossed the hollow on a high bank, pierced by a two-arched bridge for the passage of rain-water. This seemed an ideal spot to lay the charge. It was our first try at electric mining and we had no idea what would happen; but it stood to our reason that the job would be more sure with an arch under the explosive because, whatever the effect on the locomotive, the bridge would go, and the succeeding coaches be inevitably derailed.

Back with our camels, we dumped the loads, and sent the animals to safe pasture near some undercut rocks from which the Arabs scraped salt. The freedmen carried down the Stokes gun with its shells, the Lewis guns and the gelatine with its insulated wire, magneto and tools to the chosen place. The sergeants set up their toys on a terrace, while we went down to the bridge to dig a bed between the ends of two steel sleepers, wherein to hide my fifty pounds of gelatine. We had stripped off the paper wrapping of the individual explosive plugs and kneaded them together by help of the sun heat into a shaking jelly in a sandbag.

The burying of it was not easy. The embankment was steep, and in the sheltered pocket between it and the hillside was a wind-laid bank of sand. No one crossed this but myself, stepping carefully; yet I left unavoidable great prints over its smoothness. The ballast dug out from the track I had to gather in my cloak for carriage in repeated journeys to the culvert, whence it could be tipped naturally over the shingle bed of the water-course.

It took me nearly two hours to dig in and cover the charge; then came the difficult job of unrolling the heavy wires from the detonator to the hills whence we would fire the mine. The top sand was crusted and had to be broken through in burying the wires. They were stiff wires, which scarred the wind-rippled surface with long lines like the belly marks of preposterously narrow and heavy snakes. When pressed down in one place they rose into the air in another. At last they had to be weighted down with rocks which, in turn, had to be buried at the cost of great disturbance of the ground.

Afterwards it was necessary, with a sandbag, to stipple the marks into a wavy surface; and, finally, with a bellows and long fanning sweeps of my cloak, to simulate the smooth laying of the wind. The whole job took five hours to finish, but then it was well finished: neither myself nor any of us could see where the charge lay, or that double wires led out underground from it to the firing-point two hundred yards off, behind the ridge marked for our riflemen.

The wires were just long enough to cross from this ridge into a depression. There we brought up the two ends and connected them with the electric exploder. It was an ideal place both for it and for the man who fired it, except that the bridge was not visible thence.

However, this only meant that someone would have to press the handle at a signal from a point fifty yards ahead, commanding the bridge and the ends of the wires alike. Salem, Feisal's best slave, asked for this task of honour, and was yielded it by acclamation. The end of the afternoon was spent in showing him (on the disconnected exploder) what to do, till he was act-perfect and banged down the ratchet precisely as I raised my hand with an imaginary engine on the bridge.

We walked back to camp, leaving one man on watch by the line. Our baggage was deserted, and we stared about in a puzzle for the rest, till we saw them suddenly sitting against the golden light of sunset along a high ridge. We yelled to them to lie down or come down, but they persisted up there on their perch like a school of hooded crows, in full view of north and south.

At last we ran up and threw them off the skyline, too late. The Turks in a little hillpost by Hallat Ammar, four miles south of us, had seen them, and opened fire in their alarm upon the long shadows which the declining sun was push-

ing gradually up the slopes towards the post. Beduin were
past-masters in the art of using country, but in their abiding
contempt for the stupidity of the Turks they would take no
care to fight them. This ridge was visible at once from
Mudowwara and Hallat Ammar, and they had frightened
both places by their sudden, ominous, expectant watch.

However, the dark closed on us, and we knew we must
sleep away the night patiently in hope of the morrow.
Perhaps the Turks would reckon us gone if our place looked
desert in the morning. So we lit fires in a deep hollow,
baked bread and were comfortable. The common tasks had
made us one party, and the hill-top folly shamed every one
into agreement that Zaal should be our leader.

Day broke quietly, and for hours we watched the empty
railway with its peaceful camps. The constant care of Zaal
and of his lame cousin, Howeimil, kept us hidden, though
with difficulty, because of the insatiate restlessness of the
Beduin, who would never sit down for ten minutes, but
must fidget and do or say something. This defect made
them very inferior to the stolid English for the long, tedious
strain of a waiting war. Also it partly accounted for their
uncertain stomachs in defence. To-day they made us very
angry.

Perhaps, after all, the Turks saw us, for at nine o'clock
some forty men came out of the tents on the hill-top by
Hallat Ammar to the south and advanced in open order. If
we left them alone, they would turn us off our mine in an
hour; if we opposed them with our superior strength and
drove them back, the railway would take notice, and traffic
be held up. It was a quandary, which eventually we tried to
solve by sending thirty men to check the enemy patrol
gradually; and, if possible, to draw them lightly aside into
the broken hills. This might hide our main position and
reassure them as to our insignificant strength and purpose.

For some hours it worked as we had hoped; the firing
grew desultory and distant. A permanent patrol came confidently up from the south and walked past our hill, over
our mine and on towards Mudowwara without noticing us.
There were eight soldiers and a stout corporal, who

mopped his brow against the heat, for it was now after eleven o'clock and really warm. When he had passed us by a mile or two the fatigue of the tramp became too much for him. He marched his party into the shade of a long culvert, under whose arches a cool draught from the east was gently flowing, and there in comfort they lay on the soft sand, drank water from their bottles, smoked, and at last slept. We presumed that this was the noon-day rest which every solid Turk in the hot summer of Arabia took as a matter of principle, and that their allowing themselves the pause showed that we were disproved or ignored. However, we were in error.

Noon brought a fresh care. Through my powerful glasses we saw a hundred Turkish soldiers issue from Mudowwara Station and make straight across the sandy plain towards our place. They were coming very slowly, and no doubt unwillingly, for sorrow at losing their beloved midday sleep; but at their very worst marching and temper they could hardly take more than two hours before they reached us.

We began to pack up, preparatory to moving off, having decided to leave the mine and its leads in place on chance that the Turks might not find them, and we be able to return and take advantage of all the careful work. We sent a messenger to our covering party on the south, that they should meet us farther up, near those scarred rocks which served as screen for our pasturing camels.

Just as he had gone, the watchman cried out that smoke in clouds was rising from Hallat Ammar. Zaal and I rushed uphill and saw by its shape and volume that indeed there must be a train waiting in that station. As we were trying to see it over the hill, suddenly it moved out in our direction. We yelled to the Arabs to get into position as quick as possible, and there came a wild scramble over sand and rock. Stokes and Lewis, being booted, could not win the race; but they came well up, their pains and dysentery forgotten.

The men with rifles posted themselves in a long line behind the spur running from the guns past the exploder to the mouth of the valley. From it they would fire directly into the derailed carriages at less than one hundred and fifty yards, whereas the ranges for the Stokes and Lewis guns were about three hundred yards. An Arab stood up on high behind the guns and shouted to us what the train was doing – a necessary precaution, for if it carried troops and detrained them behind our ridge we should have to face about like a flash and retire fighting up the valley for our lives. Fortunately it held on at all the speed the two locomotives could make on wood fuel.

It drew near where we had been reported, and opened random fire into the desert. I could hear the racket coming, as I sat on my hillock by the bridge to give the signal to Salem, who danced round the exploder on his knees, crying with excitement, and calling urgently on God to make him fruitful. The Turkish fire sounded heavy, and I wondered with how many men we were going to have affair, and if the mine would be advantage enough for our eighty fellows to equal them. It would have been better if the first electrical experiment had been simpler.

However, at that moment the engines, looking very big, rocked with screaming whistles into view around the bend. Behind them followed ten box-wagons, crowded with rifle muzzles at the windows and doors; and in little sandbag nests on the roofs Turks precariously held on, to shoot at us. I had not thought of two engines, and on the moment decided to fire the charge under the second, so that however little the mine's effect, the uninjured engine should not be able to uncouple and drag the carriages away.

Accordingly, when the front "driver" of the second engine was on the bridge, I raised my hand to Salem. There followed a terrific roar, and the line vanished from sight behind a spouting column of black dust and smoke a hundred feet high and wide. Out of the darkness came shattering crashes and long, loud metallic clangings of ripped steel, with many lumps of iron and plate; while one entire wheel of a locomotive whirled up suddenly black out of the cloud against the sky, and sailed musically over our heads to fall slowly and heavily into the desert behind. Except for the flight of these, there succeeded a deathly silence, with no cry of men or rifle-shot, as the now-grey mist of the explosion drifted from the line towards us, and over our ridge until it was lost in the hills.

In the lull, I ran southward to join the sergeants. Salem picked up his rifle and charged out into the murk. Before I had climbed to the guns the hollow was alive with shots, and with the brown figures of the Beduin leaping forward to grips with the enemy. I looked round to see what was happening so quickly, and saw the train stationary and dismembered along the track, with its wagon sides jumping under the bullets which riddled them, while Turks were falling out from the far doors to gain the shelter of the railway embankment.

As I watched, our machine-guns chattered out over my head, and the long rows of Turks on the carriage roofs rolled over, and were swept off the top like bales of cotton before the furious shower of bullets which stormed along the roofs and splashed clouds of yellow chips from the planking. The dominant position of the guns had been an advantage to us so far.

When I reached Stokes and Lewis the engagement had taken another turn. The remaining Turks had got behind the bank, here about eleven feet high, and from cover of the wheels were firing point-blank at the Beduin twenty yards away across the sand-filled dip. The enemy in the crescent of the curving line were secure from the machine-guns; but Stokes slipped in his first shell, and after a few seconds there came a crash as it burst beyond the train in the desert.

He touched the elevating screw, and his second shot fell just by the trucks in the deep hollow below the bridge where the Turks were taking refuge. It made a shambles of the place. The survivors of the group broke out in a panic across the desert, throwing away their rifles and equipment as they ran. This was the opportunity of the Lewis gunners. The sergeant grimly traversed with drum after drum, till the open sand was littered with bodies. Mushagraf, the Sherari boy behind the second gun, saw the battle over, threw aside his weapon with a yell, and dashed down at speed with his rifle to join the others who were beginning, like wild beasts, to tear open the carriages and fall to plunder. It had taken nearly ten minutes.

I ran down to the ruins to see what the mine had done. The bridge was gone; and into its gap was fallen the front wagon, which had been filled with sick. The smash had killed all but three or four and had rolled dead and dying into a bleeding heap against the splintered end. One of those yet alive deliriously cried out the word typhus. So I wedged shut the door, and left them there, alone.

Succeeding wagons were derailed and smashed: some had frames irreparably buckled. The second engine was a blanched pile of smoking iron. Its driving wheels had been blown upward, taking away the side of the fire-box. Cab and tender were twisted into strips, among the piled stones of the bridge abutment. It would never run again. The front engine had got off better: though heavily derailed and lying half-over, with the cab burst, yet its steam was at pressure, and driving-gear intact.

The valley was a weird sight. The Arabs, gone raving mad, were rushing about at top speed bareheaded and half-naked, screaming, shooting into the air, clawing one another nail and fist, while they burst open trucks and staggered back and forward with immense bales, which they ripped by the rail-side, and tossed through, smashing what they did not want.

There were scores of carpets spread about; dozens of mattresses and flowered quilts; blankets in heaps; clothes for men and women in full variety; clocks, cooking-pots, food, ornaments and weapons. To one side stood thirty or forty hysterical women, unveiled, tearing their clothes and hair, shrieking themselves distracted. The Arabs without regard to them went on wrecking the household goods, looting their absolute fill. Camels had become common property. Each man frantically loaded the nearest with what it could carry and shooed it westward into the void, while he turned to his next fancy.

Seeing me tolerably unemployed, the women rushed, and caught at me with howls for mercy. I assured them that all was going well; but they would not get away till some husbands delivered me. These knocked their wives off and seized my feet in a very agony of terror of instant death. A Turk so broken down was a nasty spectacle: I kicked them off as well as I could with bare feet, and finally broke free.

Lewis and Stokes had come down to help me. I was a little anxious about them; for the Arabs, having lost their wits, were as ready to assault friend as foe. Three times I had had to defend myself when they pretended not to know me and snatched at my things. However, the sergeants' war-stained khaki presented few attractions. Lewis went out east of the railway to count the thirty men he had slain; and, incidentally, to find Turkish gold and trophies in their haversacks. Stokes strolled through the wrecked bridge, saw there the bodies of twenty Turks torn to pieces by his second shell, and retired hurriedly.

Ahmed came up to me with his arms full of booty and shouted (no Arab could speak normally in the thrill of victory) that an old woman in the last wagon but one wished to see me. I sent him at once, empty handed, for my camel and some baggage camels to remove the guns; for the enemy's fire was now plainly audible, and the Arabs, sated with spoils, were escaping one by one towards the hills, driving tottering camels before them into safety. It was bad tactics to leave the guns until the end, but the confusion of a first, overwhelmingly successful, experiment had dulled our judgment.

Ahmed never brought the camels. My men, possessed by greed, had dispersed over the land with the Beduins. The sergeants and I were alone by the wreck, which had a strange silence now. We began to fear that we must abandon the guns and run for it, but just then saw two camels dashing back. Zaal and Howeimil had missed me and had returned in search.

We were rolling up the insulated cable, our only piece. Zaal dropped from his camel and would have me mount and ride; but, instead, we loaded it with the wire and the exploder. Zaal found time to laugh at our quaint booty, after all the gold and silver in the train. Howeimil was dead lame from an old wound in the knee and could not walk, but we made him couch his camel, and hoisted the Lewis guns, tied butt to butt like scissors, behind his saddle. There remained the trench mortars; but Stokes reappeared, unskilfully leading by the nose a baggage camel he had found straying. We packed the mortars in haste, put Stokes (who was still weak with his dysentery) on Zaal's saddle, with the Lewis guns, and sent off the three camels in charge of Howeimil, at their best pace.

Meanwhile, Lewis and Zaal, in a sheltered and invisible hollow behind the old gun-position, made a fire of cartridge boxes, petrol and waste, banked round it the Lewis drums and the spare small-arms ammunition, and, gingerly, on the top, laid some loose Stokes shells. Then we ran. As the flames reached the cordite and ammonal there was a colossal and continuing noise. The thousands of cartridges exploded in series like massed machine-guns, and the shells roared off in thick columns of dust and smoke. The outflanking Turks, impressed by the tremendous defence, felt that we were in strength and strongly posted. They halted their rush, took cover, and began carefully to surround our position and reconnoitre it according to rule, while we sped panting into concealment among the ridges.

It seemed a happy ending to the affair, and we were glad to get off with no more loss than my camels and baggage, though this included the sergeants' cherished kits. However, there was food at Rumm, and Zaal thought perhaps we should find our property with the others, who were waiting ahead. We did. My men were loaded with booty, and had with them all our camels, whose saddles were being suddenly delivered of spoils to look ready for our mounting.

We asked if anyone were hurt, and a voice said that the Shimt's boy – a very dashing fellow – had been killed in the first rush forward at the train. This rush was a mistake, made without instructions, as the Lewis and Stokes guns were sure to end the business if the mine worked properly. So I felt that his loss was not directly my reproach.

Three men had been slightly wounded. Then one of Feisal's slaves vouchsafed that Salem was missing. We called every one together and questioned them. At last an Arab said that he had seen him lying hit, just beyond the engine. This reminded Lewis, who, ignorant that he was one of us, had seen a negro on the ground there, badly hurt. I had not been told and was angry, for half the Howeitat must have known of it, and that Salem was in my charge. By their default now, for the second time, I had left a friend behind.

I asked for volunteers to come back and find him. After a little Zaal agreed, and then twelve of the Nowasera. We trotted fast across the plain towards the line. As we topped the last ridge but one we saw the train wreck with Turks swarming over it. There must have been one hundred and fifty of them, and our attempt was hopeless. Salem would have been dead, for the Turks did not take Arab prisoners. Indeed, they used to kill them horribly; so, in mercy, we were finishing those of our badly wounded who would have to be left helpless on abandoned ground.

We gave up Salem and prepared, heavily, to march away. Of our ninety prisoners, ten were friendly Medina women electing to go to Mecca by way of Feisal. There had been twenty-two riderless camels. The women had climbed on to five pack saddles, and the wounded were in pairs on the residue. It was late in the afternoon. We were exhausted, the prisoners had drunk all our water. We must refill from the old well at Mudowwara that night to sustain ourselves so far as Rumm.

As the well was close to the station, it was highly desirable that we get to it and away, lest the Turks divine our course and find us there defenceless. We broke up into little parties and struggled north. Victory always undid an Arab force, so we were no longer a raiding party, but a stumbling baggage caravan, loaded to breaking-point with enough household goods to make rich an Arab tribe for years.

My sergeants asked me for a sword each, as souvenir of their first private battle. As I went down the column to look out something, suddenly I met Feisal's freedmen; and to my astonishment on the crupper behind one of them, strapped to him, soaked with blood, unconscious, was the missing Salem.

I trotted up to Ferhan and asked wherever he had found him. He told me that when the Stokes gun fired its first shell, Salem rushed past the locomotive, and one of the

Turks shot him in the back. The bullet had come out near his spine, without, in their judgment, hurting him mortally. After the train was taken, the Howeitat had stripped him of cloak, dagger, rifle and headgear. Mijbil, one of the freedmen, had found him, lifted him straight to his camel, and trekked off homeward without telling us. Ferhan, overtaking him on the road, had relieved him of Salem, who, when he recovered as later he did, perfectly, bore me always a little grudge for having left him behind, when he was of my company and wounded. I had failed in staunchness. My habit of hiding behind a Sherif was to avoid measuring myself against the pitiless Arab standard, with its no-mercy for foreigners who wore its clothes, and aped its manners. Not often was I caught with so poor a shield as blind Sherif Aid.

We reached the well in three hours and watered without mishap. Afterwards we moved off another ten miles or so, beyond fear of pursuit. There we lay down and slept, and in the morning found ourselves happily tired. Stokes had had his dysentery heavy upon him the night before, but sleep and the ending of anxiety made him well. He and I and Lewis, the only unburdened ones, went on in front across one huge mud flat after another till just before sunset we were at the bottom of Wadi Rumm.

This new route was important for our armoured cars, because its twenty miles of hard mud might enable them to reach Mudowwara easily. If so, we should be able to hold up the circulation of trains when we pleased. Thinking of this, we wheeled into the avenue of Rumm, still gorgeous in sunset colour, the cliffs as red as the clouds in the west, like them in scale and in the level bar they raised against the sky. Again we felt how Rumm inhibited excitement by its serene beauty. Such whelming greatness dwarfed us, stripped off the cloak of laughter in which we had ridden over the jocund flats.

Two days later we were at Akaba, entering in glory, laden with precious things, and boasting that the trains were at our mercy. From Akaba the two sergeants took hurried ship to Egypt. Cairo had remembered them and gone peevish because of their non-return. However, they could pay the penalty of this cheerfully. They had won a battle single handed; had had dysentery; lived on camel-milk; and learned to ride a camel fifty miles a day without pain. Also, Allenby gave them a medal each.

From Revolt in the Desert, *T.E. Lawrence, Jonathan Cape, 1927.*

APPENDIX II
SAS CHRONOLOGY

July 1941:
The SAS, then designated "L" Detachment, raised in North Africa by Lieutenant David Stirling. Total strength 6 officers, 60 NCOs and men.

Nov 1941–Jan 1943:
SAS patrols raid German and Italian airfields and installations in the Western Desert, destroying over 250 aircraft on the ground. Stirling, now Lieutenant Colonel, captured January 1943. A second SAS Regiment is created by the founder's brother, William "Bill" Stirling, and a large waterborne element developed, known as the Special Boat Section.

Feb 1943–Dec 1943:
1 SAS renamed SRS (Special Raiding Squadron) and put under the command of Lieutenant Colonel Paddy Mayne. The Special Boat Section becomes the SBS (Special Boat Service). SRS raids in Sicily and Italy, 2 SAS fights in Italy.

Jan 1944:
SAS units, less SBS, formed into SAS Brigade under command of Brigadier R.W. McLeod.

June 1944:
SAS parachute into France before D-Day. SAS order of battle for D-Day:

HQ SAS Brigade
1st SAS Regt   2nd SAS Regt
3rd (French) SAS Regt   4th (French) SAS Regt
5th (Belgian) SAS Regiment

1944–45:
1, 2, 3, 4 and 5 SAS serve in, variously, France, Belgium, Holland, Italy and Germany.

Oct 1945:
SAS Regiments disbanded. 3 and 4 SAS go to French Army; 5 SAS go to Belgian Army.

1949:
21 SAS Regiment (TA) (Artists), a territorial unit, raised and based in London.

1950:
Major J.M. Calvert raises the Malayan Scouts to fight Chinese Communists in Malaya.

1951:
The Malayan Scouts and M Squadron 21 SAS combine to form 22 SAS.

1952–57:
22 SAS in Malaya.

1958–76:
22 SAS serve in the Gulf, in Oman, Dhofar, Aden.

1963–65:
22 SAS in Borneo during "Confrontation" war with Indonesia.

1970:
SAS deployed in counter-terrorist role in Northern Ireland, in Britain and elsewhere.

1980:
Princes Gate.

1982:
The SAS in the Falklands.

1991:
SAS serve in the Gulf War.

1998:
SAS in Serbia and Kosovo.

2000:
Operation Barras, Sierra Leone.

2001:
Afghanistan.

2003–
Iraq.

ACKNOWLEDGEMENTS

F OR THEIR HELP in the preparation and publication of this book I am grateful to the "A Team" at Constable & Robinson: Claire Muzzelle, Adrian Andrews, Sarah Moore, Claudia Dyer, Eryl Humphrey Jones and Pete Duncan.

The editor has made every effort to locate all persons having rights in the selections which appear in this anthology and to secure permission for the usage of said selections. If any errors have been inadvertently made, they will of course be corrected in future editions. Any queries regarding the use of material should be addressed to the editor c/o the publishers.

"Victor Two" is an extract from *Victor Two* by Peter "Yorky" Crossland, Bloomsbury Publishing plc, 1996. Copyright © 1996 Peter Crossland. Reprinted by permission of Bloomsbury Publishing Plc.

"Urgent Fury" is an extract from *US Rangers* by Ian Padden, Bantam Books, Inc., 1985. Copyright © 1985 Bruck Communications, Inc.

"Cockleshell Heroes" is an extract from *Fighting Marines* by Patrick Pringle, Evans Bros, 1966.

"Operation Struggle" is an extract from *The Frogmen* by T.J. Waldron and James Gleeson, Evans Brothers Ltd, 1950.

"The Drop" is an extract from *Daedalus Returns*, Hutchinson, 1958. Trans W. Stanley Moss.

"The Battery at Merville" is an extract from *Red Beret* by Hilary St George Saunders, Michael Joseph, 1950. Copyright © 1950 Hilary St George Saunders.

"Bandit Country" is an extract from *Green Beret, Red Star* by Anthony Crockett, Streamline Publications, 1958. Copyright © 1958 A. Crockett.

"Emergency Exit" is an extract from *Beyond the Chindwin* by Bernard Fergusson, Fontana Books 1955. Copyright © 1945 Bernard Fergusson.

"Rung Sat" is an extract from *US Navy SEALS* by Ian Padden, Bantam Books, Inc., 1985. Copyright © 1985 Bruck Communications, Inc.

"The Colombian Job" is an extract from *The Shooting Gallery*, Victor Gollancz, 1998. Copyright © 1988 Gaz Hunter. Reproduced by permission of the Cassell Group.

"One Night in the Aegean" is an extract from *The Filibusters*, Methuen, 1957. Copyright © 1957 John Lodwick.

"Citadel" is an extract from *Skorzeny's Special Missions* by Otto Skorzeny, Robert Hale, 1957.

"The Pass of La Molina" is an extract from *Green Beret* by Hilary St George Saunders, Michael Joseph, 1949. Copyright © 1949.

"The Lofoten Raid" is an extract from *Lofoten Letter* by Evan John, William Heinemann, 1941. Copyright © 1941 Evan John.

"Storm in the Fjord" is an extract from *Commandos in Action* by Graeme Cook, Hart-Davis MacGibbon, 1973. Copyright © 1973 Graeme Cook.

"The Attack on Rommel's HQ" is an extract from *The True Book About Commandos* by Richard Arnold, Frederick Muller, 1954.

"Desert Patrol" is an extract from *The Desert My Dwelling Place* by David Lloyd Owen, Cassell & Co., 1957. Copyright © 1957 David Lloyd Owen.

"Hunted" is an extract from *Going to the Wars* by John Verney, Collins, 1958. Copyright © 1958 John Verney.

"Pantelleria" is an extract from *Being the Story of "Apple" of the Commandos and Special Air Service Regiment* by J.E. Appleyard, Blandford Press, 1946.

"Operation Jumbo" is an extract from *Banner over Pusan* by Ellery Anderson, Evans Bros., 1960.

"Underwater Taxi" is an extract from *The Ship With Two Captains* by Terence Robertson, Evans Bros, 1957.

"Eagle Claw" by Ian Westwell is an extract from *Elite Forces: Green Berets*, Orbis Publishing, 1986. Copyright © 1986 Orbis Publishing.

"Jungle Fighters" by Jonathan Reed is an extract from *Elite Forces: SAS* edited by Richard Williams, Orbis Publishing, 1986. Copyright © 1986 Orbis Publishing.

"Interrogation" is an extract from *The White Rabbit* by Bruce Marshall, Evans Bros, 1952. Copyright © 1952 Bruce Marshall.

"Operation Leopard" is an extract from *The World's Elite Forces* by Bruce Quarrie, Octopus Books Ltd, 1985. Copyright © Octopus Books Ltd.

"Recon" is an extract from *LRRP: The Professional*, Frank Camper, Dell Publishing, 1988.